# Networked Cultures
## Parallel Architectures and the Politics of Space
### Peter Mörtenböck and Helge Mooshammer

# Contents

**Connectivities** 7
Peter Mörtenböck and
Helge Mooshammer

## NETWORK CREATIVITY 13
Peter Mörtenböck and
Helge Mooshammer

**Interviews** 28
Margarethe Makovec,
Nataša Ilić, Gerald Raunig,
Katrin Klingan

**Borderline Cases** 36
Windsor/Detroit

**Unbounded** 46
Irit Rogoff

**Interviews** 52
Kyong Park, Srdjan J. Weiss,
Branka Ćurčić

**Extended Enterprises** 60
Moscow

**Interviews** 64
Olga Lopoukhova, Straddle3

**Forums of Culture** 69
Barcelona

## CONTESTED SPACES 75
Peter Mörtenböck and
Helge Mooshammer

**Interviews** 88
Claudia Zanfi, Ursula Biemann,
Philipp Oswalt

**Slatewalls** 97
Chinese Markets

**Casting Nets** 100
Adrian Blackwell

**Les Olympiades** 110
Paris

**Interviews** 112
Ayreen Anastas and Rene Gabri,
Eyal Weizman, Erden Kosova

**Metro City** 124
Istanbul

**Interviews** 130
Despoina Sevasti and Poka-Yio,
Stefano Boeri, Pablo de Soto

## TRADING PLACES 141
Peter Mörtenböck and
Helge Mooshammer

**Arizona Market** 164
Brčko

**Interviews** 174
B+B, Matei Bejenaru, Helmut Batista,
Asya Filippova, Oliver Ressler

**Transient Traffic** 186
Istanbul Topkapı

**Visiting Stalin** 192
Moscow Izmailovo

**The politics of 'cityness' and a world
of deals** 202
AbdouMaliq Simone

**Thank You USA** 210
Prishtina

**Interviews** 219
Marjetica Potrc, xurban, Jesko Fezer,
Tadej Pogačar

## PARALLEL WORLDS 231

**Gunners & Runners** 232
London

**Parallel Worlds** 241
Peter Mörtenböck and
Helge Mooshammer

**Interviews** 256
STEALTH, aaa, Igor Dobricic

**Parallel Worlds** 265
Marina Gržinić

**Interviews** 271
Campement Urbain, Vasıf Kortun,
Jochen Becker, Marko Sančanin

**Conversions** 282
Berlin

**Interviews** 288
Oda Projesi, Iacopo Gallico,
Ricardo Basbaum

**Horizons** 297
Rio de Janeiro

**Biographies** 306
**Index** 315
**Credits** 318

Informal market along the Byzantine city walls and Londra Asfaltı, an arterial road to the west, Istanbul, 2005

Universidade do Estado do Rio de Janeiro (UERJ), 2005

# Connectivities
## Peter Mörtenböck and Helge Mooshammer

Political conflicts, humanitarian disasters, wars and migrations – we live in an age of global unrest and discontinuity. The worldwide movement of populations, burgeoning social mobilizations and the incessantly changing form of the neoliberal economy are generating the energies of a new world order in which we are all constantly challenged to negotiate reality and make deals. Amidst this disintegration of traditional orders, access to networks and the development of connectivities are assuming an ever greater significance for the way we inhabit and configure our environments: as processes in which contours emerge and gradually take on form. Against the background of this structural transformation, networks have also become one of the most prominent concepts relating to the search for new forms of social cohesion and solidarity. The question as to what forms such connectivity should take is not only theoretical in nature but above all a question that points to the self-induced multiplicity of spaces that is continually generated by connectivities throughout the world and that in the process changes our own spaces of action and continually generates them anew.

Networks both structure and constitute an operational field for these proliferating global entanglements of people, places and interests. They become incorporated in space in different ways: in the form of translocal zones of action, community support structures, expanded spheres of influence, spatial superimpositions and intensive contacts and contaminations. However, these expansive forces are accompanied by tendencies to violent segregation and a global dynamic of the fragmentation of living spaces. Top-down visions of the planning and control of environments thus impinge on the bottom-up realities of pulsating metropolises and experimental structures of networked self-organization. This development is generating geocultural tensions, conflicts and clashes everywhere and is investing the task of designing architectures of connectivity with a particular political urgency.

While official reactions in terms of cultural and planning policies for the most part consist in the search for means of stabilization and restraint, the dynamics of deregulation are giving rise to a situation characterized by global parallel systems in which we seek out separate connectivities: parallel architectures, parallel societies, parallel lives. The engagement with these developments on the part of art and architecture in recent years has resulted in a new form of praxis founded on collective production, process-guided work and transversal project platforms. Such a 'disciplineless' praxis of unsolicited intervention in spatial contexts renders legible the dysfunctional rules of planned spatial and cultural containment and creates an avenue for generating new forms of circulation amidst the political efforts to conceal this failure. It makes use of existing networks, expands and changes them, gives rise to new circuits and thereby sketches a mobile geography of self-determined utilizations of space and culture.

Our project *Networked Cultures* aims neither to present this development as a contained movement nor to localize it within the particularities of a specific geographic or institutional context. We are far more interested in its propinquity to a plethora of other self-authorized structures, regardless of their scale – grey markets, informal commerce, alternative economies and migratory practices as well as the innumerable, minor, barely discernible attempts to establish self-determined sociality in the midst of the reconfiguration of our environments. Such an idiosyncratic propinquity confronts us with the fundamental construction of the modalities of cultural and social experience – with spatial production that is unsolicited and unlimited and that opens up an experiential sphere outside prescribed forms of political representation. These projects exert an effect – albeit one that is difficult to classify – in the realm of political reality, but at the same time they also open up an exterior space that allows for a redistribution of roles and activities beyond the conceptual frameworks commonly applied to discourses of education, planning and societal organization. What forms of cultural interaction and what social environments emerge in the context of such a new mode of production of space, politics and knowledge?

This book interrogates the meanings of this change together with the meanings of artistic, architectural and cultural engagement in these dynamics. It traces a variety of strands along which the *Networked Cultures* project itself has developed. First, attention is focused on the phenomenon of network creativity by following the routes of networks laid out by artists, architects, urbanists, curators and activists. The site that is hereby opened up marks an arena of engagement with the relationship between space and conflict and leads to an interrogation of contested spaces across Europe and beyond, examining the architecture of conflict, and discussing models of geocultural negotiation. Investigating their modus operandi, the focus then shifts to governmentality and self-government by examining the organizational matrix of black markets, informal settlements and the accompanying parallel economy. Responding to these global realities, the parallel worlds of mobility and migration, 'travelling' communities, digital worlds and other counter-geographies are discussed in relation to a politics of connectivity and the emerging 'archipelago of the peripheries'.

*Lost Highway Expedition, Novi Sad, Summer 2006*

During our exploration of these questions we had the very good fortune to encounter numerous dialogue partners ready to share their work and experiences with us. These interactions generated a complex form of connectivity which found its way into the structure of our project and which we have endeavoured to express in the structure of this book. The following contributions have thus been conceived of as a collection of dialogues that aim less to deal with a predefined object than to form new objects collectively. This goal has been pursued, on the one hand, in a series of conversations on urban interventions, public art projects and architectural experiments, which we conducted with architects, artists and curators over a period of two years and excerpts from which are presented here, and, on the other hand, in a series of essays that offer specific perspectives, narratives and interpretations which help to open up the thematic sites of this book.

Building on the network logic of this project and the new spatial creativity of globalized realities, the *Networked Cultures* project has also utilized and will continue to utilize other platforms. These include a compilation of the conversations with our dialogue partners in the form of a film archive enclosed in the book as a DVD, a website comprising a database, images, texts and dialogues (www.networkedcultures.org), and not least the ongoing manifestations of the project in institutional and public spaces. The diverse paths that this project has taken since its inception in 2005 mean that we owe a debt of gratitude to an immense number of people who have accompanied and supported us on our journey. In the course of the project, many of these people have become participants, collaborators and friends. New connectivities have been created, new ground broken.

**Peter Mörtenböck** and **Helge Mooshammer**
have collaborated on a range of art, architectural and curatorial projects as well as on academic research and writing that engages with the spatial and cultural effects of geopolitical transformation. Since 2005 they have been working on the *Networked Cultures* project, an international research platform based at Goldsmiths, University of London. They have contributed to many exhibitions worldwide, including the 7th and 8th Venice Architecture Biennials (2000 and 2002). Their most recent books include: *Die virtuelle Dimension* (2001), *Visuelle Kultur: Körper-Räume-Medien* (ed. 2003) and *Cruising* (2005). Through their work they have been involved with numerous universities and art schools. Currently, Helge Mooshammer is a Senior Research Fellow at the Institute of Art and Design, Vienna University of Technology, and teaches visual culture at Goldsmiths, London. Peter Mörtenböck is Professor of Visual Culture at the Vienna University of Technology and Visiting Fellow at Goldsmiths, University of London.

www.networkedcultures.org

# Network
# Creativity

*Lost Highway Expedition*, discussion at [mama]
Zagreb, Summer 2006

# Network Creativity

## EUROPE LOST AND FOUND

*Network struggle… does not rely on discipline: creativity, communication and self-organized cooperation are its primary values.*[1]

In the spring of 2006 the two translocal urban research networks School of Missing Studies and Centrala Foundation for Future Cities invited interested parties to participate in a spatial experiment that was intended to have the character of an expedition. Whereas expeditions are usually a means of exploring remote regions, the *Lost Highway Expedition* followed a route through the Western Balkans. The remote aspect of this collective journey was thus not conceived in terms of place but in terms of time, in the sense of bygone time of ideological community formation in the Socialist Federal Republic of Yugoslavia (SFRY). However, the project was not concerned with a nostalgic retrieval of lost conceptions and values but with developing paths for the future on the basis of the travel experiences of a self-organized community.

The core of this aesthetic and social experiment comprised a collective journey along the 'Highway of Brotherhood and Unity', a section of highway begun in 1948 but never completed. At the time, its collective construction was seen as a means of linking the major cities of the SFRY in both an ideological and infrastructural sense. Following years of violent conflict and economic and social upheaval, the Western Balkans – the name coined for this territory after 1991 – is today associated with an area whose unifying characteristic is above all to be found in the long-term exclusion of the majority of its inhabitants from EU Europe, even though the highway that was rebuilt by private companies following the destruction wrought by the Balkan wars is now being reclaimed as a part of the pan-European Corridor X within the infrastructure of the EU.[2] One of the questions confronting the members of the expedition concerned the meaning inherent in such a connection between places, ideologies and memories and the meaning it might acquire. The original invitation to join the expedition put it in these terms:

'The *Lost Highway Expedition* will begin in Ljubljana, and travel through Zagreb, Novi Sad, Belgrade, Skopje, Prishtina, Tirana and Podgorica before concluding in Sarajevo: It will comprise two days of events in each city and one day of travel in between. The events may include guided tours, presentations and forums by local experts, workshops involving the travellers and local participants, discussions, exhibitions, radio shows, picnics and other events that can be organized by the host cities themselves. Members of the *Lost Highway Expedition* do not have to travel or stay together and can enter and exit the expedition for any length of time and at any point. Participants are responsible for organizing, supporting and realizing their own journeys. The expedition is meant to generate new projects, new art works, new networks, new architecture and new politics based on the experience and knowledge gained along the highway.'[3]

Novi Zagreb, 2006

In August 2006, the shared search for an experimental community brought hundreds of participants from a wide range of backgrounds into contact with independent organizations, initiatives and cultural producers from the nine different regions spanned by the expedition. Some participants spent a month travelling the entire route, while others accompanied the expedition for only a few days. Some immediately found themselves integrated in a collective group process, while

others launched their own initiatives in dialogue with the event. In order to maintain the decentralized structure of the expedition, participants were deliberately left to define their own projects, plan their own time and make their own contacts. The concept of swarming perhaps best describes the way in which knowledge of the expedition spread, the way the vaguely delimited groups moved from section to section, converged again and subsequently disseminated the knowledge generated during their journeys in different and only partly interconnected projects – exhibitions, seminars, workshops and publications.[4]

The experimental network structure via which these activities could be disseminated and which led to a range of unanticipated encounters and findings is not the only important parameter in this context. Important, too, are the intellectual concentration and range of these new knowledge formations, which are interrelated with the way the traversed localities are linked with external networks, including the geocultural assemblages and mobilities embodied by the initiators of the project themselves. The initial platform, Europe Lost and Found, consisting of Azra Akšamija, Ana Dzokic, Katherine Carl, Ivan Kucina, Marc Neelen, Kyong Park, Marjetica Potrc and Srdjan Jovanovic Weiss, constitutes a plurality of translocal relationships and interrelated cultural references that extends far beyond the effective capacity of concrete group dynamics. The current exchange involving Ana Dzokic and Marc Neelen between Belgrade, the capital of turbo-culture, and the architectural stronghold of Rotterdam; the link forged by Azra Akšamija between post-war Sarajevo and academic institutions in the US; the different, marginalized places that Kyong Park's work in Asia, North America and Europe brings together; the connection made by Marjetica Potrc between forms of self-organization in the Western Balkans and Latin America; Srdjan Jovanovic Weiss's nomadic architectural enterprises between Novi Sad and Philadelphia – all these links are creating a mobile network structure with which a plurality of local features can be projected as a translocal opportunity.

What enabled the socio-aesthetic experiment *Lost Highway Expedition* to become more than a self-referential group experience was the space of action that was generated by the collaboration of the project's initiators and that absorbed new actors and formulated an expanded political space. The power of this space reflects the degree to which subjectivity can express itself in a diffuse and fragmented form and lead to efficient aesthetic and political connections via a reorganization of this diffusion. In this sense, the potential of the situation generated by this expeditional experiment can be read more as a merging of aesthetic productions and geocultural realities in a concrete form of spatial praxis than as an encounter between like-minded individuals.

In connection with her project *Timescapes* on the experiential topography of Corridor X, which formed one of the most heavily used guest-worker routes from south-eastern Europe during the 1970s and 1980s, Angela Melitopoulos sees a potential in the inter-operation of different spatial logics: 'The logical basis of the B-Zone is its tie to the A-Zone, but the fragmentation of the B-Zone can follow other logics that could alter both zones substantially.'[5] The question of which communities are generated by infrastructures and networks is dependent on their utilization. The concrete embodiment of migratory interconnections, the traversable reality of the Western Balkans and the contacts provided by the initiators to local initiatives together with access to political discussions, specialized city tours and social activities served to

anchor the expedition in spatial reality and prevented the search for a new 'temporary society' from being oriented solely to the process of the group or a diffuse concept of globality. This anchorage in the provisional formations of a concrete geocultural reality meant that a level was available beyond that of micro and macro-organization which allowed the possibilities offered by one relational structure to be used to gain a new understanding of other structures. The relationships between these many anchor points and the actualization of their potential in the collectively undertaken journey fashion, as it were, the connection sought by the expedition between the loci of the Western Balkans and other geopolitical regions.

In this sense, network creativity not only implies that networks are generated in a creative way but also emphasizes that networks cultivate a morphological structure for creativity. The artistic projects produced during and in the wake of the expedition form archives of knowledge that in turn allow for an extension of the expedition beyond those involved in situ to include a growing number of dispersed participants. The productive power of the network thus consists in its morphological openness, which makes it possible constantly to forge new connections from each of its nodes without necessarily being linked to a legitimizing and controlling origin.

Members of the expanding Roma community in Novi Sad, Serbia, many of whom have been expelled from Germany where they initially sought refuge after being forced out of Kosovo in 1999

## SITES OF ACTION

Whether in the form of transnational political initiatives, global economies, new technologies or urban social movements, networks are the distinctive characteristic of spatial organization in the twenty-first century. Networks have changed our forms of cultural coexistence and communication just as they have the way in which we produce and experience spaces. Cities, regions, countries and continents are being experienced less and less as fixed territories and increasingly as fluid and contested landscapes, formed and mobilized by networks of integrating realities. Networks are a form of organization, an operational politics and a generative process. On all these levels they foreground the relationships between objects rather than the objects themselves. Network thinking revolves around connections, processes and courses of action that create exchange and link things with one another. Such thinking maintains logics that are oriented to the intensity, range and quality of relationships. And it generates forms of knowledge that accrues from conversations, dialogues, interactions and interventions. At the beginning of the new millennium networks have become the most powerful figure of thought operating on the way we conceive the organization of our world: networks dominate the prevailing structures of cultural, economic and military power. They are the digital age's ubiquitous object of desire, a new force that directs our feelings, thought and action with the promise of a flexibilization of our relationships and an expansion of our possibilities.

Thus, there seems to be little difference between activity and outcome in the politics of network operation. To some extent, as Michael Hardt and Antonio Negri note in their discussion of distributed relationships, the organization becomes an end in itself.[6] That is to say, network organization is both *content* and *achievement*. It entails the act as well as what is produced by the act. As networks are largely defined through the performative acts in which they congregate, they gather topological presence through an ongoing transfer of relationality, meanings and values into the realm of political action. This process does not contend for a new static category of space, but draws attention to performativity as the fundamental logic of social life today. It implies changes characteristic of agency in relation to networking as such, but also reverberates in new organizational and spatial patterns as well as in the production of network actors themselves.

The global reality of the concurrency of the diffusion and consolidation, expansion and restriction, opening and delimitation of social and spatial organization suggests that the types of produced orders will often be contradictory and disputed, that networks can comprehend tasks of both linkage and isolation, and that the existence lived in networks is not antithetical to a life in parallel worlds. Neutral zones do not exist without relationships, and relationality does not exist without isolation. The conflict-laden multiplication of flows of goods, people and information and the concurrent proliferation of encapsulated zones, special areas and extra-state regions show that we can assume neither a change of spatial organizational forms, nor a dichotomy between defined territory and network, nor the inferiority of one spatial form as opposed to the superiority of another. The challenge associated with an investigation of network creativities lies in tracing the strategic alliance between both forms, identifying the politics of power expansion and searching for spaces of action within the operation of these politics. What do the enmeshments of art, architecture and politics that form into networks look like in specific terms? What forces can these encounters liberate and what opportunities do they offer for the formation of self-determined forms of action and collaboration? What sorts of free spaces can develop in the midst of an all-embracing network situation and how does such spatial creativity relate to collective processes?

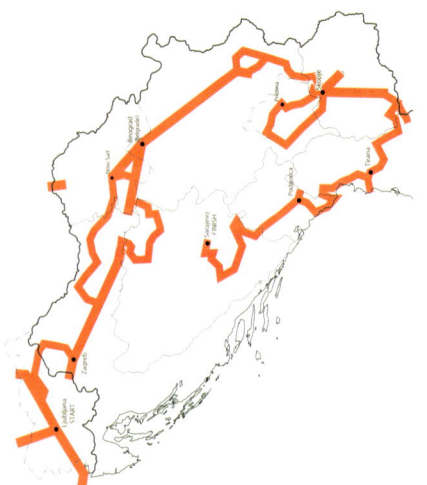

Lost Highway Expedition, Summer 2006

Before going into the organization of network creativity in more detail, it will be helpful to explain what we understand as constituting the expanded field of art and architecture that we want to use as a central reference point in our inquiries. Our focus here is less on the praxis of planning and design and their theoretical analysis and contextualization than on the newly emerging intellectual praxis of architecture. In the context of political and social questions, this praxis is producing interventions, experiments and laboratory-like situations in order to generate a new understanding of architecture via an investigation of spatial interconnections and participation in social and physical transformations. The concept of architecture employed here thus relates above all to those processes in which questions of public and social space, questions of territoriality, cultural difference and the politics of mobility, are addressed via participation in the design of project flows rather than via the level of object design. Such an architecture, which is removed from the autonomous sphere of architectural production, is now locating its operational capacity in temporary and practically oriented alliances, in the collective investigation and production of spatial situations and in the creative subversion of organizational forms. This process often results in a deliberate displacement and blurring of the roles, areas of competence and cultural dispositives via which a project is supposed to be made recognizable and assessable as a form of architecture. Many of the practices considered here are directed not only against the institutional structures in which they are supposed to be represented but also use culture as a radical dispositive in order to produce their own referential systems for social encounters and forms of material expression that alter our ideational world.

This framework also helps to elucidate our reference to art via the tension between artistic production and the prevailing obsession with the immaterial production of creativity as an ever increasing part of the overall production of cognitive capital. Social and creative capital are the new world markets of the late capitalist politics of growth, which in the past two decades has generated a specific change in the relationship between art and the economy via the circuits of money, institutions, curatorial activity, exhibition operations and art criticism. Marina Gržinić describes the new relationship as 'civilizational kinship', which presents itself to the First World as a natural and unavoidable process and involves surmounting cultural borders in order to extend this 'civilizational alliance' into undeveloped territories that have been excluded by the state.[7] One has only to recall the short-term strategic investment by the West in cultural infrastructures and exhibition programmes in the Balkans and Eastern Europe following the fall of the Iron Curtain and the effects of new 'location decisions' and the rapid severance of relationships. On the other hand, it should be noted that dissident networks have formed in the wake of these developments, networks that have brought together individuals from the artistic and economic fields with squatters, activists NGOs and local community projects and that have created autonomous production sites. In the region encompassed by the former Yugoslavia alone, dozens of such network sites have emerged, including the Centre for New Media_kuda.org in Novi Sad, [mama] in Zagreb, Metelkova in Ljubljana, Prelom kolektiv in Sarajevo, CZKD (Centre for Cultural Decontamination) in Belgrade and Press to Exit in Skopje. These and similar sites are important reference points when we refer to practices that claim the artistic field as part of their radius of action. The field that is thereby generated contains loosely linked communication and collaboration platforms in which artists, architects, intellectuals, media activists and many other individuals have joined together to develop their project alliances in the interstitial zones of the institutionalized art field and to operate them on a largely autonomous basis.

These expansive networks based on informal social organization are interwoven with the politics of global deregulation via a complex process of interaction. In order to extend boundaries and to exert control over larger areas, this politics also needs unregulated spheres where other interests gain access and dissolve the logic of cause and effect into multidirectional co-implications. Thus, it is precisely at the point where global deregulation is reflected in the experience of social realities that it also becomes an instrument that can be used against it. By abrogating the network-like expansion of formal structures it simultaneously facilitates diversions of ends and the striking of unanticipated paths. This reversal makes manifest two important characteristics of network action. On the one hand, instructions are not simply transferred from one place to another; rather, instructions are utilized, altered for one's own purposes and, if necessary, directed against the instructors. In other words, we are speaking here of network action's characteristic of transformation. This is linked in turn with the other characteristic: it is not only the case that the information moved over network channels can abrogate something but that the gesture of informing and abrogating itself represents a transferable technology.

Gas station near Ruma, Serbia, 2006

In its video and text installation *A/S/L (Age/Sex/Location)*, the Raqs Media Collective, a group of media practitioners based in New Delhi, uses the different masquerades of identities in chat-rooms and call centres to shed light on migratory experiences between online and offline worlds, between centres and peripheries. The group writes: 'Data outsourcing displaces the "Centre-Periphery" binary, by creating a fluctuating continuum between discrete spaces through the telematic pipelines of the new economy... In the context of online labour, the transformation of identities is an index of the reified, object status of the call centre worker, an Othering, of the self. The call centre worker performs at two levels; once as a disembodied Midwestern "Ruth", and alongside as a polymorphing chat-room diva. She clocks in at the call centre, and logs into the chat-room within the course of the same workday, at the same workstation.'[8] 'Ruth' embodies different marginalities with different levels of access to what identifies itself as the centre. The marginality of the position of call-centre workers consists in the connection of their own economic situation with the territorial marginality of their location. However, with its performances and protocols, the online conversation itself generates and reproduces centrality in that it supplies the centre of today's global economy.

Members of the Roma community collecting reusable materials Novi Sad, 2006

Another site of this simultaneous separation and intertwinement of network and territory, virtual space and real existence, can be found in Romanian internet cafes, where young people work in shifts to train the avatars of clients in faraway California. 'Power levelling' is the common euphemism for this improvement in remote 'gold farms' of the opportunities for avatars in virtual gaming worlds. In China, the largest market for virtual gold farms, hundreds of thousands of gaming workers ('gold farmers') labour in this specialized business in continuous shifts to produce virtual commodities and market them via international brokers.[9] The network of gaming industry sweatshops in Asia and eastern Europe reinforces the authority of territorial distance in a very similar way to a proposal by the Austrian Minister of Justice in 2004 – allegedly for financial reasons – to operate an Austrian-financed prison on Romanian territory for Romanians convicted of crimes in Austria. The exchange enabled by this authority provides space for an expansion of interventions across the borders of territories, as also seen in the case of the more than 1,000 secret CIA flights over the territory of the European Union[10] and other secret operations involving the outsourcing of labour, the application of law and organization. The deployment of extra-legal enclaves and camps such as Guantánamo Bay or the networks of 'black sites', the jargon for secret prisons operated outside one's own national territory, attest to a new dimension of the fragmentation of geographical clarities, one which consciously deploys shadowy presences, camouflages and cover-ups as tactics in order to establish fluid borders. In an instrumental respect, this fluidification points to an incessant reconstitution of the conditions governing the establishment of connections. In a spatial respect, it means a radical transformation of places into a permanently floating apparatus that serves to steer flows and currents. This offensive ambiguity accelerates the deterioration of fixed alliances and creates a climate in which it is no accident that art and architecture become network actors amidst the current upheavals in geocultural spaces. The ubiquitous deterritorialization of sites is being accompanied by a diminishment of their material and conceptual attachment to the physical and empirical singularities of a place and a corresponding increase in nomadic and migratory currents in which change takes place. Discursive sites, fictional self-formations and relational spatial practices have become key aspects of creative engagement.[11] At one end of the spectrum we find globally dispersed collective practices und temporary project platforms such as the *Lost Highway Expedition*, which track the multifaceted process of global spatial transformation. At the other end we find the competition between biennale festivals to present extraordinary places and images of our time. In each of these cases, the new sites that are formed are constituted by systems of practices that are not exempt from social, economic and political pressures. In her widely discussed essay, 'One Place After Another', Miwon Kwon emphasizes the particular relationship between mobility privileges and cultural and economic power. In reaction to the conditions of a mobilized market economy, she argues, compensation fantasies and a hidden complicity with the privileges of nomadic self-organization are spreading in the art and architecture industries as a counterpoint to tendencies to fragmentation and alienation. Art and architecture are discretely profiting from the acceleration of the circuits of attentiveness to 'undiscovered' sites.[12]

Taking this idea a step further entails looking beyond a critique of art and architecture as stooges of global economic forces. In recent years, experimental approaches have increasingly coalesced around platforms that confront the rapid consumption of one place after another with a model of self-organized creation. Networks are the new sites that are being shaped by dialogues, connections, allocations, superimpositions and intersections. The orientation to the site has thus morphed into a creative participation in translocal spaces of action. These spaces of action are places of participation growing out of a constant negotiation of the conditions of taking part, i.e. out of a constant subversion of expected functionalities and a shifting of definitions of what actually constitutes participation. They are not tied to a specific duration or concrete place and yet are based on principles of mutual responsibility and shared horizons. The goal of many projects is the disruption of the linearity of development processes, jurisdictions and role prescriptions in favour of a horizontally layered sphere of collective production, the changes of which constantly throw up new questions. In contrast to the participatory projects of the 1960s and 1970s, the concern here is not with the production of a concrete identity-establishing place but with a form of involvement that is achieved via participation in networks. In his *A Grammar of the Multitude*, Paolo Virno writes of this physiognomy of 'participation in the foreign': 'The *many*, in as much as they are *many*, are those who share the feeling of "not feeling at home" and who, in fact, place this experience at the centre of their own social and political praxis.'[13] The decisive transformation that takes place in a society without substantial communities lies in the change from the specific to common places,[14] from the location in specific communities to an orientation to principles of reciprocity and the public intellect as a common resource in any situation. This strengthens the level of the common, conspicuous singularity, the level of identity-less and circulating self-organization at which artistic and architectural production operates today in an all-encompassing state of transformation. This state is not only an object of its engagement but at the same time defines the most important parameters through which it takes effect.

Hotel Jugoslavija
Located in New Belgrade, Serbia, and opened in 1969 as one of the most luxurious hotels in the region, it was used as an accommodation for celebrities and high officials visiting Belgrade; designed by Lavoslav Horvat; bombed by NATO alliance on 7 May 1999; in 2007 Casinos Austria announced plans to transform it into a luxury casino

## PLATFORMS OF POLITICAL ACTION

Novi Sad Radio and Television (RTNS) building bombed by NATO alliance on 3 May 1999

In their investigation of social and cultural change, network practices in art and architecture are not based on the reclamation of an external sphere but rather lay claim to a space inhabited by many in order to effectuate processes of communication and collaboration. These investigations are less interested in a configuration of analytical depth than in bringing together forces that have to do with a particular question, in the collective production of a continually reshaped polymorphism. They aspire to an expansion of the prevailing field of reference and as a result often alter the framework of their own enquiry in the course of their development. Their continuously self-organized and autopoietic behaviour generates the conditions under which situative spaces of action form. The articulation of different interests and the extension of scope thus emerge as the most urgent task of a project culture that aims to provide scope for change in an interactive context involving many different motivations. In order to achieve this, the current spatial organization of interests is comprehended as an oscillation within networks and the movements of its transformation are followed. Networks are not an arbitrary option but a fact of the change in forms of political and social coexistence. The articulation of political engagement via creative thought and action thus faces a dual task: on the one hand, that of evading the prescribed situation by changing the rules of the game, and on the other that of multiplying and intensifying latent and lateral relationships.

The 'Fresh Motel' along the highway E70 in western Serbia, 2006

Network Creativity

In the words of the Raqs Media Collective: 'To do this, the practitioner probably has to invent, or discover, protocols of conversation across sites, across different histories of locatedness in the network; to invent protocols of resource building and sharing, create structures within structures and networks within networks. Mechanisms of flexible agreements about how different instances of enactment can share a contiguous semantic space will have to be arrived at. And as we discover these "protocols", their different ethical, affective and cognitive resonances will immediately enter the equation. We can then also begin to think of art practice as enactment, as process, as elements in an interaction or conversation within a network.'[15] Thus, in recent years two interwoven approaches have emerged that attempt to open up culture to the investigation of alternative aggregations and forms of action. One approach is based on the further development of a cartographic praxis in art and architecture that attempts to express urban transformation via the complex tension linking society and space to one another. Alongside these mapping projects a processually oriented praxis is developing that connects separate places and communities and creates symbolic sites of political manifestations or counter-manifestations. Both forms of geocultural engagement give expression to the way in which artistic praxis can explore possibilities of intervening in the production of knowledge archives and becoming politically operative via cultural effects.

Finished villa on Fruška Gora mountain near Novi Sad, Serbia, 2006

The value of the first approach lies in its capacity to generate snapshots of a globalized culture that attempts to structure transnational flows in accordance with their own logics. In the interaction of the globalized world with a variety of parallel worlds, the crises, conflicts and imbalances characterizing processes of societal change are brought to light. In addition, these protocols generate new forms of the symbolization of sociocultural transformation, in which the depiction of translocal networks plays a fundamental role. Here, territorial realities are distanced from the familiar framework of geographical representation and are instead articulated via spatial relationships and the extension of territories to include ideational worlds, flows, contexts, images and peripheries. The ideational worlds and cognitive interconnections generated by way of this cartographic praxis show that mappings represent not only a powerful model of the exercise of power and control but also an instrument of change. As Bruno Latour argues, 'Images demonstrate transformation, not information.'[16] The aesthetics of dissident cartographies and the way in which they point to existing power constellations or articulate new social structures open up an additional dimension that facilitates interventions in symbolic worlds and the creation of new symbolic relationships.

Unfinished villa on Fruška Gora mountain near Novi Sad, Serbia, 2006

The interventionist projects of the second socio-aesthetic approach utilize the fact that the neo-liberal restructuring of environments affects different spatial types in different localities, which, above and beyond their differences, form a network of strategic points for the reformulation of geographical zones, boundaries and intersections. To be able to operate translocally, the global market requires different instruments for the coordination of local procedures: technological information systems, political regulation and international marketing. Such spatial-political instruments are often corrupted in artistic practices to the extent that they are interrupted, redirected and utilized for one's own purposes. In the midst of the networked apparatus of translocal societal ordering processes, economic and military operations, these practices articulate their resistance by making use of the structures, procedures and possibilities of network production outside the assigned role pattern. In their movement through physical and social spaces, they create new models of order, relationships and situations. The central question for such an approach concerns how, when drawing on network resources and network capacities, zones of autonomy can be created vis-à-vis the utilization of intellectual creativity for the expansion of cognitive capitalism.

Put another way, this form of approach involves an exploration of the possible ways in which networks not only offer a model of the efficient organization and economic valorization of creativity (as in the cases of culture marketing, art tourism and cultural industries) but are also a model of societal self-organization.

Along the highway E70 in western Serbia, 2006

The process of rethinking this type of creative production, which has been increasingly emerging over the last 10 years in the expanded fields of art and architecture, involves a change in the relationship between one's own work and that which represents cultural experience. This altered approach to production is no longer concerned with designing a space for cultural experience but, on the contrary, with facilitating cultural experience that creates a space whose contours are not yet fixed. That which the type of creativity we are considering here refers to thus has much more to do with a communal organization of cultural and spatial production than with the creation of monumental spaces *for* culture. It is participation that generates the site rather than the site generating participation. To use Mika Hannula's term, this 'politics of small gestures' consists in art and architecture participating in processes of meaning production that take place in the politicized public sphere without taking part in the competition to produce the most eye-catching product.[17] Under the conditions of the all-appropriating cultural turn in globalization, this creativity therefore often expresses itself most forcefully by retreating from the circuits of the industry of the spectacle and engaging in the networked production of a series of such gestures, sketches and experiments. This process, as Félix Guattari formulates it in *Chaosmosis*, involves a denormalization and displacement of organizational mechanisms (research, exhibition, planning, etc.) in which production acquires meaning, a mobilization of levels of consciousness to reconstruct 'an operational narrativity, that is, functioning beyond information and communication, like an existential crystallization of ontological heterogenesis'.[18]

A decisive aspect of this mobilization lies in the experience of the upheavals that are taking place, i.e. in the plurality of situations in which the global change in production and communication forms establishes points of contact with the lives of individuals, rather than in a changing transcendent schema of temporal and spatial distribution and organization. In the radical case, these experiential moments are found in the sudden change of social systems, as in the case of Eastern Europe, or in the explosion of informal settlement forms on the peripheries of many large European cities. In other cases, such moments are found in micro-situations in which the forces of globalization become locally concentrated and new economic nodal points develop, lay claim to unregulated spaces, seek new staging posts for the commercial cultural industries or force urban quarters to be reshaped in the interest of geopolitical or urban-strategic speculation. All these situations are shaped by experiences of upheaval and not by experiences of rule observance. Decisions cannot resort to a constraining framework of norms formulated by the state or another form of authority. The categories of experience are defined by individuals and thus facilitate a production of subjects that were not present as such previously. The plane of reference deriving from these experiences and the situation immanent to them is the plane of the anthropological normality of life, the level of many momentary contacts, friendships and bonds as well as disagreements, enmities and fears. The experience of upheaval thus transects many levels of everyday existence in which a necessity for new decisions always enforces itself, new qualities emerge and new alliances are formed. What is decisive is therefore neither a prepotent global sphere nor an essentialist local mindset but rather the uneven terrain of unforeseen occurrences, irritations and disturbances, which emerges in the moment of confluence between unequal forces and provokes a whole series of unforeseen paths and situations.

## POTENTIALITIES

The formation of networks facilitates a shift from an enforced participation in upheavals to a *utilization* of these upheavals. The logic that is mobilized in this movement provokes a new relationship between context and situation, between space and time. It generates a series of upheavals in what Antonio Negri describes as the economically administered removal of time in our epoch: 'Time is removed – the mind is, as Gertrude Stein wants, a space; theory is the geography of this space. Time is a transcendental schematism accomplished because presupposed. Therefore it is ecstasy of effectual Power, of the capitalist analytic of subsumption.'[19] It is precisely this geography that is affected in terms of its central anchorage when in experimental praxis maps are not read but rather made use of and laws are not observed but rather utilized. The difference between reading and making use of, between observance and utilization, lies in the possibility of a negligible deviation from what constitutes the respective prevailing norm. This possibility emerges when the time removed from space is brought into play again: the time to traverse geographically fixed borders, the time to explore new spaces, the time to experience collectively. For many network actors, collective enactment, valorization and experimentation relating to structures of deregulation and the production of a 'cognitariat' (Franco Berardi) decoupled from capital represents a more effective means for shaping reality than a purely oppositional attitude in terms of engagement and a universal counter-theory in terms of conception. The artistic or architectural work integrated in this shift is no longer a space that can be traversed but rather a time that is lived through. Network action is thus an endeavour without a guarantee of success, an endeavor to achieve simultaneity and to create conditions that facilitate this. The self-organization of creative praxis is based on a shaping of time in which form is a question of the production of relationships. At this point urban production meets the contemporary articulation of art practices.

High-rise construction located in New Belgrade, Serbia, designed by Mihajlo Mitrović (1972-1980)
The 30-storey residential tower and the 26-storey office tower are connected by a bridge structure located on the 26th floor

Artistic and architectural praxis thereby shifts attention from the conditions of the respective place and its institutional actualities to the complex potentialities inherent in every situation. It formulates an approach that sees the political possibilities of change less in the external explanation of a local situation, in the critical analysis of its layers and depths and in the planning of strategies than in the actualization of the potential of the prevailing contradictions, conflicts and ambiguities of a situation. The integration of architecture in the continual flow of network forces has led to the fact that it is also beginning to look for its action logic beyond an analytic and planning intervention in spatial configurations and to develop a new interest in collaborations with practices relating to the appropriation and utilization of prevailing situations. Interim uses, provisional spatial solutions, ephemeral buildings and relational architecture are common catchphrases used to describe this architecture of upheaval – an architecture that has become fluid and that supports different spontaneous articulations of spaces of possibility without interpreting their fundamental instability as a deficiency. Provisional forms of cultural participation are forming in the convergence of networks.

Along the highway E70 in eastern Croatia, 2006

Provisional solutions are commonly thought of as a form of compensation that is supposed to counterbalance existing deficits: a deficit in terms of infrastructure, accommodation or public assembly sites but also a deficit in terms of jail cells or experientially enriched urban space. Such provisional solutions fulfil specific functional requirements. They play a strategic role for the dynamic unfolding of forces of nation-state government and post-Fordist production. However, what if we were to briefly leave aside the stipulation of functionality and employ a concept of compensation understood as a mode of production that is not tied to the idea of a deficit? What if we were to comprehend compensation as a type of production that acts from within itself, beyond a relationship to that which is lacking or prescribed by way of a particular logic? Such a mindset distances the concept of compensation from the field of local, economic, political and historically bound dependencies and the knowledge that supports and maintains these dependencies. This leads to a shift onto unstable ground that offers as yet unknown utilization possibilities, which it can liberate or refuse in equal measure. Such a concept of compensation is indicated by the ontology and politics that Giorgio Agamben discerns in the significance of potentiality for this endeavour: '[Potentiality] is that through which Being founds itself *sovereignly*, which is to say, without anything preceding or determining it (*superiorem non recognoscens*) other than its own ability not to be. And an act is sovereign when it realizes itself by simply taking away its own potentiality not to be, letting itself be, giving itself to itself.'[20] If we follow Agamben in seeing this capacity in the radical freedom from the compulsion to actualize, the question arises as to the way in which art and architecture can intervene in the distribution of ways of being to the extent that a wealth of splinter worlds forms out of the mobilizing forces of upheaval, worlds whose intensities and aggregations represent something new beyond the dominant reference system.

Can the connectivity of networks provide a relational framework for the production of aesthetic provisionalities with which the instabilities of our contemporary state can be appropriated and lived out? Can inherently unstable network action facilitate sustainable political participation in which deregulation is utilized for a shifting of empowerment from a centre to an archipelago of peripheral existences? Is such a model restricted to an exclusive space of artistic production or can such a potential also be discerned in the prevailing realities of global networks? For instance, states such as Nigeria, Cameroon, Kenya, Uganda, Somalia, Rwanda and South Africa are now being linked together by the boom in rapidly growing mobile phone networks across Africa. In a period of only 10 years, from 1998 to 2008, the number of mobile phone users on the continent has grown from 2 million to over 150 million, and an ever-increasing number of private telecom companies are sharing in the high profits offered by this new and largely unregulated market. One of the first initiatives to take advantage of these thriving mobile phone networks is the Kenyan M-PESA: international money transfer via SMS. It is predicted that in the near future this system will be used to transfer over 100 billion US dollars annually to the continent by African emigrants, money that will play a significant role in accelerating economic growth. This development is being interpreted by neo-liberal intellectuals as heralding immense economic and social changes resulting from private-sector activity rather than state and international aid provision, while leftist economists are warning of the dangers inherent in the interplay of micro-enterprises and precarity. Meanwhile the new technology is finding new forms of use in Kenya. The Nairobi People's Settlement Network (NPSN), for example, uses mobile telephony and the internet to organize massive resistance to slum clearances in the pursuit of profit. In 2006 Kibera in Nairobi, Africa's largest slum region with more than 80,000 inhabitants,[21] was the site of the first self-organized meeting of activists from a range of slum areas, who used flash mobbing to oppose corruption and exploitation. Their spontaneously coordinated gatherings at sites where clearances had been scheduled resulted in the prevention of bulldozer deployment and the creation of new structures of understanding. With the help of the well established mobile phone network, the population thus selectively transformed the micro-enterprise structure and its calculated predictability into a system of unforeseen self-coordination and made the network technologies of domination into an instrument of communal emergence.

On the border between Bosnia and Herzegovina and eastern Croatia, 2006

In this variable geometry of networks lie the structural preconditions for collective action.[22] Networks constitute attractive action alliances not because they form a closed power structure but because they promise the possibility of transformation. In the moment of upheaval they become reservoirs for the hope of finding collective possibilities of participation and change. As a result, network action constitutes a continual regrouping and reshaping of goals and components that allow for the transformation of sites of passive experience into sites of resistance. Transformation is itself thus claimed as a site of resistance. Network creativity repositions the enforced participation in upheaval as a form of utilization in which the network becomes not a means but a site of its own transformation. Put another way, what we are designating here as a network encompasses a topological tension between the connectivity of this structure and the ideas and meanings continually being developed by its actors.[23] The role of this tension consists in fending off the topological stability that would transform the network into fixed structures with an inherent identity. In a political sense, network action is thus based on a concept of deformation: networks form topological possibilities from which new protagonists are generated as network effects. This means that there is a fundamental asymmetry between the prevailing morphology of a network and its actors, an elementary moment of non-recognition and conflict, which is incorporated in the relationship between present and future structures. This asymmetry does not only provide the basis for a reshaping of the individual within a new relational ethics. It also shapes the unstable site of network creativity through an incessant and irreducible transformation of ends that are never given.

1. Michael Hardt and Antonio Negri, *Multitude: War and Democracy in the Age of Empire* (London: Hamish Hamilton, 2004), 83.
2. Ivan Kučina, 'The Instrumentalisation of Friendship', in *Lost Highway Expedition*, ed. Alenka Gregorič (Ljubljana: Galerija Škuc, 2006), 49.
3. See http://www.schoolofmissingstudies.net/sms-lhe.htm
4. One of the first print publications arising from this project is the photo collection *Lost Highway Expedition Photo Book*, eds. Katherine Carl and Srdjan Jovanovic Weiss (Rotterdam: Veenman Publishers, 2007).
5. Angela Melitopoulos, 'Corridor X', in *B-Zones. Becoming Europe and Beyond*, ed. Anselm Franke (Barcelona: Actar, 2006), 158.
6. Hardt and Negri, ibid. note 1.
7. Marina Gržinić, 'Performative Alternative Economics', in *Alternative Economics, Alternative Societies*, ed. Oliver Ressler/New Media Center kuda.org (Frankfurt am Main: Revolver, 2005), 22.
8. Raqs Media Collective, 'A/S/L: Age/Sex/Location', in *Geography and the Politics of Mobility*, ed. Ursula Biemann (Cologne: Verlag der Buchhandlung Walther König, 2003), 84f.
9. Ge Jin, 'Chinese Goldfarmers in the Game World', *Consumers, Commodities & Consumption*, vol. 7, no. 2 (May 2006).
10. As the British newspaper *The Guardian* reported on 27 April 2006, an investigation by the European Parliament concluded that between 2001 and 2005 the CIA conducted over 1,000 secret flights transporting alleged terrorists across the territory of the European Union. See online: http://www.guardian.co.uk/world/2006/apr/27/usa.topstories3
11. Claire Bishop, 'Antagonism and Relational Aesthetics', *October* 110 (2004): 51-79; Grant Kester, *Conversation Pieces: Community + Communication in Modern Art* (Berkeley, CA: University of California Press, 2004).
12. Miwon Kwon, 'One Place After Another: Notes on Site Specificity', *October* 80 (1997): 88.
13. Paolo Virno, *A Grammar of the Multitude: For an Analysis of Contemporary Forms of Life* (New York: Semiotext(e), 2004), 35.
14. Ibid., 38f.
15. Raqs Media Collective, 'X Notes on Practice: Stubborn Structures and Insistent Seepage in a Networked World', in *Immaterial Labour: Work, Research & Art*, eds. Melanie Gilligan and Marina Vishmidt (London and New York: Black Dog Publishing, 2004). See online: http://www.raqsmediacollective.net/texts1.html
16. Bruno Latour, 'There is no information, only transformation', in *Uncanny Networks: Dialogues with the Virtual Intelligentsia*, ed. Geert Lovink (Cambridge, MA: MIT Press, 2002), 157.
17. Mika Hannula, 'The Blind Leading the Naked – The Politics of Small Gestures', in *Art, City and Politics in an Expanding World: Writings from the 9th International Istanbul Biennial*, ed. Deniz Ünsal (Istanbul Foundation for Culture and Arts, 2005), 193.
18. Félix Guattari, *Chaosmosis: An Ethico-Aesthetic Paradigm* (Bloomington, IN: Indiana University Press, 1995), 85.
19. Antonio Negri, *Time for Revolution* (London and New York: Continuum, 2003), 53.
20. Giorgio Agamben, *Homo Sacer. Sovereign Power and Bare Life* (Stanford, CA: Stanford University Press, 1998), 46.
21. See Robert Neuwirth, *Shadow Cities: A Billion Squatters, A New Urban World* (London and New York: Routledge, 2005), 67-99.
22. Manuel Castells, *The Power of Identity*, 2nd edition (Oxford: Blackwell, 2004), 156.
23. Tiziana Terranova, *Network Culture: Politics for the Information Age* (London: Pluto Press, 2004), 155f.

On the highway E70 between eastern Croatia and Serbia, 2006

**PM/HM:** < rotor > has instigated an enormous network of collaborations between creative practices in southeastern Europe. How did you come to pursue this curatorial approach of connecting with other initiatives?

**Margarethe Makovec:** Anton Lederer and I launched < rotor > in the mid-1990s as a kind of laboratory of discovery. For us it was some sort of work in progress or, let's say, a learning-by-doing process. We discovered a very interesting area in Graz, the second-largest town in Austria. It was the district called Gries and at the time densely populated by war refugees from the former Yugoslavia. So we moved into a shop at street level and started out by focusing on what we found around us. What's more, the border to Slovenia is quite close, about 30 kilometres from Graz. So during this same period, we also began travelling a lot. Soon we discovered that it's the same distance from Graz to Vienna as it is to Ljubljana. Everything developed organically, and I think we learned most by curating exhibitions on our own.

We've always had a wide range of interests: one of them involved putting together exhibitions and discussing political issues in Austria as well as in a larger European context. Others concerned establishing an artist-in-residence exchange programme and an archive on contemporary art from southeastern Europe. These interests provided the basis for everything else, including travelling and meeting people. Actually we're almost more interested in making and sharing contacts than keeping them to ourselves – the latter would probably make us feel somewhat claustrophobic. We've always wanted to spread the information we gather. We like doing research, and talking to artists and everyone else who happens to be around. If you travel to Kosova and see how Prishtina or Peja (Pec) works, if you meet these very young artists in their 20s, and you see the contexts they're operating in, then it's easier to bring them into another, let's say, European curatorial context.

**PM/HM:** Using the umbrella term Middle-South-East (MSE) Meeting, you've organized several trans-European gatherings of artists and cultural producers. The most recent one took place in Prishtina/Kosovo in November 2006. How has this operational format evolved over the years?

**Margarethe Makovec:** It started with Manifesta 3. when Gregor Podnar was artistic director of Škuc Gallery in Ljubljana. Gregor asked us and five other institutions to curate an exhibition at Škuc Gallery. For the opening day of Manifesta, we organized a kind of conference to which each of us invited five people – so we were quite a large group at the first MSE Meeting. And it showed that a network already existed – a fine moment considering our networking aspirations and the fact that such attempts sometimes turn out to be a bit superficial. If you bring three curators together, it's not a network, and especially not one that has grown. Anyway, we continued in this spirit and arranged gatherings, which we called MSE Meetings. Middle-South-East is a term that is quite open in all directions. In 2002 < rotor > organized a more internal meeting with a large number of participants. *Balkan Konsulat* was a direct result of this meeting. The idea of this project was to work out a way to present networking and the people who enable a certain art scene, for instance, Erden Kosova in Istanbul or Michael Koleček in Prague. With *Balkan Konsulat* we tried to establish a platform to present partner art scenes and their respective work philosophies. For the exhibition *Balkan Konsulat Prague*, for instance, Michael Koleček opened his network to include works from German, Polish and Slovak artists. The 2004 meeting in Graz revealed

still another layer of MSE's fluid character, as it also involved people from, e.g. Holon and London. Middle-South-East is truly growing in all directions. The last meeting took place in 2006 in Prishtina where the situation was and still is rather unstable, so I think meeting there was in itself an important political statement.

**PM/HM:** What challenges does one face when engaging in such a variety of different locations? Do you think there are ways of developing a sense of sustainable community among people working in very different situations?

*real*utopia*
Art in the Gries quarter of Graz, May–October 2003
Information kiosk in Griesplatz

## Margarethe Makovec

*Balkan Konsulat proudly presents*
Exhibition series, October 2002 – November 2003

4th MSE Meeting
Prishtina, Kosovo, 24-26 November 2006
Exhibition of works by Astrit Ibrahimi at The Kosova Art Gallery, Prishtina

**Margarethe Makovec:** Of course, all these countries are really different and their art scenes are, too. For example, in most of these countries there's no money and no art market. If you look at the art scene in Bulgaria or Romania, for instance, new spaces of contemporary art are just beginning to emerge, following the example set by the Soros Centres, which covered the field in the mid-1990s. There are so many different developments and political backgrounds. Tito's Yugoslavia was different from Ceausescu's Romania. And this means their work conditions and art histories are very different, too. And so our focus has always been on meeting people who have a certain interest in exposing these developments in their work. These people are not directors of institutions in the usual sense. Some of them have launched archives of their own in private spaces, like Lia and Dan Perjovschi in Bucharest. Out of necessity, they've developed a different method for bringing things together. And as always, if you're not part of a particular scene, then you're considered an outsider. And normally this means you'll have to bring money with you if you want to do a project. But through <rotor>, we feel like we belong to this big 'family'. There's a very strong feeling of trust within the group we work with, because we're constantly trying to connect people. As always, it's important to think about the format of your work. In the case of *real\*utopia*, for instance, we involved a lot of artists from the MSE region in a public art project in Graz. We were interested in how people who were originally from Turkey but had lived in Austria for several years would react to an art intervention by a Turkish artist. This in itself is an interesting question, but when the work is shown on a prison wall, it has still another layer of context. For us it's more interesting to work in such frames.

**PM/HM:** It seems that archival work plays an important role in structuring the knowledge production of such projects.

**Margarethe Makovec:** Absolutely, it all started as a working archive for Anton and me, especially for curating exhibitions. For quite a long time, there was a lack of information about contemporary art in southeastern Europe. So we began concentrating on updating the data in our archive. These days, a lot of people come to use it. It's not public in the sense that we have regular office hours, but in the sense that people can work here and we provide them with all the material they need. In a way, it has become the real backbone of our work, and for others, too. For example, B+B from London have done research in our archive. I guess it's just about using all one's contacts and working with people who share similar concerns. This is an interesting and contagious process, and we think it's really how things should be. What we've observed – not only in our own field but also in other contexts – is the omnipresence of networks. A lot of them aren't meant for the long term, sometimes they aren't even meant to outlast a single event. That's not our plan, as we've never been interested in immediate results. Our MSE Meetings, for example, have more to do with sharing information. People often tend to begin by thinking about results, but then you suddenly have 15, 20 or 30 people sitting there together, and they all come from different backgrounds and directions. So in the end you have all sorts of ideas, but no specific results. And yet when there are results after all, as with *Balkan Konsulat* or large MSE Meetings, then they have come about naturally. You have some ideas and you just work on them.

# Nataša Ilić

**PM/HM**: You're part of a collective of female curators with a very distinct agenda reflected in the group's name, 'What, How and for Whom'. How does this relate to the conditions of working in Zagreb?

**Nataša Ilić**: We – there are four of us – started our group in 1999. We're curators and like to call ourselves a 'curatorial collective'. The name of our collective is What, How and for Whom, which is abbreviated WHW. But we've always pronounced it 'veh-hah-veh', and this can be seen as a form of resistance to the English language. We started when the social situation in Croatia was finally beginning to change, after a long decade under a very right-wing government, in very isolated cultural and political circumstances, with a very oppressive atmosphere, and war, of course. So, in the late 1990s it finally felt possible to move about, to breathe, to do things. A number of non-governmental organizations had come into being earlier; they stemmed from the alternative cultural movement of the 1980s. Then in the 1990s, they all became involved in issues related to human rights, refugees, the war, and so on; yet they were in no way specifically involved in cultural production.

There was a magazine called *Arkzin* that existed within the framework of the anti-war campaign. It was a network of 30 anti-war organizations from very different backgrounds. This magazine was probably the only platform in the 1990s for critical reflection on social reality. In 1998, it published a book for the 150th anniversary of the Communist Manifesto, and Slavoj Žižek wrote the preface. When the book was published nothing really happened: the newspapers didn't mention it; evidently no one even dared to reflect on communism and our socialist past, not even through such a symbolic gesture. We were then asked to do a show: it was hoped that we would invite other artists and make some kind of cultural event out of it that would, in turn, bring about some reflection or reaction. We took the work extremely seriously; we started with a small, not very ambitious project with Croatian artists, but then, as it developed, our ambitions grew. Also, the entire social situation changed over the next year and a half. Anyhow, in 2000, when we held the exhibition in collaboration with *Arkzin*, which still existed at the time, we did so with the net.cultural club [mama] and the Croatian Association of Artists, in this very official space for the visual arts. In the end the exhibition was called *What, How and for Whom*, and was now dedicated to the 152nd anniversary of the Communist Manifesto; approximately 50 artists from all around Europe participated.

In addition we organized a number of other shows that presented works outside the main exhibition space. At the time it was also extremely important to set up lectures, roundtables and discussions: this was the first time cultural practitioners from Serbia and Bosnia were invited to the same show – and not only to exhibit but to discuss as well. We invited people like Frederic Jameson, Richard Barbrook and Mark Terkessidis. So that's the story of our first project and how we came together. The show turned out well not only because we were happy with how it looked, but also because a lot of people came to see it and there was talk of it internationally. In fact for years it was rumoured we were doing many things in Zagreb, but for a long time no one actually came to see anything – now the situation has changed.

**PM/HM**: In light of Yugoslavia breaking up into a number of smaller entities, how do you perceive the scope of the cultural realm you're working in now? How do you deal with this situation in which the local is clearly marked off and everything beyond it is immediately international?

**Nataša Ilić**: How do we deal with this form of the local you're implying we have? One in which we immediately

*Novine Nova 2*
Gallery Nova Newspapers, no. 2, cover, 2004

*What, How and for Whom*
Dedicated to the 152nd anniversary of the Communist Manifesto, book cover, Zagreb, 2000

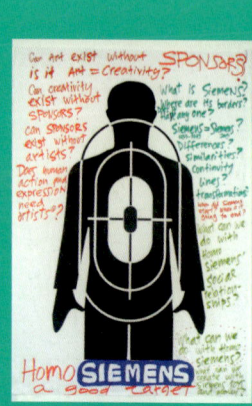

*Blancos*
Grupo de Arte Callejero, 2004
Collective Creativity exhibition, Kunsthalle Fridericianum, Kassel, 2005

Network Creativity Interview

30

past three years have evolved around the notion of normalization, because society really has become normal. I mean, we are no longer experiencing the crisis we once had in common with certain fringe groups in Europe.

PM/HM: The experience of crisis is often described as a testing ground for political imagination. Does this still apply to the current transition in Croatia, the transition from emergency and crisis to a phase of normalization?

Nataša Ilić: Not really. I'm afraid, in a general way, we've contributed to normalization, and this is what has enabled us to take part in international contexts at times of urgency. Moreover, I don't believe these times of crisis have led to more imagination. Though maybe what they have forced us to do – and this does not only apply to the 1990s but also to the socialist experiment in Yugoslavia – is to look at it all with much more appreciation than I remember our doing in the 1980s. Back then I was full of spite for the political gestures around me. What now interests me is the conceptual idea of ex-Yugoslavia, and not more. And this is so because I'm really distressed about our present political system; sometimes it seems to me that people in post-communist countries are more

distressed than elsewhere. This has a positive side, because it makes many of us more critical – wh ch means we don't just take things at face value. And it's one of the reasons why we don't trust so-called normalization. This has, among other things, to do with the fact that we've analyzed it all and now see it as a mere lid under which everything suppressed is still brewing and waiting to explode.

There was one particular project – originally entitled *Normalization* and realized as a platform with both Istanbul and Sweden – where our initial idea was not just specific to the Croatian context. Rather it was related to the mix of welfare state in Sweden, and to Turkey's desperate attempt to approach the European Union in a way that reminded us of post-war Croatia. Though the project could just as well have taken place somewhere else. As a matter of fact, there has been lots of talk of normalization everywhere recently.

Radek Community and Non Governmental Control Committee, work in progress
*Collective Creativity* exhibition, Kunsthalle Fridericianum, Kassel, 2005

become international and turn into something else as soon as we open the door? True, this is the case. I think for us, such international collaborations are extremely important for several reasons. For one, it has to do with the problems all post-communist countries face in certain respects and the fact that validation comes only from the West. So our internal position and positioning becomes important too; it's hard for officials to dismiss us once we have good international contacts.

This builds up our reputation in a way that would probably work differently if I tried to do the same thing in Germany, where it's quite natural, if you run a space, to work both internationally and locally. But for us the local context is more important: all our projects are simply trying to address social urgencies. Such urgencies have, however, undergone transformation over the last six years, so that we now no longer call them urgencies, but normalization. All our programmes in the

# Gerald Raunig

**PM/HM:** What was your initial motivation to establish the European Institute for Progressive Cultural Policies (eipcp), and how is its particular institutional form linked to the objective of your work?

**Gerald Raunig:** First let me say that my remarks cannot be seen as representative of eipcp. We have developed our institute collectively and on many different levels at the same time, so my perspective mustn't be (mis-) understood as even remotely panoptic. Rather, mine is a subjective history to which other histories must be added. My colleagues Andrea Hummer, Raimund Minichbauer and I worked intensively at IG Kultur Österreich in the 1990s, and at the end of the decade we began wondering how the network of cultural initiatives could be sensibly transnationalized. There were perhaps two reasons why we quickly rejected the idea of creating an additional European 'civil society network' like those that had been popping up in the cultural sphere since the late 1980s. The first pragmatic reason was that, in contrast to other cultural scenes that had formed their own European networks – e.g. those of theatre-makers, art educators and even socio-cultural centres – the point of departure for our autonomous cultural work and cultural initiatives was a much more heterogeneous and much less coherent setting in the various nation-states of Europe. Secondly – and this has more political weight – many of these networks had very quickly become lame lobbyists or EU consulting enterprises, primarily due, in my opinion, to the conservative effect of their member structures, which did not realize their participatory and critical potential on this highly abstract network level, but which ran the risk of becoming components of a meshwork of 'European governance'.

So, after one or two years of discussion and research, we decided to describe our undertaking as an 'institute' and to conceive of the network in such a way that we could develop a new praxis of transnational exchange via a loose network of correspondents. In thematic terms, the commitment to establishing an *institute* (symbolically on the last day of 1999; the association was founded only later) put the focus on a discursive, non-representationist praxis – whereby the presumptuous ring of the institute's name (European Institute for Progressive Cultural Studies') reflected, in equal measure, the old context of cultural networks, their fixation on state and supra-state cultural policy, and an attempt to create an ironic distance. At that point in time it was not entirely clear to us just how necessary it would become to consider the problems of all the components of the institute's name. Over the years some actors of our institute (mainly Therese Kaufmann, Raimund Minichbauer and myself) ventured, more or less successfully, to preserve the critical link to European cultural policy.

The final factor determining the positioning of the institute was surely the political developments in Austria in 1999/2000, when a resistance movement attempted to fight the reactionary government of Wolfgang Schüssel and his conservative party, which was in a coalition with Jörg Haider's FPÖ. Although the movement did not achieve its goal of ending this racist coalition, it was very effective in its politicizing efforts, and it was decisive for the institute's focus on an activist praxis. At the same time, it provided a foundation over the next few years for an intense exchange of ideas among most of the institute's main actors, even though some of them, such as Stefan Nowotny, Boris Buden and Hito Steyerl, more or less moved nomadically throughout Europe.

**PM/HM:** How does the project *republicart*, which was developed in the framework of the European Commission's Culture 2000 programme, sit within the structure of eipcp? In what way did you respond to the above issues in this project?

**Gerald Raunig:** With *republicart* (2002-2005), we managed – in a second phase after founding the institute – to establish a small base in Vienna and Linz and to successively develop a praxis specific to eipcp, transnationally linking the discourse at the interfaces of art production, theory formulation and activism by primarily using the methods of art projects, exhibitions and discursive events (from larger conferences to our workshop format). The quality of our workshops, in particular, is based on the concentration and intensity of the discussions, which involve no more than 10 invited guests. The danger of producing a small elitist circle is averted at the publication level. The publications of eipcp are its showpiece, first and foremost the multilingual web journal that we subsequently named *transversal*. From the outset, multilingual publication has entailed using the platform of the network not only to go beyond the scope of the mostly national discussion forums, but also to publish consistently in at least three languages. Over the years a specific multilingual editorial routine has evolved that has us working together with Aileen Derieg, Marcelo Expósito and many others on a praxis of exchange that promises to produce more than the mere translation of texts from the original language into another tongue.

**PM/HM:** To what extent have these experiences influenced the approaches taken by your current projects *transform* and *translate*?

**Gerald Raunig:** With the projects *transform* and *translate* (both 2005-2008), we are expanding the praxis tested in *republicart* to include very different thematic fields – namely, the field of institutional critique on the one hand and the discourse on 'cultural translation' on the other. Now that we have entered a third phase in the development of the institute, this thematic and institutional expansion has made it necessary to consider the development of eipcp as a 'project institution' (Stefan Nowotny, Birgit Mennel). In addition to the danger of internal structuralization processes at the institute, we must consider the fact that, with the greater visibility over the last few years, very different formations of desire have crystallized in relation to the institute, partially originating outside its borders. Two to three years after the start of the *republicart* project, its website, in particular, attracted a growing stream of positive feedback, suggestions for improvement and offers for collaboration. However, in the last few years there has also been a growing number of unfriendly projections onto the institute. Naturally a precarious project institution like eipcp has no easy time in preventing the engagement with this criticism from becoming polemical and in rendering the opening process productive. Although it has little support from local and national funding agencies, the financing it receives from the Culture 2000 programme creates a fairly good foundation to carry out critical projects largely unhampered by impertinent governance demands, even if the institute remains mired in the conditions of neoliberal governmentality.

# Katrin Klingan

**PM/HM:** *relations* is a multi-stranded project initiated in Germany and oriented towards its eastern neighbours. What were your motivations in starting this project and what expectations did you have?

**Katrin Klingan:** The original initiative came from the German Federal Cultural Foundation, which has had a special focus on eastern, southeastern and central Europe since 2002. I was invited to conceive a multilateral exchange project with Germany. My first thought was to ask what it meant to conceive an exchange project for these specific regions, on the one hand, and for this 'state body', on the other. This involved quite a few questions. Due to the collapse of socialism and the wars in former Yugoslavia, many of the countries in eastern Europe were, and still are, undergoing extensive and rapid transition. They were, and are, negotiating their forms of government, their pasts and, in part, even their borders – in fact, nothing other than their entire cultural, social and political identity. In the process, they've been overwhelmed by a capitalism operating largely without any restrictions, a factor which has further accelerated change. Given this situation, my task was initially to create structures for an exchange that would take these different paces and points of departure into account, and this meant also different expectations. At the same time, we saw ourselves confronted with a well-established public-funded support system – devised to result in long-term and sustainable cultural exchange – that had to perform a difficult balancing act: on the one hand, the system aimed at contributing 'something' constructive on unfamiliar territory, to help a project or an idea on its way; on the other hand, it also had to take into consideration the diverse criteria of funding institutions, criteria both expressly set and implied. At *relations*, we didn't want to export ideas from Germany, nor did we want to import cultural assets from eastern Europe. For this reason, all our projects started with discussions with artists and intellectuals – we asked them questions, for instance, about which aspects of their respective social realities should be brought to the public's attention by means of art. We then linked these local debates to international discourses in a second step. Hence many of the projects supported by *relations* have established 'platforms': representatives from different social groups and cultural institutions have cooperated and generated artistic projects and actions within a certain organizational and thematic framework.

different local contexts that connect art, everyday life, theory, politics and history, and relate them to issues prevalent in Germany. So it was much more about understanding why intellectuals and artists are really interested in certain topics and why they're so convinced they have to discuss them within their societies. This approach automatically generated an array of projects. The thematic diversity ranged from an international film project, a culture magazine on Moldavian television, the setting up of an alternative fine arts academy in Kosovo, to an archive project dealing with contemporary art of the 1950s in Poland and the artistic reconstruction of eastern Europe's post-war art history. Let me give you just one example, the project *Missing Identity* in Kosovo: the basic impulse of the artists and theoreticians who conceived the project was to develop a sensibility for the non-existent, for what's missing in their society. Therefore they founded the first gallery for contemporary art in Kosovo called EXIT as well as an alternative art academy that offered courses on contemporary art and cultural theory free of charge. Within this very project, art and theory open up a different culture of communication, one that questions prevailing social hierarchies and discourses on national identities. We

**PM/HM:** The projects you've created in collaboration with so many people in Sofia, Chișinău, Warsaw and other European cities come in many different formats, ranging from the book project *East Art Map* to political platforms, performances, debates and on-site interventions. How did this variety of formats develop?

**Katrin Klingan:** There were never any formats to start with. They evolved in the process. For me it wouldn't have mattered if the projects had only produced publications. So, the formats weren't part of *relations*'s initial interest. Our goal was to formulate overarching questions out of the

're-arranging', colloquium of *relations* project partners
Halle an der Saale, 2004

then encouraged cooperation between *Missing Identity*, the Städelschule (a state art academy) and the Portikus (an exhibition space), both in Frankfurt/Main. Since the mobility of Kosovo's inhabitants had practically come to a standstill, we initiated a broad student exchange project called *ACADEMY REMIX*. The outcome of this cooperation was not only, as we'd planned, collective works and exhibitions, but also an international symposium at Portikus, entitled 'What is an art academy today?'. In Germany, where this question had long seemed answered, the confrontation with a completely different world of experience gave the issue a new lease on life. And this is precisely what we were aiming at: focusing less on providing assistance and more on stimulating discussion.

**PM/HM**: Do you think there's potential to explore this further on other levels and that there's also a sort of 'informal' market emerging around these kinds of discourses?

**Katrin Klingan**: As far as the project *relations* is concerned, we knew from the very beginning that this would be a window of opportunity for several years, for precisely four years – and indeed it has been an enormous window, one that nobody else has been given on an institutional level with national funds in Europe. But the result of four years of *relations* is not only evident in the collaborations, exhibitions and publications, in the films, TV programmes, archives and alternative institutions developed within the *relations* framework.

The result also includes the process of mutual interaction and negotiating differences. This is also what I meant when I talked about 'platforms' earlier: here cultural exchange meant communication, a communication that dealt with the unpredictable and conflicts; moreover, a space was created for what needed to be developed first. What was exchanged here had simply not taken place in the individual countries before, nor could it be simply archived in museums. Rather, what has emerged is a network of relations and thematic focal points that reaches beyond geographic-political borders, the various languages and cultural differences; you can call it a network in flux, one that will continue on after *relations* has come to a close. In this respect, *relations* is not more and not less than a time splinter highlighting a more comprehensive development that takes place day to day in the search for dialogue and inter-cultural encounters. Regarding the 'informal markets' around these discourses: as a rule, analysis based on the social sciences seeks to delineate problems and identify their causes. In contrast, *relations* seeks to promote discussion. We've tried to bring these two approaches together and to understand and transmit how specific problems in specific places are being discussed. What visions of future artists and intellectuals are developing there? What vocabulary is being used, what kind of artistic language and practice? We cooperated with intellectuals and artists who tackle explosive themes and want to make a difference. The goal was to develop visions, to initiate discussions in the local context and make them comprehensible to an outside public. For us, combinations and confrontations between different actors, from both the artistic as well as the cultural and political fields, are extremely productive. We are concerned with the process of confrontation, and again and again with the necessary adjustments that emerge from this confrontation. When it works well, this leads to unexpected thematic turns and extends our vocabulary. In the end, nobody takes exactly the same position as they had before; or there are at least three more concepts for their original position.

We are thus concerned with productive disputes, so that afterwards we'll be at a different relay station and able to enter into new relations. Within such categories, terms like 'informal' and 'formal' are no longer relevant.

# Borderline Cases
## Windsor/Detroit

Downtown Windsor, 2006

Grand Circus Park, view from the Book Tower
Downtown Detroit, 2006
The border cities of Detroit (US) and Windsor (Canada) have suffered a dramatic decline following the 'restructuring' of the automotive industry in the 1970s.

Downtown Windsor, 2006

The former Michigan Theatre in Detroit, 2006, built in 1926, now used as a car park

SHOE REP
Windsor Shoe Repair
Peggy's Alterations Since 1984
SPECIALIST IN LEATHER
Dry Cleaning
258-9996
ELINE
& TAX SERVICES
INCOME TAX
BOOKKEEPING
BUSINESS PLAN
E: 256-3439
CANADIAN &
U.S.
DRY
CLEANING
ALTERATIONS
SUEDE
&
LEATHER

OASIS
Restaurant & Bakery
افران الواحة

FARES TRAVEL
WORLD WIDE TRAVEL
FROM Y FW NDSOR
UBA MEXIC

Along Wyandotte Street, the so-called 'Lebanese Street' in Windsor, 2006

Downtown Windsor, 2006

40

View from the Wintergarden of the Renaissance Center in Detroit (General Motors World Headquarters) across Detroit River to the Casino Windsor, 2006

ADULT
ENTERTAINMENT

1065
MOSQUE AND SCHOOL
OF AHLUL.BAYT
USE THE SIDE
DOOR PLEASE
أهل البيت
يرجى استخدام الباب الجانبي
1065

Mosque and School of Ahlul-Bayt on Wyandotte Street, Windsor, 2006

Along Wyandotte Street, the so-called 'Lebanese Street' in Windsor, 2006

Along Wyandotte Street, the so-called 'Lebanese Street' in Windsor, 2006

Ransom Gillis House, Brush Park, Detroit, 2006

Along Wyandotte Street, the so-called 'Lebanese Street' in Windsor, 2006

# Unbounded

## Irit Rogoff

Where and how are the limits which bound us established? Is the loosening of those limits synonymous with some form of liberation? Or are there certain undercurrents of concern that the response to removing boundaries might result in other and ever more vigilant modes of control? The task to hand is not one of liberation from confinement, but rather one of undoing the very possibilities of containment.

The concept of the 'unbounded' that I am attempting to put forward here seeks to marry, to bring closely together, spatialities and disciplines, i.e. certain contemporary territorial conditions, with others that frame our understanding of intellectual work today. This is surely an odd conjunction, a set of material circumstances that define spatial designations which I would like to set up in dialogue with a set of intellectual states, set up not as a causal relation but rather as one of metonymy. I am attempting this because on the one hand I see quite a few similarities between the two arenas and because on the other I believe that the framing conditions of our lives can never be that separate from the substance of what we spend those lives doing, even when these are not obvious to the naked eye. In both cases the active process of destabilization, of not having a sure and bounded ground from which to operate, is primary. Secondly I feel as if our critical lives have been much shaped by a struggle against boundaries – those of the nation-state and those of disciplined knowledge – and that the 'unbounded', which had in the past some liberating resonances, has recently returned to haunt us through the entire gamut of fears circulating within this current moment; and we must differentiate between age old fears and contemporary fears, for as Massumi has said, 'Fear is the barometric effect of contemporary capitalism.' At the level of the state there are fears concerning the inability to locate and identify enemies and fears about the inability to actually protect civilian populations from terrorist attacks, while at the level of knowledge production there are fears concerning the unravelling of institutional boundaries as sites of knowledge and fears about the lack of historically grounded knowledge as we move closer and closer to a 'trans-disciplinary' or to an 'undisciplined' intellectual practice. And so it seems we have to return to this conundrum of the 'boundary' once again, even though we may feel we have already covered that ground in a previous phase of our work, but now propelled by more recent fears and recent developments.

So first to some of these perceived similarities: the spatiality of the past few years has been characterized by an ever-increasing mode of destabilization in which notions of 'the terroristic', highly manipulated by state rhetorics, have made severe inroads into stable notions of territorial protection. Within these, previously militarized borders, which acted as barriers between 'us' and any perceived threat from the outside, have lost their logic and efficacy. Terroristic strategies have rendered boundaries as protective limits redundant, while the antagonism of some migrant populations towards the broad arena of Western capitalism and imperialism which forced their move and their sense of being besieged by multiple inhabitations and split loyalties, have led to the emergence of ever more hysterical discourses of perceived 'enemies from within'. On the other hand, in the arenas of intellectual work, an ever-continuing dissolution of disciplinary bastions of yesteryear, in which neat divisions could be sustained, and which in turn sustained notions of expertise, of deep scholarship and of grounded truth claims have also been eroding.

It is my claim that these two share certain conditions which I persist in seeing as having some form of potentiality, despite the many fears and concerns that the inevitable loosening of both sets of boundaries are certain to arouse.

Clearly, there are other understandings of 'unbounded', namely those that refer to global economies, to global warfare and to what Deleuze has termed 'control societies', whose material and conceptual implications are far from liberating or progressively transformative. The claims for a '"borderless" world of free movement of goods, capital and people, of flows travelling incessantly across regions and nations, of unstoppable global networks spanning ever more corners of the globe' (3Cs: counter cartographies collective) are neither convincing in their triumphalist vision nor convincing as a force for progress per se at any level. I shall return to these later, for the tension between bounded and unbounded is far more interesting than moralizing claims for freedom on the one hand and as the site of fears of that which is not materially and historically specific of one, and only one, set of conditions, on the other. Yet, the potential to elicit a language from a set of contemporary conditions with which we may counter the inevitable division and containment that are the daily work of all forms of boundaries, is too tempting to pass up without at least an effort to grasp it. As in the case of the present volume, *Networked Cultures*, the desire here is always to try and trace other relations, relations that extend beyond their natural parameters and emerge as the politics of connectivity.

Over the past few years our understanding of what can be contained within a boundary line has shifted considerably. Within the systems of globalization, neither labour nor capital can be bound in relation to a location. Similarly in the political rhetorics of 'the war on terrorism', claims for borders that ensure national security have not only proven unsustainable but in the process have redefined our understanding of the relations between space and its breaching. The trials and tribulations of identities on the move that test the limits of containment enacted by national boundaries and the inclusions and exclusions of citizenship and belonging have shown up the degree to which the containment and division practiced by borders have failed to do just that. Instead of bureaucratically regulated divisions we have the constitution of extra-territorial spaces for the containment of 'illegal immigrants', such as camps and centres for refugees and asylum seekers, or border settlements that produce 'passage' as permanence. Other formations that defy location are made up of the entanglements and mixings of vast populations of those who inhabit the grey zones of unsanctioned but necessary labour in reluctant host cultures, or as discussed above those 'unassimilated' into a single national narrative.

At the same time, in the intellectual world of transdisciplinarity, thought cannot be contained within traditional boundaries of its own genealogy. Our ever more complex operations of either 'arriving at a truth' or 'living out a truth' have taken us on considerable detours from the paths laid out by disciplinary protocols. Thought has taken on a more and more relational dimension with the ability to use our own passages as the mapping logics for connecting phenomena and artefacts and conditions which could not have been co-joined or related within any of the logics we had inherited. The conjunctions of fact and fiction, of experience and learned principles, the permissions to start in the middle and to recount our narrative in whatever voice comes to hand, the demise of the ability to pronounce judgement in some kind of Olympian mode, the recognition that 'criticality' is a condition of double inhabitation in which one can see through the causes of a condition while at the same time having to live out its consequences – all of these have come together to a knowledge which is not just 'situated' as critical movements such as Feminism and Post-Colonialism advocated as necessary, but is also embodied and performed.

Every activity surrounded by a 'borderline', be it one of national identity or one of disciplinary identification, puts into practice the parallel logics of division and containment. Countering the claims of such divisions and containments for purposes of 'security' on the one hand and of 'truth' or 'knowledge' on the other hand seems to me to be central to much critical work at present. Thus, the conditions of our lives and the means of critically thinking them out, of the need not to liberate ourselves from any specific mode of confinement but to critically dismantle the very notion of the ability to contain have converged in this moment of the 'unbounded'. Precisely those moments that seem to be characterized by stricture are the ones in which we can fully express our investment in the necessity of the possible.

Giorgio Agamben, in *Homo Sacer*, opens up a discussion of the relations between order and localization, a spatial conjunction which grapples with being named within the annals of culture. Those moments in which the law is suspended and order is unlocalized and which he terms 'state of exception' are paralleled in his argument by acts of specific localization that nevertheless are not sustained by order. The bio-political space, which results from the 'unlaw' inhabiting the 'law' within this state of exception renders unbounded the sphere of the social. Agamben, following Carl Schmitt, has here stressed the relation between location, order and law and the extent to which these build on one another. Its dangers are that 'unlaw' masquerading as 'law' becomes increasingly naturalized as 'states of exception' that drag on and on, and bureaucracies and regulating authorities emerge to cope with these, as can be seen in the ongoing conflicts in Iraq, Afghanistan, Congo, Rwanda, Chad, Palestine, Ethiopia, to name only a few highly visible ones.

However productive, this is however an understanding of 'unbounded' in which order and disorder, law and unlaw, norm and exception cannot be uncoupled from one another. Starting from elsewhere, as the famous anecdote advises (two lost tourists ask a local for directions on how to get somewhere; after long consideration he advises them, 'if I were you, I wouldn't start from here') might allow us to think potentiality. To this end I wish to take up Jacques Derrida's concerns with that which establishes 'the limits of the possible' as well as Brian Massumi's notion of 'everyday fear' and Nikos Papastegladis's notion of 'ambient fear' as points of departure for conjunctions between spatial understandings and intellectual procedures which seem to me to uniquely characterize the present moment. Instead of those coupled terms, I wonder what it would be like if we inhabited the seam between them, if we traced it again and again and thereby produced it as an inhabitation. To this end it seems to me very important to spatialize the workings of the unbounded as process rather than as state. To some extent one never fully arrives at an unbounded but strives towards it.

Borders, to paraphrase Jacques Derrida, serve to do nothing more than establish the limits of the possible.

Therefore, while borders that have been expanded, stretched, revised or interrupted may produce a temporary sense of satisfied achievement with regard to an expanded field of possibilities, in reality they continue to re-establish those limits behind slightly redrawn lines. And these limits of the possible work to ground a finite notion of thought, or thought that cannot leap beyond what it knows how to know. In relation to questions of territoriality, the entire discussion of breaching boundaries has linked borders and boundaries to legal statuses. Permissions to escape, permissions to travel, permissions to stay, permissions to work and permissions to take part in civic society are all negotiated in relation to the boundaries that divide and contain and that are sustained by a palimpsest of endlessly negotiated legal regulations.

As a device of such demarcations, the border is the line that needs to be crossed into a safe haven, away, for example, from the tyranny of evil in narratives of both the Second World War and the Cold War. Concurrently, it is the line at which demonized threats from the outside are held at bay and waves of ejected or disaffected migrants are either kept in or kept out of the protected entity. Thus the logic of the border is actually far less one of containment than one of division. Those concepts of division fluctuate between the concrete boundaries and between hostile and geographically embedded adversaries, such as warring nations and safe havens, running the gamut all the way to symbolic cultural permissions for transgression, of 'crossing a line'. It is this tension between internal fantasmatic border crossings and external collective armed containments that give the 'border' its current cultural frisson, its cachet as a term of political exchange, which articulates a set of potentially rich cultural contradictions whose manifestations have been concepts such as 'border writing' or the 'Border Arts Workshop'.

Other manifestations of the border are of course those of the heavily armoured and barricaded lines of division between two segregated national entities – this is a border whose integrity must be maintained at all cost, and those who attempt to pierce, breach or contravene it pay a bitter price, doomed to stay in a place of danger and misery or be kept out of the promise of safety and adequate conditions. But it is of course the 'law' that underpins the relative 'legality' and 'illegality' of subjects on the move, and not the very act of crossing over a border.

Foucault has often said of geographical metaphors that they always build on juridical maxims that in turn are sustained by political ideologies: 'Let's take a look at these geographical metaphors. *Territory* is no doubt a geographical notion, but it is first of all a juridico-political one: the area controlled by a certain kind of power. *Field* is an economico-juridical notion. *Displacement*: what displaces itself is an army, a squadron, a population. *Domain* is a juridico-political notion. *Soil* is a historico-geological notion. *Region* is a fiscal, administrative, military notion. *Horizon* is a pictorial but also strategic notion.'[1]

And so it becomes clearer and clearer to us that what we are dealing with in the process of trying to *unthink* borders and boundaries is a multifaceted apparatus in which territorial ownership and control veer between the occupation of place, the entitlement to it and the ability to marshal it into a controllable domain via some semblance of coherence. However, the highly controlled and regulated spaces that are defined by the state or the law or the inherited historical jurisdiction are equally writ with fear that works against any possibility of coherence but is highly manipulated in the struggle for cohesion. As Brian Massumi has said, 'A central concern [of this book] would have been to highlight the materiality of the body as the ultimate object of technologies of fear, understood as apparatuses of power aimed at carving into the flesh habits, predispositions, and associated emotions – in particular, hatred – conducive to setting social boundaries, to erecting and preserving hierarchies, to the perpetuation of domination. Although the organizing concept would have been low-level fear, naturalized fear, ambient fear, ineradicable atmospheric fright... special attention would have been given to fear to the extreme, to the great symphonies of collective hysteria, panic and national paranoia.'[2] Massumi addresses what he calls 'the saturation of social space by fear' and my question is what has that saturation by fear done to actual territorial materiality and to the possibility of conceiving an identifiable territory which is governed purely by that which frames and bounds it? The more recent moment is one which has been characterized by 'the terroristic', and its hallmark has been, more than anything else, the suspension of spatial certainties: exploding bodies, exploding cars, exploding buildings, an ambience of constant security announcements and metal detectors and exhortations to maintain constant vigilance and suspicion have resulted in what a recent film poster has called 'A slippery, shivery meditation on age-of-terror angst, and a brilliantly told tale from a first-time director' (*Hotel Habitare*, 2007). This inability to place the feared other, the feared event, outside of a protected territory is at the heart of a new 'ambient fear' and the futile attempts by Western governments to eradicate it by trying, in a furious and futile manner, to re-establish some semblance of protective boundaries. 'After September 11th,' says Nikos Papastergiadis, 'the fear of the other could not be contained within either a single territorial entity, or confined to a given place of origin. Fear was ambient, and initially the war was not to be fought against an enemy with a conventional army, but against the concept of terror... The boundlessness of the "war against terror" sent a chilling message not only in relation to the ambiguities of place and identity in global politics, but in the suggestion that a world with infinite terror implied that vigilance and war never ends... The twenty-first century began by re-mobilizing the emancipatory metaphor of "permanent revolution" into a slogan of dread.'[3]

And so this 'ambient fear' which has imploded the investment in and dependence on secure boundaries is one half of the current de-stabilization I am speaking of, while the other is the inability to bound knowledge within the perimeters of disciplines, or genealogies or methodologies which produce it in the same kind of division and containment of which I spoke earlier. That territorialities and intellectual paradigms are deeply steeped in one another is clear, and as Foucault stated, 'Once knowledge can be analysed in terms of region, domain, implantation, displacement, transposition, one is able to capture the process by which knowledge functions as a form of power and disseminates the effects of power'.[4]

How can we characterize this moment, which has seen through the movement from interdisciplinarity to multidisciplinarity to transdisciplinarity. Inter-disciplinary work as we experienced it in the 1980s was a model of additive enrichment;

a disciplinarity was expanded and extended via the importation of various materials and histories and methods from other disciplinary bases. And so we had an expanded sociology enriched via anthropology and psychology or an art history enriched through social history and media studies. But not only was this dogged by Derrida's previously quoted exhortation that 'boundaries, whether narrow or expanded, do nothing more than assert the limits of the possible', we can all also remember Barthes's lament of interdisciplinarity, which he likened to a process in which boxes of books are dragged around the border lines of disciplines and left there to agitate and produce effects while never actually managing to produce a new object of study. In the ensuing developments, methodologies from different fields of knowledge challenged and clashed with one another and vied between empirical grounds and self-conscious inclusions of subjectivity and reflexivity, but somehow managed to leave the very notion of 'methodology' undisturbed. An assumption remained that in order to approach a research project one had to have an a priori method that would enable you to arrive at a set of previously anticipated results. As those of us who fill in endless applications for grants and funding know, this is still largely the demand. But in our actual work we have a different experience of embarking on an intuited set of urgent matters and of letting the problematic and its materials elicit some kind of operating procedure, one that might surprise us and might result in an unexpected mode of challenge, and along the way take in all the voices and narratives and incidents which daily rewrite our fields of inquiry.

The transdisciplinarity of a more contemporary moment moves from being cumulative to being transformative. As Griselda Pollock has argued, 'I propose the transdisciplinary as a research operation replacing the "and" or "inter" with the idea of a creative current and a transformative movement that allows us to think forward via Freud and Warburg: what matters is the spaces we create for scholarly work, the environments for research as networks for creative interaction and perpetual translations.'[5] Perhaps with the objective I have here set myself, to try and articulate the process of the unbounded in relation to intellectual practice, I have some minor concerns of whether 'transdisciplinarity' might not nevertheless keep us in relation, and perhaps even a defiant relation, to the very disciplines we are in process of transcending. Arguing an 'unbounded' of knowledge production would perhaps move 'transdisciplinarity' towards an 'undisciplined' practice in which new objects of study might be produced. Very recently, at a gathering of performance theorists and performance artists and philosophers, I saw a model of knowledge production which takes place in the moment, through small fictions that produce between them an extensive connective tissue of reflection, which really did produce a platform of knowledge, and which I am not yet able to name. The great interest of this platform of knowledge for me is that it did not rely on any previously articulated knowledge, though practiced by people with very evidently considerable knowledge. That prior knowledge informed the practice was evident as something to build on without having to recuperate, rehearse or refer to it. This form of knowledge production and manifestation did not seem to involve telos, territoriality or ownership. In short, this was not knowledge as a legitimating force but as a set of enabling possibilities. For some time it has seemed to me that our moment of knowledge production is one in which transdisciplinarity *encounters* practice and that it is this encounter which is important; it is in the encounter that the work of 'unbounding', of refusing containment, takes place. Beyond the disciplines and materials that make up this field, it is the encounter itself, an active and performative cultural moment, that is central to the operations of contemporary knowledge production.

Producing new objects of knowledge does not always follow the simple logics of naming them. The Istanbul Biennale 2007, *Not Only Possible but Also Necessary – Optimism in the Age of Global Warfare*, located its *optimism* in the increasing force of the non-planned city, with its informal economies and shadow plays between quasi legality and profitability. This serves the role of loosening the top-down model of urban becomings from macro to micro – but is this really a theorization of 'optimism'? For is optimism not a drive? Is it not the recognition of potentiality rather than of possibility? Is it not the operations of the will rather than of opportunity? If we turn a situation riddled with limits and constraints into one of possibilities, have we partaken of some form of unbounded knowledge production? In short, I am uncertain whether transforming conditions and eliciting certain principles from the modes by which these conditions are lived out (i.e. informal economies far more reflective of conditions of globalization than the declared aims of multinational corporations) are in fact the production of new knowledge.

Much more interesting I find Deleuze's notion, which before and during 1968 identifies certain seminal moments as 'short-circuits where the future breaks through into the present, modifying institutions in its wake'.[6] To my ears this sounds like a template for a certain unbounded knowledge production, for it is not cumulative from below but rather the performance of an impossible reverse temporality, one in which the breach comes in the form of that which is not yet possible to conceptualize or to name, but nevertheless is here among us and shaping us. I started off by wondering whether it may be possible to undo the very possibilities of containment. Do the unstable spatial conditions of the terroristic, in which it is not boundaries but vigilance that define security, and in the non-linear sites of knowledge production that come into being through encounters and through the side-effects of future winds gushing through them, contain perhaps some insights into what 'unbounded' states and processes might be like? The 'relational geographies' of contemporary knowledge, in which links are produced through our passages and our narratives and in our and many other, less than sanctified voices, produce that very inhabitation of the seam which is constantly worked over, like an obsessive line of embroidery that spills over its allotted space and cannot settle down. Here the 'unbounded' is not a liberation of having overthrown boundaries but rather a constant worried working and reworking of them, inhabiting them, as it were, that results in their inability to sustain their divisive capabilities.

1  Michel Foucault, *Power/Knowledge: Selected Interviews and Other Writings 1972-1977*, ed. Colin Gordon (New York: Pantheon Books, 1980), 68f.
2  Brian Massumi, *The Politics of Everyday Fear* (Minneapolis, MN: University of Minnesota Press, 1993), 2.
3  Nikos Papastergiadis, 'Ambient Fears', unpublished paper, 2001.
4  Foucault, ibid. note 1.
5  Griselda Pollock, 'Interdisciplinary/Crossdisciplinary/Transdisciplinary', *CentreCATH Documents*, no. 1 (Leeds: University of Leeds, 2004).
6  'Gilles Deleuze in conversation with Antonio Negri', in Gilles Deleuze, *Negotiations 1972-1990* (New York: Columbia University Press, 1995), 170f. Trans. from *Futur Antérieur* 1 (Spring 1990).

# Kyong Park

**PM/HM:** You were one of the initiators of the *Lost Highway Expedition*, an experimental gathering that brought together a multitude of individuals, groups and institutions along the unfinished 'Highway of Brotherhood and Unity' in former Yugoslavia. What were the reasons for instigating this self-organized collective journey through the Western Balkans?

**Kyong Park:** At the very end of 2004, Marjetica Potrc and I took a 12-city tour in four weeks, a prelude to the *Lost Highway Expedition* (LHE). During the tour, we presented our works and met many of the people we ended up working with later during LHE. On the trip, we became aware of the emergence of new networks that were beginning to link the now separate republics and autonomous regions of the so-called Western Balkans. We sensed the energy and desire to move on from the horrific events of the 1990s, and form a better future with new ideas and initiatives. All this inspired us to think up a project that might extend these emergent links. And perhaps by travelling through these cities in one continuous link, we would be able to open a new 'passage', one that would be different – in nature if not in scale – to Tito's incomplete 'Highway of Brotherhood and Unity' and the EU's proposed 'Corridor X'. This was also the starting point for *Europe Lost and Found* (ELF), which involved inquiring into what kinds of links and networks were being formed in the transitional states of post-YU and pre-EU, and whether such temporal and temporary webs would be able to reconcile two historically confrontational territorial frameworks. i.e. communism and capitalism or democracy and autocracy.

Yes, this is a heavy subject to tackle, though it doesn't have to be if we take a more informal and bottom-up position, which anyway fits the region better. Moreover, the incompleteness of the utopias of previous regimes was perhaps not due to the ill conception of their original ideas, but rather to the finality of the reality resulting from their bad practices. Fittingly, LHE – the first stage of ELF and our first expedition – created a situation where more people could engage in what I call 'nomadic practices'. And it is important to say that these differ from contemporary practices of networked culture, which are largely conceived through digital cultures. In contrast, 'nomadic practices' reinvest in the importance of real space and time by making a physical expedition the primary instrument of cultural, economic and political exploration, where knowledge and information originate from real experiences. Furthermore, an expedition – with its notion of traversing unknown territory – sufficed, as was our intention, to avoid various external preconceptions about the region, especially the widely popular assumption that the countries of the Western Balkans were an exotic and primal version of civilized Western Europe. And by not constructing an all-encompassing concept or definitive strategy, LHE left the participants room to contribute to the program while we were moving through the cities. This also reduced any hierarchical and centralized tendencies of the participants who came from outside the region, especially as most of the region had once been subject to the Habsburg and Ottoman empires and was now affected by the economic superiority of the EU. Instead, we merely constructed a platform for new cultural practices, one that would be able to function as a fragmented peripheral system within the landscape of Balkanization. The idea was to create common intellectual and experiential spaces where outsiders and insiders would be able to operate on equal and mutual levels of exchange. At the same time, this undefined platform levelled things between project initiators and participants. Hence, LHE is a post-ideological and non-centralized system, structured to accommodate the essence of networked culture, i.e. individual innovations within a shared intellectual world.

**PM/HM:** How do you see experimental collective investigations such as the *Lost Highway Expedition* in relation to the current geopolitical urgencies? Does this form of collective action promote a performative politics of cultural engagement?

Tirana 2006
A view of the periphery of Tirana, where every building seems to be under construction, virtually all informal

Podgorica, 2006
A socialist housing in Podgorica, formerly known as Titograd

**Kyong Park:** For me, the most interesting aspect is the relationship between the individual and the collective. And I use the word collective rather than collaboration not because the *Lost Highway Expedition* was staged in the territory of a past collective, but because our generation exists in a period engaged in making future collectives. The difference here is that the collective in the past was a top-down social utopia, whereas today we are seeing the emergence of bottom-up social practices. The latter assumes the existence of individual freedom without any centralized belief with its governing infrastructures, and underscores the importance of the individual. The most useful definition of globalization depicts it as a process that brings the two social trajectories that I mentioned earlier into a confrontational state that can be negotiated in space; i.e. in cities, regions, continents and beyond. The fact that no clear definition of globalization exists suggests that it is not an entity, but rather a temporary process related to the historical transition from a centralized top-down social system to a fragmented bottom-up social system. In this sense, the Balkanization of the Western Balkans and its re-emergence via bottom-up locality is an important opportunity for the transitional process called globalization. And the slowness with which the Western Balkans are being absorbed into the EU – besides the obvious economic differences – may be related to the cultural political gap between the highly Balkanized territories and the centralizing, if not standardizing, ambitions of the EU. Furthermore, in a period when the Balkanized system is being assimilated into a more generalized system, the former may be gaining relevance over the latter in the EU. This means, for example, that by the time Serbia becomes eligible to join the EU, the EU may not exist anymore. Other areas where Balkanization may be more practical than assimilation include Iraq, the Kurdish territories, Palestine and Kashmir. On a global scale, it has to do with the 'Functioning Core', i.e. the Northern Hemisphere, and the 'Non-Integrating Gap', i.e. the Southern Hemisphere, as defined by Thomas Barnett in his book *The Pentagon's New Map*. Within the global and urban politics of exclusion and inclusion, LHE – with its 'nomadic practices' – is about cutting a bottom-up path through top-down territorialization. The informal process and miniscule scale of LHE reflects the nature of the fragmented collectivism of Balkanization, which is now also being called 'globalization from below'. The value of disenfranchized cultural projects like LHE should not be judged by the scale of their actions but by their growing merit in relation to their context.

**PM/HM:** There is a similar trajectory of experimenting with institutional structures in the case of the *International Centre for Urban Ecology (iCUE)*, a nomadic laboratory for future cities, which you founded in 1998. Which directions do you see emerging through such experimental institutions and what can we expect from them in the future?

**Kyong Park:** If I may take my own practical experiences as a reference, the first possibility is for cultural institutions to become nomadic, both in location and subject. Probably only through such flexibility will they be able to act both globally and locally, and not be contaminated by unilateral devices of cultural imperialism. Outsourcing and multinationalizing of cultural projects and institutions are already underway, as can be seen in how the German Federal Cultural Foundation has implemented projects like *relations* and *Migration*. Though I see these processes as a kind of return to Said's *Orientalism*, because this foundation is a top-down state fund, no matter how independent and experimental it might be and, indeed, is. The second possibility is for cultural institutions to be more renegade and go beyond 'alternative' or 'underground' frameworks. The closest anyone has ever come to achieving this radicalization of cultural institutions is probably to be found in the culture of 'freedom fighters', for their images and spiritual states oscillate between aesthetics and religious ideas, in a kind of repetition of art history. Of course such a radicalization is incredibly difficult for cultural projects and institutions to achieve or even desire. Yet as the global village becomes more political – and this is inevitable – it may not be too far-fetched to expect cultural institutions to go renegade. And this would give cultural projects and institutions even more reason to be as nomadic as freedom fighters.

Sarajevo, 2006

Informal houses under construction in the rural region outside of Novi Sad, Serbia, 2006

*Lost Highway Expedition* stopped for a ball game at Novi Sad's handball stadium, fenced off by the city authorities. Design and activism by Normal Architecture Office and kuda.org to preserve this stadium from destruction succeeded in altering urban planning. Their proposal to make the stadium part of a newly found youth centre is currently pending

**PM/HM:** To engage with different spatial challenges you have developed a system of different formats that are at the base of your work. What are the underlying ambitions of such an approach?

**Srdjan Jovanovic Weiss:** The issue is that I think I am trying to develop a complex system at the start rather than simply complicate a system given a priori, and in that sense the complexity is explored further together with the work itself. So it is an issue of learning with complexity, which makes its own openings and at the same time there are more openings than limitations. For instance my major collaborative exchange is with the Normal Architecture Office, NAO, which is a spatial practice attempt to propose space, design, expression, curating. It is a kind of practice experienced on an everyday-basis rehearsal of skills, that you can bring to any project in terms of scale, but it is architectural, it can be designed-related and it can be, let's say, art representation-related. By exchanging some of expectations from architecture and art NAO can then subvert those fields, gain a bit of freedom within each project. For example in 2007, we collaborated with Yona Friedman for an exhibition at the Drawing Centre in New York which involved all three directions in NAO: urbanism, art curating and architectural installation. The idea to collaborate came from our meeting with Friedman in his apartment studio in Paris, which in itself is arranged as a complex, but loose set of objects and pictures which he lives with.

The second collaboration is with the School of Missing Studies. If NAO is a collaboration based on proposals, SMS is a research platform for cities marked by abrupt transition. School of Missing Studies is not an alternative school in the traditional sense. I think the idea of having an alternative school is immediately cut in its roots of actually having a significance, to be taken seriously. So, School of Missing Studies involves a number of people in its core, architects, artists and curators who felt their own cities are abruptly converted and participants in the loose network. First research projects took place 'at home': Belgrade, New York, Rotterdam and the members of the group were invited to work with other cities like Munich, Halle, Moscow. Participants are diverse and often distinct and thus the range of topics start from any that can generate missing knowledge on abrupt cities to the actions that can be organized and networked. So, SMS is a place where I can be free to self-organize, engage different actors from the loose network of friends, new practitioners and also others. Now, the third collaboration is a test of whether some of NAO and SMS methods can be reflected

*Lost Highway Expedition*, hosted in Novi Sad by kuda.org, included presentations by Srdjan Jovanovic Weiss on Serbien post-socialist architecture and by Jill Magid on her work on intimacy in public space

in the sphere of high professionalism and architecture. I have collaborated with Herzog & de Meuron Architects from Basel, Switzerland on such a platform. H&deM started as a collaborative studio between architecture and art, take Remy Zaug or Thomas Ruff for example, and has today developed into a tight design company. My initial discussions with Jacques Herzog and Pierre de Meuron were about the curious necessity in the large office: how to be more efficient in terms of developing and grasping knowledge rather than emitting it all the time in form of design? The idea was, that if we can maintain the standard of not just making projects but also making concepts and points, then we may have that high professionalism considered conceptual and not only necessary. H&deM is currently collaborating with AMO on a study for the future of Haus der Kunst in Munich, a Nazi building from 1937 today showing high art. Departing from Jacques Herzog's question 'are buildings that were once abused for ideological or commercial purposes forever tainted, or are buildings stronger than ideologies?' we clearly are in front of a problem: node (building) versus network (ideology). And so, these three collaborations together basically form what I can tell I am doing.

# 55 Srdjan J. Weiss

**PM/HM:** What does it mean to work with a format like the School of Missing Studies on the Western Balkans as you did on the occasion of *Lost Highway Expedition*?

**Srdjan Jovanovic Weiss:** The format of School of Missing Studies is not an alternative university. It does not want to emulate or make a master class, or try to be replacement for a traditional school. It is not in the condition to be an alternative university like for example the Prishtina university was during the Kosovo crisis. The School of Missing Studies always had a chance to expand and shrink its participants beyond the core members without engaging the core member themselves. The big difference between Normal Architecture Office and School of Missing Studies in the method is that NAO meets and solves issues as a spatial practice. School of Missing Studies is more anarchic in a sense that it does not have meetings and the idea is to actually use that opportunity to self-organize for an actual action. The biggest action so far for SMS was the *Lost Highway Expedition*, which had 350 participants in total, and it was not meant to be a caravan, but a self-organized expedition with timelines of moving in and moving out at any possible moment. The genesis of the *Lost Highway Expedition* project, and its network of collaborators, came again from an idea coming from a network member in Skopje, Macedonia, during another SMS project held in Belgrade. This idea was further discussed and developed into a project by all current SMS members. The intention was to break the idea of the identity capsule which all cities in the Western Balkans are in at the moment into a network, information highway. The idea is that one can see culturally what is going on and you can without calling yourself a network be able to relate knowledge about these post-socialist cities connected by infrastructure built during the socialist system. The very nature of relation that you can call collaboration had not been defined a priori, but left to emerge and become distinct during a period of discussions with a loose network of partners. Thus each city was seen through a distinct aspect, all together forming a web of topics that could even be seen in a single city. The thresholds had not been defined before they were actually crossed. If you think of an exhibition in the historic context, whoever is first somewhere is the one who upholds the project, but I think that today it is not about being first but really about not having that as an issue at all. This is very important because the idea of being first enhances the danger of restricting nostalgia, of not releasing nostalgia as a force on its own. For the *Lost Highway Expedition* it was extremely important that dynamic relationships between participants and disciplines are at the same time the form of researching knowledge. If you travel or if you are on an expedition it kind of makes you different from going from A to B on a specific task, but experience the expedition as a source of knowledge and not only as a source of prescribed direction.

To be able to release this potential, SMS had to radically expand the field of action and get even looser. Originally invited by SMS to give a lecture in Belgrade, Kyong Park, who is an established spatial practitioner, became one of the key figures in the *Lost Highway Expedition*, as well as Marjetica Potrc, who is also a very established artist coming from the architectural education. And as well as Azra Akšamija, a young artist-architect. There are also highly active participants from the *Lost Highway Expedition* who became key figures in the process. For this to work as a non-hierarchical network we still needed to form a new organization, registered as Centrala Foundation for Future Cities, as a producer of the expedition. It was also extremely interesting to observe how the approaches to knowledge creation and its exchangeability have been different among all the key figures from SMS and Centrala. For instance, Kyong Park would have one idea about it that comes from his experience about a loose organization which then acquires a very strict casting and leadership. My idea was that we can have loose casting of characters but a strong network organization. Practicing that and other inversions of established methods was extremely important because we have learned so much to recreate any temporal organization to specific actors which fulfil it or make it be.

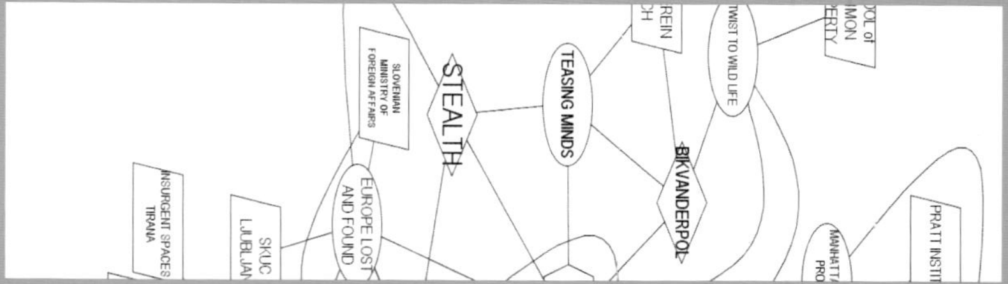

**PM/HM:** If a research operation is characterized by such instabilities, how can one create knowledge that feeds back to this array of different matters?

**Srdjan Jovanovic Weiss:** It makes it a polyphonic strategy. But at the same time it empties itself from the need to become the bureaucratic exchange of expertise, which in traditional institutions is becoming the exchange of authority. So the authority I think is never really getting a chance to develop, and everyone in this process is vulnerable, or let's say all are encouraged to be vulnerable. The feedback is generated out of this kind of vulnerability as a dialogue. It is interesting that vulnerability and feedback resonate in multiple fields, from *Lost Highway Expedition* as a loose network to tight and immense organizations dealing with space such as Herzog & de Meuron. What would it actually really mean to establish a research cell in a highly efficient and world-famous office of architecture in relation to vulnerability? It may prove impossible. The degree of vulnerability of any such spatial practice seems to define the sort of feedback one can expect to be surprised with. Trying to learn with the information that comes in in every single node, every single city is a case in difficulty, but also its potential. It may help learning to go beyond certain issues of metaphors that have been definitely imposed over the Western Balkan territory – Balkanization is one of them. It has been used as a metaphor for many kinds of conflicts that involves disintegration of more than two entities. So in fact we have a kind of a metaphor floating around as a technology of interpretation without an actual content beyond the metaphor. Between Ljubljana, Zagreb, Novi Sad, Prishtina and so on the metaphor prevents the constellation of places. You don't have a constellation of actual knowledge that can go with the technology of interpretation and influence it. The projects like *Lost Highway Expedition* can 'see' where this content can come together and then be branched off into strategies of architecture, strategies of curating or art making. The branching off here is seen as a practice of positive Balkanization. With it we can understand or deliberately misunderstand certain misuses of the process of fragmentation which have been wishful thinking in different places like the European Union or the Americas. If there is anything like geopolitics today, this kind of collective and non-utopian action is a micro-thing, a collective project based on the potential of personal, loose networks.

**PM/HM:** kuda.org has become an important node in an alternative media network that is spreading across Europe and facilitating a direct exchange of information and ideas on a transnational level. How did the political situation in Serbia influence this particular format of combining new media art with political activism?

**Branka Ćurčić:** Basically, kuda.org was established in 2000 after what appeared to be democratic changes in the country. At the periphery this also meant the 'democratic' redistribution of public funds and so more possibilities for cultural institutions to be funded by the state. Though this was just one of the factors triggering the establishment of kuda.org as a new cultural institution. There were actually many other reasons why it was initiated. The people who started it were already pursuing quite interesting art careers during the 1990s – e.g. Association Apsolutno (www.apsolutno.org), whose work, though exhibited abroad, was mainly related to contemporary art practices in Serbia during those hysterical war years. While participating in many exhibitions and events in Europe and the US, the members of Apsolutno and later founders of kuda.org experienced one specific, let's call it, consequence of the 1990s, for in most cases this was very uncritical and self-centred. In contrast, kuda.org has not been about art production but about establishing a platform that is more oriented toward discussion and analysis. So the idea from the beginning was to energize space and create tension: we wanted to invite as many people as possible from the field of international art as well as new media practice and theory to present their views, explanations and experiences. It was not exclusively connected to new media. It also had a more political art context.

**PM/HM:** Can you expand on what it means to work collectively on political urgencies in terms of the actual projects you've been involved in, for instance the *Trans_European Picnic*?

**Branka Ćurčić:** It's interesting to have an international context, to work with people outside the country who can give you different kinds of input and new perspectives on your own practices. But, it's also very important to work with people who are locally based, independent groups and artists, and so create the potential for local networking and a local scene. More and more of the people we've been working with have been, on the one hand, in institutions – official institutions – the Museum of Contemporary Art or the Cultural Centre of Novi Sad. We want to figure out what's possible with official cultural institutions, especially when it comes to bigger projects, like organizing the *Trans_European Picnic* or holding the *World-Information.Org* exhibition in Novi Sad. On the other hand, we try to create a balance between this and working with artists, youth groups and independent organizations that speak the same language as we do.

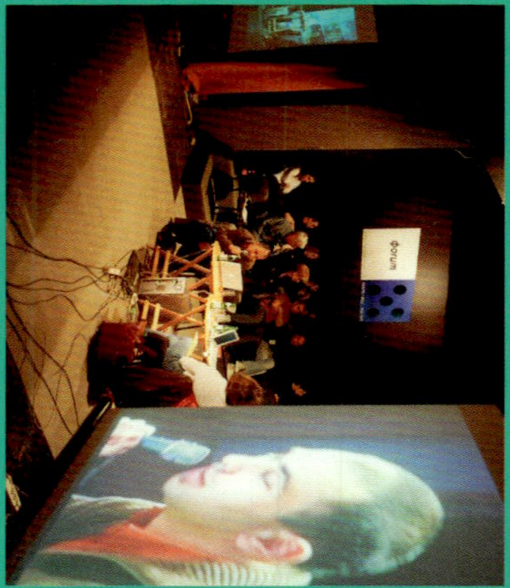

As far as the *Trans_European Picnic* project goes, it was very interesting for us to try to think about opposition to Europe, about being outside of the

*Trans_European Picnic*
Novi Sad, 29 April – 1 May 2004

# 58 Branka Ćurčić

European Union. One friend defined this position as not-yet-EU (which in our case sounds ever more cynical as time passes). We were interested in seeing how such opposition came into being and established or re-established itself through different kinds of influences: historical background, heritage, the present political situation, growing markets, but also culture as an increasingly important unifier.

For us, it was quite a big and uncertain event, and we were not really sure of the outcome. The idea was to do it in Novi Sad, which is still outside the EU, at the new border of this new Europe. In collaboration with V2_Institute for the Unstable Media from Rotterdam (www.v2.nl), we brought more than 50 different people together – artists and media activists from our own country, from the region and from different parts of Europe, not only the EU. In structure, it was a complex event, because we organized many public discussions, project presentations, screenings and performances, and ultimately this picnic that somehow wrapped up everything. Communication with the local population was very important to us, because it seemed that nobody knew or cared about what was going on with EU enlargement. There was not much public interest in things happening immediately outside the border, especially in the case of the former communist countries.

It was a quite interesting event with respect to heritage and the historical tensions that have always existed here. It enabled the discussion of diverse aspects of these issues. We also tried to introduce some historical facts about why this specific location was chosen as the site for the *Trans European Picnic*. So we introduced the history of the Petrovaradin Fortress, which is located on the shore of the Danube in Novi Sad and was originally built to mark the border: it was a military construction for defending the Austrian-Hungarian Empire from the Ottomans. Before having our picnic there, which was also where Tito used to hunt, we went to the Chapel of Peace near Novi Sad. Built at the very end of the seventeenth century, just after peace was signed between Russia, Venice and the Austrian-Hungarian Empire on the one side and the Ottoman Empire on the other, it's actually a monument commemorating this event. The building is a rotunda with four entrances, symbolizing the equality of the parties signing the treaty, which happened at a round table, the first ever used for such a diplomatic act. We're at the border, an almost military site, but there are still some things about it that are more about coming together than dividing; though the event itself brought out many critical views on EU mobility and migration policies, labour organization, and imperatives of cultural differences, etc.

**PM/HM**: It seems there are two levels of networks at stake: one is operating on the international level and the other toward the production of local platforms, such as your work with youth groups. How can art bring these different levels of organization together? Do these two levels share an interface?

**Branka Ćurčić**: I'm pretty sure there are possibilities, big possibilities, for two different levels to come together. In fact I think they're doing so all the time through what we do. At times this is oriented more towards personal contacts; at other times, towards specific projects. I can't comprehend all the possible levels of development of another network, so it's very difficult to say. In one case, where we worked together with local youth groups, it somehow went very well, because a local network already existed. Some of our people already knew a few people on the other side, at the potential network, from another context (i.e. Susanne Lang and Florian Schneider). So we thought we should try to connect these young people and activists from Brandenburg with the Novi Sad crew – independent youth groups that are very anti-nationalist, an attitude of ever-greater urgency in Serbia as of late. This alone was motivation enough for people to start working together. Another question relates to how they in fact collaborate and whether it's possible to talk about actual networks. Ultimately it seems to be more about different nodes from existing networks collaborating with nodes from other existing networks. And the nodes are changing. All the same, new networks or not, it's very exciting.

# Extended Enterprises
## Moscow

Gorbushka, Moscow's largest electronics market, 2006

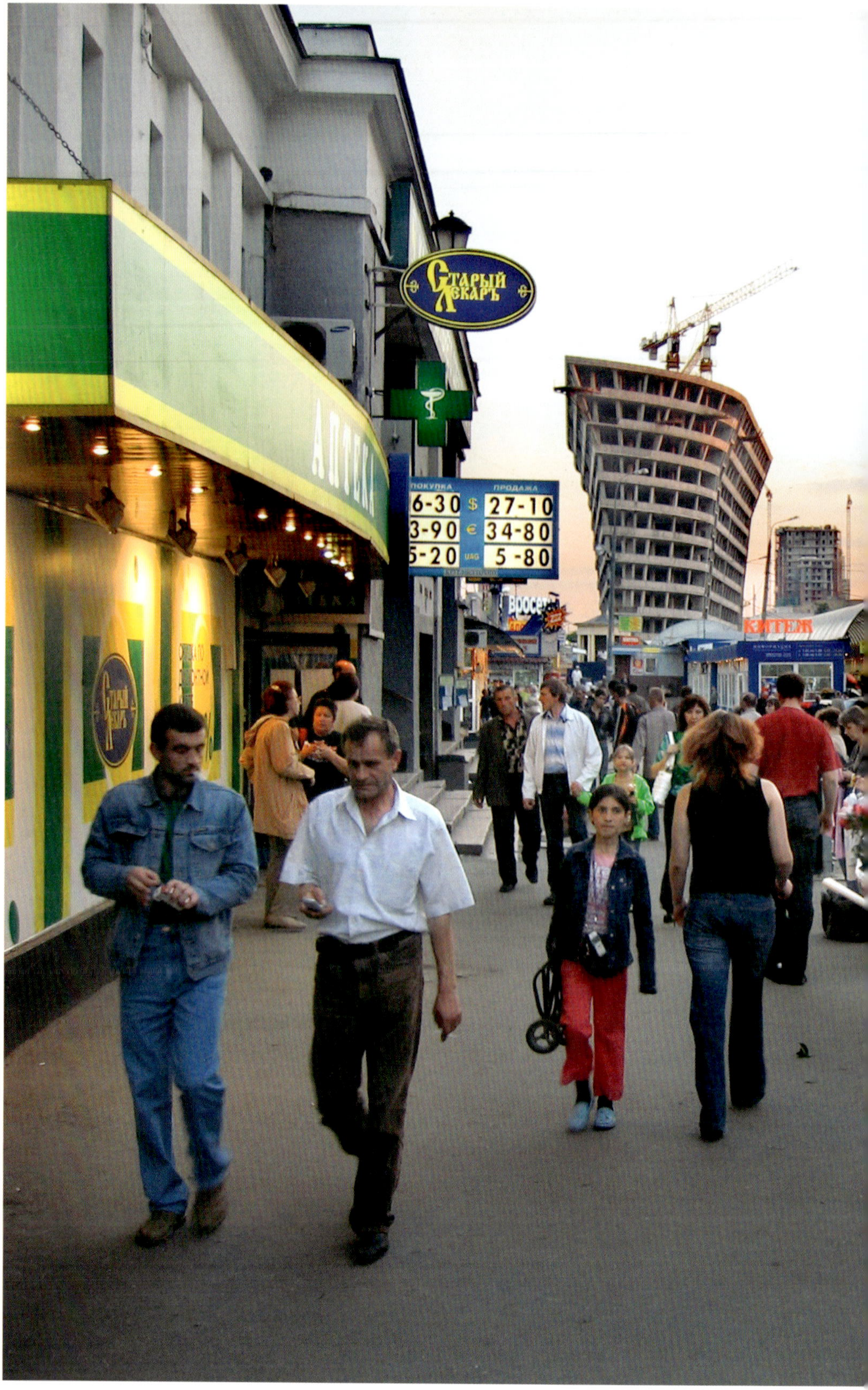

Next to Kievsky Railway Station, Moscow, 2006

# Olga Lopoukhova

**PM/HM:** How did it come that you moved into the former garages of the Red October chocolate factory, right in the heart of Moscow, and started running the joint art platform ARTStrelka?

**Olga Lopoukhova:** ARTStrelka appeared on the Moscow scene in a somewhat strange way, as is often the case in Russia. It had to do with private contacts. One day in a restaurant, Vladimir Dubossarsky, a well-known Russian artist, made the acquaintance of the owner of these premises, Artjom Kusnezov, a Moscow oligarch, who is also connected with Guta Bank. They met and had a nice conversation, and it came up that the Red October chocolate factory might have to move, and no one had a clear idea about what to do. Vladimir was oddly attached to the area – 10 years earlier he had had his art studio in the neighbourhood. We went to see the grounds for the first time in June 2003. We walked around and saw the yard with all these old garages that were not used regularly. They were really dirty, but we thought it would be interesting to do something in them. So we met and discussed it with the owner of the Red October factory, and he gave his okay. We agreed on a price and it was very low, given the location: the Kremlin, the House of Government, the Cathedral of Christ the Saviour, the Monument for Peter the Great and Tretyakov Gallery are all within a mile or less. The rent was set at the time and has not gone up since: 150 dollars per square metre a year. That's not bad. For example, even in the south of Moscow, if you want to rent an office building, it would be somewhere around 700 dollars. Once the centre and our area have been gentrified, the price per square metre is sure to go up to around 150,000 dollars a year. We decided that we didn't want the place all to ourselves and invited our friends to join us. We asked people we knew, because we hoped that way to guarantee a certain standard, I mean, we wanted it to be about real art and not salon painting. But we had one demand: there was to be a joint opening on the last Saturday of each month. And now the entire Moscow art scene knows that the last Saturday of the month is ARTStrelka's. And we've also tried to do things outside the garages during the openings as well – performances or other events, especially in the summer, when we also host festivals, present videos and so forth. Red October has enabled us to work here, but they don't support us financially, nor does the local government or the Ministry of Culture or private sponsors, but we're still here, and in September 2007, we celebrated our three-year anniversary. From the very beginning, we'd been told to reckon with only about two years, because the area was supposed to be gentrified. Yet so far, there hasn't been all that much progress, Red October is still in operation, nothing has been destroyed and only the bridge – which was under construction when we opened – was inaugurated this past September. But from the very beginning we knew that it would be a temporary project. We've known this all along, and have always thought, okay, we'll just do our best, and then we'll see what happens; we don't have any special hopes regarding the future, and we've no idea where we'll move when we have to. We're just working and taking advantage of the opportunity right now. Somebody reminded me recently that even at ARTKlyazma, the annual festival we once organized every autumn on the shores of the Pirogovskoe Reservoir, we had just been filling a gap between the old situation – a half-destroyed former rest house – and the new one – a golf club, yacht club, and so forth. But for three and a half years, we used those grounds, and put together catalogues and festivals. And not long ago someone told me that it's been included as an example in schoolbooks for social science since last year. So that's already something. It's gone down in history.

**PM/HM:** There are a lot of transient spaces in Moscow that accommodate the arts in an almost accidental manner, and this has more to do with certain economic occurrences than political will. So how does the political relate to art production in Moscow today?

**Olga Lopoukhova:** We're part of an island, a strange artistic community amid economic and political activities here, and we really enjoy it. In the 1990s, artists and most of the intellectuals had some kind of illusion – they thought they were in a position to have some effect through the Yeltsin movement. I remember my own experience when I spent four hours trying to vote in the election. First I was told it was impossible because I wasn't

ARTStrelka, Moscow, 2005
Birthday party for Vladimir Chaika

ARTStrelka, cluster of art spaces occupying the former garages of the chocolate factory 'Red October', courtyard with billboards, Moscow, 2006

ARTStrelka and the rebuilt Cathedral of Christ the Saviour Moscow, 2006

registered there. Then the police came and wanted to cart me off. After a bit, when they had understood what was going on, they allowed me to stay. I had to argue my point for another two hours before I received permission to vote. So I was active in my own way. too. During these times it was much easier to bring people together and we really were under the impression that we would be able to have an impact – 1991, when there was the first coup d'état, and then again in 1993, when there were all these demonstrations. But now in the Putin era, things have changed; it's much more apparent that demonstrations make no difference. For example, several days ago, on the occasion of Russia Day (independence day) there was this huge demonstration of young people. They wore special uniforms and T-shirts sporting the word 'local', which meant as much as 'We're local people'. So here were several thousand schoolkids from the Moscow region and they were in this demonstration, but it was organized by the Kremlin. So people today actually prefer just to pursue their own interests and not interfere too much in politics, because it's all really useless nowadays.

**PM/HM:** What does this experience of political domination mean in terms of developing some sort of future for an independent art site like ARTStrelka?

**Olga Lopoukhova:** In Russia the phenomenon of occupying former industrial spaces emerged a bit later than in the rest of Europe. It started three years ago, quite sporadically and unexpectedly, when Artplay and ARTStrelka opened almost simultaneously, and afterwards, just a bit later, Fabrika. Now the next huge and ambitious project, Winzavod, is in a former winery close to the centre of Moscow. Still, we don't consider ourselves to be anything like an organization; instead we think of ARTKlyazma and ARTStrelka as projects. And a project has a beginning and an end. Nevertheless, if you're involved in a project, you'll have much more energy than if you're part of an organization that will continue to exist for another hundred years after your death. We must work on our projects step by step, and do our best to use them, and get energy out of them, because, we know, they won't last forever.

In Russia it's impossible to plan anything. But when you're really doing things, the next step just presents itself to you when it's needed. That's how it was when we organized the ARTKlyazma festival: everything just happened at exactly the right time. So, I guess, sometimes we suffer more from a lack of new artistic ideas than from a lack of space. Though back then the situation was such that it was impossible for young artists to show their work and ARTKlyazma was the only platform where they could do so. This meant young unknown artists were showing at the festival together with artists like Oleg Kulik or Dubossarsky&Vinogradov, and they were all published in the same catalogue. So this gave us the opportunity to give a much broader picture of what was going on. But even if it had been possible for us to continue putting on this festival for another ten years, I don't think we would have done more or better in comparison to the first festival, because nowadays there's also the Moscow Biennial and other non-commercial spaces where people can exhibit. There's Fabrika, Strelka, Winzavod and a lot of galleries. With all this is going on, something new will emerge – which is why we don't have any special strategy or believe what's happening now has to last forever.

# Straddle3

**PM/HM**: In 2000 you initiated the multifaceted *context weblog* that samples new cultural context. How does this online network relate to other activities of the Straddle3 collective?

**Josep Saldaña**: Straddle3 works in the ubiquitous and pervasive realm of architecture and urban computing. An initial moment in building the network was a series of events that we did, called *Openfridays* (www.straddle3.net/openfridays). We began with an appropriate tool – the *context weblog* (www.straddle3.net/context) – an emerging cultural observatory that offers information about art, science and technology, and has several formats. Actually, these weblogs are 'information capsules', and we published them every week between 2000 and 2006. They constitute the basic material for our other projects; it's like a research continuum that provides us with theories and practices for thinking about more commercial projects or for people who ask us to do something. We have developed it all by mapping, sampling and experiencing new cultural contexts. In fact, *context weblog* allows us to research and train how we do things in relation to a networked view of the world, and this is the most important factor. In the process, we've developed related projects that permit us to extend our investigations to social networks. This was also the point of departure for *Openfridays*, an event that enabled the creation of different social networks in Barcelona. For example, we're now in Can Ricart, the oldest industrial complex in the city and one that the authorities would like to destroy. Industries and creative spaces are located in this industrial complex. The synergies in it are very interesting and it's a very good place to be. It's something we want to retain and not demolish. Obviously, the City Council's problem with the complex has to do with aesthetics, as it would like it to be cleaner and more directly integrated into Poblenou, an industrial neighbourhood that is being gentrified for the new economy... It all has to do with money.

**Joan Escofet**: My architectural interest relates to the energies here (www.nau21.net). Walking down the street, you can find people who are working close by and with whom you might collaborate. It's easiest to build a network, if you can actually see one another. We're happy with virtual networks but real networks mean communicating face to face. And even though it seems that collaboration is possible with literally everyone around the globe, physical contact is something that drives networks forward.

**Josep Saldaña**: This is one of the characteristics of scale-free networks. There are nodes that have a lot of links and others that have a few. It's by consciously making use of these features that we can construct networks adapted to different projects. *Openfridays*, for example, was part of *Dorkbot Barcelona* (www.dorkbotbarcelona.org), where people do strange things with electricity. It's now a global network. It's a very concrete network for electronic artists. At the same time, we can contribute to the *ParcCentralPark*

*Openfridays*
context network, 2002–2005

Can Ricart
Barcelona, 2005

network, which deals with problems of urban public space in our area (www.citymined.org/projects/parccentralpark.php). Our experiments have made me understand these projects as a kind of laboratory for *context weblog*. On another scale, they also work as urban laboratories for testing ways for the city to grow. Actually, humankind has become an urban species. Urban issues are extremely relevant for all of us.

**PM/HM:** Your *context weblog* highlights processes of sampling as an integral part of networks. What potential does work from others have for you?

**Josep Saldaña:** For me, the work of others is our very basis. What we're doing is absolutely impossible without the network, without the work of others. We use contemporary tools – aggregating knowledge that people wish to share with others. This is the most important phenomenon today: the sharing of knowledge, i.e. cooperation and open content. In fact, *context weblog* is a remix of different materials that are in the network. Of course, it also involves our own work, our own contribution, but the materials for building the blog are in the network, and we respect and always credit the work of others. Knowledge and advancement are impossible without cooperating together. For me, competition makes no sense in this field.

**Joan Escofet:** The building blocks are actually the people themselves. For each project you can think about the different profiles of those who might be able to bring together what you need to build something. That's how we work: *context weblog*, for example, wouldn't exist if it weren't for the aid of a programmer we met through our involvement in *Indymedia Barcelona (barcelona.indymedia.org)*. It's about meeting someone in one project and then collaborating with them on something else. Though we also see all the competition and we talk about it sometimes – because for us it's strange that people working in open contexts are susceptible to running after fame.

**Josep Saldaña:** At the root of this kind of competition is the problem of the evolution of content, of knowledge, which is so accelerated that it throws previous business models into a crisis. How to survive in this new era? I think the only way is by continuing to share content. In fact, the web shows that content is not a static, closed product, and has become more open, context aware and socially embedded. It's a whole different era. The same goes for architecture. Maybe one day we'll be

Can Ricart
Barcelona, 2005

able to design context-aware architecture, in all senses of the word – because the topics we're pursuing in *context weblog* are ones that will obviously affect contemporary architecture. For example, the oil crisis or climate change, cross-cultural phenomena or the ubiquity of computing. All these things already affect, should affect or will one day affect contemporary architecture.

**PM/HM:** This notion of shared knowledge and competence also lies at the heart of *Fada'iat*, an ongoing project that tries to set up a self-organized and uncensored exchange of information

67

and places, too. But I think we've more in common with a number of projects whose roots go back to the US than to the city we're working in. We've more regular personal contact with people there than here, for instance with the people from *Leonardo*, a network and journal on art, science and technology that has existed since 1968. In some ways this affects how open we are, but in others it doesn't. Networks facilitate contact with people who are on the same wavelength, and it doesn't matter where you live.

The prototype for it was developed for a patio at the Castle of Guzmán el Bueno in Tarifa in 2004. This is an on-going project that still has to be implemented.

**Josep Saldaña:** Actually, each part of the world is a synthesis of the whole. Many European cities have become extremely important Islamic or Arab cities, and it's not important if such a city is in the North or the South. I think this isn't relevant anymore. Contact between Tangier and Barcelona can be more intense than between Tangier and Tarifa, which are geographically but not necessarily emotionally closer. Moreover, people's imaginations in Tangier can be more similar to those in Barcelona than to those in the south of the country. Paradoxically, such locations are very important. Just think of New Orleans and the people living there. Then again, people in these places move often. We've close contact with the whole world and with specific locations at the same time. This generates conflict and tension but also opportunities for architecture.

**Joan Escofet:** This kind of nomadic life has its own needs. I think the prospects are good for services conceived for contemporary life. Our own work is affected by locations

involved designing a project called the *Observatory of the Straits*, which was conceived as a media lab observatory and was to be built in an old castle in Tarifa (Spain). We presented this project together with *hackitectura* and other groups to Tarifa's City Council.

across the Straits of Gibraltar. What role can architecture play in such an endeavour?

**Joan Escofet:** With *Fada'iat* (www.fadaiat.net) we collaborated in different ways. The most important

[recerca + producció + formació + comunicació ]: per un nou art de viure

**CAN RICART : RECONFIGURANT LA CIUTAT**
la ciutat europea contemporània està formatejada segons 'windows'
incapaç de tenir accés al codi font de la programació (linux)

INDUSTRIA

**CAN RICART**
un espai públic del segle xxi,
productiu, creatiu, obert, en xarxa ...

digital hub

ESPAIS CREATIUS

PATRIMONI

cap a la ciutat interactiva amb un sistema operatiu obert

**MANI-FESTA-ACCIÓ**
divendres 16 desembre 2005, a les 19.00 hores
rambla del poble nou - ramón turro (devant de l'aliança del poble nou) - metro L-4 - poble nou

Can Ricart
Campaign poster, 2005

# Forums of Culture
## Barcelona

Can Ricart, 2005

Torre Agbar
Designed by Jean Nouvel (2001-2004)

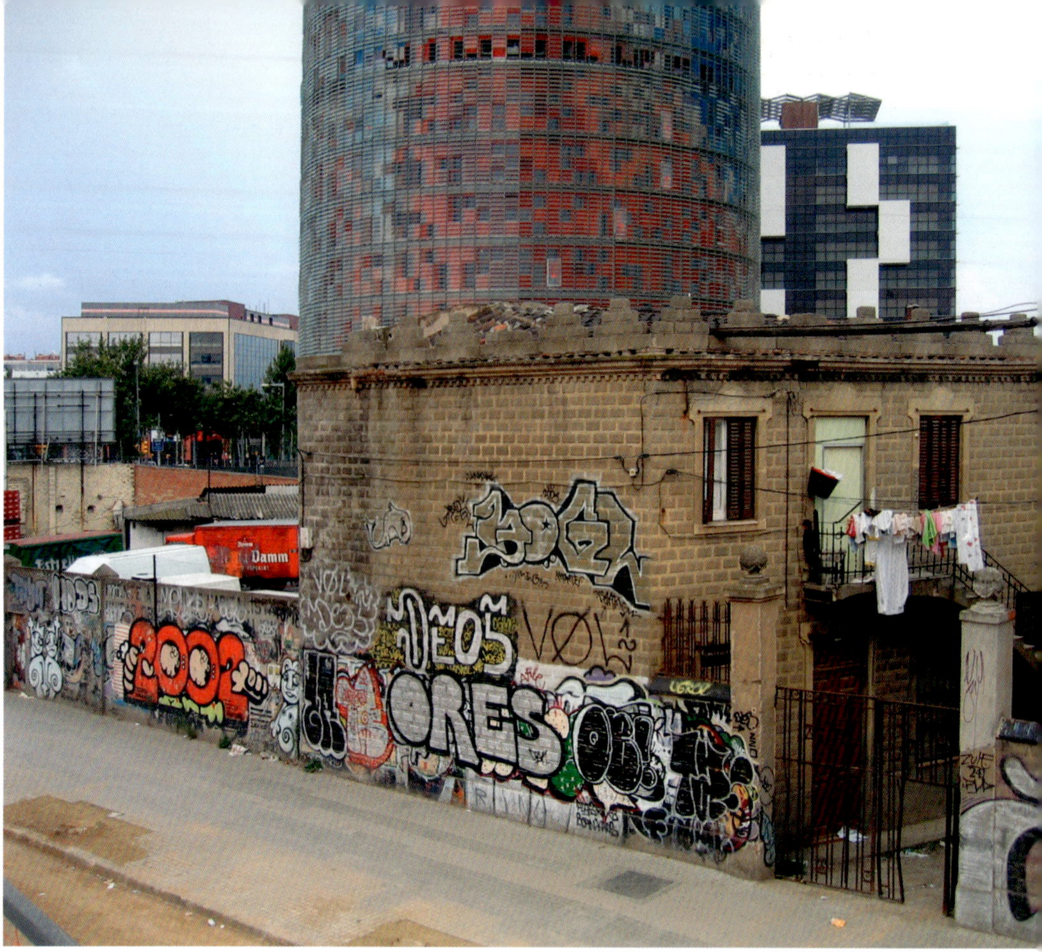
Damm

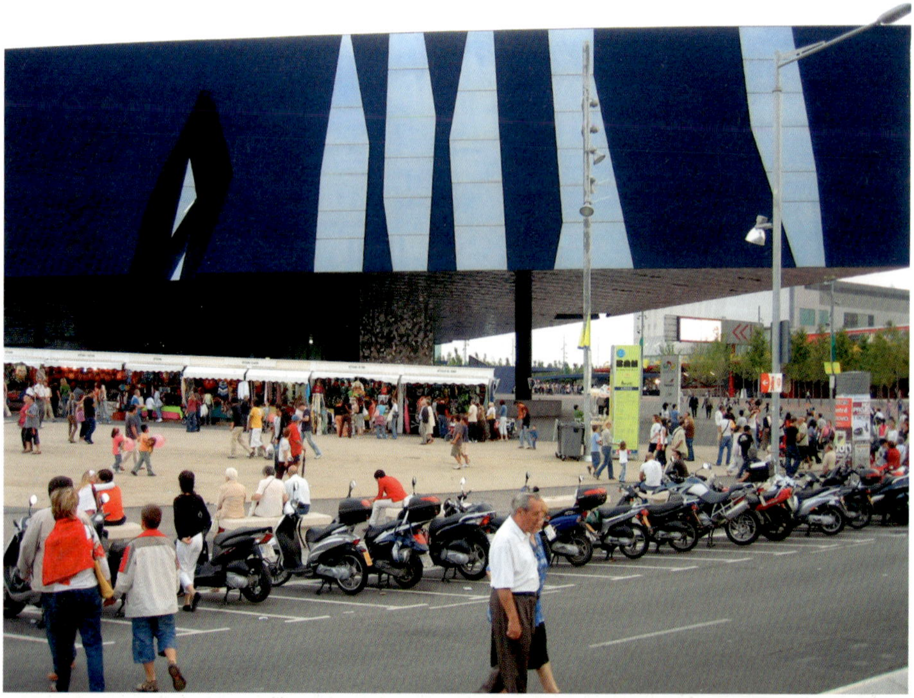

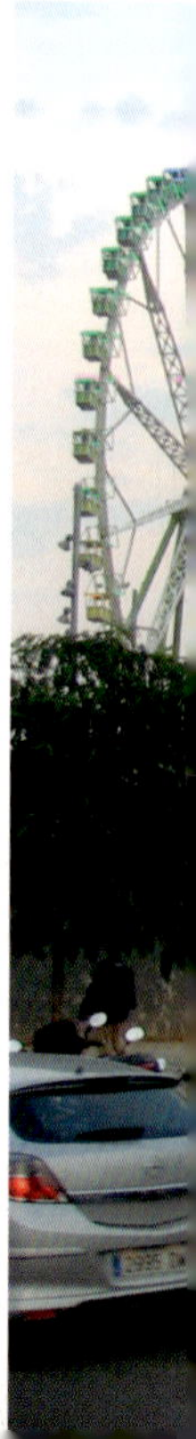

Southeast Coastal Park and Auditoriums
Designed by Foreign Office Architects (2002-2004)

Can Ricart
A historic factory complex in Poblenou occupied by small workshops and studios until early 2036, which has become a focus of conflict between planning authorities and local initiatives

Forum Building
Conference and exhibition centre at the coastal end of Avinguda Diagonal, designed by Herzog & de Meuron (2001-2004)

# Contested Spaces

Centre of Prishtina during the 'Thanksgiving Days for USA', 20-23 November 2006

# Contested Spaces

## TRACING CONFLICT

What is conveyed by the US-led invasion of Afghanistan, the riots in the French banlieues, the electronic fortification of the EU's outer borders, the torture flights of the CIA and the British Anti-Social Behaviour Orders for unruly youth, aside from headlines of a 'growing cultural threat'? They are all signs of a dynamic process involving progressively fragmented global conflicts. Such conflicts are characterized by the simultaneous disintegration and consolidation of 'place' as the theatre where they occur. The differences between the individual conflicts, in terms of both their initial conditions and management, manifest themselves in the local realities of the global shifts of capital and life. Struggles over the dominance of a specific ideology or social group thus meet increasingly mobilized cultures. Efforts to create and maintain an intrinsic global 'whole' by means of spatial-political acts of violence are challenged by clandestine networks that operate in a broad illegal sphere extending from terrorism to informal self-help. In this situation – in which the UNCLCS,[1] for instance, is dividing up the extended mining rights to ocean beds among empires old and new – what significance can a project like *Solid Sea* by the group Multiplicity assume if it grasps the purported extraterritoriality of the Mediterranean as a space containing not only natural resources but also the victims of the distribution struggle between the Global North and South?

In the two decades since the proclaimed end of the Cold War and the 'stable balance of power', the multiplying relations between conflict and space have become one of the most pressing issues in geo-cultural research. In the engagement with conflict terrains over the past few years, various aesthetic approaches that focus on the forces and dynamics of conflict instead of its harmonization have gained momentum. What they all have in common is the simultaneous critique and use of prevailing conflicts, a.) as political acts that constitute spatial organization, and b.) as phenomena that operate on a translocal level. Their distinctive characteristic is the different ways they access areas of conflict and the formats they develop. Proceeding from these differences, we can identify a variety of methodological approaches, each of which establishes its own field of action. The first approach, which uses records, maps, archives and diagrams, aims to produce alternative knowledge of the conditions of conflicts and the borders they create. A second approach challenges the operability of conflicts by intentionally creating disruptions and confusion – not only laying bare the form of the conflict and its operative strategy, but also establishing its own field of action. A third aesthetic mode of operation deregulates conflict-produced borders by means of a concentrated intensification of cross-border forms of action. Finally, a fourth approach responds to the growing fleetingness and mobility of conflictual forces by creating its own mobile, virtual spaces where conflicts can be engaged in and negotiated.

Eyal Weizman's studies of the political space created by Israel's late-modern colonial occupation are a key example of the first methodology. Using diagrams, maps, film footage and historical research, Weizman traces the transformation of a multi-ethnic region into an all-consuming military landscape: all elements of this landscape – settlements, buildings, streets, bridges, hills, trenches and dams – have become strategic tools in the Israeli-led transformation of the Occupied Palestinian Territories. Fashioning these elements into political weaponry is part of a complex pedagogical programme of the Israeli state, which is guided by practice and creates spatial facts. Weizman's work highlights the manner in which Israeli state policy shapes not only complex territorial structures, but also the organization, format and legitimacy of its operations in a series of elastic inclusions and exclusions. The logic governing the development and construction of this border system gives birth to a completely new world, one that intertwines walls with tunnels, checkpoints with elevated pathways and road blocks with air corridors, thus producing a vertical stratification of different mobility rights. This conflict policy and the territories and networks it produces are not merely exposed for a specific geographic case study. Weizman also shows that state military operations are not the sole claimants to this type of working method. In other words, the research into the architecture of this conflictual space does not critique the operation of concrete state and military power by presenting it as specific, but by transferring its logic to a wealth of other contexts. In these contexts it brings forth the components of terminologies and counter-terminologies that themselves compile knowledge of a new field of articulation.

Research into the unequal effect of borders also forms the basis of the abovementioned work by Multiplicity. Its atlases of the Mediterranean bring to light the ambiguities surrounding the growing territorial solidification of this region. The Mediterranean is predominantly depicted as the cradle of civilization, as a place of encounter between different cultures. However, on a more quotidian level, it is also a place where the global division between North and South is being implemented under a regime of electronic borders, military patrols, undocumented border incidents and the rhetoric of illegality and national security. It is a contested geography of journeys and border crossings, each with its own intention and purpose. The maps drawn by Multiplicity show the different movements of disadvantaged and advantaged groups, creating a geography of stark contrasts determined by the territorial logic of a one-sided world order. In this connection, Ursula Biemann studies just how this logic intervenes in a colonial fashion in the spatial order beyond the border – and the way it is undermined by self-created forms of logic. Drawing on a growing archive of documentary video footage, Biemann explores various geophysical conflicts, not in a top-down view, but from the perspective of creating social living spaces. Such micro-policies of survival trace a complex network of detours, back doors, underground channels, hiding places, tunnels and tricks that make up everyday life beyond the border. In work on the Spanish-Moroccan border region around the enclaves of Ceuta and Melilla, Biemann investigates how, in the interplay between technological control mechanisms and illegal border crossings by smugglers and migrants, the border is simultaneously sealed off and porous: on the one hand, the profitable supply of the global market for goods is promoted, and on the other, the undesired flows of people to Europe is prevented. The contested border is transformed into a camp for an army of border crossers and day labourers. As formulated by Giorgio Agamben in *Homo Sacer,* their bodies become a bio-political border, a zone where it is impossible to distinguish between interior and exterior, exception and rule, legality and illegality.

Thousands of miles away, Ayreen Anastas and Rene Gabri tracked the spread of this mobile zone across the entire national territory of the United States in a project called *Camp Campaign*. On their journey they made contact with local communities, activists and intellectuals, gathering material for a cartography of the history of encampments. Their map shows a geography of temporally and spatially dispersed camp situations which mark out a hidden matrix of political space in the US – a bio-political horizon determining the political relevance of life. Marked on this map are military camps, tent cities, working camps, reservations, rendition airstrips, scenes of protest, relocation centres, relief camps and civilian campsites. The spread of these camps across the entire territory of the US shows the suppressed traces of a polycentric conflictual terrain: a disintegrated outer border that multiplies within in order to project itself onto the outside world. As Victor Burgin writes: 'Repression acts not so much on the trace itself as upon *connections* between traces.'[2] Burgin compares the analytic process to the act of exposing dangerous, hidden relations: it severs well-established ties, making it possible to create new relations by reconfiguring current patterns. Viewed this way, the value of a map like Camp Campaign's lies not so much in the fact that it sheds light on suppressed traces as in the fact that it provides the chance both to recognize the connections between the various articulations and inscriptions of a ubiquitous camp and to produce new traces of the imagination.

*Solid Sea 01 – The Ghost ship*
Multiplicity, documenta 11, 2002

A desire to challenge the politics of the border by insisting on the existence of border activities and by intensifying these activities also constitutes the motivation behind cooperative platforms between contested border areas. The borders of post-state federations, above all the European Union, seem to function as hermetical seals, but these federations in fact pursue a policy that aims for the control and management of mobility. The emerging network of filters and channels ensures that the border is sufficiently porous for the economic advantages of global migration flows. For greater control of labour and production, the authority associated with the spatial borders of state territory is transformed into a flexible, mobile authority of civic control. Instead of keeping immigrants at bay by means of hermetic seals, such federations use immigrants by forcing them into illegal employment and black markets.[3] A highly idiosyncratic, goal-oriented economy arises on the other side of the border, one consisting of textile manufacturers, telecommunication businesses, refugee camps, labour migrants, intermediary dealers, human traffickers, legal advisors and non-governmental organizations (NGOs). Forces of production and migration meet in narrow border channels, forming a marginalized territory of contested enclaves, buffer zones, military areas, protective strips and no-man's-land: an intensified supply and negotiation space of geopolitical warfare, one that aesthetic practices regard not only as their subject but increasingly as a sphere of activity.

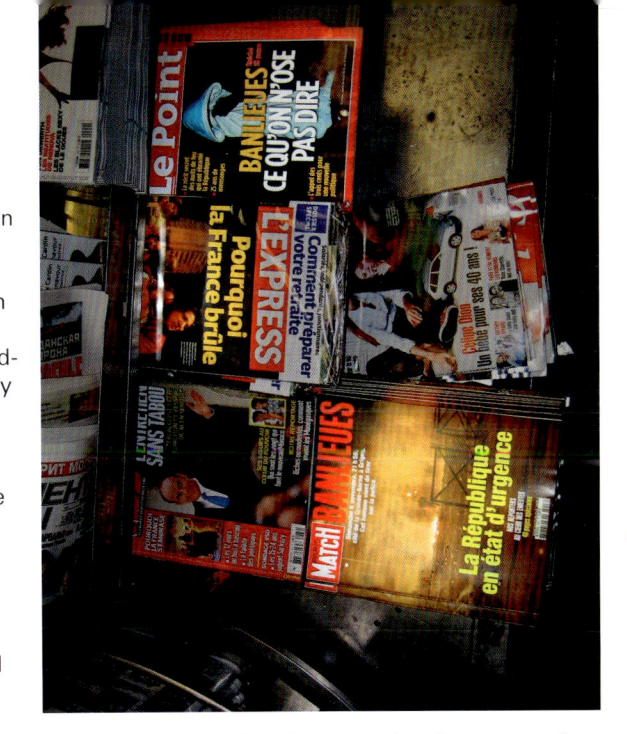

An important point of reference are the transnational network activities associated with *Fada'iat* ('through spaces'), a project that regularly holds workshops, seminars and joint happenings along the Straits of Gibraltar. Since 2004, this network of various groups in Spain and Morocco has been attempting to create a multiple social and infographic terrain that allows a community to emerge that can defend itself against policies of spatial division and urban cleansing. One of the most important goals of this initiative – which is formed by architectural and media collectives such as hackitectura, Indymedia of the Straits and Straddle3 – is to jointly establish a free, cross-coastal communication zone linking the Spanish town of Tarifa with Tangiers in Morocco – a zone that promotes dissident knowledge and temporarily suspends the clear divide between North and South in the region. The network deploys satellite dishes, WiFi links and mobile architectures as civil technologies in the struggle against the border geography dominating the region and its further implications for all of Europe. Its sphere of action extends beyond any single concrete locality, as shown by the activities undertaken against urban redevelopment policy in the city of Barcelona, specifically the protests against the axis created for the 2004 Universal Cultural Forum. This axis runs between Jean Nouvel's landmark building, Torre Agbar, and the new park on the seafront, where buildings by Herzog & de Meuron and Foreign Office Architects have been attracting an international urban public. In the middle of the axis is the former Can Ricart industrial complex, which looks back on a different neighbourhood history and has become the symbol of the tenacious struggle by the local population of Poblenou to reconquer public space. When the Cultural Forum was built, this local culture was marginalized and vilified as obsolete. Bringing together different population groups at a variety of events, including discussions, exhibitions and street festivals, the protest by the local population was supported by a large network of artists, architects and media activists, who called for collective public planning processes and more sustainable spaces of cultural co-existence. The focus of such protests is not the demand for integration, but efforts to explain the exclusionary process underlying social homogenization. As Jacques Rancière put it: 'Politics is not about integrating the excluded in our societies. It is about restaging matters of exclusion as matters of conflict, of opposition between worlds.'[4]

In this situation, networks become important platforms of action, since they create the opportunity to overcome a dependency on offers of participation and, instead, to actively question the conflictual mechanisms and regulatory powers concealed behind rites of participation. Since the creativity involved in producing such self-empowered participation in urban or geopolitical processes is not pooled in a single central body, but dispersed across networks, the form of involvement in these processes does not operate via central authorization, but via self-authorized participation in network activities. This has changed the prevalent forms of critical intervention: only on one level does the fabric joining areas, subjects and interests represent a concrete spatial locality in the sense of geographic proximity. On another level, these urban social movements mobilize a trans-territorial network that sets different nodes of social restructuring in relation to one another. In this politically motivated process, the network is at once the product and producer of social movements. Instead of representing interests by means of homogenizing logics of identity, its strength lies in the joint, cross-border execution of acts of change.[5] These acts show that borders and border regions are highly imaginary constructs, brimming with illusions, false memories and myths. Operating in these areas entails crossing the thresholds of both physical and imaginary space.

## EXCEPTIONS

In 2007, the Heidelberger Institut für Internationale Konfliktforschung (Heidelberg Institute for International Conflict Research, HIIK) recorded 328 political conflicts throughout the world, of which 130 were of a violent nature. Its annually published 'conflict barometers' and 'conflict panoramas' indicate the strength and quantity of these conflicts and reconstruct the development of crises, wars, negotiations and peace agreements. The result is a geography of conflictual intensity displaying a specific constellation of regions, countries and continents as a single conflict zone spanning the globe. This zone is distinguished by 'the clashing of interests (positional differences) over national values of some duration and magnitude between at least two parties (organized groups, states, groups of states, organizations) that are determined to pursue their interests and achieve their goals'.[6] On the maps of the HIIK, this conflict zone – in the form of an archipelago – lays siege to a 'low-conflict' inner zone covering Western and Central Europe, North America, Japan and Oceania. Its contours coincide conspicuously with those of another geography: the global 'territorial security system' that, developed over the past few years, uses electronic sensors, infrared cameras, naval convoys, air patrols, fences and fortifications in a bid to banish 'conflicts' from the shielded interior. The EU's Schengen Information System, the military fortification of the EU's outer borders, the Israeli West Bank barrier, the SIVE (Sistema Integrado de Vigilancia Exterior) surveillance system between Europe and North Africa, the razor-wire fencing along the Spanish enclaves of Melilla and Ceuta, the United States-Mexico barrier ('Tortilla Wall'), the technologically armed Australian Coastal Defence, and the Demilitarized Zone (DMZ) between North and South Korea – this ring of defence technologies, which is supported by state and international doctrines, partitions off an economically prosperous inner area. Surrounded not only by conflicts but also by this technological defence ring, the Global North appears as an enclave in a seething international conflict.

The ever-denser chain linking symbolic sites of conflict creates a figure of exteriorization that shifts the focus of conflict from within to without. The image created by the HIIK masks the deliberate elimination of difference that Henri Lefebvre describes in conjunction with the elimination of all that eludes the dominant urban policy of homogenization and normalization: 'What is different is, to begin with, what is excluded: the edges of the city, shanty towns, the spaces of forbidden games, of guerrilla war, of war.'[7] In the politics of global economic control, a conflictual space is always a space of exclusion, a space on the periphery, a space that defies abstraction. Conflicts are supposed to take place off the beaten trail, at places whose contiguity cannot be broken but harnessed ideologically. The power of abstraction operates under cover: it spreads via fragmentations, zonings, borderlines, crossings and penetrations. As the policy of concealment becomes more complex, so, too, does the set of instruments it employs and the spatial structures it produces.

The range of high- and low-tech mechanisms used by the military to enclose prospering areas, together with the conflict zones of the HIIK, portrayed as a world map, marks out the paradoxical policy of the global re-territorialization of conflict: although conflicts are never related to issues that are strictly territorial in nature, attempts are increasingly being made to present them as territorial disputes that can be resolved by fortifying these areas. The realities constructed in this dynamic – the cleansed spaces of the First World – do not represent homogenous containers, but the effects of a spatial policy based on spatial abstraction and global homogenization. As part of this policy, resistant territories are not longer fought over, but bracketed out, placed under quarantine and enclosed in order to produce a dualism of inner and outer spheres. Enclaves in which other enclaves are embedded signal an equilibrium that can only be maintained by a sophisticated border system. What emerges is a complex spatial organization of intertwined inner and outer zones. As a result of this organization, social conflicts are not so much regulated as defended against. Both the increased fortification of space in the form of an agglomerate of hypertrophic protective cells and the enlargement of scale from the urban to the regional and continental serve to create the illusion that complex systems of experts are required to create a balance in

Street vendors on the Spanish Steps in the centre of Rome, upon being alerted of a plain-clothes police operation, 2006

the tensions that supposedly originate in the properties of space. The difficult balance of urban and geo-cultural morphologies, so the argument runs, is the successful result of rational conflict control. This process, which is shaped by architectural methods (the organization, design, construction and representation of spatial structures), exposes a globally operating spatial praxis that is founded on fragmentation and dispersal – a praxis in which detention camps, secret prisons and military camps function as the smallest unit. Forming on the other side of the border are autonomous enclosures such as gated communities, all-inclusive resorts, enclosed malls, fenced-off campuses, leisure parks and their all-purpose mobile form, the sports utility vehicle (SUV). Viewed on a large scale, 'functional' zones are thereby created vis-à-vis the complexly structured zone of unrest and hotspots.

In 2001 Great Britain introduced a new Terrorism Act to prevent terrorist activities. Section 44 of the Act enables the government to treat any form of deviant behaviour as a state of exception and to deal with it accordingly. Since then, the police have stopped and questioned more than 30,000 people each year without a compelling reason. Emergency authorities are potentially expanded to include all areas of political life and can be used by the police at any time as the legal basis for stop-and-search operations. The Terrorism Act represents an extreme manifestation of the elastic border, offering maximum flexibility in an effort to monitor the interior life circumscribed by the power of the sovereign. This elasticity is designed as a projection onto the future, as a mobile and virtual border that can be executed wherever future conditions make it necessary. The border is directed against a largely undefined exterior whose threatening nature is first ascertained in the act of its execution. This makes the creation of a border into an act of performative knowledge production. The border gains legitimacy, as it were, by establishing a hostile nature; and in its most elastic form, it gains legitimacy from an ideology that envisions a ubiquitously hostile urban environment, one that extends from the micro-areas of urban gang warfare to the hideouts of terrorist networks organized in the suburbs.

The use of conflict and crisis in the visual aesthetics of the media, in the design of crisis spaces and in the global policy of conflict management goes hand in hand with the guiding concept of conflict management that gives conflict avoidance priority over conflict engagement. Here conflicts are almost exclusively discussed in terms of 'defusing tensions' and 'clarification', and the most refined state of conflict is seen in crisis prevention. This traces back to an understanding of crisis derived from the ancient Greek verb *krínein* (to 'separate' or 'discern'), wherein 'crisis' means 'decision' or 'decisive turning point' – a break with an existing situation at its most sensitive developmental point and the emergence of an exceptional state. This turning point – as the most pressing point for a decision on action – contains not only the chance to avert the threat of a crisis and to restore normalcy, but also the opportunity to radically reconstruct the subject. If we approach conflict from the perspective of consolidating an order that is governed by general norms, we can only ascertain this turning point ex posteriori – at a point, that is, when the crisis has already been overcome. It is different if we approach conflict as the singular expression of a decision concerning action, that is, if its radius of action is positioned outside the norm. Here the potential of the decision-making power circulating in conflicts points to a fundamental separation between the norm and its application. At the most extreme point of the crisis, both spheres keep the greatest distance to each other if the application of the norm is annulled in order to assert the norm's validity. Put differently, cognition of the norm takes place from the perspective of extremes, via the point of exception. A fissure opens up – one that Agamben describes as the topological structure of the state of exception. 'That is, the state of exception separates the norm from its application in order to make its application possible. It introduces a zone of anomie into the law in order to make the effective regulation [*normazione*] of the real possible.'[8]

Padua, 2006
In response to claims about drug-related crimes and violent behaviour the municipality of Padua (Italy) erected a three-metre-high steel wall around a housing estate mainly occupied by African immigrants. The police also set up permanent check-points to control access to the estate

According to Agamben, this lawless space has increasingly advanced to the centre today. As peripheries have grown more fluid and mobile, the exception, as a territorial form, is shifting from the edge to an encampment within the political centre. Banishment no longer entails expelling something to the margins of geo-cultural existence, but rather rending and dividing co-existence at the heart of the social order. The state of exception has therefore become the organizational principle of a social crisis that appears to be ubiquitous: it does not lead to normalization, but, under the banner of the fight against terrorism, it serves as a permanent provisional arrangement and a form of government. The 'camp' is the architectural expression of this government, an instrument of control over the body that gains legitimacy through crisis scenarios and that brings about the work of other apparatuses, protocols and authorities. This process removes the negotiation of conflicts from the public sphere and delegates it to experts. Under this new crisis management, the object of public debate is no longer the contents of the crisis. It is shifted to a constellation of professional crisis forums whose work is geared toward efficient action. Consistent with this thinking, all involvement with conflicts is regarded as successful only if it results in their elimination. Conflicts are subordinated to a conflict-free state, which becomes a mandatory goal: conflict only makes sense when it is engaged in with an eye towards its resolution.

## MOBILE DIVISIONS

One of the central spatial effects of this policy is the dispersal of conflict and violence from international space to the territories within states[9] – specifically, to the space of the city, in which conflicts become tangible. At the same time, these effects are linked to a network of remote spaces that not only provide support, alliances and cooperative forms, but also ensure that conflicts are shifted, suppressed and subdued. The city as a political form originates in a contingent, polycentric play of expansionary and isolationist forces. This kind of urban system does not reveal itself as a place of geographically determined social processes, but as the focus of political conflicts.[10] As new conflicts arise from this complex fabric today, they direct our attention towards new ways in which the presence of social exteriority is constituted and expressed. Closer attention to these shifts is all the more urgent, as, from the perspective of the global market economy, the city is increasingly becoming a construct that can be dismantled and shifted. To protect market interests, the lines of a conflict, which have become mobile, are adapted to a set of ephemeral assemblages which they observe over the short term, but which they will leave at some point. Regions of conflict are therefore not geographic sites, but discourse-evoked (trans-) localities that themselves produce the subjects of conflicts parallel to shifts in global market conditions. Replacing the city, the flexible concept of community is capturing attention as a new level of reference. The consequence of this shift is that the community itself, and no longer the city, is threatened if the security of 'common' interests appears jeopardized.[11]

Corresponding 'protective measures' have included the creation of police cordons and the construction of three-metre-high walls around apartment buildings in Padua occupied by North African immigrants (summer 2006), as well as the issuance in Great Britain of so-called Anti-Social Behaviour Orders, designed to banish certain individuals from public space. When migrant youth culture is portrayed as intent on burning everything to the ground – as during the most recent riots in the French banlieues – effective propaganda is created for the spatial control of social classes. If we were to trust the narratives produced by mainstream media reports, we would have to conclude that this potentially dangerous situation can be found in all parts of the Western world and that it seeks to produce micro-conflicts in cities everywhere – with the result that defences need to be mounted in an ambivalent, all-encompassing territorial context. The omnipresent enemy emphasized in these stories initiates ever more restrictive policies of socially based 'urban security'. As Negri and Hardt imply in *Multitude*, one consequence is that, in the war against such abstract enemies, the limits of security measures are rendered indeterminate, both spatially and temporally. Wars against abstract concepts or social practices are acts of governmentality that are indistinguishable from most other forms of political activity. Reproducing all aspects of social life, they can be extended anywhere irrespective of spatial or temporal boundaries.[12] In this process, the suspension of normal civilian 'rules' in the quest for civilian 'decency' mobilizes a form of bio-power that flexibly produces or reinforces social hierarchies in line with prevalent value systems or opinion polls. Instead of engaging with a geopolitical situation that cuts across separate categories of violence and peace, the city of panic[13] seeks to isolate and ghettoize zones of unregulated violence from purified and patrolled zones of harmony.

Described by Anthony Vidler as the 'war ideology of the plan',[14] the deliberate destruction of the city is not an external evil, but part of a programme that is transforming urban life under the aegis of a neo-liberal 'urbanization'. The social conflict produced in this transformation process functions as an evoked construct that provides the desired framework for the forces of transformation. Conflict and the denial of conflict are both intrinsic components of the urban condition and embedded in its spectrum of political action. If conflict is declared to be something that cannot be fit into twenty-first century conceptions of citizenship, it is defined as a state of exception that exists outside the bounds of urban society. Such representations promote a system whose goal is to preserve power, one that is rooted in two seemingly antithetical initiatives: the deliberate provocation of conflict and the simultaneous exclusion of conflict as a public sphere. This double-edged strategy aims for protective control following the triggering of the conflict – control that can be used to 'resolve' the conflict and take the transformation process in the desired direction.

From the demise of the New Economy and the rise of the global protest movement to the emergence of the militant network of the global jihad and the violent attacks on the World Trade Center and Pentagon – the manner in which centres of social power have perceived the network has changed. Once viewed as a tool of trouble-free control, it is now feared as a source of uncontrollable danger. In this regard, networks have replaced the most powerful figure of modernity: the threatening figure of the masses in the nineteenth and twentieth centuries. Elias Canetti's concept of the masses as a symbol of being *touched* by the unknown has given way to a trope of being *connected* with the unknown. Increased mobility, accelerated contacts and the declining relevance of spatial distance – as an expression of our sense of proximity and distance – have allowed new parameters to emerge and generated not only a new connective quality, but also elements of uncertainty and fear: fear of the unchecked spread of global epidemics, fear of terrorist networks and fear of a profound social, financial and military crisis in the old centre of world power. The network has become a diffuse symbol of the enemy, one encrusted with fears – just as diffuse – of disintegration, transmission and contamination. In the widespread talk of a 'war on terrorism', the network has become a useful tool to give fear a place. Of infinite scope, this place can be experienced everywhere – which is why it must also be reorganized, monitored and protected everywhere by political leaders. The use of the 'network' concept cleverly disguises a global policy of regulatory mechanisms that attempts to control network dynamics on the one hand but must provide space for its expansion on the other to achieve its own goals.

It is not only the spread of networks but also the defence against them that shapes the spatial form of crises. These defences include the security architecture of gated communities, the walls enclosing states in the Israeli-Palestinian border conflict, the use of electronic fences to seal off the European continent from North Africa, as well as Dubai's planned resort project *The World*, designed as a miniature universe and man-made refuge. Now that the network enemy is at home on all scales, no single scale is off-limits when it comes to attempts to avert the crisis. The struggle taking place in these zones over how to design the state of crisis demonstrates that the network is no antipode to border policy. In policies of spatial distribution and spatial control, networks play an important role in efforts to strategically secure borders and expand border regions. The intelligence of networks and their logic of flexible combination and control is needed to provide a dynamic challenge to the

Arsenal
Concrete letters barrier outside Arsenal's new Emirates Stadium, promoted by the British Home Office as a 'good example of elegant counter-terrorism design', London, 2006

accelerated interaction between distant nodes. To cite Bruno Latour, like the border, the network is a concept and not a spatial object[15] – it is a divided fiction that, dependent on the desired type of spatial and social organization, gives rise to a particular material form.

## CONFLICT POLITICS

In our reflections, we therefore do not wish to address networks as *places* of conflict and crisis – which is the case when terrorist networks are described as the sources of conspiratorial violence, or networks are seen as the 'problem spaces' of globalization.[16] Of primary interest to us is how networks can be seen as a situational *form* of transformation, as a spatial manifestation of upheaval that has largely emancipated itself from any direct link to local topographies. Networks mark out a socio-spatial process whose properties emerge from a situation rather than essentially existing in local or historical conditions. The dynamic form of such processes is shown by many examples: with the emergence of the money market and the exchange of goods, services and balance-of-payment funds across borders, the mercantilist trade networks of the seventeenth century produced both cross-border competition and new control instruments, one being the 1651 Navigation Act, which established a closed trade zone over large areas of the world. This competition and new set of instruments shaped the crisis of the absolutist state. Each new generation of expansionary technology introduced in the nineteenth century – the railroad, telecommunications, electricity – gave expression to the crisis affecting the patronage of Western civilization over ever-growing colonized regions. Later, in the twentieth century, the network architecture of guerrilla warfare, taking the concrete form of the underground tunnel begun by the Viet Minh in the late 1940s, played a central role in the tactics of the Vietnam resistance. Yet this network architecture also provided an effective structure for the crisis in Western power during the Cold War. In 1969 ARPANET[17] – the first data transmission network and the predecessor to the Internet – emerged from the context of the US state security crises but also helped shape this crisis with its sophisticated distribution of information flows, designed to ensure security.[18] In much the same way, today's internationally networked NGOs do not passively reflect but formatively influence the crisis in nation-state government caused by globalization. Similarly, in the period after 1989, the social networks in Eastern Europe, which originated in the age of Real Existing Socialism, have not only cushioned the sudden disruptions of state regulations and welfare authorities, but also transformed them into a new set of instruments for cultural co-existence under the conditions of unregulated self-enterprise.

This metonymic relationship between crisis situations and network formation provides us with a form-giving model that does not isolate spatial renewal from crisis-ridden spatial conditions, but regards this space as a source of generative potential for new forms. Networks are transformational spaces, and precisely that is their strength. In light of this quality, networks can be seen as fluid peripheries organized around a central void. The best way for such a structure to grow and change is if it refuses a clearly outlined central project. In a deliberate, active process of dispersing attention and obfuscating a middle figure, networks open up paths that circumnavigate a central emptiness. These paths crystallize around something that exists, not as a clearly drawn object, but as an indeterminate region, as a gap that cannot be filled. They repudiate not only their past, but also the clearly defined form of their future as a joint project. Entirely committed to the terrain of the present, structural control and collaboration must be created anew at every moment. Networks are an expression of an ongoing beginning. This geometry of transformation makes possible an upsurge in spontaneously designed, flexible, temporary spaces, especially in remote and less stabilized regions in which labour migration, economic deregulation, social separation and religious movement have created a spatial patchwork of migratory infrastructures. These infrastructures consist of kiosks and minibuses, prayer rooms and pickup points for day labourers, transit camps and street kitchens, social clubs and local radio stations. New social spaces are not being created in place of or atop existing ones, but in the middle of existing socio-cultural orders.[19] The transformation of these economies provides an expansionary space for networks – one in which new cultures seize ground.

Businesses in East London, 2006

In this way, networks are able to create a place where conflicts are handled in a different way. Ernesto Laclau and Chantal Mouffe show that the creative potential of conflict lies in its ability to keep blind totality at bay.[20] This totality is oriented toward two poles: the first is reached by measures of cleansing, and the second by measures of harmonization. In the first case, the democratic public sphere is conceived as a cleansed space of individual expression; in the second, as a harmonized social whole. For both, conflict is a force that undermines the genesis of the functioning spaces of democratic society. But if we assume that the potential platform for articulating a global public sphere – the network of transversal interaction – is not a structure that can be planned and fixed, but that it represents the transfer of ideas and debates to the arena of politico-spatial action, then conflict is the criteria for creating and appropriating spaces of democratic co-existence. So conflict is precisely the condition that is required for their genesis and growth. It functions as a force of negotiation that is carried from moment to moment, a force that, in many small steps, structures our understanding of the future in relation to the past. The fundamental potential contained in conflict is that it opens up possibilities for political action, of which violence is just one.

However, in official policy, conflicts are negotiated in mitigation processes whose endpoint is not a dynamic state of embraced difference but a struggle over the control of what is excluded. As Judith Butler argues, the state of being human is defined by a matrix of inclusions and exclusions in which spectral existences justify an endless warfare against the phantasmal infinity of the enemy: 'It is not a matter of a simple entry of the excluded into an established ontology, but an insurrection at the level of ontology, a critical opening up of the questions, What is real? Whose lives are real? How might reality be remade? Those who are unreal have, in a sense, suffered the violence of derealization... Violence renews itself in the apparent inexhaustibility of its object.'[21] It is indicative that, although the debate on the use of rights performs a central ethical and political function, the relationship between law and justice has no greater meaning in the expanding discussions on political and economic spatial control.[22] The apparatus underling a legal practice is not the result of its own nature; it is a changeable, contingent construct of political and theoretical engagement. There is an idiosyncratic commonality between the denial of this connection and the denial of the link between the organization of violence and urban life: their construction as incompatible zones and the consciousness this creates (i.e. that there can be no place for dissent in the law and no place for conflict in the city) are related to a particular conception of culture in which difference poses a danger. The ideological function of the agreement between law and justice therefore coincides with the normative organizational design of the city as a non-violent zone of civilization.

If, as Georg Simmel writes in 'The Sociology of Conflict', engagement in conflict is intended to serve an 'uncultivated' release of tension between opposing forces,[23] this opposition must pre-exist as a structure of different characteristics that can only be related to one another by means of their susceptibility to a harmonization process aiming for the well-being of 'culture'. However, that which is cultural is neither the *source* of the conflict nor an *alternative* that can be abstracted from it – as argued by Homi Bhabha in his discussion of hybridity. Rather, it is the *effect* of distinguishing practices that create authority: 'A disposal of power, a negative transparency that comes to be agonistically constructed *on the boundary* between frame of reference/frame of mind.'[24] The insistently used concept of a clash of civilizations is an effect of power – an effect with which certain traits, bodies, gestures, discourses and desires of a culture are identified.

This practice, which operates on a discursive and material level, results not only in the growing fragmentation of spatial co-existence, but also in the institutionalization of conflicts in a policy of global division. Conflicts become the dominant framework for determining the way a certain territory and a certain population are perceived. Architecture is an expression of this policy. It creates divisional lines, trenches, fortifications and partitions within an elastic geography of interior and exterior zones surrounded and organized by a large number of players. As Eyal Weizman writes, the architecture of the frontier is not simply 'political' in the sense that it is manifested in political, ideological and economic controversies. Rather, it is 'politics in matter',[25] a form of political conflictual practice. 'In this context the relation of space to action could not be understood as that of a rigid container of "soft" performance. Political action is fully absorbed in the organization, transformation, erasure and subversion of space.'[26] It is precisely this overlapping of space and politics that, on the one hand, makes conflict all-encompassing and, on the other, determines its irresolvability, thereby opening up the opportunity to performatively create spatial meaning. Space is not merely a 'container' for our action. Nor is architecture a container for politics, and nor are cities, regions and states containers for the seething conflicts within. Conflicts are shaped by mental geographies and their physical enactment. Space is thus a possible form for articulating conflicts – a very concrete form of conflictual practice and not a container for conflict. Conflict does not reside outside our existence. It is lived out and spatialized by all of us.

untitled, Dan Perjovschi
*Leaps of Faith*, Nicosia, 13-29 May 2005

1. UN Commission on the Limits of the Continental Shelf.
2. Victor Burgin, *The Remembered Film* (London: Reaktion Books, 2004), 82f.
3. Sandro Mezzadra, 'Borders/Confines, Migrations, Citizenship', in *Fada'iat: Freedom of Movement, Freedom of Knowledge* (Barcelona, 2006), 178.
4. Jacques Rancière, 'The Abandonment of Democracy', *Documenta Magazine*, no. 1-3 (2007), 459.
5. Brian Holmes, '"We Are the Media": The Dream of the Transnational-Popular', in *Populism Reader*, eds. Lars Bang Larsen, Christina Ricupero and Nicolaus Schafhausen (New York: Lukas & Sternberg, 2005), 23f.
6. *Conflict Barometer 2007: 16th Annual Conflict Analysis* (Heidelberg Institute for International Conflict Research at the Department of Political Science, University of Heidelberg, 2008), ii. Online: http://www.hiik.de/konfliktbarometer/pdf/ConflictBarometer_2007.pdf
7. Henri Lefebvre, *The Production of Space* (Oxford: Blackwell, 1991), 373.
8. Giorgio Agamben, *State of Exception* (Chicago, IL: University of Chicago Press, 2005), 36-40.
9. *Conflict Barometer 2007*, ibid. note 6.
10. Stuart Lowe, *Urban Social Movements* (London: Macmillan, 1986), 2.
11. Jordan Crandall, *Under Fire 2: The Organization and Representation of Violence* (Rotterdam: Witte de With, 2005), 25-37.
12. Michael Hardt and Antonio Negri, *Multitude: War and Democracy in the Age of Empire* (London: Hamish Hamilton, 2005), 14.
13. Paul Virilio, *City of Panic* (Oxford and New York: Berg, 2005).
14. Anthony Vidler, 'Photourbanism: Planning the City from Above and Below', in *A Companion to the City*, eds. Gary Bridge and Sophie Watson (Oxford: Blackwell, 2001), 35-45.
15. Bruno Latour, *Reassembling the Social: An Introduction to Actor-Network-Theory* (Oxford and New York: Oxford University Press, 2005), 131.
16. Aihwa Ong and Stephen J. Collier, *Global Assemblages: Technology, Politics, and Ethics as Anthropological Problems* (Oxford: Blackwell, 2005).
17. Short for 'Advanced Research Project Agency Network'.
18. Sadie Plant, 'Network Wars', *Blueprint*, September 1998: 26-27.
19. Stefano Boeri, 'Eclectic Atlases', in *USE – Uncertain States of Europe* (Milan: Skira, 2003), 445.
20. Ernesto Laclau and Chantal Mouffe, *Hegemony and Socialist Strategy: Towards a Radical Democratic Politics*, second edition (London and New York: Verso, 2001).
21. Judith Butler, *Precarious Life: The Powers of Mourning and Violence* (London and New York: Verso, 2004), 33.
22. Samantha Besson, *The Morality of Conflict: Reasonable Disagreement and the Law* (Oxford: Hart Publishing, 2005).
23. Georg Simmel, 'The Sociology of Conflict: I', *American Journal of Sociology* 9 (1903): 490.
24. Homi Bhabha, *The Location of Culture* (London and New York: Routledge, 1994), 114.
25. Eyal Weizman, *Hollow Land: Israel's Architecture of Occupation* (London and New York: Verso, 2007), 5.
26. Ibid., 7.

# Claudia Zanfi

**PM/HM:** How does the network structure of aMAZElab and MAST (Museo di Arte Sociale e Territoriale) relate to specificities of the annual *Going Public* project and your interest in collaborating with communities within the realm of art?

**Claudia Zanfi:** *Going Public* is a complex on-going project of reflection, research, creative production and cultural exchange that has established itself in an interdisciplinary area. The main subjects are mobility, migration, memory, borders, new geographies, Mediterranean countries, the Middle East and the public sphere. One of our central targets is to organize meetings between local people and international artists, architects, sociologists and writers, and let them work together. We started the project in Modena (Italy) for the International Festival of Philosophy in 2002. Since then we have invited artists to become 'tutors' for local communities on a new issue each year; together they do research and develop visual works, which are then presented in public spaces and implemented in debates, film and video screenings, walks, seminars, etc. All this can be seen in our publications – which I don't like to call catalogues of an exhibition, as *Going Public* is not just an exhibition. It's a real act of cultural activism, especially in how it confronts contemporary living and inhabiting cities. This is a very strong characteristic of *Going Public*: the title itself already refers to this quality, namely that of actively going out into the public domain. We started by using places and platforms of mobility: train stations, bus stations, gas stations – though not as 'galleries' but as collaborative spaces where some of the workshops took place. For example, at the first edition of *Going Public* we had some banners put up by Multiplicity that questioned the city and the relation between local and global. The banners were positioned as flags on the platforms of the main station and they formulated a set of questions. The people waiting for the trains could sit there, read the banners and start to think about these questions. They could enter into a kind of dialogue with the installation, one that had nothing to do with the aesthetic perception of an artwork. For example, one of the questions was 'How is European space changing?' – and this is, of course, quite an important question to think about while travelling by train.

**PM/HM:** The various editions of the *Going Public* project seem to cover Europe and the Mediterranean not only in a geographical sense but also in terms of cultural urgencies. In most cases, you have done this by moving outside the centre. How does this shift of attention reflect the changing geopolitical situation in Europe?

**Claudia Zanfi:** In 2005 we were invited to Larissa (Greece), because they had heard about our *Going Public* projects. By the way, we really like the idea of our project growing like a seed, sprouting up here and there. So the new Larissa Contemporary Art Centre invited us to submit a project similar to that of *Going Public*, i.e. to work with local communities and in public spaces. Larissa is one of the least known cities in Greece, the only larger city not at the sea, located in northern Greece, not far from the Albanian and Macedonian borders. It's a really ugly city that evolved without urban planning. But the most interesting cultural and political movements, for example the trade union movement, started in Larissa. Initially we only planned a small edition of *Going Public*, entitled 'Communities and Territories', but it turned out to be huge. The aim was to focus on bordering territories and local communities, on migrations and the flux of people, on the activities of small communities living in Larissa, communities that came from the Balkans and eastern Europe (e.g. Roma, Vlachs, and refugees from Albania and Serbia) as well as Russia (Pontians) and Asia. We found the most peculiar things and attitudes there. For instance, the main military base for aircraft guarding Greek territory against the Turks is in Larissa. We were walking in the streets and talking while dozens of interceptor aircraft kept crossing the sky. All these intersections were very interesting for our work, for the research published in the book and for the artists invited, including Adrian Paci, Rirkrit Tiravanija, Maria Papadimitriou, Maya Bajevic,

*The Memory Box*
Gianmaria Conti, project for *Atlante Mediterraneo*, Nicosia, Cyprus, 2006

*The Farkadona Case*
Hariklia Hari, project for *Communities and Territories*, Larissa, Greece. 2005

Starco Square, Beirut, 2006

Pablo Leon de la Barra, Marjetica Potrc and others from Cyprus. We also invited Carlos Basualdo to a public debate, open to everyone in the city and the students of the University of Thessaly in Volos.
We can call Larissa a 'state of exception' as defined by Giorgio Agamben's theory. It has more than 300,000 inhabitants, but there is no centre except for a very small historical one. It's built in a very chaotic way; there are many 'satellites', in the sense that every community has its own circular neighbourhood. If you draw lots of circles or bubbles, then you have a map of Larissa. It's not a gated city in terms of urban fabric, but it's one in social terms. There are many different communities of migrants. Greece is in the middle of this huge migratory movement between the East and West, especially in relation to the Balkans. Due to the war in the Balkans, the fall of the Berlin Wall, the collapse of communism and the situation in post-communist societies, Greece has become a route for different migrating groups. Once people migrated to Russia and Ukraine and other communist countries; after 1989 these same people had to leave again. This double flux led to gated communities inside the city. For example, there is a very interesting case near Larissa: the community in Farkadona. It's made up of Greeks who lived for almost 30 years in Russia; they returned to Greece but still speak only Russian with one another. After 15 years in Farkadona, this community of Pontian Greeks still lives in 200 iron containers, 25 square metres per family, and every year the municipality promises to give them real homes.

**PM/HM**: Such projects can be very successful within a kind of international discourse, but how do they affect local circumstances, and in particular the communities involved?

**Claudia Zanfi**: Well, take the Farkadona community we were just talking about. A team founded by Hariklia Hari (who is an architect) was involved in our *Going Public* project. For it, the team started doing important research on the Pontian Greeks and organized legal demonstrations against the municipal authorities, programmes for housing and a community newspaper called *The Argonaut News*. Such activities don't involve the kind of research where you can maintain distance. We're not biologists or scientists; first and foremost we work with human beings. By practising visual art and contemporary culture, we talk to people and activate a dialogue. The project in Farkadona was very important, because it motivated the community to come out of limbo and raised its self-awareness. Prior to the project, the leader of the community rarely visited the municipal authorities to say, in the name of the community, 'we're fed up with having to live in containers', and nothing ever happened. Then they started a newspaper together with the lead artist, and of course a newspaper is a voice, so thanks to it they were able to make themselves heard. They also took up residence in the radio stations of the cities of Farkadona and Larissa, which meant they had an even stronger voice with which to reach the public. This is when things started to change. Of course, this doesn't happen in every case and every community, but if we obtain even one result like this one, we feel that the project makes sense, that it's successful, not only in the artistic community, but also in society, and that's important to us.

# Ursula Biemann

**PM/HM:** *The Maghreb Connection* is a collective undertaking that relates more to producing new knowledge than accumulating art in a traditional curatorial context. What is the significance of this kind of research in which you meander between curatorial and artistic practice?

**Ursula Biemann:** I understand my curatorial work as an expansion of my own artistic practice; it's a way of forming a mutual context. When you speak of transit migration in the Maghreb, including trans-Saharan migration from West Africa, it's a complex topic and a huge geography with lots of key locations. It's more than a single person can handle. You have to depend on other people to cover different sections of migration paths, raise specific issues and document different locations: Lampedusa, migration gates in Morocco, the Nile Delta. But it's a relief to know you can focus on your own small distinct area because the others are elaborating on theirs, and together these works will establish relations across the entire region. We don't need more reductive representation there. For *The Maghreb Connection*, I started a network with people I had worked with in the past and others just joined in; for instance, I had heard of a couple who were working on Lampedusa, a crucial location that we had been wanting to cover anyway. The project grew organically over a number of months before we settled into a group. In fact our collaboration turned into a network all by itself; there was no defined collective structure that had us actually sitting around the table and making decisions together, but we shared a lot of information. The aim of our research was to produce new knowledge, so we went on location and gathered a lot of information from people who were involved in migration studies, local NGOs or directly with migrants, and were documenting migration gates, nodes and relays in the mobility network. In a second phase, we developed diverse artistic projects with this material. In the process we wrote substantial research texts for the publication. This happened at a time when we were in the middle of editing videos and everything was still a construction site. It was during this process of articulation that the collaboration in the group became most intense. The day after the opening in Cairo, we held a conference on migration politics and art, with speakers from, for example, Observatorio Technologico del Estrecho, an activist network on Spanish-Moroccan border issues, as well as Maghrebi scholars doing research in France. The majority of those attending the conference came from Morocco, Lebanon and the larger Middle East – for it was a regional project. The exhibition got a lot of media attention. TV journalists wanted to know more about this unusual curatorial project and they immediately understood that the artworks hadn't been chosen from a position of authority, but that the whole project had grown in a 'workshop' fashion, as one of them called it. They were surprised to see a conference on migration politics set in an art exhibition, especially one where the two were so closely related. They recognized the potential of the art context to trigger a debate in a country where public debate is restricted. *The Maghreb Connection* continues to grow and new artworks are being developed for an upcoming exhibition in Beirut.

**PM/HM:** In most of your works there's an interest in the interaction of all kinds of networked economies with everyday community situations. What can be achieved by bringing these minor encounters and side events to the attention of a wider audience?

*Sahara Chronicle*
Video essay by Ursula Biemann, 34 min., 2006

*Black Sea Files*
Video essay by Ursula Biemann, 43 min., 2005

*Sahara Chronicle*
Video essay by Ursula Biemann, 34 min., 2006

*Crossroads at the Edge of Worlds*
Video essay by Charles Heller, 37 min., 2006

**Ursula Biemann:** To stay with the example of *The Maghreb Connection*, one of the motivations was clearly to counteract the repetitive simplistic representation of boat people in the media. Unless you take specialized literature, the images reproduced in the media present poor Europe being overwhelmed by an enormous invasion of people who want to enter it. To start with, we felt the need to show that this form of migration is not a problem that has emerged suddenly but a well-grounded social practice with local ties and historical roots. In addition we wanted to open up a whole range of discussions and research subjects around the issue because reductive representations also tend to be misleading. There had to be something to gain from deeper levels of analysis and presenting audiences with the complex web of spatial and social relations we both observed and created during our research. Some of us had a particular interest in spatial configurations, because it is striking how different transnational spaces overlap and intersect in this region. There are all these subversive, clandestine formations, and they exist side by side with high-tech plans to create a giant transnational harbour in the southern section of the Mediterranean Basin. One of the artists from Cairo has been doing work on Chinese migrants who have moved to Cairo. For there is not only migration from the South to the North but also a considerable flow of lateral movement within Africa, a lot of which involves the Chinese. For my part, I wanted to make the network itself visible by going to some major gates in the Sahara. In Niger, I filmed the departure of sub-Saharan migrants as they were packing and leaving on desert trucks, when everything still seemed possible to them. I filmed these quiet scenes in an unexcited way, like an everyday event. I also interviewed some key figures of the organization, 'coxers', as they call themselves, and a Tuareg ex-rebel leader who gave his sophisticated analysis of this space of mobility, one that has always been occupied by the Tuareg socially, if not politically, and which they now have repurposed for a giant migration transit business. People have established a web of connections and they use it to move through these vast spaces; this web is also a complex social and not just physical system of underground relay stations. You have to be able to rely on a lot of people, if you want to make it. These networks are mainly fuelled by economic activities that have emerged from them – the desert cities are booming – because everything has to do with survival, and people automatically find ways to capitalize on this. The more furtive the network, the more coded and difficult it is to visualize it. In their spatial organization these networks are geographic but it's the sort of geography that has to do with networked thinking rather than with a classical sense of spatial determination.

The clandestine, coded nature of the system and the highly emotional existential stakes involved in the operation make it extremely difficult to find adequate representations. You can capture activities at a number of logistic hubs, even if the rest remains out of sight. What we're looking at, then, is an off-Broadway play of geopolitics where you only get to see the side events. However, if you were to choose not to deconstruct the powerful players of this web, but set them aside for once, and managed not to fall for simple victimization clichés, you might start to see how the migrants themselves shape and give meaning to the process. To pay attention to such inventive social practices is a lot more interesting, because it leads to the complexity of social textures. For ultimately there's no simple way to tell the story of trans-Saharan migration. I think the wider audience knows very little about the finer facets of migration. With our work we can contribute to diversifying the discussion and making it more complex.

THIS IS THE STUFF OF MOVEMENT.

**PM/HM:** Speaking about the ambiguity of informal networks that accompany migration: informal economies are sites of exploitation, yet there are also moments of creativity connected to these arenas of survival. What are the implications of artistic investigations into these conflicting worlds, e.g. in your work on the global sex industry?

**Ursula Biemann:** The condition of women in the global sex industry ranges from forced prostitution to self-determined migration, which means the term itself encompasses these ambiguities. In the trafficking of women you have to look really hard to find any empowering moments, as their bodies and labour are almost entirely governed by others. Many women, the majority I'd say, experience economic exploitation regularly but they also create huge economies in the process, shadow economies and spaces of survival in the cracks of global capitalism. It's interesting to see exactly how they go about this and at the same time, to subvert the idea that global capitalism is something all-pervasive that has a grip on the whole world, for this is not at all the case. To show how people are constantly subverting this concept is a way to draft counter-geographies. Subverting and circumscribing borders is, of course, the most visible effect of this. There's a desire for self-determination and a savoir-faire of migration; simultaneously there are these other technologies developed to manage and control it. These two tendencies are constantly in friction with one another and sites where this friction becomes visible are interesting places. This became very clear in my research for *Remote Sensing*. International sex workers have a very strong network, one that has been in the making for over a generation. Some of them even have long-standing relations, as they first began

*Remote Sensing*
Video essay by Ursula Biemann, 53 min., 2003

*Black Sea Files*
Ursula Biemann, 2005
Oil cartography, designed in collaboration with Hosoya Schäfer architects, Zurich

*Sudeuropa*
Video by Raphael Cuomo and Maria Iorio, 38 min., 2005

لمبيدوسا

arriving from Southeast Asia at the end of the Vietnam War. This is a history we shouldn't forget; not everything started with globalization. First, all you see is the exploitation – the magnitude of exploitation is just unbelievable – and the fact that women are addressed in their sexuality by global capitalism is outrageous. There's undeniably a sense of sacrifice and victimhood. But after a week or two, the more I spoke with these women, for example in the Philippines, I had to acknowledge their position, which they spoke about in such normal, unspectacular terms. I entered a different level of conversation and began to see the small things they've managed to achieve, including the fact that they help their families to survive. In my video, it's not so important to state my personal position but to open a range of conflicting positions regarding prostitution and trafficking, including the ethical choice of engaging in sex work. That's when black-and-white vision blurs and you start to enter a grey area, a zone of negotiation, and this is what I've been most interested in over the last years. To open up a discursive space has been one aesthetic strategy; the other has been to invent new images for the transnational mobility and global network, both real and virtual, that these women have created in the process.

*Sahrawi refugee camp*
Photograph by Armin Linke, 2004

93

**PM/HM**: Your recent projects *Urban Catalyst* and *Shrinking Cities* deal with questions of urban shrinkage and provisionality by employing a variety of approaches ranging from calls for ideas and academic research to on-site interventions, exhibitions and public debates. Did this methodological hybridity grow out of the urban situations addressed by your projects themselves or is it more a manifestation of a particular kind of collaboration?

**Philipp Oswalt**: There is an unplanned phenomenon emerging in cities, one in which vacant spaces are used on a temporary basis by different actors. Vacant lots and buildings become available resources for actors who have little capital but have the energy and the willingness to generate public activities or cultural activities, social activities and so on. The question involved in the *Urban Catalyst* project was: Is there anything planners can learn from these unplanned phenomena? And should we instrumentalize, copy, support or enable them? So the project wasn't limited to the analysis of this informal urbanism, but also engaged in the question of what to do. In a similar way, we also pursued different case studies in our *Shrinking Cities* project – this was essential for this project and could be more intensely developed within its scope. Doing so not only enabled us to understand the different urban conditions better, but also the different cultures of urban research.

Regarding the involvement of artists, we had this interdisciplinary principle on different levels of the project, which meant the curatorial team included a mix of people, namely an art curator, an editor from an architecture magazine, a sociologist and an architect (myself); we also had contributors from dozens of different disciplines. On the one hand, such an interdisciplinarity is necessary and unavoidable if you engage in a subject that can never be completely covered by a single discipline. Someone from outside comes in and may be fairly naive and question some of the taboo issues of your discipline. This can be very productive. On the other hand, interdisciplinarity is creating extreme problems in communication: each profession has its own criteria, and they often don't match. Certain questions are very important for artists, others, for architects – and they are often contradictory. So this becomes an issue, because if you have different criteria, you cannot simply combine them, as nobody would be able to fulfil them equally; this means you need to prioritize and say, okay, this is more important than that. The point is how to manage this process so that something consistent comes out of it.

**PM/HM**: Aren't such demands for consistency also prone to instrumentalizing the potential of experimental urban practices in favour of hegemonic urban interests?

**Philipp Oswalt**: If we're talking about *Shrinking Cities*, for instance, then it was more about establishing a think-tank for urgent questions. Building up awareness, initiating a discourse (setting an agenda) and developing knowledge were important to us. By doing this, we wanted to have an impact on how people think and how they act. What then becomes critical is how to communicate the work being done. I'm not afraid of being didactic. I respect the fact that art normally isn't

*Shrinking Cities*
Exhibition at the Centre for Contemporary Culture Halle (ZfzK Halle) in the former train station of Halle Neustadt, Germany, November 2005

untitled, drawing by FLAG/Bastien Aubry, Dimitri Broquard, 2005

# Philipp Oswalt

in such a project. Of course there is a significant difference if an artwork engages in the analysis of a given situation or in active interventions. In the first phase of the *Shrinking Cities* project, we focused on the first aspect; later on, on the second, which might be considered the more problematic sphere.

Generally speaking, there is a fundamental difference between the logics of urban planning and the art world. In the art world it's very common and more or less the norm (not to say a must) to focus on conflicts and contradictions, and criticize existing conditions, while in the urban development context you are expected only to speak in the affirmative, offer solutions and positive scenarios. Both attitudes are limited and similarly one-sided. This problem manifested itself early on in our project title 'Shrinking Cities'. While it was – unsurprisingly – positively received in the art context, it was at the same time the very reason why we had (and still have) on-going problems with urban planning departments and municipalities or even professional organizations of architects. In Manchester the head of the architects association wanted to halt our work, and in some German cities local politicians stopped exhibitions already in preparation.

*Shrinking Cities*
International Pavilion, 10th International Architecture Exhibition, Biennale di Venezia, 2006

activities with no lasting effect. This is a very dangerous and anti-political attitude that obscures certain discussions and provides amusements by offering interesting art or not-so-interesting art, and this becomes a kind of pseudo-activity in itself.

**PM/HM**: How has this danger of shadding and veiling differences in the urban fabric been circumnavigated by the *Shrinking Cities* project and what has been the response?

**Philipp Oswalt**: There is a multitude of possibilities for artists to engage

the German ministry for building to investors and municipalities, everybody engages artists for urban development projects. Basically you could say: if they get stuck with their problems and have no clue what to do, they invite artists who then simulate some urban activity or meaning that has been lost. It gets especially dumb if there are vacant shop fronts, and people and artists are invited to do some temporary activity in them for a few weeks. By doing this, conflicts and political issues, crises in the real estate business or the urban planning profession are covered up by a surface of cultural

didactic and probably also shouldn't be didactic. But I find the current fear and taboo status of didactics in the cultural context very problematic. If you look back into the history of political protest or the labour movement, it has always been essential to be outspoken and clear in trying to reach others. Today it has to be done with a different attitude, as we have doubts and see contradictions as an important part of our work. But being didactic doesn't have to imply knowing conclusively or providing final answers.

Now to your question: it has become very fashionable to involve artists in urban development, and there's no neighbourhood in Germany that has not been affected at least once by some kind of artist involvement. From

95

The very interesting and challenging character of a subject like shrinking cities is that you're facing fundamental problems, and not only pragmatic and technical questions. These problems are to a large extent a question of values, conceptual modes of judgement and are quite political – for example, the question of real estate or property: How is property organized and conceptualized? How would other forms of dealing with property open up new possibilities? Or another major clue to the problem is migration: Do we accept migration or not, and how do we deal with it? If you work with a politician – a mayor, a minister or the head of an urban planning department – and you raise this kind of question, it's very difficult to find anybody who is willing to commit themselves on the issue, and this is true even though migration is a prime force in defining the causes and effects of shrinkage and therefore provides major clues for new modes of action.

But for us it was necessary to take the liberty to ask questions that go beyond normal modes of practice, even though it meant losing contact with the government. So the possible political impact of such an approach is rather indirect. What we tried to do is to influence thinking on the subject and by doing this, we hoped, of course, to change the practice of action in the long run, too. I strongly believe, that for certain modes of work it's absolutely necessary to refrain from direct policy consulting. Instead we must develop a discourse to stimulate ideas and different ways of thinking, and hope that this will in the long run have some impact on what is actually done in cities.

*Shrinking Cities*
Exhibition at the Centre for Contemporary Culture Halle (ZfzK Halle) in the former train station of Halle Neustadt, Germany, November 2005

# Slatewalls
## Chinese Markets

Psyrri, Athens, 2007

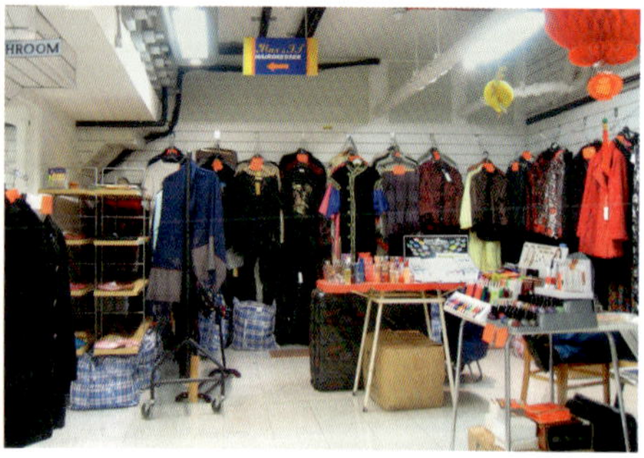

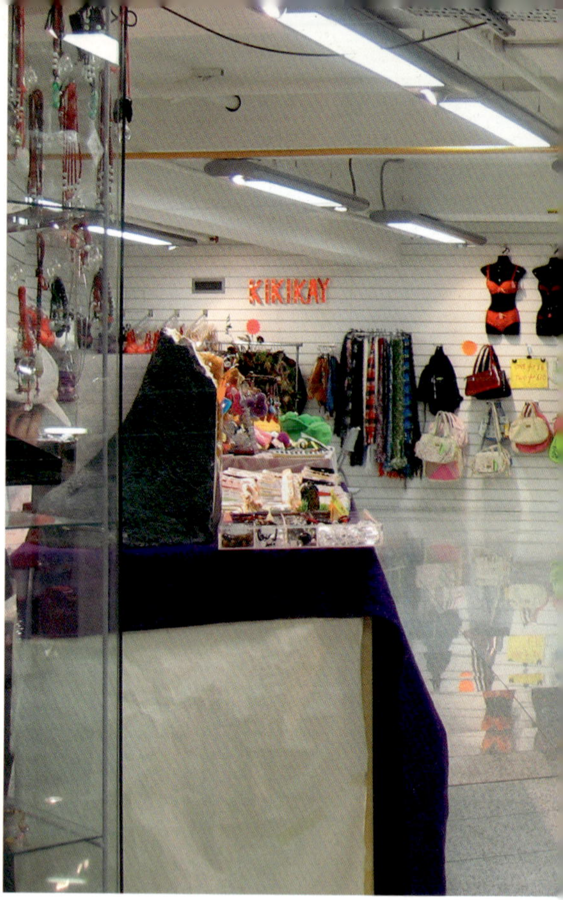

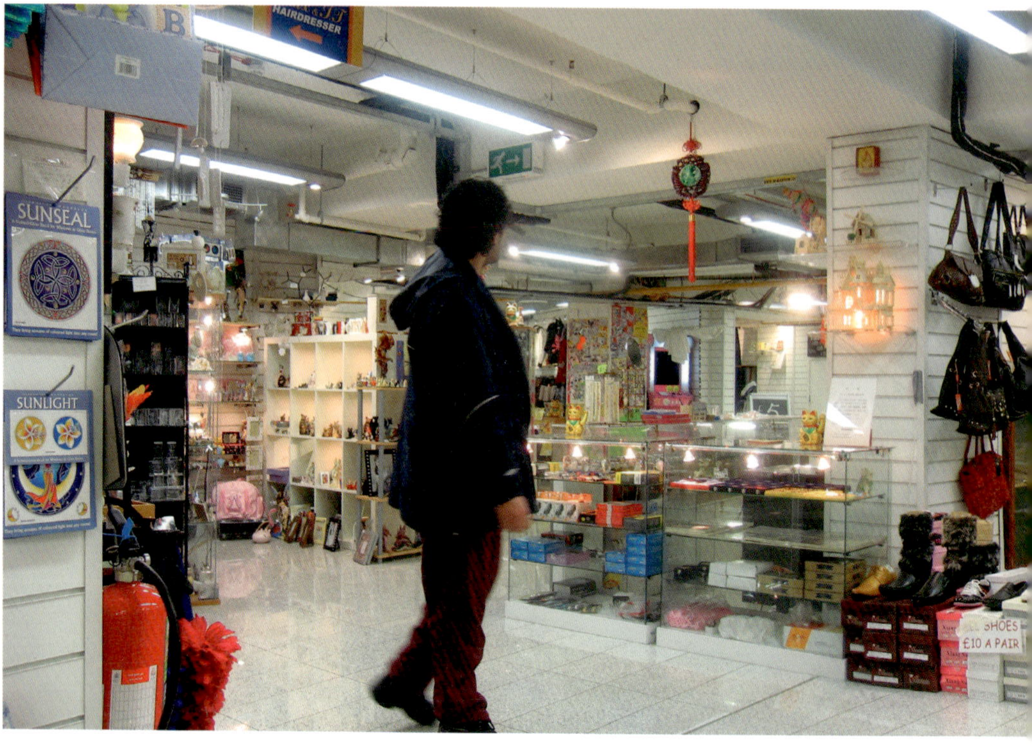

The ubiquitous slatewall, a shop fitting system that allows for flexibility in the display of changing stock, widely used by retailers of 'Chinese' merchandise

China Town on Charing Cross Road, London, 2007

# Casting Nets

## On the Co-Constitutive Dispersions of Governance, Production and Urbanization in Contemporary China

### Adrian Blackwell

*The rural component of Chinese civilization was more or less uniform and it extended everywhere that Chinese civilization penetrated. It, and not the cities, defined the Chinese way of life. It was like the net in which the cities and towns of China were suspended... Chinese cities were but knots of the same material, of one piece with the net, denser in quality but not foreign bodies resting on it.[1]*
Frederick Mote – The Transformation of Nanking 1350-1400

*This is no longer a capitalism for production, but for the product, which is to say, for being sold or marketed. Thus it is essentially dispersive, and the factory has given way to the corporation.[2]*
Gilles Deleuze – 'Postscript on Societies of Control'

The contemporary movement of people from the Chinese countryside into the cities has been mirrored by a corresponding move of cities into the countryside. Beijing's New Development Zones, the networked industrial/agricultural fabric of the Yangzi Delta and the factory villages of Shenzhen's Bao'an County and Dongguan are each specific illustrations of the ways in which cities are currently decentralizing. This paper compares the urban forms of these three urban conurbations, in order to locate this decentralization in relation to coincident dispersion of governance and production: the devolution of the central government's authority and the breaking apart of state-owned industries. This generalized situation of dispersion, characteristic of neoliberalism around the world, brings with it a specific set of contradictions in China where it confronts the forces of an authoritarian and still Keynesian state, processes of primitive accumulation and strategies of ideological interpellation. These apparently Chinese characteristics in turn reflect back on neoliberalism in general, asking us to look at the similarities between these and strategies of governance, production and urbanization in the rest of the world.

### DECENTRALIZATIONS OF GOVERNANCE AND PRODUCTION

Since 1978 and the initiation of Deng Xiaoping's market reforms, there has been a steady dispersion of governance downwards from the central government in Beijing to provinces, urban municipalities, rural townships, villages, families and individuals. It is no surprise that this has been closely paralleled by a decentralization of the primary factors of production, because at the end of the Cultural Revolution land, labour and capital were almost entirely controlled by the state. In fact the two processes of devolution have been co-constitutive. Martin Hart-Landsberg and Paul Burkett have argued that economic processes unleashed in the late 1970s have driven state policy ever since.[3] But despite the rising dominance of a capitalist mode of production, the central government has managed to retain control over the primary repressive and ideological state apparatuses throughout the transition, controlling of the military and guiding the direction of local policies through a sequence of loose directives, operating across a spectrum from 'formal laws' to 'policy declarations and general pronouncements',[4] creating a flexible process that has allowed executive power to remain concentrated, at the same time that economic planning and experimentation has been diffused across the country.

The process of reform was felt first in rural areas during the period 1978-1984,[5] starting with the transformation of rural communes into villages and townships under the 'Household Contract Responsibility System'. This legislation was initiated by peasants themselves, when in 1978 farmers in Anhui Province began secretly organizing themselves according to households rather than production units. Their experiments were first acknowledged by local authorities and subsequently adopted by the central government, which eventually implemented the system across China in 1981.[6] The second key element of rural reform was the liberalization of rural industry that had been promoted throughout the Maoist period, first during The Great Leap forward and later with the Commune and Brigade Enterprises (CBEs). Already profitable during the Cultural Revolution, they were renamed Township and Village Enterprises (TVEs) after reform.[7] The expansion of TVEs during the reform period was one of the key tools in the first phase of marketization in China, developing quite differently within each regional economy. The third essential reform was a two-part increase in the price of agricultural products: an increase in the price paid for a household's production quota and the deregulation of the price of over-quota production, introducing a dual pricing system.[8]

These reforms increased household incomes in rural areas quickly between 1978 and 1984, but after 1984 the emphasis of reform shifted to the urban areas, and since then the socio-economic gap between urban and rural residents has greatly increased.[9] Wang Hui, former editor of the literary journal *Dushu*, has argued that these urban reforms, constituted a devolution, or transfer of political and economic power from the central government to lower levels, 'a process by which relations of social advantage were reorganized under state direction by the transfer and apportionment of resources that had previously been directly controlled and distributed by the state itself'.[10] This redistribution of assets from the public sector to the emerging private sector was a process where political power was exchanged for economic power, often within families and between generations.[11]

The urban reforms began in 1979 by granting new administrative powers to municipalities, through the naming of four special economic zones (SEZs). In 1986, the State Council generalized this early exceptionalism by promoting cities as privileged engines to drive regional and national growth.[12] Techniques were introduced to allow municipalities to jump administrative level and at the same time increase the territory assigned to them, such that power has been dispersed to the four SEZs, 14 Open Coastal Cities, and four provincial-level municipalities: Beijing, Tianjin, Shanghai and Chongqing.[13] The active power of cities increases the closer they sit to the central government within an administrative hierarchy, so this process has also been one of power consolidation within certain cities and the corresponding disempowerment of many rural areas.[14] A second mechanism of devolution was the breaking apart of state-owned enterprises (SOEs). During the Maoist period these industries were attached through a vertical chain of command directly to the central government, skipping municipal levels of control.[15] In the reform period, however, this line was loosened. In 1983 legislation was introduced to allow companies to hire contract workers,[16] and in 1988 bankruptcy legislation terminated urban workers' rights to lifetime employment.[17] Private shareholding experiments began in experimental work units in 1984, public shares were first offered on certain Shanghai and Shenzhen companies in 1992, and a public shareholding system was finally adopted across the country in 1997.[18] The third strategy of decentralization involved the opening of real-estate markets. Land in China remains under the ownership of the state, but the liberalization of private land development processes since the mid-1980s has been one of the prime drivers of the urban economy. The transfer of land through a leasing system was made legal in 1986 under the Land Management Law, and revised in 1988 to allow for long-term leases and again in 1991 to authorize the sale, rental and transfer of leaseholds. In 1995 urban residents were given the rights to own their homes,[19] and banking reforms quickly followed to allow consumers to secure mortgages for home ownership, ushering in the property boom of the late 1990s.[20] These rural and urban reforms initiated a process of original accumulation as the foundation for a properly capitalist economy. Over the past 30 years China has seen the proletarianization of both rural peasants and the privileged communist working class and the creation of a substantial bourgeoisie primarily from the bureaucratic echelon of the communist social structure.[21] However this process of class composition has also been a process of deterritorialization and reterritorialization, in the most literal senses of these two concepts. Within the reform process, people were dislodged from their land, workplaces, communities and homes and subsequently relocalized within changed situations.[22]

## DECENTRALIZATION OF CITIES IN CHINA

The devolutions of governance and production listed above have each had unique spatial effects on what was the primarily rural character of China in the late 1970s. In the countryside the fast development of Town and Village Enterprises from 1985 to 1995 began to bring some of the characteristics of urban life to the countryside in both the Yangzi and Pearl River Deltas. At the same time, the urban reforms have pushed the extension of urbanization into surrounding agricultural areas, creating an uneven patchwork of migrant housing, village industries, high-tech clusters, gated communities, artists' villages and high-intensity farming. In the Lower Yangzi Delta, for example, the countryside between cities is populated at densities that closely parallel those of many North American cities,[23] suggesting the emergence of a new form of diffuse urbanization.

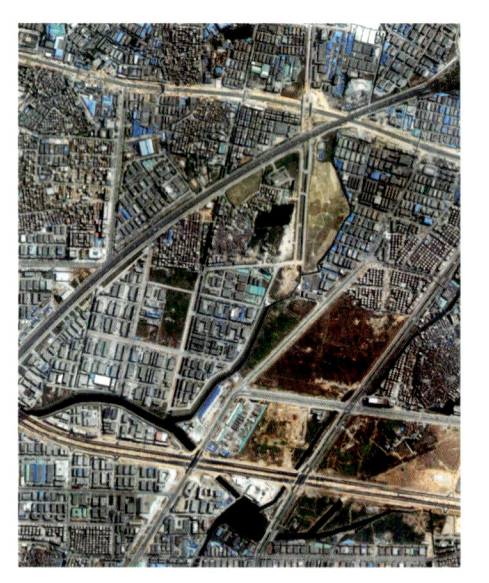

Google Map of Pearl River Delta: Factory Territory

German urban designer Thomas Sieverts has argued that the *Zwischenstadt*, the in-between city, has become the predominant pattern of urbanization across the globe.[24] The centred and concentric city has been superseded by a dispersed network of urbanization, pulled apart by the increasingly rapid circulation of information, capital, commodities and labour. In North America and Europe the decentralization of both industry and housing, beginning in the early part of the twentieth century and accelerating in the wake of the Second World War, acted as the spatial foundation for the long process of the mobilization of capital found in the globalized production chains that have emerged since the 1980s.[25] Here Guy Debord's prescient argument that urbanism lays the foundation for all other capitalist separations is confirmed.[26] Urbanism acts in advance of other processes of production, because it reterritorializes capital in fixed assets, making relocation difficult and forcing its utility on the future.

If the 'in-between city' is both the urban tissue of neoliberal capitalism and one of its preconditions, the decentralization of Chinese cities is also co-constitutive of Chinese neoliberalism. Spectacular economic growth has been driven by the industrial powerhouses of the Pearl River and Yangzi Deltas and their rhizomatic geographies of production. These vast industrial peripheries are unprecedented urban formations, founded on the apparent contradiction between the unbounded expansion of the cities themselves and the Chinese regulation of the boundary between city and country through the household registration system, or *hukou*, which indelibly marks each person as either an urban citizen or a peasant. Moving from the country to the city is easy and necessary today, in order to match labour to booming industrial and service economies, but it is nearly impossible for peasants to gain permanent rights of residence in the cities in which they work, leaving them in a precarious position. It is important to understand this system not merely as a relic from the earlier communist regime, but rather as a recently renovated technique for modulating labour markets, creating a historically unparalleled rise in social and economic inequity.[27] As a result of this system of regulation, the in-between cities of the highly populated coastal regions are filled with migrant farmers. They live on the urban edge, because it is cheaper and less controlled than the city. Also the villages on the edge appear familiar in structure, and migrants are not subjected to the discrimination and discomfort they feel in the city. Like the indeterminacy of this space itself, peasants are caught between the urban and the rural: named farmers in official and unofficial discourses even when the work they do is industrial or service work and they live in urbanized areas.

The downloading of power and responsibility to municipalities and the early reliance on local experimentation has meant that each peripheral region has unique trajectories of dispersion. In the Pearl River Delta foreign direct investment overdeveloped the countryside to create a continuous production zone. In the Yangzi Delta, villages and towns urbanized through the profits of TVEs, creating locally determined meshwork of farming and urbanization. Finally, in Beijing, the urban periphery has been transformed through real-estate development, high-technology zones and cultural industries into a heterogeneous archipelago of differentiated uses and users.

## PEARL RIVER DELTA: FACTORY TERRITORY[28]

The Pearl River Delta, with its long history of mercantilism, vast Cantonese diaspora, familial and language connections to adjacent Hong Kong and Macau and distance from the heart of the country, was seen by Deng Xiaoping as the ideal place to experiment with capitalism within China. The Special Economic Zone of Shenzhen has developed more quickly than any other city in history, from a series of agricultural and fishing villages in 1979 to a city of over nine million people today. Its fast development has been driven by the proximity of mobile capital and the need to find a spatial fix for the declining profitability of Hong Kong's manufacturing sector. When China opened the SEZ to foreign direct investment, the low cost of labour on the mainland was too much for Hong Kong capitalists to pass up. While considerable sums were invested in the SEZ, the most lucrative spaces for investors turned out to be the Town and Village Enterprises directly to the north in Bao'an district and Dongguan.[29] Hong Kong business people used their personal connections with villagers to develop working relations for which they provided capital, machinery, technical and managerial expertise; local farmers provided land, and labour was provided by migrant workers from across the country. As a result the local farmers have become wealthy from land development in collaboration with their Hong Kong neighbours.

This pattern has produced a web of industrial urbanization over a unified territory from Guangzhou to Shenzhen on the east side of the Delta, and with slightly less intensity on the west. Each former agricultural village acts as a development corporation in order to profit from its land, creating a production landscape that has very few of the monuments, residential districts or commercial areas of a traditional city and yet employs over 11 million migrants in its factories. The architecture of this area is repetitive, multiplying a very limited set of building typologies: export-oriented factory buildings; dormitory housing, where most migrant workers live; new high-rise farmers' villages, which rise four to seven stories as apartment housing for those migrants who do not live in dormitories; and finally the remnants of traditional courtyard houses in the pre-reform villages. Pun Ngai and Christopher Smith have called the process of production in this zone a 'factory dormitory regime', in order to emphasize the precarious and intertwined living and working conditions of migrant workers in the PRD. This concept also highlights the decisive spatiality of this production pattern, with its monotonous walled compounds, its guards and curfews. These apparently contingent working arrangements rely on short-term contracts to prevent labour organizing and take the physical form of a work camp, in order to create a system of 'labour on tap'.[30] Here the networked and apparently self-organizing development at the macro scale is sharply contrasted with the hierarchical and structured design of the factory themselves.

**LOWER YANGZI DELTA: URBANIZATION IN THE COUNTRYSIDE**[31]

While rapid development in the PRD has been driven primarily by concentrations of mobile capital, management expertise and distribution networks, in the Lower Yangzi Delta, rural urbanization has occurred more slowly and has been generated by local forces.[32]

The internal stimulus for this local development came from the long tradition of agricultural and textile industries in the region. Its trading towns, interconnected waterways and fertile farmland have made it the most productive region of China since the Tang Dynasty. The external stimulus has been the expansion of state-owned enterprises in the mid 1980s. Existing TVEs were subcontracted by these larger urban companies to produce parts, creating proprietary relationships between particular TVEs and SOEs, allowing SOEs to grow without necessitating physical expansion onsite.[33] Using Karl Marx's processes of formal and real subsumption, Daniel Buck argues that through this arrangement rural labour was formally subsumed into the capitalist processes,[34] while existing production systems were consolidated and integrated into capitalist markets without transforming the labour process itself.[35] The relatively prosperous period from 1985 to 1995 allowed for the expansion and profitability of both the TVEs and the SOEs in the region, with workers in the TVEs receiving benefits and job security similar in kind, if not quantity, to that enjoyed by urban workers.[36]

However, by the mid-1990s industries in the Yangzi Delta began to experience competitive pressures from producers in the south and were forced to restructure their productive relationships. As a result the non-competitive relationships between TVEs and SOEs were scrapped. TVEs were thrown into competition, wages were forced downward, and jobs were no longer secure. Many were forced out of business during this process and the salvageable ones were privatized, bought by foreign or local investors. Buck points to this violent transformation as the real subsumption of labour, through which social relations themselves were radically reshaped to conform to capitalist processes.[37] This crisis forced local farmers into a model of development similar to that pioneered in the south. Local farmers now use their accumulated capital and land-use rights to develop housing for a migrant labour force, hired at reduced wages, to work in restructured enterprises. This process constitutes the 'capture of the country by the city'.

The countryside is stratified by class like urban spaces, with the local farmers constituting a local bourgeoisie while migrants work the fields and factories.

Until the late 1990s the non-competitive relations between TVEs allowed the village collectives significant powers of self-organization, and the resultant urbanization of the countryside proceeded as an unprecedented integration of housing, farming and industry. Around Hangzhou, local farmers' houses have been rebuilt to four to six floors, in order to function as apartments for migrant labourers and decorated to project a sense of urbanity and affluence. These intensified villages run in linear formation, directly following the linear typologies of former settlements. Tendrils of each village link to other communities, creating an almost continuous web of urbanization on top of a surface of open fields. The farmland itself is divided into long and narrow strips of different crops, running perpendicular to each linear village. Interspersed between housing and fields are low one-

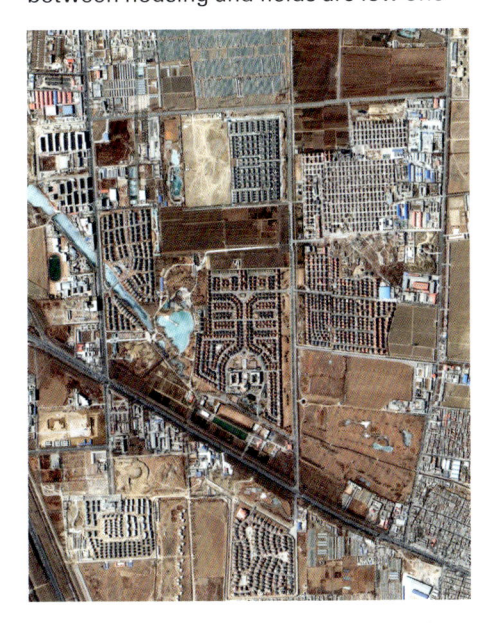

Google Map of Beijing periphery: heterotopic urbanism

storey sheds for heavy production and four- to six-storey warehouse buildings for lighter assembly and textile manufacturing. This integration of different uses resonates with radical proposals to reorganize European city space at the end of the nineteenth century: Peter Kropotkin's vision of the integration of manual and brain work in an industrialized countryside and Ebenezer Howard's proposal for 'Garden Cities of To-morrow'.[38] Despite its recent restructuring, the landscape urbanization of the Lower Yangzi Delta constitutes one of the closest actually existing approximations of these bottom-up development strategies.

## BEIJING PERIPHERY: HETEROTOPIC URBANISM[39]

The periphery of Beijing is different from the delta regions, because it does not have a dense regional network of industrial development. Beijing has always been relatively isolated from other cities rather than contiguous with them. During the Ming and Qing Dynasties, as the capital of the Chinese Empire, Beijing was a walled city with little periphery. By the fall of the republic in 1949, the city had hardly expanded beyond its Qing borders. However, with the move of the capital from Nanjing back to Beijing, the city developed rapidly after 1949, to act as a model for all of communist China. Until the early 1990s, when private development steadily overtook it, the work unit, the *danwei,* formed the basic building block of Beijing's development. This cellular expansion based on autonomous *danweis* was loosely guided by central planning initiatives which proposed an urban form divided by radiating greenbelts, creating a fractured and suburban form. Beijing Architect Lu Xiang has called this spatial structure, which dominates the city's form from the second to the fourth ring, a 'heterotopic city', conjuring up Michel Foucault's heterotopia to describe how complete yet separate each of these worlds is.[40]

Since 1990 Beijing has rapidly accelerated its expansion, with the completion of the second and third ring roads in the 1990s, the fourth in 2001 and the fifth in 2003. Frederic Deng and Youqin Huang have described the dual character of Beijing's contemporary sprawl: the city's 'Development Zones' leap-frog beyond its urbanized areas, designating vast swaths of agricultural land for future development, while agricultural villages, uncertain of their own futures and with limited tools for development, 'gradually become ghetto-like, sprawling migrant enclaves'.[41] Local village collectives consider ways to intensify their production and participate in capitalist markets, some renting land for small industries, specializing in taxi services or renting out failed TVEs as artists' villages. In Beijing, the development of villages has mostly remained at a single story, although new buildings are now being constructed two to three stories tall. Next to these villages sit residential suburbs: in the northeast of the city are gated suburbs for foreign professionals; to the north on the central axis are expensive high-rise apartments overlooking the Olympic green; in the west along the Badaling highway is Huilongguan, 'sleep city', an immense commuter suburb of medium-rise buildings, housing professional migrants in the health care and software sectors. Beside these diverse types of housing sit Maoist industries like Capital Steel, set to close before the Olympics, and the Dashanzi Electrical zone, already transformed to cultural uses. New industrial development consists primarily of high-tech and creative industries: Zhongguancun dwarfs all other zones, with its software development parks rising like a cloud of smoke northwest of the university district on maps of Beijing; Yizhuang Science and Technology Zone in the southeast and areas like Fengtai in the southwest fill out the picture but are tiny by comparison.

If development in the Pearl River and Yangzi Deltas proceeds as a network of repetitive typologies, the Beijing periphery is a patchwork of heterogeneous forms. Villages in the edge city have been constrained from developing vertically so they are filled in in ad hoc ways, making them appear far less affluent than the villages of the south. Here the emphasis has shifted to culture, and the edges of the city are developed as required to facilitate these new industries.

## DECENTRALIZED CONTROL AND RETERRITORIALIZED PRODUCTION

Urbanization has cast its net across vast territories of China's coastal conurbations, acting as an important foundation for the transformations of neoliberal governance. In their work on the changing state and land system in China, George Lin and Samuel Ho point to the evolution of the Chinese state since 1978 from a centralized and localizable entity to a 'strategic and relational' configuration predicated on the negotiation between different levels and forms of governance.[42] This model resonates with Michel Foucault's expansive theorization of governmentality as the triangular interaction between *government*, the biopolitical administration of the population, *discipline*, the training of individual bodies, and *sovereignty*, the law and the legitimate exercise of force.[43] His theorization posits a field in which to locate heterogeneous powers, from self-government to the administration of territories.[44] Thomas Lemke has argued that Foucault's study of the 'Chicago School' economists[45] leads him to understand neoliberal governmentality as 'a political rationality that tries to render the social domain economic and to link a reduction in state services and security systems to the increasing call for "self responsibility" and "self-care"'.[46] In China, apparent contradictions between the party's sovereign power, intrusive biopolitical control and neoliberal self-discipline appear equally at home in the dispersed neoliberal forms of Foucault's triangle of governmentality.

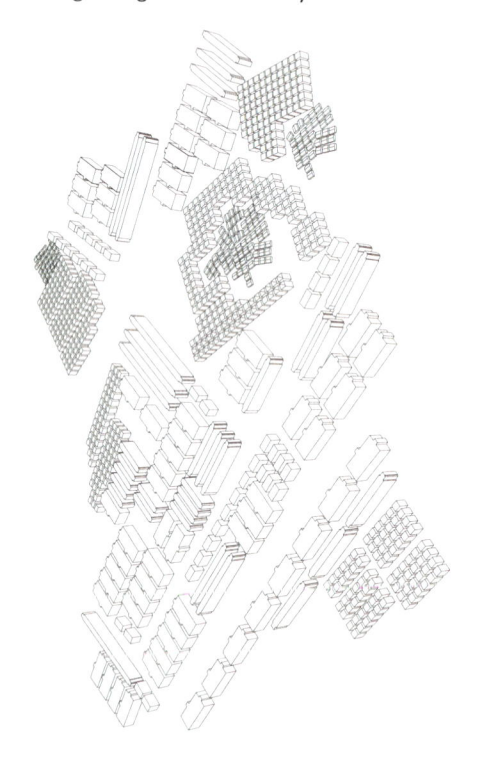

Typical urban composition in the Bao'an Factory Territory

Since 1978, Maoist biopolitics have been transformed to allow for more flexible regulation of the population. In order to open labour markets, peasants were freed from the land, necessitating the renovation of the *hukou* system from a system of walls to one of mobility and variable controls: temporary permits, registration, licenses to apply for and fees to pay.[47] This radical act turned the *hukou* into an axiomatic system of modulation; farmers are deterritorialized by the low profits of farming, but they are prevented from reterritorializing themselves, and are instead left in permanent flux, never at home in their places of work. For its part discipline has been downloaded from the state to individuals in the neoliberal China. The founding act was the household contract responsibility system, and more recently the move to individual home ownership has almost completely replaced the socialist right to accommodation within work units. In both cases, debt has replaced disciplinary enclosure as a means of control.[48] Post-Mao discipline is enacted on a radically individuated subject, indelibly marked by the one-child-only policy. The primary characteristic of the new workers is the extreme precariousness of their ways of life, which has become a new form of discipline, one consolidated through the workers' independence and homelessness. Finally, transformations can be seen in sovereign power, which Foucault defined as the power to 'take life and let live'.[49] In China, the state has retained this right since 1949, but in 1981 Deng Xiaoping downloaded this authority from the national to the provincial courts, inaugurating a 'fast-track criminal justice system', which human-rights groups claim has executed over 10,000 inmates a year.[50] The massacre in Tiananmen Square in 1989 has not been repeated, but the state has augmented its human surveillance networks, with internet monitoring and repression of activism.[51] At the same time the state has used the devolution of powers as a means of evading the political fallout from unpopular actions, as individuals can now jump scale and appeal to the central government for justice, allowing the sovereign state to act as benevolent arbiter, making urban space an important locus of contestation.

If the spatial function of governance in all three of its coincident registers is to manage people and territories, then the mission of neoliberal capital is internal and external expansion. Marx has named three essential processes of capitalist integration, which we have already introduced above: primitive accumulation, formal subsumption and real subsumption. Thinking in terms urban development, these three processes deterritorialize, territorialize, and reterritorialize both land and labour: freeing it, integrating it into capitalist processes, and restructuring it for capital's use. Like Foucault's historical progression of diagrams of power, these three terms are related by Marx to consecutive historical moments of capitalism, and yet they occur and recur at different speeds and under diverse circumstances, such that we find them sitting side by side under conditions of globalized neoliberalism. As Paolo Virno claims, today 'the production models which have followed one another during this long period re-present themselves synchronically'.[52]

This synchronic triangulation of processes of capitalist integration also presents us with a diagram upon which to locate the productive forces within the three variations of the Chinese *Zwischenstadt* discussed above. Buck illustrates this through his history of the Yangzi Delta, where the process by which the city has extended its reach into the countryside shifted from formal subsumption in the mid-1980s to the more violent restructuring of real subsumption after the crisis of over-production in the mid-1990s. In the Pearl River Delta, the export-oriented production zone was constructed by liberalizing the *hukou* system to allow migrants to work in cities under experimental labour conditions.[53] Here real subsumption followed primitive accumulation without mediation. In the periphery of Beijing, migration and endogenous development stumble forward in an unruly way. We find processes of primitive accumulation alternating with non-systematic processes of formal subsumption of rural labour within heterogeneous industries.

In advance of these processes captured in the nets of urbanization, and again in response to them, peasants and workers have been making and remaking space in China. In her analysis of the female factory workers of the Pearl River Delta, Pun Ngai observes that these women are following their desires to escape the paternal and hierarchical worlds of their rural villages, migrating to the cosmopolitan edge cities of the factory territory. The fact that this journey is also one of pain and exploitation forces them into new forms of creative resistance against authoritarian governmentality and exploitive labour relations. Pun argues that these women's actions constitute a 'minor genre of resistance',[54] but the force of migration by those who now live divided, half peasant, half worker, threatens to transform China once again. The complex endogenesis of in-between cities has produced a new terrain of contestation over production processes, technologies of governance and forms of subjectivity.

1. Frederick Mote quoted in John Friedman, *China's Urban Transition* (Minneapolis, MN: University of Minnesota Press, 2005), 35.
2. Gilles Deleuze, 'Postscript on Societies of Control', in *Rethinking Architecture*, ed. Neil Leach (London and New York: Routledge, 1997), 309-313.
3. Martin Hart-Landsberg and Paul Burkett, *China and Socialism: Market Reforms and Class struggle* (New York: Monthly Review Press, 2005).
4. Richard Walker and Daniel Buck, 'The Chinese Road', *The New Left Review* 46 (2007): 62.
5. Wang Hui, *China's New Order* (Cambridge, MA: Harvard University Press, 2003), 48.
6. Justin Yifu Lin, 'The Household Responsibility System Reform in China: A Peasant's Institutional Choice', *American Journal of Agricultural Economics* 69 (May, 1987): 410-15.
7. Louis Putterman, 'On the past and future of China's Township and Village-Owned Enterprises', *World Development* 25, no. 10 (1997): 1640. The growth of CBE/TVEs actually slowed from 30% per year between 1971 and 1978 to 16% per year between 1978 and 1983.
8. Wang Hui, ibid. note 5, 48-49.
9. Ibid., 49.
10. Ibid., 50.
11. He Qinglian, 'China's Listing Social Structure', The *New Left Review* 5 (Sept-Oct, 2000). See also Russell Smyth, 'Asset-Stripping the Chinese State-Owned Enterprises', *Journal of Contemporary Asia* 30, no. 1 (2000): 3–16; X. L. Ding, 'The Illicit Asset Stripping of Chinese State Firms', *The China Journal*, no. 43 (2000): 1-28.
12. Laurence Ma, 'Urban Administrative Restructuring, Changing Scale Relations and Local Economic Development in China', *Political Geography* 24, no. 4 (2005): 484.
13. Ibid., 492.
14. Ibid., 494.
15. David Bray, *Social Space and Governance in Urban China: The Danwei System From Origins to Urban Reform* (Stanford, CA: Stanford University Press, 2005), 129-130.
16. Hart-Landsberg and Burkett, ibid. note 3, 41.
17. Walker and Buck, ibid. note 4, 43.
18. Ma Shu Y., 'The Chinese Route to Privatization: The Evolution of the Shareholding System Option', *Asian Survey* 38, no. 4 (April, 1998): 383-387.
19. Walker and Buck, ibid. note 4, 46-47.
20. Deborah S. Davis, 'From welfare benefit to capitalized asset: the re-commodification of residential space in urban China', in *Housing and social Change: East-West Perspectives*, eds. Ray Forrest and James Lee (London and New York: Routledge, 2003), 186.
21. Walker and Buck, ibid. note 4, 42.
22. Gilles Deleuze and Félix Guattari, *Anti-Oedipus: Capitalism and Schizophrenia* (Minneapolis, MN: University of Minnesota Press, 1983), 225.
23. Andre Marton, *China's Spatial Economic Development: Restless Landscapes in the Lower Yangzi Delta* (London and New York: Routledge, 2000), 70. See also Friedman, ibid. note 1, 35-55. In the countryside of the Yangzi Delta population density is 750-1260 persons per sq km. For a listing of urban densities in North America see City Mayors http://www.citymayors.com/statistics/largest-cities-density-125.html (accessed November 25, 2007).
24. Thomas Sieverts, *Cities without Cities* (London: Spon Press, 2003), 48-68. See also parallel discourses around Landscape Urbanism: Charles Waldheim, 'Landscape as Urbanism', in *The Landscape Urbanism Reader*, ed. Charles Waldheim (New York: Princeton Architectural Press, 2006), 35-53.
25. Thomas Sugrue, *The Origins of the Urban Crisis* (Princeton, NJ: Princeton University Press, 1996), 153-178.
26. Guy Debord, *Society of the Spectacle* (New York: Zone Books, 1994), 119-127.
27. Dennis Tao Yang, 'Urban-Biased Policies and Rising Income Inequality in China', *American Economic Review* 89, no. 2 (1999): 306.
28. This section draws on field work in the Pearl River Delta's Factory Territory in Shajing in June, August and December 2005, and June 2006. See Adrian Blackwell, 'Territory = Factory', *Architecture and Ideas* VI, no.1-2 (2007): 50-67; Adrian Blackwell and Xu Jian, 'New village = cellular structure of the factory territory', *Urban China* 12 (August, 2006): 88-93.
29. David Harvey, *A Brief History of Neoliberalism* (Oxford: Oxford University Press, 2005), 136.
30. Chris Smith and Pun Ngai, 'The Dormitory Labour Regime in China as a Site for Control and Resistance', *International Journal of Human Resource Management* 17, no. 8 (2006), 1456–1470.
31. This section relies on fieldwork with Xu Jian in Hangzhou and Wuxi in May and June 2007.
32. Friedman, ibid. note 1, 35.
33. Daniel Buck, 'The Subsumption of Space and the Spatiality of Subsumption: Primitive Accumulation and the Transition to Capitalism in Shanghai, China', *Antipode* 39, no. 4 (September 2007): 762-764.
34. Ibid., 762 764.
35. Karl Marx, *Capital*, vol. 1 (London: Penguin Classics, New Left Review, 1990), 1019-1023.
36. Buck, ibid. note 33, 762-764.
37. Ibid., 764-769. See also Marx, ibid. note 35, 1023-1025.
38. Peter Kropotkin, *Field, Factories and Workshops* (Montreal: Black Rose Books, 1994); Ebenezer Howard, *Garden Cities of To-Morrow* (Cambridge, MA: MIT Press, 1965).
39. This section relies on field research conducted with my students at the University of Toronto and B.A.S.E. (Beijing Architecture Studio Enterprise) in collaboration with students at Tsing Hua University's Department of Literature and Professor Meng Yue Tsing Hua / UofT, in May and June 2007.
40. Lu Xiang, 'Beijing: Post-Big-Yuan City', *Urban China* 3 (2005): 58-63; Michel Foucault, 'Of Other Spaces', in *Politics-Poetics: Documenta X, the Book* (Kassel: Cantz Verlag, 1997), 262-272.

41 F. Frederic Deng and Youqin Huang, 'Uneven land reform and urban sprawl: the case of Beijing', *Progress in Planning* 61 (2004): 211.

42 George C.S. Lin and Samuel P.S. Ho, 'The State, Land System, and Land Development Process in Contemporary China', *Annals of the Association of American Geographers* 95, no. 2 (2005): 412. Lin and Ho refer to the work of Bob Jessop's *State Theory* (1990) for this theorization of the contemporary state.

43 Michel Foucault, 'Governmentality', in *The Essential Works of Foucault 1954-1984,* vol 3: *Power,* ed. James D. Faubion (New York: The New Press, 2000), 219.

44 Thomas Lemke, '"The Birth of Biopolitics" Michel Foucault's lecture at the College de France on neo-liberal governmentality', *Economy and Society* 30, no. 2 (May, 2001): 191.

45 Ibid., 204. Foucault refers to a number of 'Chicago School' economists in his lectures on neoliberalism, including Ludwig von Mises, Friedrich Hayek, Henry Simons, Henry Shultz and George Stigler, but focuses most closely on Gary Becker, author of *Human Capital*.

46 Ibid., 203 and Michel Foucault, 'The Birth of Biopolitics', in *The Essential Works of Foucault 1954-1984,* vol 1: *Ethics,* ed. Paul Rabinow (New York: The New Press, 2000), 73-79.

47 Wang Fei-Ling, *Organizing Through Division and Exclusion: China's Hukou System* (Stanford, CA: Stanford University Press, 2005), 80-83.

48 Deleuze, ibid. note 2, 312.

49 Michel Foucault, *Society Must Be Defended* (New York: Picador, 2003), 239-263. Michel Foucault, *The History of Sexuality,* vol 1: *An Introduction,* trans. Robert Hurley (New York: Vintage Books, 1978), 135-159.

50 Jim Yardley, 'Number of executions falling sharply in China', *International Herald Tribune,* June 8, 2007.

51 The crackdown on the China Democracy Party is one example of this. See Theresa Wright, 'The China Democracy Party and the Politics of Protest in the 1980s and 1990s', *China Quarterly* 172 (2002): 906-926.

52 Paolo Virno, *A Grammar of the Multitude: For an Analysis of Contemporary Forms of Life* (New York: Semiotexte, 2004), 105.

53 In addition to the designation of the *Shenzhen Special Economic Zone* the Chinese government gave the Guangdong provincial government the right to enact its own 'special policies', cutting its leash to Beijing. See Lin and Ho, ibid. note 42, 419.

54 Pun Ngai, *Made in China* (Durham, NC: Duke University Press, 2005), 189-196.

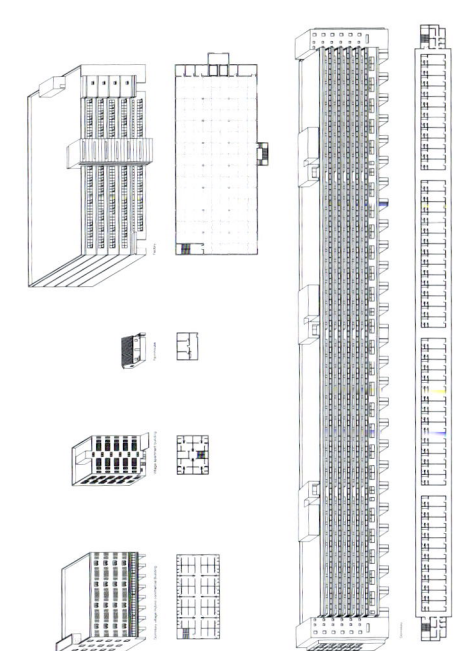

# Les Olympiades
**Paris**

A modernist housing complex in the 14th arrondissement, inaugurated in 1972, that has become one of the largest Asian quarters in Paris, 2005

# Ayreen Anastas and Rene Gabri

**PM/HM:** Your project *Camp Campaign* includes a cartography outlining your trip through the United States and highlighting particular camp sites, but also representing dialogues and meetings, encounters that you had during this journey. How did you bring together such a particular instrument with fundamental political issues and expressions of personal experience in an art project?

**Ayreen Anastas:** The project is called *Camp Campaign*; the exhibition takes its name from a script which we had prepared for it: *Project For An Inhibition in New York or How To Arrest A Hurricane*. The exhibition is one component; our preparatory research and conversations, the trip, and the map were other elements of the project. They all relate to each other, but every phase confronted its own particular set of questions.

our visits to East Baltimore or even the situation in Palestine. We formulated the following question to help give us some orientation: How is it that a camp like Guantánamo Bay can exist in our time?

Here we are not necessarily looking for a straight answer. More, we would like to open up a discussion and think about it ourselves alongside others, by introducing analogies, parallels, and retrieving histories.

**Rene Gabri:** The drive across the US was itself a kind of poetic operation, since it tracked a word (camp) and a set of related ideas through geographical space. It combined very different contexts, historical periods and circumstances with one another, sometimes uneasy associations were made. We also gave talks and presentations along the way, which challenged the participants not to isolate those camps in Guantánamo, but to see that it is one piece of a much larger and problematic puzzle, history, situation. Since we was a campaign, we also combined different modes of representation, different modes of address to the public.

**Ayreen Anastas:** The map initially was not meant to be a public document; it started instead as a practical device to help us orient ourselves, but mostly choose a route that would make most sense for our project and search. We knew we wanted to meet certain people or to visit specific places/communities. We needed to map those out to see where they were located and how we can make the most out of a line of movement through the US; that became our trip. The map gained more and more layers of information as we proceeded with the project.

We started with a line drawing of the US map that we traced ourselves. We overlapped several information

We started by asking ourselves what was a topic which we felt was critical and needed to be addressed today. This led us to think about what was happening in Guantánamo and made us want to connect it to everyday phenomena like what we had seen in

NRA Shooting Competition, Camp Perry, Ohio, 2006

Memorial for May 4 Massacre
Kent State University, Ohio, 2006

Internment Camp Museum, Tule Lake, California, 2006

112

the so-called mixed cities (non-Jewish Palestinians and Jewish citizens of Israel). Lydd and Ramlah are such mixed cities, and the authorities and planners are always concerned to keep the ratio of 80 percent Jews to 20 percent Palestinians there. Those Palestinians do not have the same status as the Palestinians in the occupied territories; they are supposedly citizens of the state of Israel.

Another investigation concerns the unrecognized villages of the Bedouins in Al-Naqab in the south of Israel. There we met with a geographer and a community organizer who explained to us their situation. The villages are declared 'illegal' because they are undesired people living on desirable land. The state of Israel would like to concentrate those Bedouins in housing projects and concrete buildings, which does not match their way of life.

**Rene Gabri:** So our 'poetic operation' also had very strong political implications. Of course, each of these phenomena have their own histories and specific questions attached, but we felt it was also necessary to begin to see what they had in common. If we continue to isolate such phenomena, we risk isolating our resistance to them.

We took the same question with us to Palestine when we went there early last year, in March. All Palestine can be seen as a camp, yet we were looking at more specific situations there and trying to record and connect them.

One investigation for example concerns urban planning in the city of Ramlah and Lydd and how it is used there to exclude and suffocate any possibility of growth for the Palestinian community within Israel in

**113** layers and maps on top, such as Native American lands and reservations, internment camps, relocation centres and citizen isolation camps from World War II, boot and military camps, former POW camps, prisons and detention centres. We also mapped cities and people we wanted to visit.

For example, Baltimore is one such density on the map. We had spent a month there before starting the tour, where we met a lot of interesting people. Our question was also investigated in Baltimore as a city and in how urban planning can create a situation similar to a camp, especially for the African-American community, which has become an unwanted 'population' or demographic for developing and selling properties in the once neglected parts of the city.

We created a legend that contained the symbols to indicate each of the above. And these symbols were distributed all over the map. So that the map gained density from which our route defined itself or crystallized.

WWII Era Munitions Plant
Crab Orchard National Wildlife Refuge, Illinois, 2006

Former POW Camp, Camp Perry, Ohio, 2006

Ford Plant, Detroit, Michigan, 2006

**PM/HM:** What are the undercurrents that connect such different geographies and how can one open up one's personal practice to engage with all these different issues arising from translocal ruptures?

**Ayreen Anastas:** What we have here are some kind of glasses that we see the world with. They are analytical glasses, filters of these realities. One basic question for example that we see relevant, is how the economic dynamics created by neoliberal policies combine with the often racist policies which underlie many of the situations we were exploring.

In other words, what motivates us is what matters to us, and the question that remains is how can we do something about it, no matter where we find ourselves. The situation may differ, yet having this kind of analysis or glasses is helpful. Otherwise one is not grounded in a way, and may lose orientation.

We are able to build lines of connections to many issues, people and classes regardless of the geographic location. In addition, there is also personal experience that adds an affinity to one case or another.

**Rene Gabri:** I would just add that there have been thinkers along the way, whose work has been absolutely critical to us (Clastres, Celan, Benjamin, Kafka, Butler, Agamben, Holmes, Harvey, Rancière). If you look for instance at the analysis offered by Giorgio Agamben in his books *Homo Sacer or State of Exception*, they are essential for offering these filters Ayreen is mentioning. But at the same time, for Agamben's own critique to have some value or validity, it needs to be interrogated further, it needs to be used (not just demonstrated), explored in specific contexts, confronted with other critiques, other lenses, other histories. I think another question which informs a lot of our collaborative work is how to connect critiques, ideas or thoughts to our own practice, to our work, to our politics, our everyday life. Because sometimes, philosophical or analytical insights are abused, instead of helping us understand things, they are used as a crutch or even worse, a barrier.

**PM/HM:** What importance does a network which is held up by a mutual horizon, like the 16 Beaver group in New York, have in such a context? How does a sense of communality develop along the need for continuous change and transformation in response to different situations?

*Fear is Somehow Our For Whom? For What? and Proximity to Everything Far Away*
Ayreen Anastas and Rene Gabri

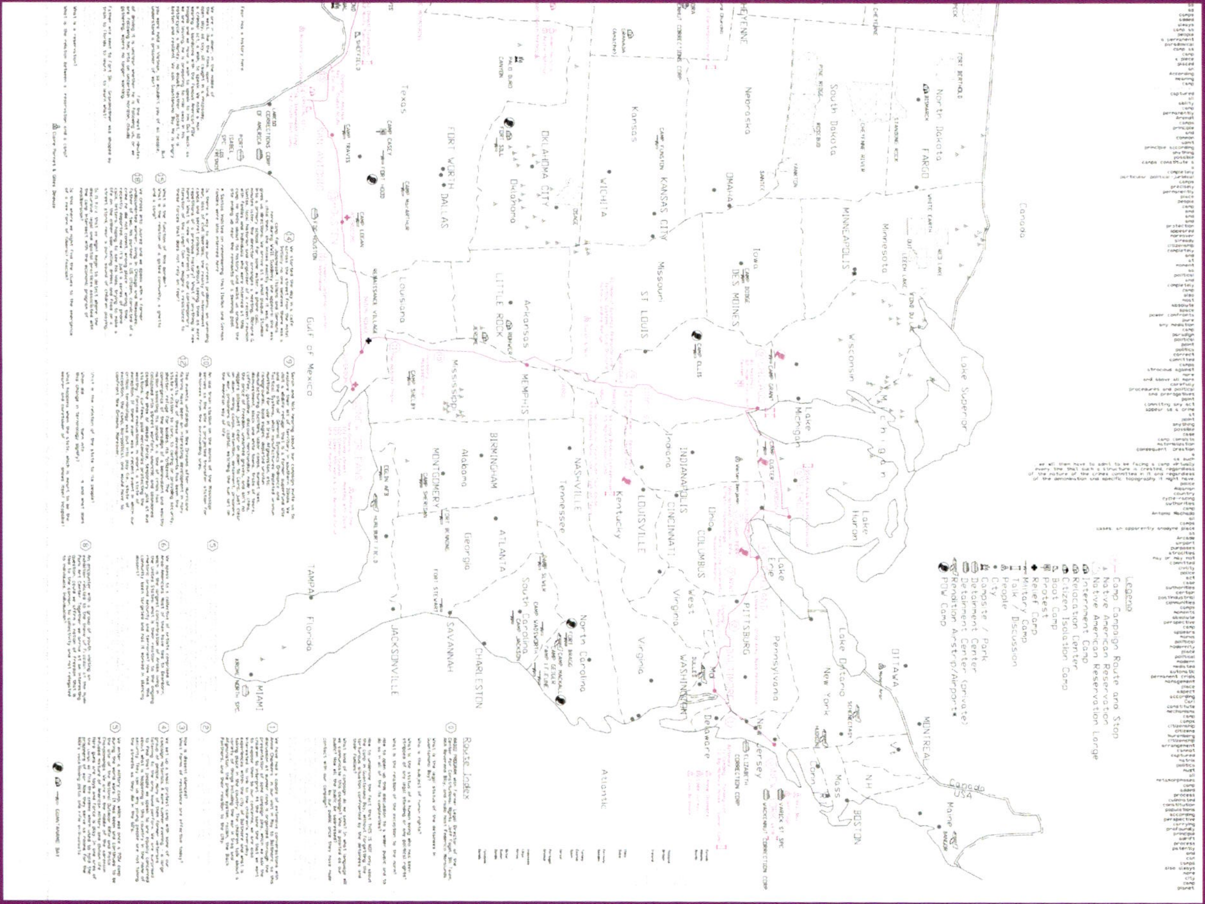

**Ayreen Anastas:** Informal and light. We meet regularly and it is part of our everyday life. We do not need funders or board members to approve our programmes. And if something comes up that is of interest to us, or needs to be addressed, we organize something in relation.

**Rene Gabri:** Our intellectual exchange is always being filtered through rigid institutions and very directed situations, from universities and museums to billion-dollar websites. We, in turn, are each asked to be small corporations, competing with one another, nominated, ranked, specialized, gaining in value and junk like this. This is deadly for thought and for life. So yes, networks like 16 Beaver (and there are many) help establish grounds for a general intellect, for sharing questions and thought. Many of our largest problems are common: they are economic questions of sustenance; they are questions of health, of our capacity to attain a voice, to be involved in a conversation about how to organize society, our capacity to think and share ideas, to be creative, to contribute to a general intellect, to consider the ecological implications of our actions, to seek social justice, to critique or resist domination if necessary... Of course, there are different

*Camp Campaign*, a journey through selected locations in the United States exploring a range of perspectives on the notions of camp and specifically Guantánamo Bay
Summer 2006

115

infrastructures which support this type of collective thought, exchange and activity; but some are unfortunately terminal, too hierarchical, too closely time to them, make use of them. We do not need to abandon the universities or museums; we just cannot let them dictate what counts or what matters.

**PM/HM:** Informality supports a mode of survival on the one hand, and provides the ground on which networked practices grow and thrive on the other hand. Deregulation as the main characteristic of new forms of spatial distribution is thus a very ambivalent phenomenon. How can one inhabit such a situation?

**Rene Gabri:** For me, informality and deregulation are highly ambiguous terms today. Fundamentally, we are being asked to make a false choice. The so-called free market has been associated with horizontality, deregulation and informality. On the other hand, the statist models of leftist politics have been critiqued as being rigid, centralized, overly regulated etc... But as we experience capitalism, we know it to be anything but a free market, anything but deregulated, anything but horizontal. It is highly regulated, with its regimes of property, borders, copyrights, trademarks, and patents. The same neoliberal agenda which seems to underwrite 'globalization' is also responsible for the most massive dispossession of the commons (i.e. privatization) and destruction of informal or cooperative spaces/economies. So, the language we employ in these contexts is riddled with ideological veils and misnomers.

I would prefer not to see a space like 16 Beaver in conjunction with 'deregulation'. I would rather see it in a long line of attempts historically at various levels of society to organize infrastructures which try to re-distribute power back to people – initiatives which resist highly centralized and controlled spaces of exchange and discourse. The rigid and hierarchical spaces have historically emerged from both right and left, they have different origins, names attached, but the effect has been the same, to concentrate power and wealth.

What is the most important thing to salvage from a leftist politics is not that statist legacy, but its insistence on maintaining a commons, its insistence to reconsider and redefine the political community, its ability to win basic rights for each and every individual (health care, education, a place to live, etc.) and its ability to connect local and more global concerns.

**Ayreen Anastas:** Well, a good way for me to address this question is by considering the Palestinian context. Authority counts on formality or a semblance of it. For me, as a Palestinian, authority has always been bad authority, it took me a long time to understand what people were talking about in Germany or here in the United States. I still may not understand it frankly, the nation-states and their governments legitimized by this thing called democracy.

A Palestinian, still today, has to live with tricks in order to survive, the tricks of the weak, because geographically,

Contemporary Private Ordnance Plant
Crab Orchard National Wildlife Refuge, Illinois, 2006

Burial Site, Trail of Tears, Illinois, 2006

116

Shoshone National Park, Wyoming, 2006

Migrant Worker Camp, near Cairo, Illinois, 2006

**117** if you need to move, you need to think of a trick. To overcome the 'formalities' of the occupier and the state machine. These 'formalities' are more of bureaucracies that hinder the life and movement of the Palestinians. So you need a permit to move from your bathroom to your living room. Poor people have a harder time circumventing these formalities.

To go back to 16 Beaver, one important point about informality is to know that we do have agency, and that we can overcome the social checkpoints and barriers, whether real or imagined. We can connect to others, talk and organize with them, collectively becoming a force that is harder to break.

Contested Spaces interview

# Eyal Weizman

**PM/HM:** In recent years you've developed a multifaceted architectural practice that has involved buildings and stage sets, as well as worked with a variety of NGOs and human-rights groups in Israel/Palestine and run the Centre for Research Architecture in London. If we understand it right, this approach has less to do with dissociating yourself from more traditional forms of architectural practice than with multiplying entanglements on various levels.

**Eyal Weizman:** Yes, to use the term you've just introduced, I've sought to entangle or immerse my work, myself, in various frameworks and media simultaneously. This form of practice seeks to extend rather than question the role of the architect. And since you've asked about the role of the architect in a network society: I've tried to have various positions within systems, so sometimes I've entered them as an architect, which in itself can work as a great camouflage. I realize that the title 'architect' still carries a weight that is unjustifiable and problematic, but it can also help one to infiltrate and engage in various other domains. One can engage in political action as an architect', that is, partake in diverse forms of activism; do cartography, spatial analysis or human rights work; curate or write – all supposedly from within the domain of the praxis itself, which is why I think it might still be considered a form of camouflage, though maybe not for long. Yet I still think these activities aren't enough. Such positions tend to be related to each other and I think we must push forms of spatial action beyond their limits and open them up further.

Multifaceted activities establish connections through various collaborative networks. To a certain extent, many of my personal forms of practice and collaboration have led to work/social relations that later fed into the round table at the Centre for Research Architecture at Goldsmiths. Initially, to start the program, recruiting was 'by invitation' only, and I naturally invited all those who were my colleagues and peers, who shared projects and/or the same world and whose work I admired from close up – which is a different critical perspective than admiring a form of practice from afar, without knowing the person or collaborating with her/him. So the outlines of a network that previously worked on a particular project, whether architectural, political or curatorial, were filled with new content in the context of the Centre. People joined us when they recognized the need to find a space to reflect on very busy and dynamic forms of practice. Most of our members are extremely active cultural producers, but realize the kind of limits and problems that 'constant networking' and constant travel and too much work involve. We realized we needed to discover a new sensibility, a new patience for ideas, to spend more time talking, reading, thinking together, than the hyperspace of the cultural planet generally allows. The group now has a very horizontal structure. It has an empty centre (as you see...) and we simply dig deeper into each other's work.

Paradoxically, perhaps, the Centre for Research Architecture sets out to question the two separate terms that make up its name. It seeks to open up the discipline and praxis of 'architecture' – understood as the production of rarefied buildings and urban structures – into a shifting network of 'spatial practices' that includes various other forms of intervention. It also contests the utilitarian, applied, means-to-ends relation between knowledge and action that is evoked by the term 'research', and the artificial opposition between theory and practice that it implies. Drawing on the vocabularies of urbanism, architecture, art, media, politics and philosophy, the Centre's mode of operation seeks to use spatial practices for an open-ended form of critical inquiry. This is the reason why the Centre has brought together a group of leading international practitioners – architects, artists, activists, urbanists, filmmakers and curators – to work collectively in a roundtable mode on individual projects. Our members engage in a unique and robust set of critical interventions in the fields of spatial and cultural politics; they deal with the built environment through documentary filmmaking, media activism, art and curating in various places worldwide.

Roundtable at the Centre for Research Architecture
Goldsmiths, London, 2006

Diagram's showing the routes through buildings taken by Israeli troops during 'swarming' manoeuvres (attack on Nablus, April 2002), OTRI, 2004

**Eyal Weizman:** At the Centre for Research Architecture, we use practice to induce new knowledge to reveal itself or, in fact, to create it, which means practice in the field is what provokes the subject of research and analysis to emerge. We don't believe you'll get very far if you try to research – let's say urban politics in a particular city or a zone of conflict or even the cultural sphere of various groups and structures – by measuring and analysing reality. In fact, it's by making provocative interventions and confronting the system, rather than passively researching it, that we believe a system will reveal itself to us in one of its various manifestations. This kind of 'provocative research' or 'action research' has its roots, strangely enough, in the operational and allows us both to organize and mobilize knowledge and connections. As I've said, my own project is not, however, merely a remnant of this process. It's a re-articulation of emptied networks that have now taken on different content. Rather than discussing our social relations, we just practise them. In other words, rather than fetishizing the relation itself, we just go on doing what facilitates our work. As we tackle problems, we try to evolve matters using whatever means appears more efficient. So ultimately, if there are new innovative forms of social engagement and they are exactly what we need at a given moment, we reflect and decide whether we want to incorporate them or not. That's what interests me: how the outline of relations can lead to the topic that sustains them, and how we might resolve problems and impasses in research.

**PM/HM:** A common assumption about knowledge is that you need to learn everything first in order to act out the knowledge you've gained. This creates a strange model of transformation where new possibilities are always linked back to the existing archive. How can different forms of knowledge be produced outside of this epistemological regime?

stand forms of theory and research as political acts and ways of space-making in their own right. Zones of conflict enable formative forces to reveal themselves clearly; conflict mobilizes form. In this sense, conflict is important to us, though not as fetishization of its iconography and righteousness, but as something that forms

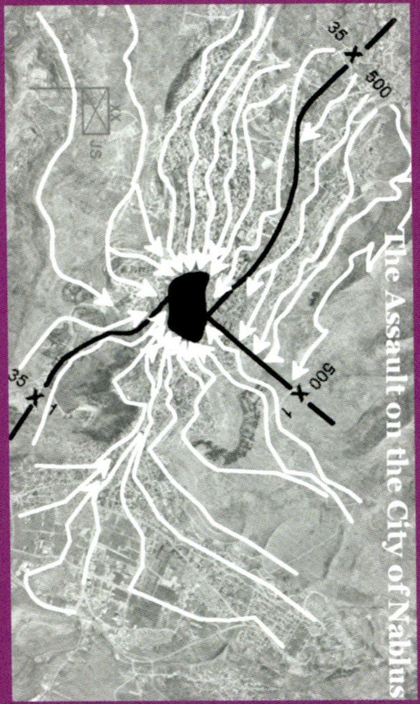

**PM/HM:** Networks often emerge in situations of spatial contestation. In what way is your research committed to these scenes and sites of conflict?

**Eyal Weizman:** I think what connects the various topics – and again some of them might appear to you much more immediately political and perhaps more 'combative' than others – is that there's a commitment to under-

I believe in the capacity of terminology to become self-fulfilling. So the word 'network' is probably right for a certain mode, a certain form of interaction, and at another level it produces the reality it names. But it doesn't sum up the entire specificity and complexity of our operation – in fact, it may even operate against it. A network defines a number of forms of social relations that are constantly in formation. Yet I don't think our meetings can be understood only in terms of a network. Yes, we're connected to various different practices, but there's also an attempt to create a zone, maybe a kind of free zone, a place of a little calm and reflection in all this hustle and little reflected action. Actually, we strive simultaneously to enhance our creativity by joining internal interaction, whilst cutting away, temporarily, the outside.

119

induced. In other words, by setting dormant situations in motion and taking a so-called pre-emptive approach, you produce the very thing state security forces have been mobilizing against and fear most. You provoke the system to reveal its inner organizations and by doing so you produce knowledge. This completely inverts the concept of intelligence and operation. If you once thought intelligence was a prerequisite of military operations and that you needed to know in order to act – well, it's the reverse here: you act in order to know. That's the essence of such research. This has influenced us – even though our ethical, moral and political position is obviously very different – and explains how action in a situation of radical ambiguity produces knowledge by effectively creating the knowledge needed. Such research has no bibliography. It's its own bibliography. Its constant practice produces its own bibliography. The philosopher Brian Massumi called this kind of action 'incitatory'. The very action incites what you will later theorize about and research. It captures the nature of how we see – artistic, architectural and cultural – practice as the production of knowledge that has not been there before.

Image demonstrating how Israeli Defence Force troops move through the walls of Palestinian homes in Nablus, 2002

mode of both humanitarian organizations and the military – though such roots might be found elsewhere too (action research is also a methodology in anthropology) but it was in zones of conflict that we encountered them. In my own personal research on contemporary military thinking, I've found that the degree of knowledge reached by intelligence agencies with regard to their various enemies, whether they be guerrillas, resistance fighters or terrorist organizations, is such that these organizations remain very opaque. In fact, the military very often pursues some kind of random action to make its enemies emerge or surface; sometimes it even 'creates' or 'accelerates' them. The minute they do, they have a form and their organizational structure becomes clear. This is when further military actions become possible. The military thus regards raids as tools of research – in other words, the idea of knowledge (intelligence) and action (raid) inverses.

In a strange way this might expose the perverse logic of the war on terror as an epistemic problem: it's about how to understand and rationalize that which confronts you, rather than how to reduce the risk of violence taking place – quite on the contrary, a greater fear of violence and terror is actually

*Leaps of Faith*
Curated by Erden Kosova and Katerina Gregos
Nicosia, 13–29 May 2005

*Rule Britannia*
Sigalit Landau, Nicosia, 2005

# Erden Kosova

**PM/HM**: *Leaps of Faith* is the name of a group show you curated together with Katarina Gregos in the divided city of Nicosia. What impact did the location have on your curatorial approach?

**Erden Kosova**: Nicosia is renowned as the last divided city in Europe, and the residents of both parts have lost their visual memory of the other side of the city. One of the main objectives of our exhibition was to facilitate circulation between the Greek and Turkish part of the city. We wanted people to move about in both parts, and so we encouraged and invited people to at least walk back and forth. The gates were opened in April 2003, but for political or psychological reasons people were still reluctant to go to the other side. Our idea was to stimulate an interest in architectural knowledge on site, and to focus on an artistic practice that could be negotiated between the different actors and create a discursive organism. We organized a film programme, bringing in works from other regions that had similar political situations, and so offered aesthetic models for comparisons between Cyprus and other locations. Lebanon, Beirut, Israel and Palestine are all near the island, just 20 minutes away by airplane. Nevertheless, there is little interest in relating to these neighbours east of Cyprus. Which is why we wanted to raise interest in political engagement of this kind, and so we organized some talks within this framework. Almost all the artists presented their works at the Goethe Institute, which is located in the buffer zone, in the UN-controlled corridor between the two territories. This was the first international contemporary art exhibition of this scale on the island. Yet, it was a humble exhibition, put together with limited resources, without support from any official local institution. It's difficult to foresee the long-term effects of the exhibition. At some point, the connections established between the two sides and between circles in each area should organize themselves and work towards certain objectives. Intellectual interventions from the outside cannot do more than facilitate existing forces. When you work as a curator, how can you avoid reproducing preconceived ideas and representational conceptions of the site and try to channel them into something else? It's a big ethical challenge to use a space that has remained unused for 31 years after a traumatic rupture. But I think there's always a way to talk about the rupture, about the other, to transform a specific memory, performatively speaking, in a progressive way. Of course, there's the risk of failing, of producing new exoticisms and representational ideas, but there's also the possibility of generating productive discussion about these contested spots.

**PM/HM**: How do these political and curatorial experiences relate to your own background, that is, to the politically oriented art scene in Istanbul in the late 1990s?

**Erden Kosova**: I belong to a generation in Istanbul that emerged around 1998-1999. Local networking was full of accidental motivations, but also political ones. We sought ways to express our energy, and then there were other like-minded people, and if they found some space, some location to meet, things developed very fast. This was the case in 1998 when a kind of collective spirit evolved locally. At the time, nobody from this young constellation was invited to international art exhibitions. So we just sat around at home talking about art practices, but then at some point things took off. European art institutions somehow discerned this energy, appropriated it to the global circuit, and suddenly artists started to produce works for specific exhibitions. The works were not produced for empty studios; they were produced for exhibitions to which the artists were invited. So, people got caught up in a different speed, things became more structured and standardized, and this had, of course, positive and negative consequences. The same thing happened to me. Through my collaboration in Graz with < rotor > gallery, I found constellations of people from nearby geographical locations who had similar concerns and experiences. We were from the same generation, we saw the same cartoons as children, we made the same jokes, we were in love with the same football players. We had different mother tongues but we had similar concerns, ways of thinking, similar political interests. I somehow insisted on keeping in touch with what I had found, and people on the other side were also pleased with collaborating with what I represented, my stories, my perspective of reading artists. I slowly started to see their perspectives too, and then I had the opportunity to travel and to produce things with them. So, there was a kind of gradual expansion of perspective, a networking.

**PM/HM**: You spoke about the energy of Istanbul as one of the key factors in shaping the local art scene. Thinking about the current urban explosion taking place in Istanbul, what are the implications of this accelerated growth and urban segregation, and how does it relate to new forms of cultural expression?

*Outside the Projects*
Anber Onar, Nicosia, 2005

*Legislated Nostalgia/Now Denial*
Katerine Attalides, Nicosia, 2005

**Erden Kosova:** There's this popular argument that Istanbul was never modern, but went directly from the pre-modern to the post-modern. The logic behind this is based on the notion of a belated modernism that tries to catch up with the standards of other megapolitan cities, but in doing so pursues completely unsustainable and strange projects. The mayor of Istanbul is an architect, and he had the idea of putting a huge whirling dervish statue on one of the islands so that it would look like some kind of statue of liberty. It was ridiculed a lot and he had to give up the idea and, instead, a smaller statue, related to Mehmed II, the conqueror of Istanbul, was erected in Kadiköy, in the Asian part of town. The Islamic movement has this obsession with Mehmed II. Why conquer a city over and over again? The agenda on the surface is nationalistic – exalting the heroic past and expressing pride in having captured the historic capital of the Eastern Roman or Byzantine Empire and ushering in a new era. But at the same time, Istanbul has been informed by a very contemporary agenda, one in which newcomers to the city, who see themselves as authentic locals, have literally to conquer Istanbul back from 'the Byzantines of the present', from a more bourgeois and Western-oriented culture.

On the other hand, those who see what is happening as the arrival of a peasant culture that spoils the urban environment are very elitist in their views, and ignore the possibility of hybrid cultures emerging between the urban and what is still in the process of developing an urban identity. 'Arabesque' culture was, for example, very important in the 1980s. This culture was not introduced by migrants from cities in Anatolia, nor was it native to Istanbul – it was something else. This music took elements from Egypt, India, Europe and other places. In the Balkans, similar cultural formations emerged. In Serbia, it was called 'turbo-folk'; in Bulgaria, 'chalga'. It had so-called oriental roots and interrupted the cultural politics of these countries, displacing the official ultra-modernism of the nation-states of Yugoslavia or Bulgaria or Turkey. So Arabesque music is somehow genuinely urban. But then the mass media struck back, inventing so-called Turkish pop, a form of mainstream music that promotes cultural homogenization. Yet contrary to the elitist position that condemns Arabesque and other similar styles of expression, I would say they provide some vague possibilities for producing new urban formations of subcultures and forms of communications.

**123**

# Metro City
## Istanbul

Caddebostan Plajları
Redevelopment of the beach front in Caddebostan, a wealthy suburb along Bağdat Caddesi on the Asian side of Istanbul, 2005

Metro City
Shopping Mall in Levent, Istanbul, 2005

126

Londra Asfaltı, Istanbul, 2005

World Trade Center Istanbul, 2005

Karaköy, Istanbul, 2005

Karaköy, Istanbul, 2005

View from the Tobacco Warehouse in Tophane, one of the exhibition venues of the 9th Istanbul Biennial, 2005

Ad hoc shooting range in Zeytinburnu, Istanbul, 2005

## Despoina Sevasti and Poka-Yio

**PM/HM:** You're both artists committed to creating platforms for experimental cultural investigations. What were your motivations for engaging yourselves in projects like A-Station, and in which way did this engagement provide a framework for curating the recent exhibitions *Suburbia – the Vast Cityscape of the Athenian Suburbs* and *Scan Istanbul – Suburbs of a 21st Century Metropolis*?

**Poka-Yio:** A-Station is a small independent art organization, an art centre, based in Athens. It started as an initiative of artists and theorists, because there were no public spaces or initiatives here that allowed for experimenting, gathering information, creating research projects or networking between different disciplines such as the fine arts, architecture and cultural studies. Our primary interest in A-Station was to put on regular exhibitions. Though from the beginning we said we wouldn't exhibit there as artists ourselves and we didn't, for instance, want to present 'traditional' group shows. Instead we hoped to create a space that would focus primarily on gathering information and lead to art production.
*Suburbia* was a first attempt to work in this multidisciplinary way with architects, photographers, artists, people from various institutions and disciplines on the chaotic imagery and unsaid history of the vast cityscape of Athenian suburbs. We aimed at concentrating more on a theoretical survey about the suburbs of Athens than just compiling an exhibition on them. This investigatory principle led to our experimenting and working in workshops, and this resulted in a kind of melting pot of different people. It's an approach that gives a broader insight into things you don't normally expect to see. Until *Suburbia*, Athens had virtually gone unnoticed in contemporary fine arts. The dirty ground-level approach to a city bursting with energy was just not there. So we created this exhibition and it actually produced the know-how subsequently used for the *Scan Istanbul* project. Despoina was part of *Suburbia* and then took over, together with Oguz Içsöz, the Turkish curator, to create the project.

**Despoina Sevasti:** *Scan Istanbul* is a collaboration between Greek and Turkish artists, architects, photographers and theorists. We worked with the Greek participants based on the *Suburbia* model before leaving Greece. And then, as soon as I arrived in Istanbul, we did preparatory work with the Turkish participants. In fact, work began about three months before the actual workshop. Though I think the whole procedure actually started when people first met. For even if we tried to give them theoretical feedback from our experiences in Athens – to make a bibliography and so on – it was mostly personal contact and collaboration that led to ideas. In the beginning it was a bit bizarre, because it was the first time young Greek and Turkish artists, architects and urban planners had met in a workshop, and the approach we adopted was quite unknown to many of the participants. So at first people were rather stunned by it all. I'd been going to Istanbul for eight years already and had thought it would be much easier, but it took some time to break the ice, though, of course, this process was very interesting in itself.

**PM/HM:** In terms of producing a research archive and making it available through artistic work, e.g. in an exhibition, what was your particular motivation for expanding your field of engagement from Athens to Istanbul?

**Poka-Yio:** There was the personal interest of Despoina and Oguz Içsöz, but apart from that you should know that in Greece we don't usually see Istanbul as a city that exudes anything futuristic, yet this is exactly what it does. As soon as we arrived, we understood that something clearly futuristic was happening right there in front of our eyes, and we wanted to understand it and explore it, because this might be what the future would be like in many places, even Europe. There's massive immigration to Istanbul and, since it's all taking place within the country's own borders, it's leading to a violent overturn of both the urban and social fabric. This means class struggles within the city are in a constant state of flux. All these phenomena are fascinating for us as artists who live in a kind of glasshouse.

**PM/HM:** The works produced in these workshops touch upon a whole array of public fantasies and hopes about Europe, hopes about urban futures. In what way does such an approach implicate art as an agent in a political process?

*Scan Istanbul, Suburbs of a 21st Century Metropolis* Workshop and exhibitions, organised by A-Station, Athens Centre for Contemporary Art, curated by Oguz Içsöz and Despoina Sevasti, Istanbul, 2003-2005

*Gültepeee*
Video by Andreas Sitorego, 3 min., 2003

*Esenler*
Video by Aylin Güngör, 8 min., 2003

scarves, but the slight differences in the semiotics of their variation – that's what's really interesting.

**Despoina Sevasti:** This particular subject is very important here in Istanbul, but no one seems to talk in depth about the real issue. It's always either women *with* scarves or women *without* them, but the entire issue is actually much more complicated. There was one Greek artist, Victoria Karvouni, who wanted to explore the different sorts of scarves women wear; for her it was about investigating the cultural differences within this phenomenon. Not all scarves are the same. Scarves have all kinds of social connotations and a variety of semiotics. She'd already done a similar work in Athens, about haircuts. We knew from the beginning that not everyone would welcome this project. Everyday hundreds of people passing by on Istiklal Street would come in and say, 'What's this? This isn't art – and, what's more, we don't like these people.' And: 'Why are you presenting such an image of our city?' Yet at that very moment, women with scarves were inside the gallery or right outside on the street. This is a very important aspect: once you leave the art community, you get completely different reactions to what we call 'art'. People can rediscover the city through

**Poka-Yio:** This is an extremely sensitive matter. Since the beginning of A-Station, we've had this issue, whether we should intervene in things or use a more passive approach. We don't want to glorify anything, nor do we want to reveal anything, or find the skeletons hidden in Istanbul's closet. That's not what we're after. What we want is a small shift away from the (art) tourist's eye – which only focuses on the spectacular historical components of the city –towards the less prominent 'underground' differences that make Istanbul what it is. These are, of course, subtle differences. For instance, we all witness women with

such a research archive and discover completely different things based on the raw, untouched material on display.

**Poka-Yio:** As I said, artists and curators are always tempted to glorify, because there are so many things that can produce a spectacular show. Especially in Istanbul, as the cityscape generates very strong images. So I think there's always a temptation to create an exhibition that might be overwhelming, even though it wouldn't do justice to what it developed from originally. From the start we said our exhibitions weren't to be as spectacular as the usual visual art shows, because this wasn't the point. We don't need to reveal everything to the spectators of an exhibition. We should just show them a web of circumstances and let them navigate a way in and out themselves. It's simple to pick five or ten images, or four or more videos, and make people say, 'Wow!' And it's easy to create a metaphor with such material – or to transform it into something else. But, like I've said, that's not the point. We just want to bring raw material to the foreground, and then let researchers, architects, artists and gallery audiences find their way through it on their own.

# Stefano Boeri

**PM/HM:** Given the dynamics of the current transformation of the cultural landscape in Europe, in which ways do you think the field of architecture needs to reinvent itself?

**Stefano Boeri:** I don't believe that rethinking the role of architecture in contemporary societies can be connected solely to enhancing the sophistication of design in our discipline. The question today is not how to intervene better in the complexities of our societies and introduce local improvements or local solutions. I don't quite trust the capacity of contemporary architecture to deal with a dimension of structural dynamics that can only be solved within the political sphere itself, and I don't adhere to the idea that architecture can update its technical tools by facing what's happening in a local context. From a certain point of view, this would just be an alibi for politicians; while from another point of view, it would be a way to eliminate the assumption that architecture is able to control and determine the future of physical environments. Instead, one of the most interesting and probably important things that architectural practice can commit itself to – and this applies more to research than design – is the expansion of knowledge with regard to what is occurring and will take place in future environments and local spaces. We've been trained to observe the surface of things, and in this sense we are adept witnesses of processes that only manifest themselves on the skin, on the physical layer of our environment. Our discipline may, in fact, be one of the most sophisticated tools at our disposal for observing the physical layer of contemporary transformations. And these can in turn be used as metaphors to describe the social and structural layer of ongoing processes.

**PM/HM:** You've described the periphery as a mobile situation in which centres become peripheries in the sense that they have moved outside the focus of hegemonic political interest and are increasingly populated by what's considered the margins of culture. So peripheries have become part of an 'archipelago' economy. How can architecture relate to this field of peripheral productivity?

**Stefano Boeri:** As architects, it's fundamental that our vocabulary represents the actual sense of things, particularly in relation to physical transformations that might be taking place. From this point of view, the notion of periphery is now extremely weak, and what happened in the Paris banlieues in November 2005 was a demonstration of this. The periphery of the contemporary European city is more like an archipelago than a ring, in terms of its geometrical distance from a city's central areas. Naples, Genoa and Paris display, for example, many peripheries or hyper-central niches. In fact, the notion of periphery should be completely redefined from our own perspective, from that of a profession that is close to the physical context. This is something we can actually do as architects, because it's our unequivocal social capacity. The fact that I've spent a lot of time in the last years demonstrating how, in my opinion, design and research operate in completely different spheres is probably connected to my personal background in Italy. As you know, this involved the experience of the Italian *tendenza* in the 1970s: Foucauldian discourse in which thinkers, such as Aldo Rossi and Vittorio Gregotti made a great effort to demonstrate how design and research, or design and analysis, should have a direct and linear relation, and attempted to illustrate how research was in fact a precondition for design or a

Centre Régional de la Méditerranée Competition, Marseilles, France, 2004; winning entry by Boeri Studio, view from the water

Centre Régional de la Méditerranée Competition site, Marseilles, France, 2004

*USE= Uncertain States of Europe*
Multiplicity, Triennale di Milano, 2002

guarantee of good design. There was also Manfredo Tafuri and his way of thinking, which was more or less oriented toward demonstrating that the preliminary task of architecture was connected with historical analyses and the social context of these analyses, and so on... This often determined a spontaneous reaction in terms of trying to establish realities in the opposite direction, where social realm and design have autonomous spheres. In fact, they work as autonomous spheres in our society – they have different methodologies and require different approaches. In the case of design, this is connected with our capacity to integrate and open up the future, to include possibilities, opinions, things, thoughts and so on. In the case of our research, it is more or less strictly connected with our capacity to actually exclude future possibilities, to select a certain possibility in order to manipulate the physical dimension, to make special social configurations, and so on. The social realm and design realm are two completely different spheres, and I trust architecture to have the capacity to combine them while conserving their autonomy. In a way, this opens up the notion of schizophrenia, which is an extremely important factor in current architecture. I think schizophrenia provides the imagery for how an architect might operate and offers a good perspective for architecture. I don't think we should abandon design, and only research and analyse the local social context. I'm sure there are many possible short circuits or unpredictable synapses.

PM/HM: You are co-founder of the research network Multiplicity, which is active not only in the field of architecture but also art and communication. What kinds of possibilities are created by working within such networked practices?

Stefano Boeri: We're talking about synapses, right? We could also use the term transfer. Interesting for me is that there are ideas that you can develop and transfer. You can observe, for example, how a concept produces fruitful effects when it moves from one sphere to another. From this point of view, there are a lot of possible synapses: for instance, a concept that is produced or developed in the course of research is suddenly introduced to art and design. In doing so, it retains all the possible misunderstandings that such a move involves – normally it produces a lot of misunderstandings anyway. Let me give you a concrete example: our Multiplicity group has done a lot of research on the Mediterranean as a solid sea, as a solid continent, as a place increasingly characterized by barriers, frontiers and pipes, border devices and so on. But if I use the idea of a solid sea as a metaphor, as an analogy, and try to translate it into a design methodology, it immediately becomes heavy and banal and stupid. But if you just hold on to it and avail yourself of it as a world – Nietzsche used the word 'world' to propose the existence of worlds more solid than stone – in your design practice and simply try to deal with conserving its nature, this can produce interesting results. For instance, the building that our architecture studio designed for Marseille, the Centre Régional de la Mediterranée, is in my view very strongly connected to Multiplicity research. Even if it is a built, physical architectural structure, and therefore not a linear effect of research on the Mediterranean, it constitutes a reaction to the concept of solid sea. It is a building capable of hosting the city within it and so is like a public space that uses the sea as a collective site.

I connect the idea of networks with the idea of sampling. Currently, at least in research, the act of sampling is becoming ever more crucial. This is because the weaker we become in designing aggregate maps of the contemporary environment, the more necessary it becomes to use the idea of sampling. Today, in order to observe or comprehend the state of things in the contemporary European city, we don't count on an aggregate view – this is because we can no longer offer any general explanations. However, what we have been able to develop is a methodology to sample different contexts in order to compare the results of the samples and try to gradually put considerations on the table. It's a gradual process of accumulating knowledge, a method-

133

create a network, to share common networks. It may sound a bit deterministic, but if you don't share some common methodological, analytical and research values, it becomes very dangerous. I think our field is important because it's one of the last fields where you're obliged or condemned to show the outcome of your work, while also revealing the criteria determining your research practices. From this angle, our Multiplicity projects have been extremely interesting for me, because with them we've been forced to conduct research and at the same time produce exhibitions, installations and so on. At the beginning this was really mad, because of the temporal and structural differences between research and installation. Yet at a certain point we also realized that applying ourselves to communication was an amazing help. We were immediately asked what we were developing and to reflect on how we might communicate the steps and ethics underlying our research. This proved very interesting because it enabled us at exhibitions to offer the public an opportunity to evaluate our criteria.

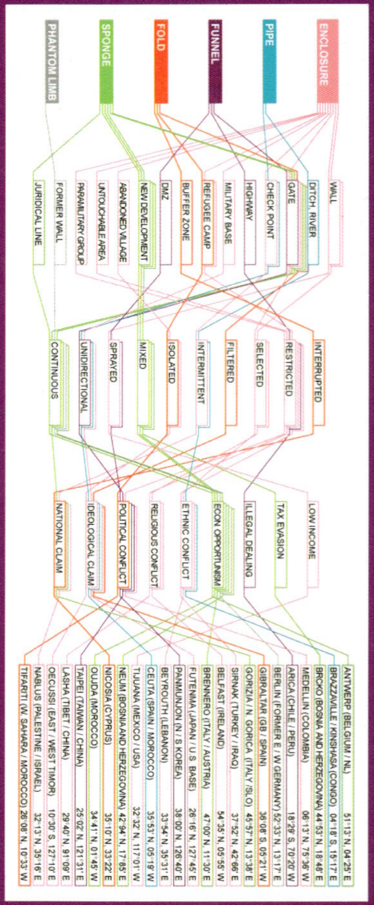

*Border Device(s) – Border Matrix*
Multiplicity, 2003

ology that needs to be locally hosted and counts on the presence of local networks. If you want to sample what is happening in the banlieues of Paris, you can go there, but it is fundamental to interface and interact with the local network. In a way networking and sampling are part of one and the same way of dealing with local spaces. It is very important to compare the idea of bridging social capitals with that of binding them, because there's an intention to introduce notions of difference. And this underscores how the presence of multicultural and polyethnic communities is necessary in order to appease our social conscience. From a different point of view, it is also important to understand the dimensions of each one of the local identities that makes up a multiethnic society. Differences are an ingredient, but they should be graduated in a very sophisticated and delicate way. So from this point of view, networks are about bringing together differences and this also applies to research: you need to share some common values, methodologies and goals; otherwise it's pure chaos or pure research 'aesthetics' and not really about accumulating knowledge. From a certain point of view – and this will help me answer your question about the field of art – it's very important to

*Solid Sea*
Multiplicity, first presented at documenta 11, 2002 – ongoing

134

# Pablo de Soto

**PM/HM**: Hackitectura.net has produced a series of critical engagements related to how contemporary space is not only structured by physical buildings but also by electronic tools such as information networks, surveillance systems or tracking devices. How has this interest in the virtual led you to focus on border spaces?

**Pablo de Soto**: The beginning of hackitectura.net was related to our activities with the Internet and the desire to go beyond the idea of space as presented to us at architecture school. We thought a new world was emerging and no one at school was talking about it. From the start we wanted to try to experience some of the new aspects of telematic networks and figure out how to achieve different levels of presence. In 2002 we held a founding event: our idea involved going to a space and linking it to, let's say, five or more different spaces in the world. At the time I had a filmmaker friend in Seville and I asked him if he was going to be working on a movie about Seville in the future, because we would like to provide a scene for it. In this scene, hackers would play a decision-making role in the city. The event was entitled *Pure Data Beta Rave* and its slogan was: 'The world is interconnected, we cannot wait any longer!'

*fadaiat*
Borderline academy, Tarifa, Spain, 2005

At the time, we weren't just working locally with video and audio, but also with remote inputs. We talked with different groups, with people in Mexico, for example, who were organizing the border hacking event in Tijuana in 2001. We learned a lot from them and we asked: do you want to tell people about your experiences via live streaming? More input arrived from Tarifa, Spain – from an activist reading a manifesto about new laws that discriminated against refugees. One year later we suggested the *Indymedia Estrecho (Indymedia Straits)* project. It was the seed of all that came afterwards.

This border in southwestern Europe is absolutely hard-core: it was militarized in 2002 when SIVE (a border surveillance system) began to be implemented. It consists of a network of sensors along the coast of Andalusia and the Canary Islands that are connected to an interception system. A new kind of control space has come into being: it's not based only on physical but also on non-physical checkpoints that migrants *sin papeles* – without papers – can't cross.

Within the context of the EU's border management policy, the Spanish state has been a pioneer in this kind of electronic defence barrier. The United States built a wall along the Mexican border with equipment left over from the Gulf War (Operation Gatekeeper, 1994), but this wall went up in a, let's say, more 'post-modern' way; it's an electronic wall that resembles medieval surveillance towers, yet also uses radar, infrared and optronic sensors. US and EU propaganda is selling the system to fight organized drug trafficking and people smuggling. But since SIVE has been in operation, boat people – who in the past crossed the Straits of Gibraltar where it was narrowest (between 14 and 40 kilometres) – have been forced to take much longer and more dangerous routes to avoid being tracked and intercepted. So here the rest of us are, living in wealthy Europe, often without any knowledge of the upgrades being made to this high-tech wall – the wall between us and the unfortunate people on the other side.

**PM/HM**: In contrast to these cases in which new technologies are implemented to secure the division of space, and separation of populations and cultures, hackitectura.net is working on strategies to develop subversive information networks that enable

*Techno-Bedouins, 2005*

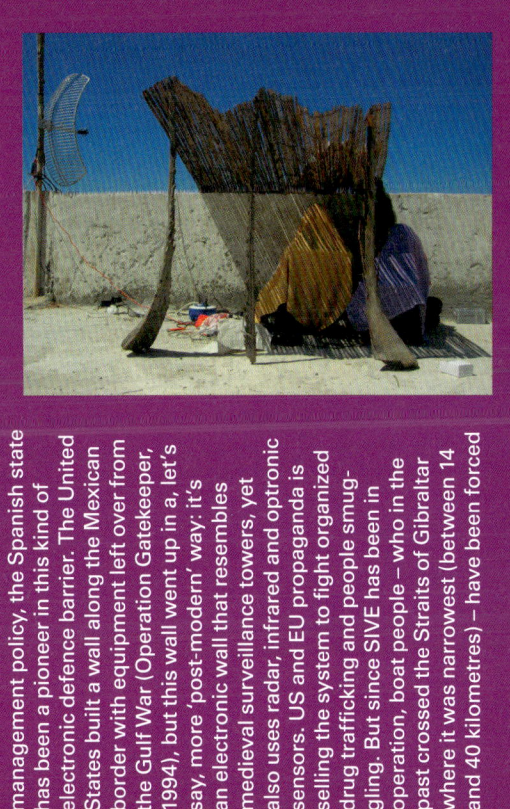

people to cross these divisions and connect different communities. What are the expectations linked to these counter-networks?

**Pablo de Soto**: As hackitectura.net, we were one of the founders of the *Indymedia Estrecho* project. It was launched in 2003 after a previously unsuccessful attempt to create a local Indymedia site in Seville. It happened within the scope of an activist and artist meeting in Andalusia to which UNIA – the International University of Andalusia – had invited us and other groups, artists and video makers. We suggested using this gathering to start an experimental *Indymedia Estrecho* project. We weren't alone in this process: people – mainly those who had been working with migrants for eight years already at the Casa de Iniciativas, a social centre occupied by squatters in Malaga – supported our independent media initiative. They had lots of grassroots know-how and practice with migration phenomena, so it was a very nice alliance.

At the beginning of the entire process there was an amazing discussion about whether we should focus on the Straits idea or create a more regional Andalusian Indymedia. We remarked that in this globalized world we have the choice, tactically speaking, to work

physical and virtual space in relation to contemporary architectural practice?

**Pablo de Soto**: While architects once reacted to undefined border spaces by saying, 'this is not for us', we now see them as spaces where new struggles and revolutions are in progress.

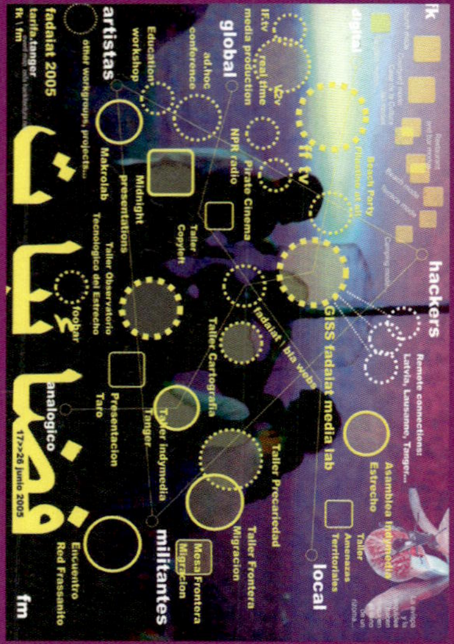

helpful to do so on both the local and global level. So if we want to change or to improve things at the southern European border, it's not enough to do so merely from the perspective of a rather northern identity. The idea was to project our identity into the ocean, into the waters in between. From the ocean – and the idea of the Straits – we would be able to see north and south, up and down...

Right now there are nodes in several cities outside Andalusia, in northern Morocco, for instance, in Tangiers and Larache – but they aren't very active. Though I can still say that at this very moment *Indymedia Estrecho* works as an information network and political platform for activists in the area; it promotes a previously non-existent Pan-Andalusian movement, as well as provides an information platform for people who want to know what is going on here: internauts from the United States, France, etc.

**PM/HM**: The *Fadaï'at* project, with which you've been involved since 2004, intervenes in the contested realities of the Moroccan-Spanish border by setting up digital infrastructures and virtual networks, and thus connecting different localities to a global realm of information. What is your take on this intertwined engagement in

Actually we had wanted to be active in such a space from the beginning. In a way I think we decided to focus on this space and make it a long-term project after reflecting on the Zapatista move-

human groups – instantaneous 2005
From *fada'iat: libertad de movimiento + libertad de conocimiento*, a book by observatorio tecnológico del estrecho, 2006

from post-state identities. Capital is global and constantly relocating companies from here to there for cheaper labour (i.e. Spanish companies have moved *maquilas* to Morocco). When it comes to workers' rights, you can fight for them in your neighbourhood; however, it might be more

The electronic border
From *fada'iat: libertad de movimiento + libertad de conocimiento*, a book by observatorio tecnológico del estrecho, 2006

136

Contested Spaces interview

ment, which has a 25-year history. Following the *Indymedia Estrecho* project, *Fadaʼiat* was our next suggestion for interfering with the Spanish-Moroccan border. This project is about symbolically opening this cruel border and improving communication from bottom to top, and so generating critical output beyond what we hear in the corporate media about what is going on in this geographical region. In 2005, during an official summit between Spain and Morocco, three sub-Saharan migrants died at the border. The border police moved the bodies very quickly from one side to the other, i.e. they died on the Spanish side and were then transported to the Moroccan side. There's a need to make this reality visible and to change how many see it: a low-intensity war is going on at the border.

A new economy is emerging in relation to this militarization. Within the EU's border management policy, Spain is pioneering new means of controlling geographies. Such territorial control technology has also been sold to Greece and to Poland for its border with Belarus.

So hackitectura.net – with its platform for tactical cartography in 2003 and its *Fadaʼiat* laboratories from 2004 to the present – strives to do strategic work for this geography and its counter-geography, similar to what others have already done in Tijuana/San Diego or Israel. Our objective is to map the border as an economic and social space with its struggles and counter-hegemonic (or reality-hacking) activities.

# Trading Places

Arizona Market
Brčko, Bosnia and Herzegovina, 2006

# Trading Places

## ARIZONA MARKET: INTER-ETHNIC COLLABORATION IN BRČKO

Not far from the north Bosnian town of Brčko lies one of the most notorious marketplaces in south-eastern Europe: Arizona Market. It has 2,500 stalls on an area covering 40 hectares, receives 3 million visitors a year and employs directly or indirectly an estimated 100,000 people. Apart from these statistics, what distinguishes the market depends on participants' perspectives and interests, and these can differ considerably. For some, it is a model of a multi-ethnic community, for others it is the largest open-air shopping mall in the Balkans, while still others experience it as hell on earth. The differences in perspective depend upon which of the numerous stages and transformations of what is commonly called Arizona Market one is referring to.

The strip of land occupied by the present Arizona Market is a part of the war zone that was fiercely fought over by Serbian, Croatian and Bosnian Muslim units because of its strategic position after Bosnia-Herzegovina had left the federal state of Yugoslavia in 1991. Besides the entities set out in the Dayton Peace Accords of November 1995, i.e. the Serbian Republic and the Federation of Bosnia-Herzegovina, the disputed territory around the town of Brčko, whose future was to be decided in an international arbitration process, was granted special status. It was placed under the direct supervision of a special supervisor from the Office of the High Representative (OHR) of the international community of states for Bosnia and Herzegovina. Along the so-called Arizona Corridor (the north-south link between Bosnia and Croatia, which divides the Serbian Republic into a western and an eastern part), thus named by the IFOR/SFOR troops, an economic hub has established itself whose importance extends far beyond the area occupied by the Special District of Brčko. In 1996, after the checkpoint set up at the interface between the three ethnic groupings had evolved into an informal meeting place where cigarettes and cattle were traded and coffee was served at the roadside, the local commander decided to encourage initial encounters between members of the different ethnic communities by establishing a 'free-trade zone', with the aim of consolidating peace. SFOR soldiers levelled several hectares of farmland, cleared the mines and supplied building materials. In next to no time, the largest informal market for goods in Southern Europe arose on the opposite side of the road to the checkpoint: with wooden huts, improvised stalls, smuggled goods and bootleg versions of brand-name goods. Textiles, food, electronic products, building materials, cosmetics, car accessories and CDs could all be purchased at favourable prices there. The cheapest goods could be acquired directly from the lorries.

Decisive for the continued development of Arizona Market was the fact that, unlike most other informal markets, it arose on the open fields with the support of the armed forces. In the years that followed, the convergence of economic activities at the site and the self-organization of this grey trade area were extolled as a model for promoting the sustained development of communications and community structures between former wartime enemies. Supplementing the simple market facilities and mobile sales, the first houses soon arose, presaging the emergence of a self-organized urbanization process on the site. As time went by, ever more bars and motels operating in these huts and houses started to accommodate a form of trade that made it increasingly difficult to sell – at an international level – the success story of peace based on the market economy. For at Arizona Market, the real money was made through prostitution and trafficking in human beings: with women and girls who were being brought in from Eastern Europe. According to reports, they were rounded up on the streets and resold like cattle from one bar owner to the next. On 26 October 2000, the international community (OHR, OSCE, UNMIBH and SFOR) announced a package of measures designed to purge Arizona Market of such illegal activities. These measures focused on regulating the issue of licences and tax revenues and relocating the market by June 2001 to a new site that would offer all the necessary facilities and safety features.[1]

The most striking thing about this strategy to regain control over Arizona Market – which ultimately culminated in the ceremonial opening of a new shopping centre in the presence of the Principal Deputy High Representative, the US Ambassador, Donald S. Hays, on 11 November 2004[2] – was the way the international community, which exercised politico-territorial control, and an international investor co-operated in privatizing public space. In February 2001, the supervisor ordered the closure of the existing market.[3] In December that year, Italproject, an Italian-Bosnian-Serbian consortium, won a tender to establish and operate a new market. The consortium signed a 20-year leasing agreement with the district administration that granted it the right to retain 100 per cent of the rental income for a period of seventeen years in return for developing the infrastructure. The project envisaged investing 120 million euro, under the supervision of the EUFOR (EU), to develop a modern trade infrastructure on an area initially comprising 60,000 square meters. In a later phase of development, a complexly structured economic and trade base for the entire southern European area was to be established, which would include multiplex cinemas, hotels, casinos and a conference centre. Italproject offered existing traders the opportunity to rent or buy stalls in module-like rooms. Resistance by landowners and traders to this total takeover was met with compulsory dispossessions. This response was justified with the argument that it was in the public interest to ensure that the district administration of Brčko complied with the agreements concluded with Italproject.[4] Demonstrations and road blockades staged to oppose the demolition of the old site were cleared by the police. As most of the landowners affected were Croatians who sought the support of nationalist groups to assert their cause, the maxim of achieving reconciliation by taking economic measures came dangerously close to fomenting an ethnic conflict as a result of what was seen as an arbitrary allocation of economic options.

Arizona Market
Gate of the Trade City of China
Brčko, Bosnia and Herzegovina, 2006

The transformation of the informal market into a shopping centre, which was intended to prevent illegal activities and, at the same time, preserve its economic vitality, signalled a critical turning point, revealing the limits of translating between formal and informal systems. The 'spontaneous' evolution of a public-urban space in the shape of an informal market surrounded by transporters and huts was replaced by enclosed fee-charging parking spaces. The coming together of diverse cultures was now regulated by fixed opening hours and private security guards. In summer 2006, there was little sign of the original Arizona Market (Arizona 1) with its thousands of wooden huts standing around a tarpaulin and metal-roofed bazaar. All that was left after the site had been cleared were a few levelled-off fallow fields – an uncanny reminder of that moment, a decade earlier, when the bulldozers started work. The present Arizona Market contains the market halls operated by Italproject and Arizona 2, a hybrid urban entity whose gravel roads and wooden verandas not only make it look like a Wild West town – a rudimentary social and economic frontier – but also conjure up images of an embryonic self-organized town where people can live and trade. A new type of local structure is emerging here which is composed of the remains of the former 'rampant' developments and the newly partitioned plots of the master plan whose module structures are being appropriated through individual aesthetics. A residential settlement has evolved polymorphously above two clearly arranged sales floors, inspired by urban models. At the same time, the wide variety of roof extensions, window apertures, balustrades and other forms of decoration signal the advent of individual inhabitation of the large-scale structures of strategic investments. The site's remarkable form reflects the struggle of official planners to control the dynamics of the black market. In this segment of the market, the convergence of the two systems has led to the proliferating parallel existence of cultural claims and practices. Here, the tension between informally and formally regulated organizational forms has enhanced the aesthetics of spatial use which Srdjan Jovanovic Weiss describes as 'turbo architecture' – a kind of aesthetics that takes its orientation from self-made truths about national tradition, rules and architectural style and invents new typologies from a combination of diffuse repertoires of forms, colours, materials and standards. Turbo architecture is one of the unconcealable and unrestrainable results of the black market. It is 'proof that architectural production depends neither on a stable market nor on a stable political system'.[5] Turbo architecture is a self-created niche marking out its own field of operation by skilfully manoeuvring through a combination of half-truths, misunderstandings and local reactions; it is the antithesis of the firmly laid-down rules of the master plan. In this sense it counterbalances the design envisaged for the new Arizona Market. Indeed, at Arizona Market, at the interface between the grown settlement and the new developments on allotted plots, 'Balkanized' house models respond to a landscape of instable policies with powerful gestures of invulnerability and success, hyper-materialism and hyper-identifiables.

In contrast to all of these facades, developments on the other side of Arizona Road point to the vital contribution that invisible labour markets have made to Arizona Market's prosperity. The far-reaching trade contacts find their official expression in the fact that Italproject is developing the *Trade City of China* on the other side of Arizona Road. The *Trade City of China* is a theme shopping centre designed to accommodate over 100 businesses that import their goods directly from China and resell them in Brčko to wholesalers and retailers. This splendid future is being made possible by hundreds of Chinese workers who are staying in a bunkhouse in a vacant salesroom that stands in the shadows of advertising hoardings. If one takes Arizona as a model of a market-oriented town-establishment project, then the *Trade City of China* is Arizona's Chinatown, and its decorated prefabricated hall a sign of changing trade relations. Arizona, being caught up in the vortex of these diverse enterprises, is also surrounded by a variety of conceptions. In their study on the Arizona Market, Harvard Business School economists, for instance, have concluded that democracy is not necessarily a precondition for launching capitalist economies. The armed forces, they argue, are more efficient than a democratically elected government at triggering economic processes, because they, like their market counterparts, go into operation when states of emergency present themselves.[6] Where the Harvard study praises the combination of a military framework and economic self-organization as a model for a perfect market-oriented state structure, others condemn the transformation process as a lost opportunity to urbanize the area from below. This shift in attention to tax revenues and ignorance about the potential that self-regulating structures contain have extinguished any hopes of forward-looking models of sustainable urban development. To cite Azra Akšamija: 'A fundamental reorganization of a situation in the case of a conflict provides the possibility to intuitively come to terms with the economic and political changes that ensue. Using the existing conditions to create new ones would have continually reshaped the market without destroying its original character.'[7]

In only 10 years, Arizona Market has been transformed from a space of bare survival into a centre of ubiquitous consumption. What was once a mere border guard post has now become a post-metropolitan territory. Hopes that Arizona Market might become a model for a self-organized town were dashed when a market arose whose existence and development were far more extensively tied up with the presence of the international defence force than that formerly generous gesture to bulldoze a few fields seemed to suggest. The UNHCHR attributes the crisis – the dramatic increase in prostitution and trafficking in women – to, among other things, the presence of over 30,000 peacekeepers in BiH.[8] Bosnia was not so much a transit country as a destination for women victims of trafficking. The SFOR troops were not only customers, but allegedly also had their share of the profits accruing from smuggling and corruption.

The 'solution', based on the model of 'urban renewal' developed in the US in the 1960s (declaring a district a problem area and thus permitting large-scale expropriation in the name of the 'public interest'), was fostered by the transformation of the legal system in the Brčko district with the help of legal advisers financed by USAID (US Agency for International Development).[9]

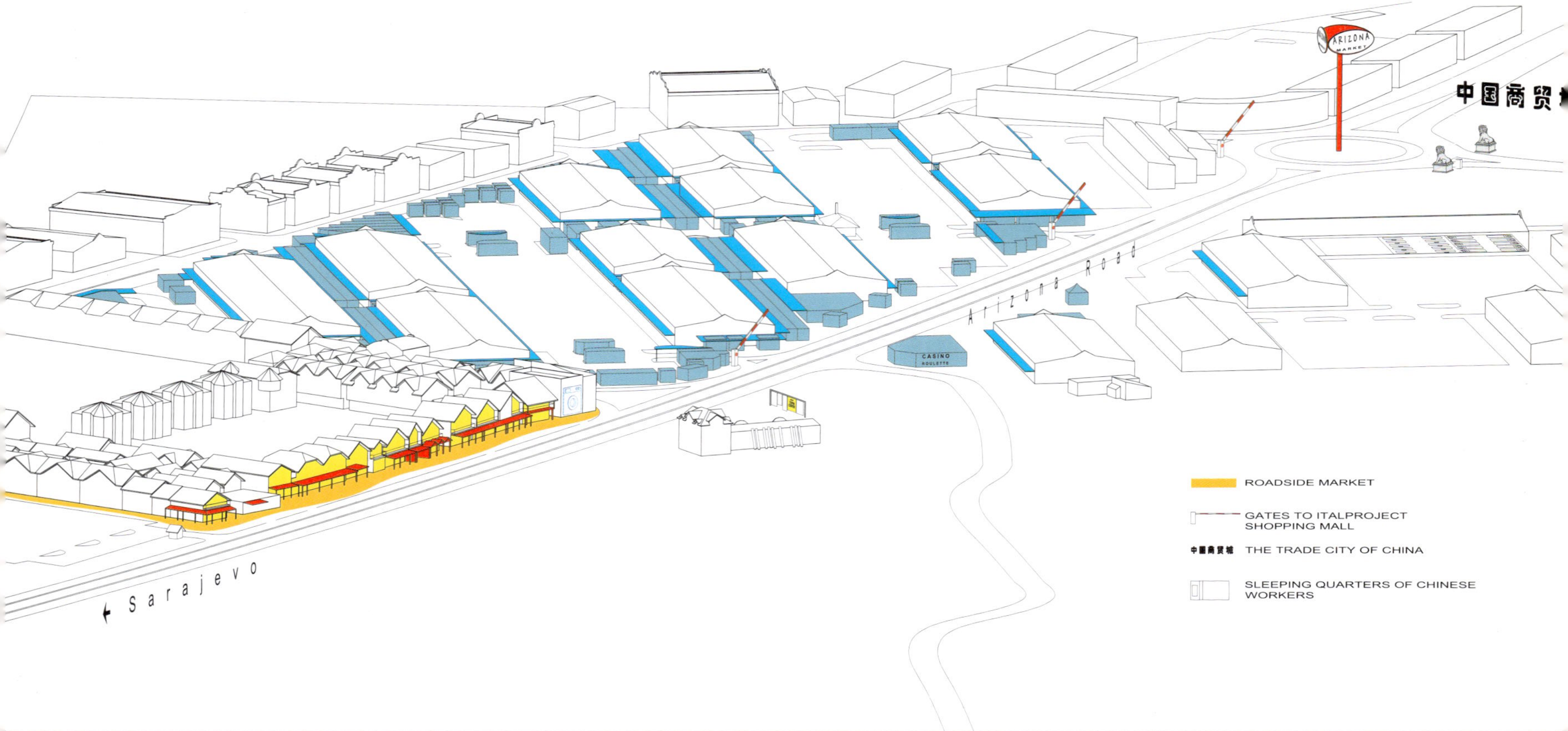

ROADSIDE MARKET
GATES TO ITALPROJECT SHOPPING MALL
中国贸城 THE TRADE CITY OF CHINA
SLEEPING QUARTERS OF CHINESE WORKERS

*Arizona Market*
After the redevelopment by Italproject
Brčko, Bosnia and Herzegovina

Nowadays, Arizona Market is characterized by two things that are ultimately related to each other. Although – or because – the international community has intervened massively in the regulation of the market, the purging of the market by means of centralized controls has been an extremely nebulous affair: on the one hand, for example, Italproject's Italian lenders are persistently not named and, on the other hand, Italproject refuses to ask where the buyers of new market properties obtain the money they need to make their purchases. Rumours range from assertions of lucrative deals being made by organized veterans of paramilitary associations and the employment of suspected war criminals, to allegations of deals being struck with former brothel-owners who are not content to rent one stall only, but invest in 'turbo penthouses' occupying several floors. The convoluted flows of international money and goods at Arizona Market may have now entered a new phase, yet the form of capitalism that prevails there now is no less 'rampant' than it used to be. Its attraction lies in an all-pervading motivation to gain some form of control – ranging from the need to survive, at one end of the scale, to international relations at the other – by seizing anything that is not yet subject to controls. All these many different levels of exchange have created the countless trade situations that one finds at Arizona Market, which promise everyone an opportunity to exploit the market to their own ends, even if this only means purchasing a cheap T-shirt.

## ISTANBUL TOPKAPI: TRANSIENT TRAFFIC

In July 2005, one of the leading forums for international architecture – the 22nd World Congress of Architecture – was held in Istanbul under the motto 'Grand bazaar of architectureS'. The central theme of the congress was the utopian idea of a pluralistic world in which cultural differences are not a source of animosity and atrocities, but a resource to help people find a way to live together in harmony.[10] The leading lights in contemporary architectural design presented their models and discussed them in the context of Istanbul's struggle for recognition as a cosmopolitan city. Outstanding engineering achievements, sustainable planning and cultural heritage formed part of a well-orchestrated protocol of declarations of intent to participate in the exclusive set of global cities. The allegorical motto of the congress as well as its point of reference – the legendary oriental bazaar that leaves no desires unfulfilled – transfigure the socio-spatial challenge posed by a rapidly expanding megacity and its hope that it will be saved by quick responses from architects and town planners.

Outside the tourist centres and escaping international attention lies a very different type of bazaar. It is composed of a vast network of provisional, informal street markets that establish themselves right alongside building sites where urban renewal plans are being realized, beneath terraces of city motorways and next to newly constructed tramway lines. These markets disappear as quickly as they materialize, only to reappear elsewhere. This bazaar is not so much a location for trading goods as

Informal market along the Byzantine city walls and Londra Asfalti, an arterial road to the west, Istanbul Topkapı, 2005

a space under negotiation. It is a threatening and threatened space which winds its way through the city from site to site and temporarily uses (as the intermediary user of the newly planned infrastructure) the wastelands along the development axes of the planned city.

Both the ambivalent form of the 'bazaar' and the schizophrenic manner in which it produces space are symptomatic of the way modern Istanbul's entire spatial development has proceeded up to now. Its present largely stems from its having developed outside the regular planning channels. Istanbul's explosive growth has seen the number of residents rise from 1 million in 1950 to 9 million in 1995 and finally to an estimated 15 million in 2005. These millions of domestic migrants from Eastern Anatolia have primarily found accommodation in illegally built dwellings, in Gecekondus built 'over night'. They make up countless villages, based on local relationships, on the outskirts of the multi-million metropolis and account for up to 65 per cent of all buildings there. There has been an influx of the rural and the dirty, from which the pro-Western middle class feels increasingly overrun. Urban researcher Orhan Esen believes that this development has resulted in Istanbul more and more losing sight of its own urban reality during the twentieth century.[11] The dominant conceptual model of the city of modernity, one based on planned intervention, has failed here. And in the rejection of the autonomously and collectively, self-built environment typical of Gecekondu culture, as well as its suppression from discourse on the contemporary city, open debate with this city has given way to shame and encouraged denial and a tendency to withdraw. It has come to the point where Istanbul is frequently portrayed as an agglomerate that cannot be represented and is doomed to decline. The result is a city without a language, in other words: a city unable to reflect upon itself in any other terms than in those of the failure, the worthless and the abject. Over the past two decades, as the number of residents and developed areas has risen, a conspicuous shrinking process has occurred that is typical of the globalized city. An increasingly large and 'invisible' city confronts a small core of globally usable infrastructural spaces. This infrastructure does not cater for a local environment, but for global processes centred on the lifestyles of the global elites, which meet face-to-face in an increasingly generic city.[12] As the city shrinks, it increasingly isolates all that lies outside the loops of global networks. In Istanbul, for example, there is a widely spread myth that the millions of residents in the undersupplied periphery have never made it as far as the Bosphorus, let alone the urban hubs of public-political activity such as Taksim Square or İstiklal Caddesi in Beyoğlu.

Informal market, Istanbul Topkapı, 2005

The merging of urban production with the circulation of state planning agents and the informal economy has created countless hybrid spaces in Istanbul. One of these arose in 2005 before the gates of the Byzantine city wall in the district of Topkapı, where the building sites of two of the main enterprises that took on the job of tidying up the city in the 1980s converge. On the one hand, a traffic network of urban motorways has been created there in the style of modernist US urbanism. On the other hand, the 1,500-year-old Byzantine city fortifications have been reinstated there in their original condition. In nationalist literature, their continual decline and the living conditions in the wretched areas bordering the fortifications had come to symbolize both the impoverishment of Istanbul and the stronghold of true Turkish values.[13] Between newly delivered and unused building materials, impassable heaps of crushed stone and 8-lane motorways, a swarm-like mass fills a black market covering several kilometres. Piles of second-hand goods and fabrics are mixed up on bare ground with new TV sets, refrigerators, pieces of furniture and computers. On days when visitors turn out in strength, several thousand people can been seen negotiating this construction site of the new Istanbul.

The informal market evokes an archaic model of a city that arises organically as trading centre at the junction of transport and trading routes. In the case of Topkapı, however, it is also moving in the shadows of official town planning, which it temporarily turns into a vehicle serving informality. This market makes use of the semi-finished building structures in a way that has less to do with their intended uses

*Transient Traffic*
Informal market along the Byzantine city walls and Londra Asfaltı, an arterial road to the west, Istanbul Topkapı

MARKET AREA

MINIBUS SERVICES TO AND FROM THE MARKET

TOPKAPI CEMETERY

or with any conceptions or images of modern urban planning than with unplanned utilization and the economic situation of the rural population that has migrated to the city. Land has been occupied here on an improvised basis, bypassing the planners. This approach is not based on how things will look after the plans have been realized, but seeks instead to realize alternatives to this process. The innovatory power of this informal economy is evident not only in its sheer size, but also in its far-reaching ramifications, with all the emerging services systems such as shuttle buses, street kitchens, middlemen, suppliers, livestock selling, the attendant forms of cultural entertainment and ad hoc shooting ranges. With its bizarre combination of modern transport systems, its symbolic sites of a national renaissance, spontaneously arising market activities, rich visual display of the intricacies of legally authorized work, its third market and informal trading, Topkapı represents more than just a coincidental clash of diverse forces. The growing perviousness of official and informal structures, the rampant appropriation of urban space and the accelerated disintegration of cultural territories are typical moments in the evolution of a city structure dictated by the new world economy, in which full control over a territory is no longer a relevant issue. In contrast to the territorially based economic forms, large and small spatial structures are evolving which circumvent the functional separation of space and embed themselves in the prevailing geography as a mesh of networks.

These observations raise the central question about the current status of planning as the once great hope of modernity. The self-organized economies of Istanbul's poor defy the goals of official planning while being inextricably tied up with them at the same time. To the authorities, these economies are undesirable developments that must be eradicated by urban planning schemes. Proceeding from this logic, modern planning projects in Istanbul are not simply endeavours to find solutions to problems linked with the city's enormous growth, but also schemes that simultaneously trigger further conflicts. A street market like Topkapı clearly demonstrates the increasing energy with which Third World cycles encounter those of the First World – yet without the spatial shields or the mediatization once considered a matter of course. The essential point here is that there is absolutely no distinct dividing line nor – more importantly – is there any set of binding rules that could serve as an operational basis for an exchange between the systems. We only know that the minibus we try to stop by waving it down really is going to stop once we are inside it. Hence, participation in socio-spatial processes, for which the informal market situated amidst the hustle and bustle of Istanbul stands, echoes the performance – used as a metaphor by Ernesto Laclau – at which we always arrive too late. We live as *bricoleurs* in a world of imperfect systems whose rules we co-determine and transform by retracing them. It is in this very moment, according to Laclau, that we find the key to (acts of) emancipation: in the middle of a performance that has started unexpectedly, we search for mythical and impossible origins but are unable to rise above the impossible task facing us. What counts, however, is that we struggle and strive to arrive at decisions that have to be made because there is no superordinate monitoring or control system. Running counter to the radical foundation of a democratic society and operational structures sketched out in the great narrations of modernity, a model of political praxis is taking shape that is continuing to develop through a plurality of acts of democratization.[14]

## MOSCOW IZMAILOVO: VISITING STALIN

Thirteen dead and 53 badly wounded: this is the result of the bomb that exploded at Moscow's Cherkizovsky Market on 21 August 2006. The dead included six Tajiks, three Uzbekis, two Russians, one White Russian and one Chinese. Among the badly wounded were many Chinese and Vietnamese. The suspects are three young Russian skinheads, who are accused of 'premeditated murder of two or more persons committed out of national hatred'. Immediately after the attack, the Moscow Public Prosecutor was still convinced that it was related to internal disputes between criminal associations of local traders, as had been assumed in the case of repeated explosions and arson attacks on Moscow markets in the past. Earlier, on 26 March 2005, the 10,000-square-metre Russian Court, the pseudo-historical wooden exhibition complex at Vernizash souvenir market, had also been the target of one such 'explosive' conflict.

Vernisazh
Mock Russian village with arts and crafts market catering for international tourists
Moscow Izmailovo, 2006

Cherkizovsky Market (often referred to as Izmailovo Market) in the northeast of Moscow, is one of the largest informal markets in the city, with connections to all parts of the Russian Federation and beyond. On an area three times the size of that occupied by the Kremlin in Moscow, 15 specialized trading areas form a rampantly growing bazaar structure that completely surrounds Izmailovo Stadium and includes all sorts of attractions: from Eurasia markets to the Izmailovo Kremlin (with a Vodka Museum), which was specially erected for tourists, the sale of arts and crafts, and a reconstruction of Tsar Alexander's wooden palace. The market's 'owners' are among Russia's new millionaires. Telman Ismailov, for instance, developed the AST group (one of Russia's largest developers) with an estimated half a billion US dollars in annual rent taken from Cherkizovsky Market. A birthday song sung by Jennifer Lopez for a rumoured 1 million dollars established him in the media as one of Moscow's new oligarchs. At the lower end of the new market-economy scale, there are thousands of migrants from Tajikistan, Uzbekistan, China and an extended Southeast Asia, who have come to seek work at the market as stall-minders, carriers and tea-sellers seven days a week. They sleep in the metal storage containers (above the stalls or on the periphery of the market) or in the cellars of the stadium. In this state of modern slavery, they are not only at the mercy of exploitative employers, but also of arbitrary police behaviour and gangs of young thugs. As a result, many of them never dare to go more than a few hundred metres from the market.

In September 2006, one month after the bombing, the vice-speaker of Moscow City Council announced that the market would be closing at the end of 2006. A few weeks later, the head of the Department of the Consumer Market of Moscow announced that most of the trading places on the site of the Russian State University of Physical Education (RGUFK) would be taken down by 1 July 2007, and the remainder by the end of 2007. This, it was said, would allow the site to be returned to its proper use, as a space where people could devote themselves to physical culture. But how is it possible to determine the 'proper' use of a space, especially in an age of global restructuring? Does its use as a venue for sports events really do justice to the original plans? Or isn't it simply a by-product, a parasitical use of its potential?

During the XXII Olympic Summer Games in 1980, the RGUFK site served as one of the locations of the Moscow Games. For the weight-lifting events, a new indoor arena, the Izmailovo Sports Palace, was erected. At the southern end of the site, next to Izmailovo Park underground station, the Olympic village was constructed in the form of a four-tower hotel complex with 8,000 beds. The stadium itself, which stands in the middle of the grounds, was built during the 1930s. It is a fragment of the envisaged 'Central Stadium of the Soviet Union' planned by Stalin to accommodate 120,000 spectators. Never completed, it also served to camouflage the 'Reserve Command Centre of the Supreme Commander-in-Chief of the Red Army, I.V. Stalin'. Ultimately, the construction of the stadium was inspired by more than purely sporting considerations. Not only was the stadium intended to be bigger than Berlin's Olympic Stadium, and its peculiar asymmetrical form designed to hold grandiose military parades at which the columns of tanks could roll into the stadium unhindered from the parade ground to the east. It was also conceived as part of a vast military infrastructure covering the entire Soviet Union. Situated 17 kilometres to the east of the Kremlin, a bunker beneath the stadium was designed as an intermediary stop-over point in case Hitler should launch a surprise attack on Moscow and the Soviet Command have to be evacuated to Samara, 1,000 kilometres away in the Urals. Consequently, sports events in Izmailovo have always been part of a far greater system of deceptions and compensatory gestures. Cultural events are just as important as strategically embedded building structures for preserving this system. Events such as these helped to sustain policies that were imitated with ever greater rapidity when the RGUFK site was converted into one of the largest informal trading centres in the Russian Federation.

Cherkizovsky Market was a product of the politics of individual initiatives promoted by perestroika. Under its banner, members of the state sports

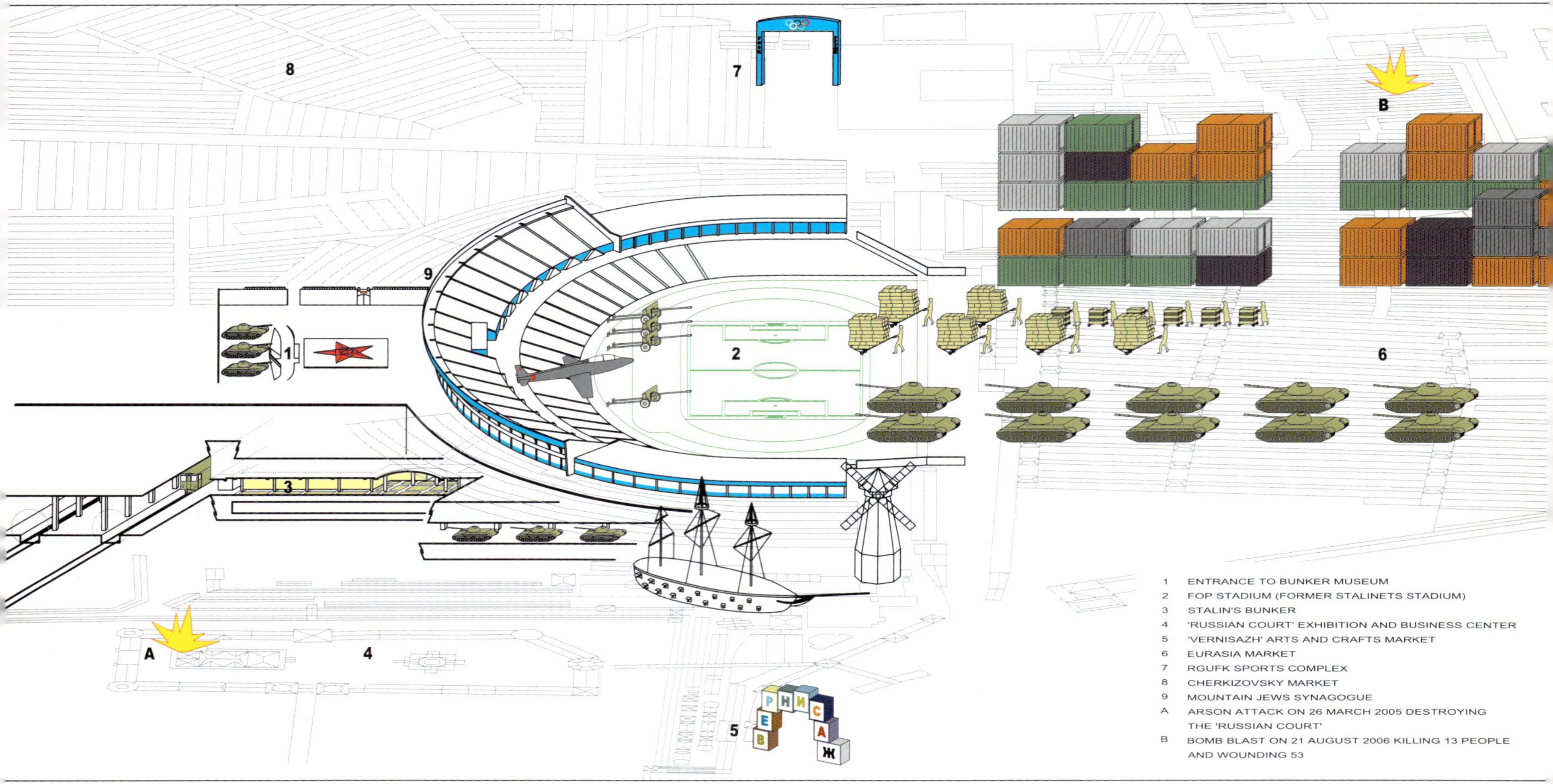

1 ENTRANCE TO BUNKER MUSEUM
2 FOP STADIUM (FORMER STALINETS STADIUM)
3 STALIN'S BUNKER
4 'RUSSIAN COURT' EXHIBITION AND BUSINESS CENTER
5 'VERNISAZH' ARTS AND CRAFTS MARKET
6 EURASIA MARKET
7 RGUFK SPORTS COMPLEX
8 CHERKIZOVSKY MARKET
9 MOUNTAIN JEWS SYNAGOGUE
A ARSON ATTACK ON 26 MARCH 2005 DESTROYING THE 'RUSSIAN COURT'
B BOMB BLAST ON 21 AUGUST 2006 KILLING 13 PEOPLE AND WOUNDING 53

*Visiting Stalin*
The sprawling Cherkizovsky Market around the former Stalinets Stadium
Moscow Izmailovo

institute began to use the grounds and buildings commercially. In June 1989, Sergei Korniyenko and a 'collective of enthusiasts' leased the stadium buildings. Under the terms of the contract, the spectators stands and the sports fields are to be available for events such as Spartakiade 2000 ('For a United and Healthy Russia in the 21st Century'). The remaining spaces, like those beneath the stands, can be used commercially. FOP, the Sports Health Enterprise founded in 1989, proved to be extremely innovative. Nowadays, in conjunction with the New Historical Cultural Centre Izmailovo (NIC Izmailovo, founded in 1995), it operates enterprises as diverse as an arbalest shooting range, the Aero Fitness Club, various bars, the Lux Sauna, the Alain Beauty Salon (up to 'European standard') and the Preobrazheniye (Transformation) School for the Spiritual Development of Man, which is run by a cosmic artist-healer.

Furthermore, FOP played a vital role in the 'rediscovery' of Stalin's old bunker. In 1994, the Iron Division club helped to organize a museum exhibition which was taken over from the Central Museum of the Armed Forces and opened as a branch on 1 September 1999. Adjacent to the bunker rooms, FOP operates a Georgian-style restaurant called Visiting Stalin, as well as a concert hall (holding 200 people) used for performances by the Prince Sergei Korniyenko Orchestra. Even though the bunker was apparently never used by Stalin himself – just as the stadium never performed the function originally anticipated – one can now book a bunker tour for a little over 100 US dollars. The price includes a visit to the reconstructed conference hall of the Supreme Command of the Red Army, as well as to Stalin's study and recreational and leisure areas, plus a dinner at 'Stalin'.

Alexander Ushakov, the General Director of Vernizash in Izmailovo, another company operating on the site, was also a member of the State University of Physical Education. He was an active combat sambo wrestler, before he became a sports trainer. Ushakov took over the flea-market site to the south of the stadium from the RGUFK. He started to construct the Vernisazh Complex, which, not unlike Disneyland, accommodates countless imitations and set pieces from Russian architecture on an area covering 20,000 square metres. Here, a mixture of Russian arts and crafts is sold alongside Soviet souvenirs such as fur hats and Matroschka dolls, amidst the folklorist scenery of an old Russian village with a fort-like Wild West touch. The Vernisazh tourist market, initiated under perestroika, highlights the great expectations placed on the Western market. The far greater part of Cherkizovsky Market confronts these expectations with the informal economy created by the new market systems in the deregulated transformation societies in the East.

Whereas the stadium was originally supposed to provide an arena for mass performances demonstrating the superiority of the political order of the Soviet Union, it has now become the archaeological site testifying to the inner emptiness of a Babylonian city-within-a-city into the cracks of which the ants of globalization have now moved. No longer do revolutionary tanks roll or patriotic armies march on the parade ground, which has disappeared beneath the Eurasia Market. Instead, thousands of carriers and tea-sellers swarm out around the endless labyrinth of its kilometres-long halls to keep this rough trading organism alive. As a central trading place for the sheer necessities of life, the Cherkizovsky Market has become the contested scene of cultural identities where attempts to reconstruct a Russian national identity encounter the complex realities of a globalized migration-economy. The progressive commercialization of even the tiniest of niches has generated a large number of unforeseen spaces for microcultural negotiations, like the one for the 3,000 Mountain Jews from the Caucasus, for whom a 20-square-metre room – laid out with carpets and located between the shoe storerooms and the sportsmen's and women's toilets in the caverns of the stadium stands – serves as a synagogue. Like the majority of the hundreds of thousands of people whose existences are inextricably tied up with the market, they, too, are both marginalized and transformed into targets of a global tug-of-war over cultural identity. To some, they are 'blacks', to some they are not orthodox enough, while some doubt whether they are Jews at all.

Whereas the owners' good contacts with the government and the mayor have led to repeated delays in implementing the plans to close the markets, a ruling to restrict the share of foreign workers at markets to 40 per cent, which came into effect on 1 April 2007, really did have a widespread impact. From Moscow to Vladivostok, there are reports of markets collapsing completely. This has not only affected immigrants working at the market, but also all those impoverished sections of the Russian population who are dependent on the cheap products available at these markets. These policies (Russia for the Russians), which are propagated by Putin, are frequently seen as a tactically motivated response to the increase in racially inspired attacks. Consequently, the bombers of 12 August 2006, who felt that there were 'too many Asians at the market', ultimately did not only kill thirteen people and wound 53 others, but also affected, with their actions, the existence(s) of an estimated five million illegal immigrants in Russia.

## MARKET COMMUNITIES

The complex transformations of the three sites dealt with here reveal how markets function as a dynamic force that generates new forms of collective exchange, and how this process relates to the aesthetics of establishing new social orders. Despite the very different ways in which historical developments and local micro-processes converge, there are similarities between the informal trading areas along the Byzantine city wall in Istanbul, the establishment of an economy in the district of Brčko and the never-ending transformation of a cultural site of national importance in Moscow. All three markets arose and expanded in a hybrid situation, meandering between informality and planning, and in a close dialogue with strategically important typologies of modern urban planning: sports and training centres, traffic buildings and facilities, and military complexes: in the stadium area of Moscow's Cherkizovsky Market; between the newly constructed rapid transport systems and the historical fortifications in Istanbul; and at a checkpoint controlled by international troops in a Bosnian war zone. These three markets are now being demolished (Moscow), or transformed into legal structures (Brčko) or forced to move to new locations (Istanbul).

The fate of these three junctions of self-organized trade is similar to that of other informal markets, following, for example, the pattern of the slow dismantlement of the Jarmark Europa at the Dziesi ciolecia Stadium in Warsaw and the removal of the Polish market near Potsdamer Platz in Berlin around the time the Wall opened in 1989. These markets are able to survive for a short while as platforms for an experimental urbanity at the micro-level of everyday life; they then give way to the political pressure to create a new architectural order, which is supposed to restore some form of normative urbanity; later, they reappear somewhere else. Although these experimental structures repeatedly disappear from the face of the earth, they leave their mark on the fabric of the city. They transport images, ideas and values between different worlds. And with their improvised technologies, infrastructures and spatial policies, they create openings for new urban situations and new links between the local and the global levels.

Cherkizovsky Market
Moscow, 2006

The term 'informal market' is a collective noun referring to widely scattered trading phenomena whose dynamics and forms of spatial materialization differ greatly in character, even though they are generally tied to political and economic transformations. At the economic level, the term applies to incomes whose generation is 'unregulated by the institutions of society, in a legal and social environment in which similar activities are regulated.'[15] Informal markets refer to uncontrolled activities by travelling enterprises operating over large areas, such as the East European 'suitcase traders' and the mobile and border-crossing networks of the kiosk trade, as well as the rampant agglomerations of temporary grey and black markets that are provisionally occupying vacated plots everywhere. The globally distributed nodes of the informal economy are usually the product of political upheavals, global economic deregulation and related migration patterns, and new working and production situations. Nowadays, they arise at the interface marking the transition from nation states to a globally oriented, neo-liberal, control society, in which the state is less a disciplinary organ than an expedient instrument for regulating 'informal' arrangements. Driven by new imperatives of social mobility and the expansion of transnational spaces brought about by the unequal movements of tourism, migration and flight, informal market types have come into being that have created, from local opportunities, novel and extreme physical configurations very different from the old centre-periphery model. These spatial structures are intermediate zones that are seized by diverse interest groups, no matter whether they are local or global, formal or informal, and own much or little capital.

Operating against centre-periphery logic, economic processes are currently spawning spatial network structures at whose intersections poles of economic development are being created that stand out against their immediate surroundings. As the economist Pierre Veltz shows in his model of the *archipelago economy*, the globally oriented homogenization of production finds itself repeatedly challenged by a dynamic network of bottom-up associations. The countless interstices in the archipelago, where people operate with social capital, trust, a shared culture and unspoken knowledge, contain a new zone characterized by the development of self-organized, small-scale social relations rich in endogenous development.[16] Within this archipelago-like overall distribution of economic power, a new type of efficiency is emerging with corresponding spatial imperatives: unlike Fordism, the efficiency of an archipelago economy does not stem from specific forms of the division of labour, but from the quality of its communications and co-ordination processes, which, due to the specific spatial distribution of actors, can only be standardized to a certain extent.[17] Informal relationship structures are needed so that these processes can spontaneously connect things outside the framework of unwieldy systems of rules. The processes that stimulate the self-organization of informal markets and direct the transactions create a lively imbroglio of actors. It is because of family ties, the prospects of a quick sale and the opportunity to sell items at other markets, and because of friendships, dependencies, liabilities and debts to suppliers, as well as unexpected twists in people's lives and the development of new relationships that people come together in an environment where they can benefit from worlds different from their own. It is not the constitution of leakage points – points where overflows are allowed to occur and the commodification of things is partially suspended – but a far more generous and inconspicuous opening up of many different worlds to each other that generates the vigorous dynamics and maximizes the turnover of the informal market.

Castle Market
Sheffield, UK, 2006

One of the most striking features of the boom in informal markets in Europe over the past two decades since the collapse of the Soviet Union has been the increasingly rapid development of external networks. This process has intensified exchange relations with markets outside Europe and, above all, with China. Operating in such extensive informal market structures means having to rely on network connections with special qualities. Relationships of trust, loyalties, favours and personal agreements determine what is known among cohesive transnational Chinese communities as 'quanxi' (relationships) between different people: exchange structures – based on personal contacts – that extend beyond formal agreements and are easy to mobilize.[18] The Russian term 'blat' stands for a similar form of transforming social into finance capital. 'Blat' relationships are dynamic, long-term, and informal in nature: from black-market deals and party contacts to the exchange of services and reciprocal assistance in everyday life. The smooth transition from social exchange to profitable business deals encourages the extensive and increasing interweaving of economic, economically caused and extra-economic phenomena. The increasingly refined channels through which goods and commodities are transported are an important instrument in this context. As labour conditions become increasingly precarious, the transport of goods and commodities becomes increasingly individualized, spreading across a large number of smaller towns and localities where finely meshed networks participate in informal trading structures. In this way, informal markets are part of a simultaneous process of geo-cultural fragmentation and expanded reproduction. They serve as models for the materialization of a new spatial order of social strata, cultures, regions and associations from which new structures of civil-societal cohesion emerge.

## COMPLICITIES

Informal markets are places of transition in more ways than one. They serve, on the one hand, as places for brief stays and are themselves often seen as mere 'transitional effects': as adapters between unregulated relationships and order. This perspective views transition as a foreseeable process whose conclusion – as the result of a series of measures – is certain from the very start. It assumes the existence of a central intention that controls change, the existence of both an order-generating plan and the latter's ability to capture a development in its totality. The concept of transition that we are referring to here sees in this process a transition to a different, as yet unknown state, whose spatial form only reveals itself later. Initially, this transition is not physical. Even so, it still generates an accelerated space which, in the case of informal markets, is saturated with a surfeit of conflicting symbols and practices of signification. Transition, at the spatial level, characterizes ambiguously formed places where the transformation and novel organization of subjectivities are possible. Thus considered, informal markets are unstable and vulnerable places that do not appear in the matrix of territorial and ideological affiliation of individuals and cultures. They are channels through which cultures outside the designated places of encounter interact directly with the forces of globalization, creating another feature of liberalized global capital markets: a flexible shadow system, whose relationship to the homogenizing forces of neo-liberal globalization is characterized, above all, by its paradoxical production of culturally heterogeneous micro-locations. Here the cultural paradoxes of globalization become evident. The traditions of self-appropriation of space and the self-organization of markets combine with the dynamics of neo-liberal globalization to create a contradictory process in which networks are formed at ever greater and asynchronous speeds, spaces are generated on a trans-territorial basis and cultural experiences are transformed.

When examining these scenarios, one cannot ignore the way neo-liberal policies are co-opting survival strategies in the Global South nor can one overlook the related expedient myths of informality that serve as an expression of emancipated individuation. Mobile and fleeting accumulation are just as attractive for the functioning of neo-liberal capital markets as they are for the organization of black markets. It is, therefore, necessary to ascertain which structural link lies behind these shared interests. Elmar Altvater and Brigitte Mahnkopf draw attention to this when they describe informality as the 'shock absorber of globalization' outside the framework of the welfare state and assistance programmes, and demand that it be understood as 'an expression of structural transformations in the relationship between global, national and local economies under the dictate of global competitiveness.'[19] This complex relationship between neo-liberal government techniques and forms of self-organization, as well as the spread of the market mentality[20] to the organization of creative processes and critical practices has led to a multiply encumbered starting point – to take up the question of how cultural experience can be organized in a way that generates space for modes of expression whose outline is yet to be defined.

Both the global art market and the ever-growing market of the creative industries determine the patterns through which the aesthetics of resistance are able to perpetuate themselves intentionally, as it were, in a spectacularized world of consumption and to become profitable in the process. Faced with the extended boundaries of the neo-liberal market, the battle – initiated within the extended field of art and architecture in the 1990s – to radicalize culture by fusing art and life is now in danger of degenerating into a commissioned parody of itself. In a climate marked by the neo-liberal 'appropriation of forms of appropriation', the control of critiques of control and the abstraction of the senses by the sensualization of abstraction, it seems wrong, at first sight, to take informal markets, of all things, as a point of departure for reflecting upon models of alternative economies in which new horizons of cultural experience can be organized outside both central controls and profit-oriented frames of reference. According to Saskia Sassen, informal markets are the low-cost equivalent of global deregulation and serve, first and foremost, as the suppliers of advanced urban economies, with the sole difference that, at the lower end of the scale, the risks and costs have to be borne by the actors themselves.[21] With her argumentation, she finds herself in the same boat as Mike Davis, who, in *Planet of Slums* (2006),

Cherkizovsky Market
Large Eurasian market in the northeast of Moscow, 2006

presents an ensemble of epistemological fallacies on informality in order to expose the strategic nature of the ideology of informal organization. From the myriad of concealed forms of exploitation and seduction to the fanatic obsession with quasi-magic ways of acquiring money (gambling, pyramid schemes, etc.) to the diminution of social capital as a result of increasing competition within the informal sector, Davis lists all the erroneous beliefs held by the advocates, such as the Peruvian economist Hernando de Soto, of an 'invisible revolution' of informal capital.[22] Instead of fulfilling the promise of greater upward mobility, the boom that began in the informal sector in the 1980s led to greater ethno-religious differentiation, as well as to increased exploitation of the poor and urban violence. Davis's notion of a counter-offensive to the neo-liberal version of informality involves strengthening trade union structures and radical political parties and, last but not least, reviving a community based on worldwide solidarity within the framework of a militant refusal to accept the assigned marginal role within global capitalism.[23]

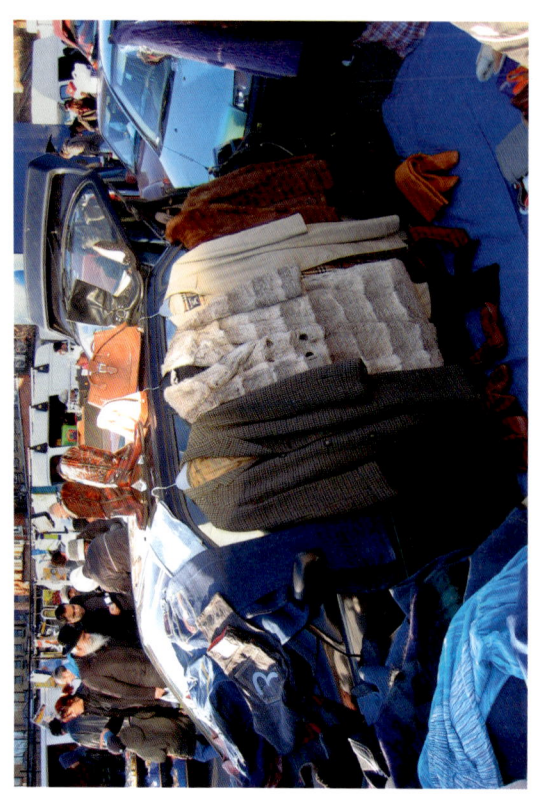

The wealth of arguments and evidence, as well as all the statistics, maps and diagrams that have been presented, seem to demand a condemnation of the state of informality – a condemnation that can draw on well-documented material on the dynamics of poverty, exploitation and oppression. The roles of power seem to be too clearly allocated and consolidated to imagine how – through the way they function – they can allow alternative social formations to develop. But what if we refuse to accept this logic for a moment and take a look at an entire series of shortcomings in the apparatus of global economic control that we have just criticized – shortcomings that can create space for social experiences outside the boundaries within which this apparatus exercises control? If one looks beyond the boundaries imposed on the world by the economic regime, one sees the manifestation of the boundary as a political space that cannot be controlled through the workings of the economy alone and which therefore creates a space for re-structuring social order. Attempts to explain informal activities from the standpoint of the totality usually ignore the way in which local spaces are changed by a large number of actors and spontaneously co-ordinated modes of behaviour that cannot be determined by knowing the overall situation. Hence, the type of habitable formation and the potential for change offered by networks of informal organizations are often overlooked. Although power circulates in such networks, people are not merely the consenting targets of those who exercise power, but, as Michel Foucault argues in his lectures at the Collège de France in 1975-1976, the relays of power. Power is a kind of arrangement: people submit to power and exercise power. Power flows through them, which means that it can be seized and redirected.[24] Hence, one of the ways of carrying out artistic interventions and thinking architecturally is, therefore, to search – beyond the world of hackneyed concepts such as slum culture, chaos economy, social mobility and transitional societies – for ideas, impressions, images and experiences that help to show ways of making local co-ordination work in these spaces of self-organized exchange, and to demonstrate how the forces of change are not appropriated or passed on in the same way as property and commodities, but are, instead, directed through networks with differentiated structures.

In these analyses of informal markets, it is not a question of establishing what the markets represent in themselves or are supposed to achieve, but of ascertaining what they can help to realize at a different level. Informal markets create a conflict-ridden terrain of accesses without explaining the principles behind accessibility. They are not a concept of space, but an expression of social praxis. We are particularly interested in the point at which transformations occur when informal market realities connect up with their specific field of application: the place where they take root, crystallize into new forms, and trigger effects that extend the field of social perception and activity. In exploring scenes such as these, we are interested, in other words, in how alternative involvement is possible – with the spontaneously emerging spaces of informal market activities and their physical and visual properties – that will enhance that logic of resistance which affects not only concrete experiences themselves, but also the horizons and modalities that organize these experiences. What we associate with this kind of commitment is certainly not the production of a map that assigns a specific activity to a specific location and represents a geography of 'sites of informal trade'. Nor are we concerned with a comprehensive typology of informal markets or a typology of the spaces in which informal trade takes place. Our interest in the complexity of local situations is mainly concerned with examining those perspectives from which the many fleeting flows of convergence, aggregation and atomization, which are characteristic of informal exchange, are themselves considered. The local space is the terrain on which the dynamic movements of countless actors are recorded, strip by strip, in scattered visual allusions, physical signs, spontaneous scenes and small organizational changes that trigger the growth of a network of 'trans-localities'.

## BOUNDARY ECONOMIES

One of the most virulent sites of conflict in recent times has been the transition from governance centred on the nation state to an ensemble of forms of governing and regulation that is increasingly attuned to the mentalities of networks and markets. As forms of cohesion change, temporary geographies with unequally saturated power constellations emerge that are particularly dependent on one parameter: mobile and short-term accumulation. Within global market realities, the spread of market techniques to all areas of life, which Foucault characterized as the main principle of neo-liberal governmentality, has created new relationships between the world and the subject. Governmentality thus works on a liberalized economy of the ontological. Each 'governmental measure', in other words, each measure aiming to direct, control and manage individuals and collectives that wants to seize some space within this structure, must first, according to Foucault, pass the 'market test'. One important aspect of the economization of the social level is the extension and naturalization of governmental activities, whose product is *homo oeconomicus*: a social actor committed to maximizing his or her personal gain.[25] Foucault also points out, however, that people never exclusively play the role of *homo oeconomicus*. The arts of government also allow the subjects to act in accordance with their own will, to deviate, and to commit misdemeanours intentionally, which might be directed against the goals of the government, because they establish markets, for instance, which allow people to gain social experiences outside the designated categories. In this sense, then, they permit activities that involve resistance and block old categories, thereby allowing new avenues for self-constitution to open up. In this way, markets can serve as settings for exposing social normalization and negotiating resistance.

In neo-liberal economics, the role of *homo oeconomicus* can be considered only as a utopian nucleus that serves to limit governmental power to those domains in which there is no risk of conflicts with the practice of social life. In this sense, it is an expedient 'interface between government and individual'.[26] As a result of both the ever greater influence of economic knowledge on social organization nowadays and the dominance of socially accepted knowledge structures that endeavour to make capital out of the most remote spheres of cultural production, conflict areas multiply whenever economic requirements and social network structures merge. The question as to how, in such a situation, economic calculation divorces social behaviour from its context and networks lies behind the Actor-Network Theory (ANT) developed by Bruno Latour, Michel Callon and John Law in the 1990s. In Actor Network Theory

– The Market Test'[27] Callon argues that markets are not embedded in networks – not even when they use their flows and intensities to generate trade. If this were not the case, the argument continues, they would be unable to produce calculating actors who settle conflicts by fixing prices. *Homo oeconomicus* and *homo sociologicus* are not, in Callon's view, opposing forces, but individual actors with perfectly stable spheres of competence.[28] Whereas in Mark Granovetter's much-cited theory of 'weak ties', social networks represent the milieu that configures markets,[29] Callon believes that it is precisely those establishments and elements (catalogues of goods, anonymity processes, financial controls, etc.) which reject networks and create space for calculability within the framework of transactions and by creating an arena that breaks down the constituents of an unregulated assemblage into its individual components. The calculability thus achieved (in Callon's theory) is based on processes of disentanglement, separation and dissolution affecting parts of a network, and on the destabilization of old relationship patterns in favour of a superior market interest. Amidst all the radically vague and flowing communication, fixations and frames are thus established which are able to act at a distance to weak social bonds. In brief: frames are placed on a fabric of fluid relationships to create a basis for economic co-ordination and transparent calculation.

This necessary process of alienation, on which the market is based (according to ANT), generates a wide range of frames and configurations in parallel to the creation of the social, psychological and communicative horizons of life. This process is advanced by a multiplicity of different interests that are equilibrated with the aid of economic calculation. As it is impossible to equilibrate everything, strategies are needed to deal with overflows. Relationships are created that do not appear in a calculated frame: as externalities that can be internalized to a certain degree, but also produce new externalities. Each transaction concluded on the market produces, in other words, business sidelines that escape the control of the central actors. For this reason, elements are also needed with which the externalities can be used to fine-tune calculated processes locally. Susan Leigh Star and James Griesemer coined the term 'boundary objects' for these elements. Boundary objects serve, on the one hand, to stabilize activities in a shared market environment and, on the other hand, to open up a market to other worlds. They have 'different meanings in different social worlds but their structure is common enough to more than one world to make them recognizable means of translation. The creation and management of boundary objects is the key to developing and maintaining coherence across intersecting social worlds'.[30] They facilitate the production of space for overflows.

If the neo-liberal drive to cheat the regulated market affects ever more people who are excluded from the rules, pressure will grow to create a different kind of exchange in which a series of agreements is annulled. As the informal market cannot obey the official rules, it can only rely on them to a certain degree. In order to maintain this trade structure, a network of informers, mediators, black marketeers, and middlemen is necessary. These networks, which are essential if an informal market is to function, form highly efficient boundary economies that can absorb the vast overflow produced by informal trade. A network generated by this collective involvement in business sidelines changes the rules by refusing to implement them.

Overflowing is also a procedure used by contemporary artists and architects to manipulate the frame for exploring geo-cultural processes in order to establish new connections. Working in a variety of different projects, they play a game with the sensory horizons against which we perceive, and enter into contact with flows of human beings, goods and capital. Through acts of networking, aesthetic and political practises change the frames in our perception: whether it be to manufacture a 'third space' for congregating, or to explore hidden phenomena, to sketch out alternative forms of exchange or to discuss the use of a certain space. A trading place altered in this way generates other by-products, a different set of encounters

Car boot sale in Holloway, North London, December 2005

outside the customary conventions. If the creation of overflow points is both a means of artistic destabilization and an instrument of control for regulating niches, then the question arises of how the two forces operate in relation to one another. Does this make it easier to finely adjust the way dominant market relations are configured, or to create a loose network of creative mergers whose activities may spawn new centres of activity and trade? To avoid espousing a model of polar opposition, we should, from the very start, view existing forces not as opposing movements, or as the clear opposition of two sides, but as a continual reciprocal play of vague figures and shadows that employs the moments of framing and overflowing as means of creating ensembles and controlling horizons without laying down rigid goals. The network-generating processes in experimental artistic and architectural activities demonstrate just how useful frames are for staking out relationship structures and co-ordinating co-operation, as, for example, in the joint production and distribution of knowledge. Drawing on analyses by the Swiss sociologists Urs Bruegger and Karin Knorr Cetina, Brian Holmes has pointed out how markets can be described as knowledge constructs. They act as epistemic objects within a sphere of technological and institutional frames. They are highly instable and variable in their nature as they always remain incomplete and changeable. This variability makes them seem alive and unpredictable. Holmes writes: 'What is at stake in the new art are framing decisions which set boundaries around productive groups (by constituting relational structures with unique parameters) and at the same time provoke displacements (by engaging processes of self-reflection and intervention on those constitutive structures).'[31] The point of this discussion on the interaction between economic controls and creative network production is not the question of frames as such, but that of using frames. In brief: the politics of their deployment.

Whether in social or in political terms, the new subjectivities emerging in the current flows of migration, displacement and resettlement become a nexus of contacts between conflicting worlds. They remain entangled but rework their entanglement within themselves, creating the subject as a fragmented battleground, as a potent and contested mobile arena. Informal markets come into conflict with the official social order because the economic system operates with different frames from those the victims of globalization need in order to survive. Owing to the pressure to exclude their sociality in different ways, the migratory economies that are linked informally with one another, also come into conflict with one another. The way in which the compensations produced by trade overflows can help to negotiate this conflict shapes the forms and realities of our coexistence. Does the establishment of such frames permit the emergence of a fruitful and shared terrain or does it signify the violent end of all differences? Does overflow result in one-sided profits or does it allow for the redistribution of shares – i.e. a self-determined reorganization of our subjectivities? A key moment in this discussion centres on operating outside existing political taxonomies. Many of the traditional taxonomies employed to gauge the dynamics of market activities are based on a conception of network structures as spatially linked phenomena with clear goals. The exact opposite applies, however, when we consider, say, the spatial reality of global network migration, where abrupt mobility,

Arizona Market
After the redevelopment by Italproject
Brčko, Bosnia and Herzegovina, 2006

Pacific Mall
Toronto, 2006

extreme uncertainty and radical openness are the defining parameters of this kind of social and economic structure. This also raises the question as to how, in the absence of stable and reliable prognoses, it is possible to calculate activities within this sphere. What is the 'market' and cognitive value of frames circulating in the informal sphere?

In a certain sense, informality veils the epistemological dimensions of trading places. Informality filters knowledge, so that only some of the activities on the market remain intelligible, while murky segments, dubious contacts and risky transactions are supposed to go undiscovered. Precisely this aspect of knowledge production – the displacement, blacking out and the active suppression of knowledge – is responsible for a great deal of those activities that define not only informal trade, but also the spatial appearance, dissolution and reconstitution of informal markets. The informal market is an instrument of concealed trade. In this sense, then, there is no logical operational structure, but only a contingent operating mechanism – a social fabric geared to opportunities, one that continually obeys the principles of reciprocity instead of being subject to the dictates of rational calculation. If they are to attract further transactions, AbdouMaliq Simone argues that forms of urban sociality arising in the shadows of the informal economy need to be able to shield themselves from the public eye, scrutiny and comparison. He writes: 'This process of assembling proceeds not by a specific logic shared by the participants but rather can be seen as a recombination of contingency. In other words, a coincidence of perspectives, interpretations, engagements, and practices that enable different residents in different positions to either incrementally or radically, converge and/or diverge from one another and, in the process of doing so, remake what is considered possible to do.'[32] One reason why framing processes are never completed when it comes to informal markets is rooted in the very nature of informal organization itself. Out of concern that such types of organization will become known, their frames are always provisional and mobile, so that they cannot be identified as having a tangible form or be assigned a familiar taxonomy. The movement of endless transfers is the dominant image of these global microstructures. Objects are transported ever further afield instead of being unloaded once at the 'right' place. The process of becoming of this particular place is rooted in the paths of movement themselves. Consequently, the process of transport is endless.

These sites of mobile and transient production, the deferral, obfuscation and active fragmentation of archival composition account for many of the activities that define informal trade as well as for the spatial emergence, dispersal and re-aggregation of informal markets: the lack of price tags, the false trade descriptions, the improvised trading places, the mutability of constellations, the devalued spaces filled with cultural hybridities, the abundance of strange objects that can be used for almost anything. They allow us to consider the potential of cultural encounters outside the formal market prerequisites of clarity, transparent calculation and disentanglement. The market, with all its hustling and bustling, creates a cacophony of sounds, voices and accents which finds its own social audience despite the fact that it does not resound in an 'ideal speech situation'. Scattered informal arrangements of stalls, trailers, trucks and tent cities arise that do not constitute what modernist planning would consider a rich form of cultural co-habitation, but as places that always exist outside the conceptual framework of urban planning. Irregularities appear that characterize the 'mosaic universe' of diasporic movements where things and beings don't converge on a totality, but assert their mutual relatedness by 'inventing junctions and disjunctions that construct combinations that are always singular, contingent and not totalizing.'[33] One could argue that the organizing principles of informal markets are not ideal blueprints for sustainable alternative economies, open community projects and new bonds of worldwide solidarity. They may, however, destabilize processes occurring within larger institutional and non-institutional ecologies that have been taken for granted for quite some time. This destabilization does not represent the transition from one system to another, but the slow and conflict-ridden process of multiplying systems in an amalgam of synchronicities that are mutually dependent and use one another. The alliance between informal and formal exchange systems spreads not through a strict process of creating frames but through never-ending entanglements in which overflows are not side-effects, but a mode of spontaneous operation, disguise, expansion and change. It is not despite, but because of this entanglement these structures transform themselves into something novel: they become amphibian forms. They multiply instead of disentangling themselves, producing a volatile body of knowledge which passes between informal global structures and the subject emerging from them.

1 Office of the High Representative (OHR) and EU Special Representative (EUSR) in Bosnia and Herzegovina, 'International Community to clean up trade at the Arizona Market, Brčko', *Press Release* (26 October 2000).
Online: http://www.ohr.int/ohr-dept/presso/pressr/default.asp?content_id=4092

2 Office of the High Representative (OHR) and EU Special Representative (EUSR) in Bosnia and Herzegovina, 'PDHR to attend the formal opening of the Arizona Market', *Press Release* (10 November 2004). Online: http://www.ohr.int/ohr-dept/presso/pressb/default.asp?content_id=33492

3 Office of the High Representative (OHR) and EU Special Representative (EUSR) in Bosnia and Herzegovina, 'Supervisory Order on the Use of Land in Arizona Market', *Press Release* (17 February 2001). Online: http://www.ohr.int/ohr-offices/brcko/bc-so/default.asp?content_id=5323

4 Office of the High Representative (OHR) and EU Special Representative (EUSR) in Bosnia and Herzegovina, 'Opening Remarks of Brčko Supervisor on land expropriation in Arizona Market at a press conference in Brčko on 25 July 2002', *Press Release* (25 July 2002).
Online: http://www.ohr.int/ohr-dept/presso/presssp/default.asp?content_id=27536

5 Srdjan Jovanovic Weiss, 'What Was Turbo Architecture?', in *Almost Architecture* (Stuttgart: edition kuda.nao, merz&solitude, 2006), 28.

6 Bruce Scott and William Nash, 'Global Poverty: Business Solutions and Approaches', paper given at the Harvard Business School conference 'Brčko and the Arizona Market' (1-3 December 2005). Online: http://www.hbs.edu/socialenterprise/globalpoverty.html

7 Azra Akšamija, 'Arizona Road', in *Designs für die wirkliche Welt. Designs for the Real World*, ed. Sabine Breitwieser, Generali Foundation (Vienna and Cologne: Verlag der Buchhandlung Walther König, 2002), 74.

8 Madeleine Rees (UNHCR Sarajevo), 'Markets, Migration and Forced Prostitution', *Humanitarian Exchange Magazine*, no. 14 (June 1999). Online: http://www.odihpn.org/report.asp?id=1054

9 US Agency for International Development (USAID), 'Bosnia and Herzegovina. ACTIVITY DATA SHEET. FY 2002'. Online: http://www.usaid.gov/pubs/cbj2002/ee/ba/168-031.html

10 Suha Özkan, 'The welcoming speech of the President of the 22nd UIA, World Congress of Architecture', *Programme* (Istanbul: UIA 2005), 10f.

11 Orhan Esen, 'Learning from Istanbul – Die Stadt Istanbul: Materielle Produktion und Produktion des Diskurses', in *Self Service City: Istanbul*, ed. Stephan Lanz (Berlin: b_books, 2005), 33.

12 Scott Lash, *Critique of Information* (London: Sage, 2001), 4f.

13 Orhan Pamuk, *Istanbul. Memories and the City* (New York: Alfred Knopf, 2005), 245f.

14 Ernesto Laclau, *Emancipation(s)* (London and New York: Verso, 1996), 79-82.

Arizona Market
First signs of urbanization: so-called Arizona 2
Brčko, Bosnia and Herzegovina, 2001

15 Alejandro Portes and William Haller, 'The Informal Economy', in *Handbook of Economic Sociology*, 2nd edition, eds. N. Smelser and R. Swedberg (New York: Russell Sage Foundation, 2005).

16 Pierre Veltz, *Mondialisation, Villes et Territoires. L'Économie d'Archipel* (Paris: Presses universitaires de France, 1996).

17 Pierre Veltz, 'The resurgent city', paper delivered to the Leverhulme International Symposium 'The Resurgent City' (London School of Economics, 19 April 2004). See also idem, *Le nouveau monde industriel* (Paris: Gallimard, 2000).

18 Anita Pozna, 'Guanxi: A safety net of personal relations in the transnational Chinese community', in *Re:Orient. Migrating Architectures*, ed. Attila Nemes (Kunsthalle Budapest, 2006), 20.

19 Elmar Altvater and Birgit Mahnkopf, 'Die Informalisierung des urbanen Raums', in *Learning from\* - Städte von Welt, Phantasmen der Zivilgesellschaft, informelle Organisation*, ed. Jochen Becker et al. (Berlin: NGBK, 2003), 24-25.

20 Karl Polanyi, 'Our Obsolete Market Mentality: Civilization must find a New Thought Pattern', *Commentary,* vol. 3 (February 1947), 109-117 [reprinted in *Primitive, Archaic and Modern Economies: Essays of Karl Polanyi,* ed. G. Dalton (Garden City, NY: Doubleday Anchor, 1968)].

21 Saskia Sassen, 'Why Cities Matter', in *Cities. Architecture and Society,* vol.1, ed. La Biennale di Venezia (Venice: Marsilio Editori, 2006), 47-48.

22 Mike Davis, *Planet of Slums* (London and New York: Verso, 2006), 178-185.

23 Ibid., 202.

24 Michel Foucault, *Society Must Be Defended – Lectures at the Collège de France 1975-76* (London: Penguin Books, 2004 [1975]), 29.

25 Michel Foucault, *Security, Territory, Population – Lectures at the Collège de France 1977-78* (Basingstoke: Palgrave Macmillan, 2007 [1977]), 349-354.

26 Ibid., 355.

27 Title of the essay is a reference to Foucault's market test of liberal governance.

28 Michel Callon, 'Actor-Network Theory – The Market Test', in *Actor Network Theory and after,* ed. John Law and John Hassard (Oxford: Blackwell, 1999), 181–195.

29 Mark S. Granovetter, 'The Strength of Weak Ties', *American Journal of Sociology*, vol. 78, 6 (1973), 1360-1380.

30 Susan Leigh Star and James R. Griesemer, 'Institutional ecology, "translations" and boundary objects: Amateurs and professionals in Berkeley's Museum of Vertebrate Zoology, 1907-39', in *The Science Studies Reader,* ed. M. Biagioli (New York and London: Routledge, 1999 [1989]), 503-524.

31 Brian Holmes, 'The Artistic Device – Or, the articulation of collective speech'. Online: *Meteors* (Université Tangente, 2006) http://ut.yt.t0.or.at/site/index.html

32 AbdouMaliq Simone, *For the City Yet to Come. Changing Life in Four African Cities* (Durham, NC and London: Duke University Press, 2004), 14.

33 Maurizio Lazzarato, 'To See and Be Seen: A Micropolitics of the Image', in *B-Zone: Becoming Europe and Beyond,* ed. Anselm Franke (Barcelona: Actar, 2006), 296.

# Arizona Market
## Brčko

CHINESE MARKET
FIRST 'ARIZONA MARKET', NOW FLATTENED
FORMER 'BAZAAR'

164

Arizona Market
After the redevelopment by Italproject
Brčko, Bosnia and Herzegovina, 2006

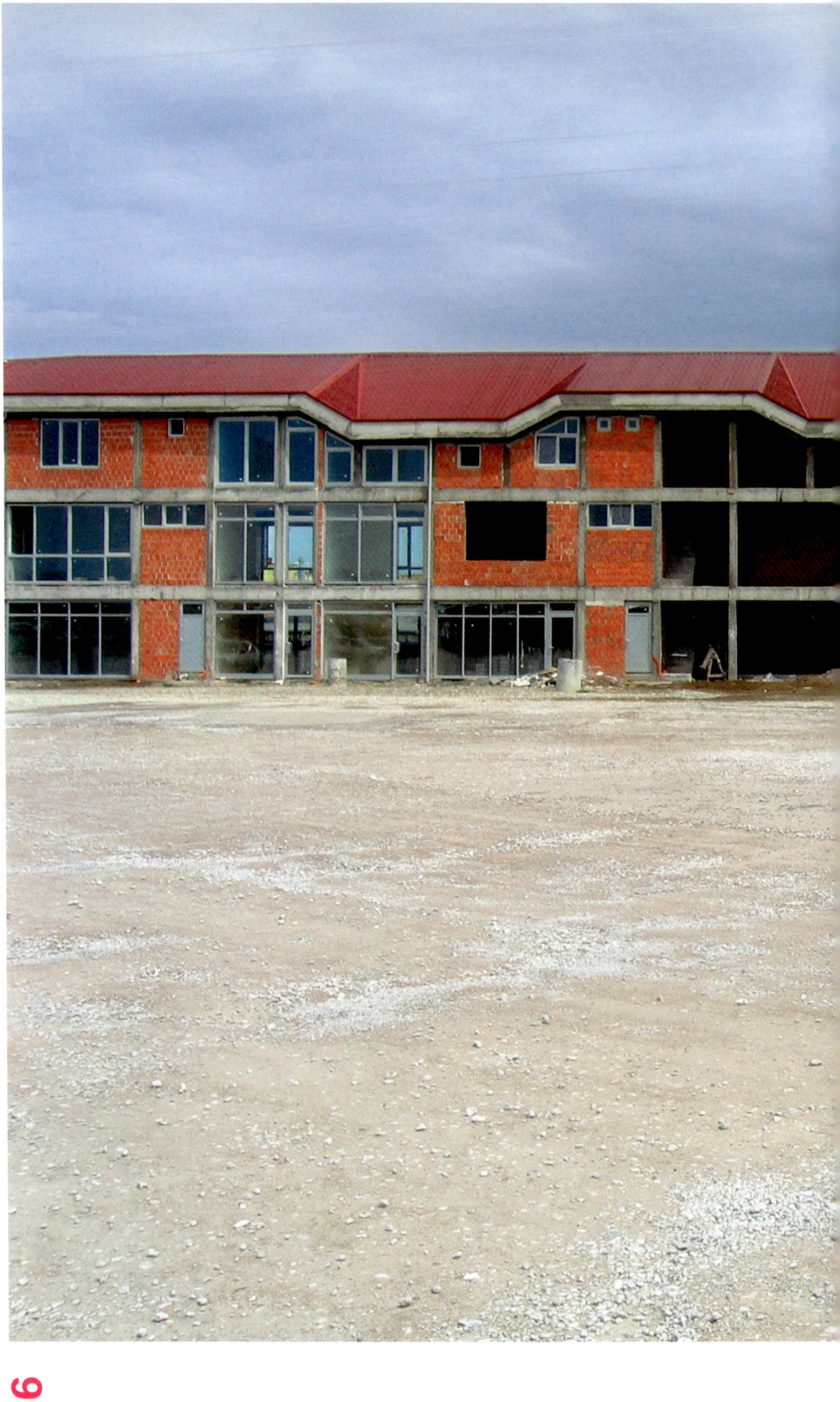

Arizona Market
Brčko, Bosnia and Herzegovina, 2006

SALON TEPIHA-ITISONA
STAZA-LINOLEUMA

OBUCA NA VELIKO KOD
JANJETA
ORANGINA

Arizona Market
Brčko, Bosnia and Herzegovina, 2006

CD
SHOP
"MM"
DVD
CD
CD

CD SHOP
DVD
MP3
DIVX
AUDIO I VIDEO KASETE
CD - DOMAĆI I STRANI
PLAY STATION
"ESTRADA-2"

CD shop and car wash along the road to Arizona Market
Bosnia and Herzegovina, 2006

Mobile CD selling along the road to Arizona Market
Bosnia and Herzegovina, 2006

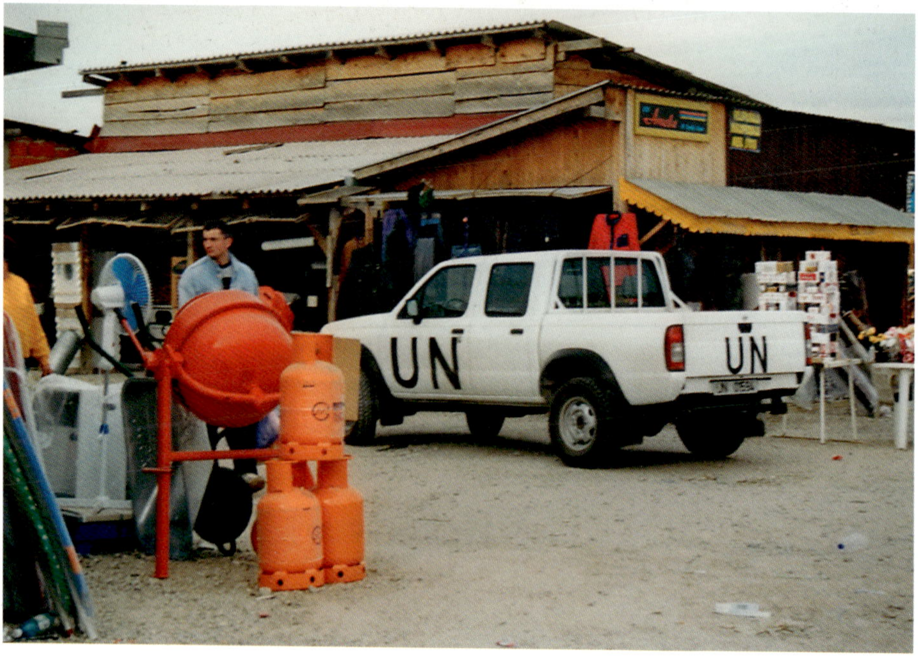
UN
UN

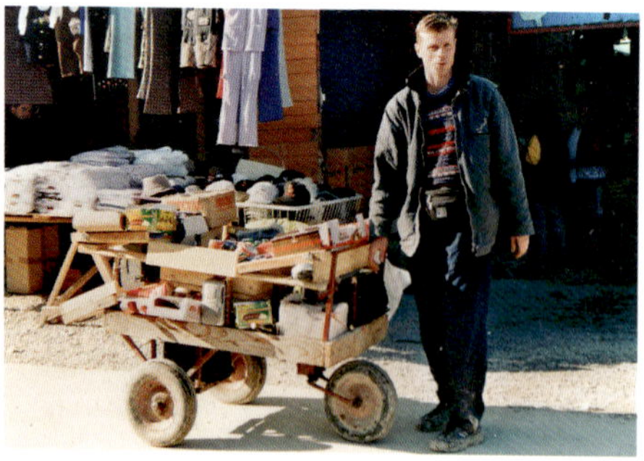

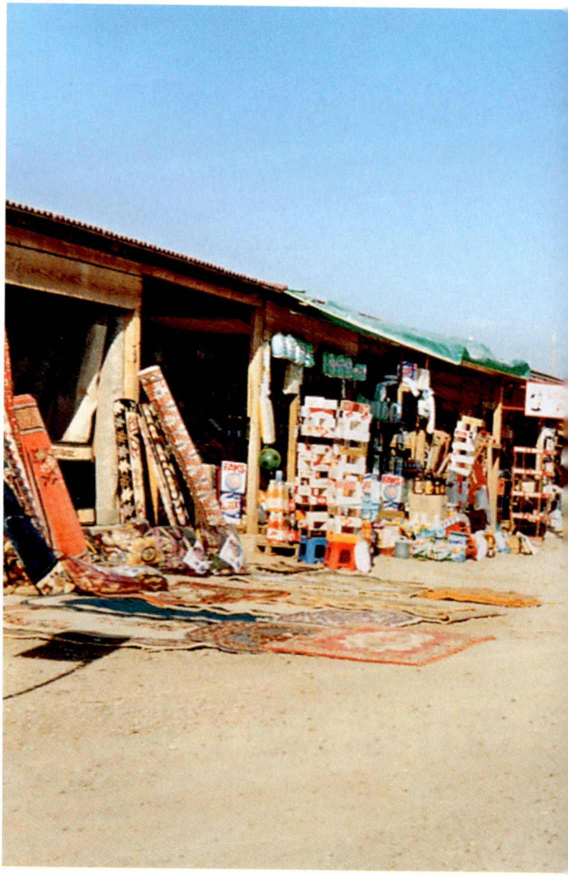

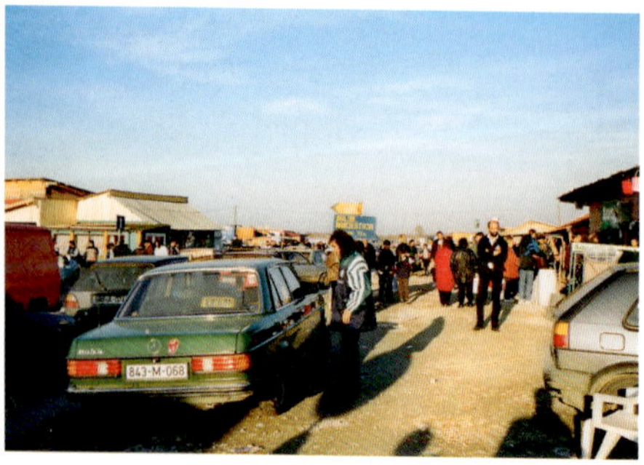

Arizona Market
First phase of the market: so-called Arizona 1, now demolished
Brčko, Bosnia and Herzegovina, 2001

**PM/HM:** Can you describe how you work together as B+B and how this collaborative curatorial practice has developed its particular approach?

**Sarah Carrington:** We were interested in looking at how you could present projects that were investigating people, or were using people, or were working with people, and how you could support the point of encounter more effectively. And also to try and create more of a terminology around that practice, because it felt like a lot of it was being simplified or dismissed or confused with community art legacies, so we were trying to look more closely at those distinctions.

**Sophie Hope:** It feels like now there are a lot of conferences, papers and symposia which investigate socially engaged art practice, and that's something that we felt has changed a lot since we've been working over the five years. But also something that's been really key to our practices is the UK context; it's our starting point. We've had a New Labour government since we've been working together and the impact on cultural policy has been so massive. It's interesting for us to find out how it's affected practice and how artists are really dealing with this issue of art being used to change social situations in quite a pragmatic way. But we are trying to think about how artists and curators can connect up beyond their own contexts by creating meeting points beyond the safety of their own back yards.

we've been really interested in finding examples that are emerging in different contexts. By demonstrating to audiences here that it's not just about New Labour, that this practice has a long legacy, and there are lots of people working around the world in different ways, and with different motivations, but they need to be given space. We're trying to inform audiences and open up ideas of what socially engaged practice might be – because I think it's such a loaded term here, now. For example, with *Trading Places*, the exhibition we did at the Pump House Gallery (London, 2004), we were bringing together examples of artists who were working with migration as an issue or working with migrants or refugee communities – and in Britain those projects are perceived as coming from a particular kind of government line, that 'you must include those who are socially excluded' and artists must make people's lives better and give voice to communities. And then we went to Vienna and found people saying, 'I want to give voices to migrants in my work', so we were interested in where was that coming from, was that to do with some sort of trend, or was it to do with a genuine social conscience, and if it was, what do they really want to change and how do they think the art is going to change it? So by bring-

ing projects from that context to the UK, we were saying that these artists are doing this not with a governmental or cultural policy baggage, so how can we access that here, and how can we learn from that approach here, and how could we also not simplify every single socially engaged project to be merely a response to funding? It's also the crisis of the left more widely. In the *Real Estate* exhibition we had in the ICA (London, 2005), we presented a project by Lorraine Leeson and Peter Dunn, which took place from the '80s to early '90s called *The Docklands Community Poster Project*. Lorraine said herself that she would

*Advanced Science of Morphology*
Neda Prlja, Novi Zagreb, 2006
*Reunion*, meeting points between critical art practices from southeast Europe and the UK

**PM/HM:** Part of your work closely follows creative practices and cultural networks in southeastern Europe; what kind of insights do you gain from this research in relation to working in Great Britain?

**Sarah Carrington:** There's such a preconceived idea about what socially engaged practice might be here, and

*Real Estate*
Billboard poster from the Docklands Community Poster Project, Peter Dunn and Lorraine Leeson, 1981-1991

174  B+B

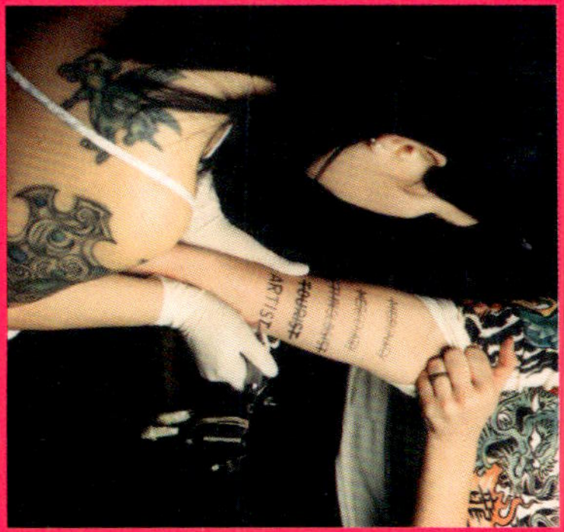

*Wild Places*
Lisl Ponger, 2000
*Trading Places*, migration, representation, collaboration and activism in contemporary art, 2004

175 never use that approach now because it was so specific to that moment; it was so anti-Thatcher and based in the ideals of the left at that time, that that's impossible now, because that sort of figure is no longer there, and there isn't the distinction at all. It's neoliberal policies in action now, and that's where culture is very useful as a kind of outlet, somehow.
We were just so interested in that history and the way that Lorraine and Peter worked so precisely with community groups, and their relationships to the local council. But it was so much directly initiated by the community with them, rather than by an agency or by a council inviting them in (which is how such projects might happen today), and so we just wanted to use that as a really important example of asking, when something isn't funded, or official in that capacity, what the potential of it is.
Nowadays, the project would be funded by the docklands corporation (the development body the community activists were working against), so that would be the difference. And they would claim that culture was really contributing to the change, that it was improving the residents' lives – whereas Lorraine was using her role to say: 'look: these people are really angry; we need to let everyone know about how angry we are, and how can I help you do that?', rather than having a brief from an agency that was about to affect communities' lives in a detrimental way.

**Sophie Hope:** Yesterday I went to see a project a friend is working on in Farnborough, as part of Slough Estates' big development project of the old Ministry of Defence airfields there and turning it into a big business and leisure park. Amy Plant is the artist and she set up a Friends scheme of local residents to decide what to do with a certain so-called 'public' patch of land within this development. I was talking to one of the local residents who was on that Friends scheme that she set up, and his motivation for being on it is because he's worried about his house price; he's worried that his house price will go down because of the business park, so being involved in the Friends scheme is a way of him having a say on the proposed development. This raises the question, how is an artist implicated in supporting values, politics or principles they might not necessarily endorse or that could even be at odds with the point of the project. A platform such as the Friends scheme is a mechanism for people with different views and concerns to make decisions about a patch of 'public space'; it is not judging people's motivations for getting involved. For example, in the process of raising awareness of shared, communal space the art project might enable people instead to find a way to protect the value of their private property. The artists/initiators have to ask themselves if they are happy to facilitate such a process – how does it fit with their own politics and is this important?

**Sarah Carrington:** In *Reunion*, we have this structure in which the partners that we're working with will help to decide on how best *Reunion* will operate, so we haven't set down a structure. I think by inviting people we already know we have common interests with, and who know about us as well, it's more like we're actually learning from each other, and again, that we can look at how we maybe don't need to rely on institutions so much; how can we use a union structure – maybe just to pretend – to strengthen our work as independent organizations or as self-organizing groups; how can we use that as a model, and potentially then impact on infrastructure in south-eastern Europe as well.

**Sophie Hope:** Our networking, through *Reunion* for example, or attending conferences and symposia, is really floating on and supported by the things that we're trying to constantly shift, change and subvert or whatever. We're being paid to network, subvert and critique. The only reason we're here and we're doing what we're doing is because there's a capitalist system that keeps it afloat. So that is our big question: how can we sink it – but then do we go down with it?

**PM/HM:** Your *Reunion* project is very fittingly positioned in this context, trying to appropriate the space of institutional boundaries that such projects are usually exposed to. How do you structure this networking process and how do you keep it political?

# Matei Bejenaru

**PM/HM:** In 1997 you initiated the *Periferic* – International Biennial for Contemporary Art in Iasi. Given this programmatic name for a biennial, how can one approach 'peripheries' in the context of globalized art production?

**Matei Bejenaru:** Iasi is in northeastern Romania and has about 400,000 people. It has its own history, which might be seen from one perspective as a sad history, because the city lost everything it once had. It used to be the capital of Moldavia. The kingdom of Moldavia came into being in the Middle Ages and, with the advent of modern times, slowly disappeared. In the mid-nineteenth century, Iasi was still more emancipated than Bucharest. The idea to build a modern Romanian state was born in Iasi, and when it happened in the 1860s, the capital was moved to Bucharest. It was then that Iasi began losing influence and power, and Bucharest began growing. Romania didn't undergo industrial development until the late nineteenth century. Bucharest became a large city, while Iasi remained a small patriarchal and archaic place. Nowadays it's an interesting town with its own dynamics and different layers of culture – but it obviously didn't have the same chance to develop and modernize itself as Bucharest did. In my opinion, real modernization began with communism. Iasi is somewhat isolated and provincial, but not to the point that people want to leave.

I studied art in Iasi in the first half of the 1990s, and after graduation other young artists from the city and I 'invented' a small independent performance festival, called *Periferic*. From the very beginning it was a platform where we could affirm our artistic identity. In the first editions of the event we organized performances, as well as round tables and discussions about the status of art in our post-communist context. We tried to understand the potential of the place by relating our artistic practices to the local situation. *Periferic* grew more and more and was transformed from a local festival to an international biennial of contemporary art. In 2001, we founded the Vector Association, a non-profit institution that now organizes the biennial, runs a non-commercial gallery and publishes Vector Magazine. With its sixth and seventh editions, *Periferic* became a visible international art event in a place that was almost unknown. Now, we're trying to decide whether we should keep a biennial format in the future or not. There are so many biennials everywhere...

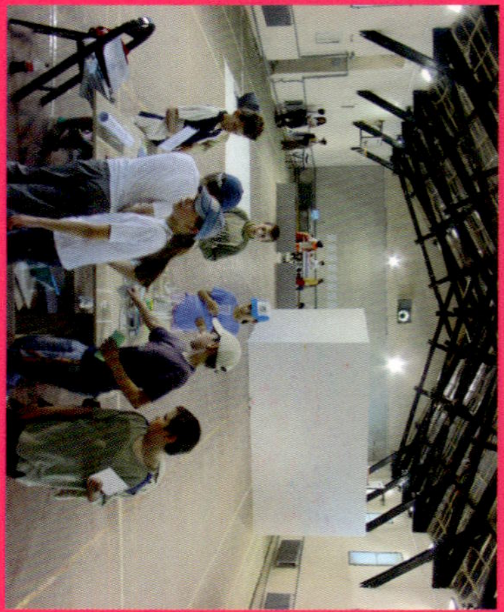

**PM/HM:** As an institution the Vector Association plays an important role for the local scene, while *Periferic* connects Iasi with the international art circuit. Given the remoteness of Iasi in terms of the art world, how has it been possible to develop such a multilayered structure?

**Matei Bejenaru:** I think it has developed gradually. First we established links with artists within Romania; then we slowly expanded by inviting artists from eastern Europe: from Hungary, Poland, Ukraine, Moldavia, Bulgaria and Turkey. After three or four editions, we'd established a network, but that network was based on personal relationships. Since 2002, I think this network has grown due to the Vector Association. For example, you didn't come here because we knew each other but because you'd heard about the project, about the fact that there was an institution where you could meet people and get information. Since 2002, the event has a certain level of international visibility, and this attracts people, especially people from the art world and professionals to examine the conditions under which art can be regarded as a gift, and what speculative components influence its realization and social value.

We're currently preparing *Periferic 8*, which will be held in October 2008. The curator is Dora Hegyi from Budapest, initiator of the Free School of Art Theory and Practice. The main topic will be 'Art as a Gift'. *Periferic 8* intends

*Why Children*
Curated by Attila Tordai
*Periferic 7*, Sports Hall of the Arts University, Iași, May 2006

*About art and the ways we look at the world* 02
H.arta, 2006
*Periferic 7 – Focussing Iași*, International Biennial for Contemporary Art, Iași, Romania, 12-30 May 2006

176

who are interested in Romania. If you Google 'Romania' in combination with 'contemporary art', 'Vector' and 'Periferic' will appear. And if you take a look at our website, you'll quickly see the event has been around for about 10 years now.
I think we're the most organized structure in Iasi to promote and debate contemporary art. There are some other independent young groups of artists – which is very good – but they don't have enough power to exist as institutions or to attract enough resources to develop projects. We have our own network in Romania and abroad. We're connected to different structures and different projects. It isn't easy, because we're in a transitional phase at the moment. Until now we've received a lot of money from abroad. We understand that for future development, for a medium- and long-term strategy, we need to find local resources. The Romanian economy is growing; there's more money available, even if it's not earmarked for contemporary art, and we have to fight to attract sponsors.

We want to continue developing educational programmes, for this is what we've been doing for a few years now. The idea is to stimulate an interest, a dialogue, and create an educated audience who needs this kind of culture. This will also encourage more sophisticated artistic production. This is important at the moment, because after we join the European Union in January 2007, we won't be receiving the same funds as we are now, though the transition will take a year or two. We need to understand exactly the kinds of money we're going to have to raise. Probably local money, from the municipality or from local sponsors... The City Council of Iasi has to support us – they can't really ignore us. Even if they don't understand what we're doing, they know we're enhancing the city's image and bringing in a lot of sophisticated people who are writing about Iasi.

**PM/HM:** How do you think this will change in light of Romania joining the EU; in other words, what impact will EU spatial policies have on your work in Iasi?

**Matei Bejenaru:** I don't think there'll be another EU enlargement towards the east in the next ten years. And I don't think it will be easy to integrate the Republic of Moldavia, on Romania's eastern border, just 20 kilometres from here. It will also be hard for Ukraine, which is another big neighbour. But Iasi might become a place of exchange for different structures and groups of artists from these neighbouring countries. More money will become available, and this will lead to the development of institutions and programmes related to regional cultural collaboration.
In 2006, we started a system of residencies, called *Backyard Residency*, a project with Novi Sad, Belgrade, Istanbul and Iasi. The aim is to encourage regional mobility and enable the exchange of ideas, because it's important for us to establish a stronger art network in the region.

Unfortunately, at present, we don't know much about each other. Romanians know very little about Macedonians, Bosnians know almost nothing about Romanians, and the Serbs have probably never travelled to Romania before. Both the Bulgarians and the Romanians are focusing too much on Brussels – they're now in a hurry to learn how to eat at the same table and follow the same rules of etiquette as Europe.

*Periferic 6 – prophetic corners*
Opening, Palace of Culture, May 2003

*Everything / Synchronisation 02*
Laura Horelli, 2006
*Periferic 7*, Iasi, May 2006

177

**178** **Helmut Batista**

**PM/HM:** As an artist and curator who has been living and working in Rio de Janeiro for many years, how do you feel about the current interest in Brazilian favelas in terms of social and political self-organization?

**Helmut Batista:** For me the favelas are just another part of the city, like Copacabana Beach. But unfortunately they are not in fact really a part of it. You won't find them on maps, even today, in 2007. I think most people who are living in these places nowadays don't think of themselves as living in a favela but feel they live in a community. There are 600 favelas in Rio alone. There are 'bad' and 'good' favelas; some even have banks and McDonalds. Some have no violence at all and others are really violent. The police can't go into many of them; there are only a few where they can. So there's a wide range of concepts for communities and small towns that organize themselves.
The favela 'Rio das Pedras' is one of the best examples of self-organization. And yet the body that keeps it under control are militia made up of ex-policemen, and they've taken justice into their own hands. They're now building themselves up into a sort of paramilitary force like in Colombia, though in these places a very different format. In these places than people do in France or Germany. People in the favelas use electricity from the system without paying. There's something like an unconscious system of wealth distribution: rich people pay large amounts to cover services to almost everyone else; poor people have to siphon off electricity and water just for the sake of surviving. They also don't pay any kind of taxes, for instance property taxes.
This has a big influence on certain aspects of the favelas and how they're built. If you don't pay for electricity, you build your house just with a hole for the air conditioner. So most of these places are very dark and the streets are very narrow, because they don't really need daylight. What's more, if you have an air conditioner, you want to keep everything closed. So the fact that electricity is 'free' makes the architecture completely different. The buildings are very close to each other and often have no windows or natural ventilation. If people suddenly had to pay for electricity, most favelas would turn into uninhabitable places – they'd be too hot to live in.

**PM/HM:** In one of your recent curatorial projects you invite other artists to travel with you across South America. Your car becomes a place of art production. Apart from that, it also exposes the role of intimacy in networking processes. What do you expect from these kinds of encounters?

**Helmut Batista:** I'm interested in building up networks. I think the only way for changes to happen in places like Rio de Janeiro is by establishing exchanges between international artists. I started the *ROAD project* with this intention in mind. Each time I make a trip I invite an artist. Am I a curator? Actually, I don't know what I am. I invite people whose work I like and with whom I can imagine having a good personal relationship. These trips are very intimate and we often stay longer than a month together, night and day. We start the trip with the intention of doing something that might seem like work; this does not necessarily mean that we'll end up working. Then we go from one place to the next and see what happens.

Célula Urbana do Jacarezinho
Rio de Janeiro, 2004

everybody pays a couple of reais per month for a variety of services, for example, to have the post delivered to their homes. Often there are no street names, so the postman has to take the post to the main community headquarters and from there people have to distribute it themselves. And although this system is very cheap, it reverses the concept of everything. It's a very ambiguous way of thinking of the city. You're part and you're not part of it. Then there are things like electricity: the public electricity company charges a lot in Brazil; I've read we pay more

ROAD project
Mobile residency, ongoing

Célula Urbana do Jacarezinho
Opening of a media and information centre in Jacarezinho, initiated by Bauhaus Dessau Foundation and the municipality of Rio de Janeiro, 2004

But it's not only about geographical dislocation. It's also about how we react to new situations. It's about discussions you don't usually have during your normal life and working time. It's not about holding meetings for two hours in a coffee bar with a curator. We are together 24 hours a day and share all our experiences. Meeting different people while travelling is surely a big part of it all and makes everything more possible and uncontrollable. It's this uncontrollable aspect that motivates us to carry out this project. You just don't know what you'll find and whom you'll talk to. So creating a network is just a side effect that happens pretty naturally.
An important part of these trips is the desire to build up a South American residency programme and network for research. Though not just for visual art, but for research in general.
So far we have made six trips. My car was confiscated on my fifth trip with Gabriel Lester, at the border between Peru and Ecuador. Paper problems and corrupt police made me lose the car, and from that moment on I had to rethink everything. The last project, Peru to Medellin, was done with the help of MED 07 (encuentros de Medellin) with artists Julia Rometti and Victor Costales and a rented car. In May 2007, a year after the confiscation and a year of struggling with Peruvian authorities, I received notice that there was nothing to be done and my car was now property of the Peruvian government. It's funny and stupid at the same time. It was a FIAT, but there are no FIATs in Peru, and the car was in urgent need of repairs. So I guess it will just rust away in some depot in Peru.
Since beginning in 2004, we've been to Argentina, Chile, Bolivia, Peru and Ecuador. I always leave my car wherever we stop and then just fly back with the artist. Until now only two of the artists have actually done a piece: João Modé, whose worked we showed at the Rio Film Festival in 2006, and during the last trip (Peru to Medellin) we finished up a project with Julia Rometti. I'm not interested in having an agenda. It's more about the

179

The question now is:
Who's going to pay for my lost car?
No foundation will do that, I guess.

just putting together shows. Primarily I'm interested in getting to know the right people in a personal sense. If the work is also nice, we have a perfect blend.

Coming back to the institutional level: I guess I have to define myself as a curator. Though this is just terminology. For me the question here is the challenge to produce something in different contexts. I invite somebody to do this and then we write all these bureaucratic papers to foundations so that they'll pay for it or at least help us. The art system just enables you to meet the right people and raise some money.

Things move very fast nowadays. Artists and curators hop from one exhibition to the other in a matter of a few days, even hours. What we are doing here is pretty much the opposite. There's so much time for real experience. This is a luxury compared to the way things are done in the institutional world of galleries and museums. After realizing six projects in three years, I think it's all coming together to form something that might be called *one* project, something that stands on its own. Doing this is also a political gesture, and the gesture itself is part of the dislocation and development of networks that is so important.

**PM/HM:** The networks you develop are critically informed by the creativity of personal friendships, while at the same time linking up with institutional settings and their demands. How do you manage to negotiate the tension between these different ends?

**Helmut Batista:** In Rio things have to be organic. Nothing happens here if you don't establish friendly connections. Actually, that's how I do things, too. On these trips I'm not interested in

experience we have together. There's no concept for an exhibition at the end. I just do a lot of kilometres and take a look at what's happening at these places and try to build up connections. We have already succeeded in bringing some Argentineans, Chileans and Colombians to Rio. Now some Peruvians are coming. So it's a long, steady and gentle work-in-progress. I call it the mobile residency programme, actually.

Célula Urbana do Jacarezinho
Rio de Janeiro, 2004

180

# Asya Filippova

**PM/HM**: PROEKT_FABRIKA is one of the most exceptional contemporary art spaces in Moscow. Can you tell us about your involvement in its formation?

**Asya Filippova**: Well, I'm the director of the factory, and this factory is a bit different from other art spaces in Moscow. Most such factories are no longer functioning production sites, but our factory still produces technical paper. It's still in operation, though of course it's very different from in Soviet times, because back then the factory was quite huge and massive, and supplied paper to all of Eastern Europe – Poland, Czechoslovakia, Yugoslavia and other socialist countries. Nowadays we produce very special kinds of paper and only for Russia. Anyway, production was reduced, and many spaces, mainly industrial workshops, became vacant. And then there was the fact that, besides being the director of the factory, I've lots of friends among artists and gallery owners. So one day I realized I might be able to offer a space for cultural projects like exhibitions. Initially, to be honest with you, my idea was quite modest. I just intended to open a space where my friends could have private exhibitions of contemporary art. I invited Elena Kuprina, who runs her own gallery, E.K. ArtBureau, to come take a look at the space. She said, 'Yes, it would be fine for exhibitions.' So we opened in January 2005, while the first Moscow Biennale of Contemporary Art was taking place. We started with a special project called *No Comment*, the spaces we had. In Soviet times, for instance, it was common practice for every plant and every factory to have a club for workers, so-called Palaces of Culture. So we also had this Palace of Culture, and one day I invited Elena Tupyseva over – she's the director of the contemporary dance company Tsekh, a well-known agency in Russia.

*Proekt Fabrika*
A contemporary arts complex occupying disused parts of a technical paper factory in eastern Moscow, 2006

*Global Photo Project*
Ivar Sviestins, 16-26 June 2006

an exhibition of young Russian artists. And then the project actually started to develop and grow on its own. Not that I planned it that way; it was not my strategy to invite theatre people or musicians or architects. But people began coming and were interested in the spaces we had. I showed her this space, our Palace of Culture, and she decided to renovate it and turn it into a venue for contemporary dance and concerts. It started sponsored by the Ford Foundation. I to grow all by itself – we just selected people with similar ideas, similar preferences, and so on.

Then, last summer the Ford Foundation invited us to New York. We went there and took part in a workshop called 'Sustainable Art Spaces', and that's when I understood that we were probably a sustainable art space, too. In the first year, maybe a hundred people came to see the exhibition and about ten people rang me up from time to time to ask about my plans, but by no means did everybody in Moscow know about us. And then suddenly a few months ago, I realized I was being literally inundated with offers, questions and ideas, which may mean this is the right moment to move on to the next level.

**PM/HM**: How is PROEKT_FABRIKA connected to places outside Moscow?

**Asya Filippova**: Well, usually everything is concentrated in Moscow itself. There aren't so many contemporary artists living in, I don't know... Saratov or Voronezh. Many artists came here quite some time ago and are now working here in Moscow, which means we mostly deal with people from Moscow and St Petersburg. Though sometimes we have joint projects with the National

Institute of Contemporary Art and the National Centre of Contemporary Art. They arrange yearly festivals of young artists and engage artists from all over Russia, because they have some departments and representatives in other towns and regions of Russia. In other words, they're in a position to set up such a network, and it enables us to collaborate with people from outside Moscow. Regarding foreign artists, well, it's absolutely absurd and strange, but it's easier for us to deal with artists from Germany, Holland or Sweden than with artists from other parts of Russia, because the rest of Russia is completely different from Moscow – actually Russia has two completely separate parts. In June 2007, I was at the Trans Europe Halles meeting in Vilnius, and I'm now thinking about joining this network of independent culture centres.

**PM/HM:** Given the economic boom of business developments in central locations in Moscow, do such experimental and hybrid spaces have a future?

**Asya Filippova:** Well, I don't think we'll be able to continue producing technical papers for another 20 years. I don't think that has a future, because it's pure madness to try to produce anything in the centre of Moscow.

At the moment our premises include three different kinds of areas: one area is production itself; the second area consists of so-called cultural spaces; and the third, offices for rent – this is the commercial sector. In the future, I think production will be relocated away from here, while the so-called cultural sector will grow and develop. Nevertheless, there will still be enough space rented out to pay the bills, space for anybody who wants to come here and wishes to rent some offices for their business... or for other commercial purposes. Anybody can come here and rent a space, but of course I prefer to deal with people who are connected with creative industries – art, advertising, photography, cinema. In the past few months a lot of people have asked about spaces for film studios, for example, maybe this will be a new branch. Though there will always be two parts, one for cultural activities, and another for commercial offices and spaces for lease – for all those who enjoy being around people who are different than they are, people who dance, sing and make installations.

**PM/HM:** Is there a network of collaborations or do the different kinds of people who have ideas for certain projects compete with one another?

**Asya Filippova:** I wouldn't say they compete all that much, not really. I was afraid it would be competitive, but I don't think that's the case at the moment. I don't know about the future, but I've heard some say there isn't enough contemporary art and culture in Moscow, not enough for the number of spaces, but I don't know. Competition doesn't exist yet, because people from, let's say, Winzavod or ARTStrelka come by, too, and we communicate and exchange ideas. And if an artist from ARTStrelka needs a space for a studio, then his or her manager or gallery owner sends the artist to me, which means artists come here and if I can offer them something then I do. I would not call this a network, but it's about contact; though then again, a very limited number of people is involved. Everybody knows everybody else, every gallery owner knows all the others, and every cultural manager in

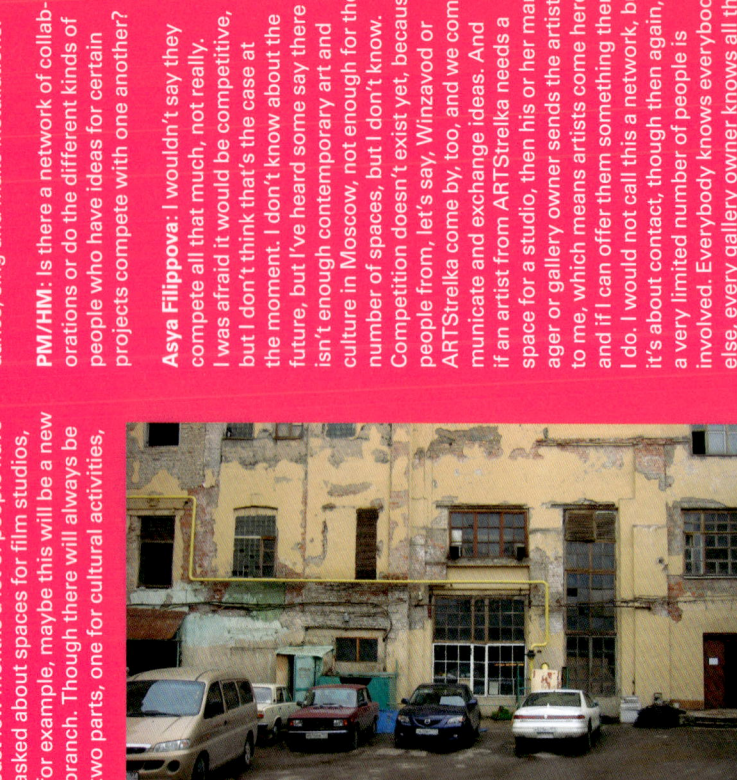

Proekt Fabrika, Moscow, 2006

Former Palace of Culture (workers' club), now used by the contemporary dance company Tsekh, 2006

Printing office of the paper factory which houses Proekt Fabrika, Moscow, 2006

Proekt Fabrika, Moscow, 2006

**183** Moscow knows most of the others, too. We communicate and collaborate, more or less. I should also mention that our factory is different from other art centres – from the start it was not conceived as a commercial enterprise. Maybe it would be better to be as well planned and commercial as some of the other spaces, but we are just completely different.

**Asya Filippova**: Well, of course, I hope people are interested in our site. But I also know lots of people come and take a look at our buildings, and are either shocked or lost – so I have mixed feelings about it all. Though I myself like things how they are. I like the appeal of this site and the people who work and live here, and they like it too, though sometimes, they come and ask me: 'Well, Asya, aren't you planning to renovate the buildings after all?' When is it going to happen?' So, yes, there's a special atmosphere, I know this and they know it as well, but it doesn't mean it will always remain this way. Of course we will renovate some things, but I hope the original architecture will not be ruined by plastic siding, business-centre architecture, and the spirit will remain the same.

**PM/HM**: Do you think that the aesthetics of this complex play a role in how artists feel when they come to your place, or are you thinking of renovating the building to enhance the cultural appeal of the location?

# 184   Oliver Ressler

**PM/HM:** Your work as an artist focuses strongly on economic issues and, in particular, on forms of alternative economics. How do you feel about the relation between such an artistic practice and political activism?

**Oliver Ressler:** In 1999 I produced an installation called *The Global 500*. It focused on the 500 largest transnational corporations and how they related to a discourse on economic globalization. The exhibition was presented for the first time some months before protests against the World Trade Organization in Seattle. I was extremely interested in what was happening there, and produced two films related to the anti-globalization movement in 2001/2002. The movement also demonstrated how Margaret Thatcher's well-known slogan 'There is no alternative!' can't be true. At the time I had some knowledge about alternative models, though not much. So I started to investigate and through some books I got further information about different concepts and models for a system that would no longer be capitalistic. The project *Alternative Economics, Alternative Societies*, which I started in 2003, is the largest I have ever worked on, and I continue to do so today. At present it consists of 16 videos on different models and concepts for alternative economies and alternative societies. Some are historical ones, such as the workers' collectives during the Spanish Civil War or the Paris Commune or workers' self-management in Yugoslavia during the 1960s and 1970s. Very elaborate new economic concepts have also been included, such as 'Participatory Economics' by Michael Albert, and concepts for a new organizational structure for society as a whole, for instance 'Inclusive Democracy' by Takis Fotopoulos or 'Libertarian Municipalism', which is presented within my project by Chaia Heller. I have also included interviews that focus more on certain methods and aspects, ones that might be of interest when considering alternative economies or societies. For example, the concept of 'Free Cooperation' by Christoph Spehr or an interview with John Holloway on changing the world without taking power. The idea of my project is to present a variety of different projects, concepts and models. Some of them come from a more anarchist background, others from a more socialist background, but all of them aim to contribute ideas for organizing society differently and fighting for such alternatives – that's why I think all these authors can be considered activists to some extent.

Within the scope of this travelling exhibition and the 16 video interviews I conducted, I have tried to give a condensed view of those aspects of the concepts that I regard as most important. The videos are between 20 and 37 minutes long, and give the audience an opportunity to access these concepts. People walk around the exhibition space and choose videos according to their interests. If they are especially interested in a concept they may go to the author's website or buy the book. I think the project *Alternative Economics, Alternative Societies* provides a helpful structure to generate discussion and make some of these concepts more accessible, and lots of activists have used it as a tool in the twenty-one cities in which it was realized over the last four years.

**PM/HM:** Your video works are available for purchase on your own website, which yields a concept different to traditional ways of distributing art; it creates a link between your work and broader audiences outside the gallery system.

**Oliver Ressler:** I try to keep the prices of my videos low so that many individuals, libraries and universities can afford to buy them. I work together with some distributors and the DVDs are sold for between 15 and 35 euros. So it's possible to buy a DVD just like a book. It's important for me not to limit the videos or my art production in general to a very small group, but to make them accessible to a broader audience. Especially since the videos are often related to social movements

*Venezuela from Below*
Oliver Ressler & Dario Azzellini, video, 67 min., 2004, stills

*Alternative Economics, Alternative Societies*
Exhibition project, 2003–ongoing

**PM*HM:** How do these documentation's of existing social and political movements introduce a notion of implicatedness which extends the given forms of political agency?

**Oliver Ressler:** I think it's clear that I'm very dissatisfied with the existing capitalist society. So the main focus of my work over the last 10 years has been on how to get rid of this society and contribute to the creation of a new one. Some projects are more on the level of analysis and critique of social reality; others focus on forms of resistance; still others – such as the two projects on Venezuela or *Alternative Economics, Alternative Societies* – concentrate on ideas that might be of importance when considering how to achieve a new society. I share many ideas with activists, and may be considered an activist myself, so that on certain occasions my position is one of a participating, involved observer. Sometimes the work provides a kind of platform for existing ideas, at other times it creates ideas that do not come directly from activist practices but may still be of great importance for activists. So for me there's no formula for how my work functions; there are different strategies and different focuses from project to project.

or resistance groups. I work on these issues because I would like to support the groups and their struggles, and I think the best form of support I can offer is by doing this work and making it available not only to people who see exhibitions or visit film festivals, but also to activists, who are usually very interested in learning about other activists' strategies and experiences, ones that might affect their own strategies.

I worked together with Dario Azzellini on two films about Venezuela. Our concepts were in both cases so clear and accessible that even people who didn't have knowledge about contemporary art understood and valued them. Many supporters of the Bolivarian process use our films for education and mobilization in their communities, and for me it is an important aspect that the films I've realized are being used

conducted the interviews. They came to Caracas even though some of the factories were in cities 15 hours away. The workers made this effort because they were, on the one hand, proud that they or their colleagues had appeared in the film and, on the other hand, they were extremely interested in finding out what workers in other factories in the country had to say about their struggles and how they organized their factories.

Since my work relies on the time and collaboration of others, I'm interested in sharing and returning the work to them in exchange. Many artworks I have produced are available completely free. In 2001 I did a magazine together with Martin Krenn that was related to the *Border Crossing Services* project; it was distributed via direct mail to 12,000 households in the border region between Austria and Slovenia. It presented what migrant organizations and anti-racist organizations in Austria and Germany have to say about crossing borders, illegalization, migration and the European politics of exclusion. It helped to reveal their viewpoints to the rural area between Austria and Slovenia, which was a highly militarized Schengen border at the time.

by the very activists without whom it would not have been possible to make them. For example, the film *Venezuela from Below*, our first collaborative film on Venezuela from 2004, is now also being distributed on the black market in Caracas. You can buy the DVD there for less than a euro. For someone who wants to see the film in Venezuela, it is probably easiest to buy it on the black market – that is, for those who missed the broadcasts of the film on TV. When we presented the film *5 Factories – Worker Control in Venezuela*, which we finished in 2006, 300 people came to the first presentation in Caracas, many of whom were workers from the factories where we

185

# Transient Traffic
## Istanbul Topkapı

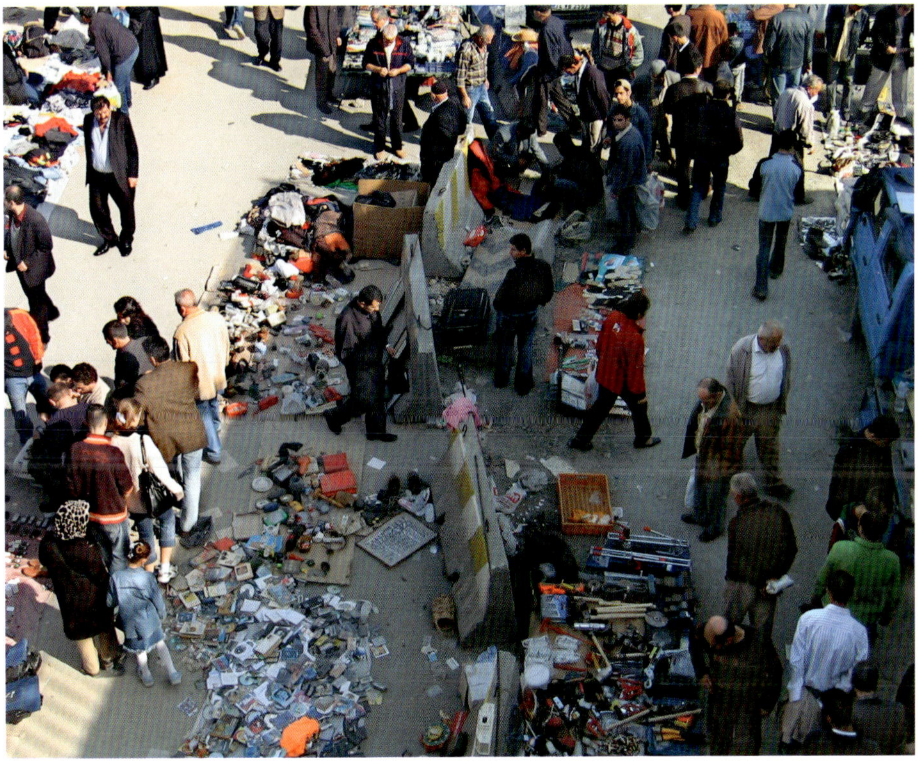

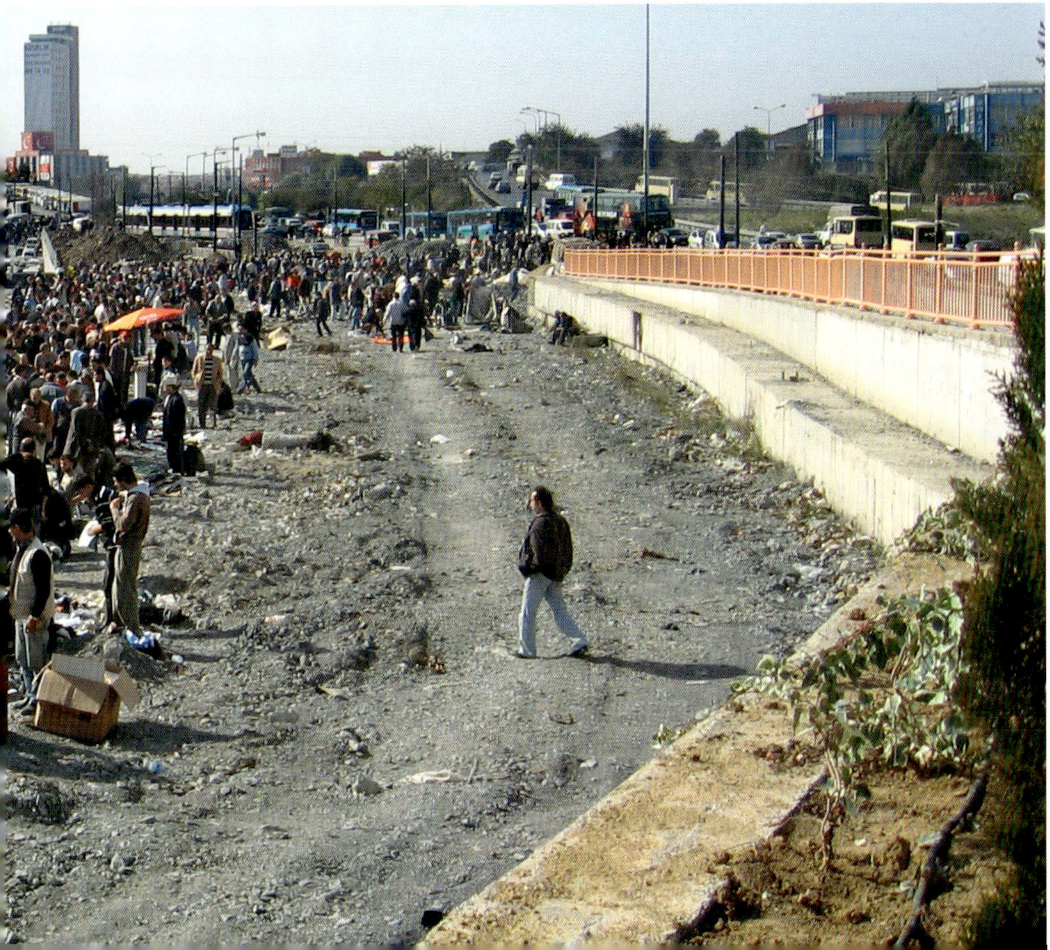

188

Informal market along the construction sites of transport projects, Istanbul Topkapı, 2005

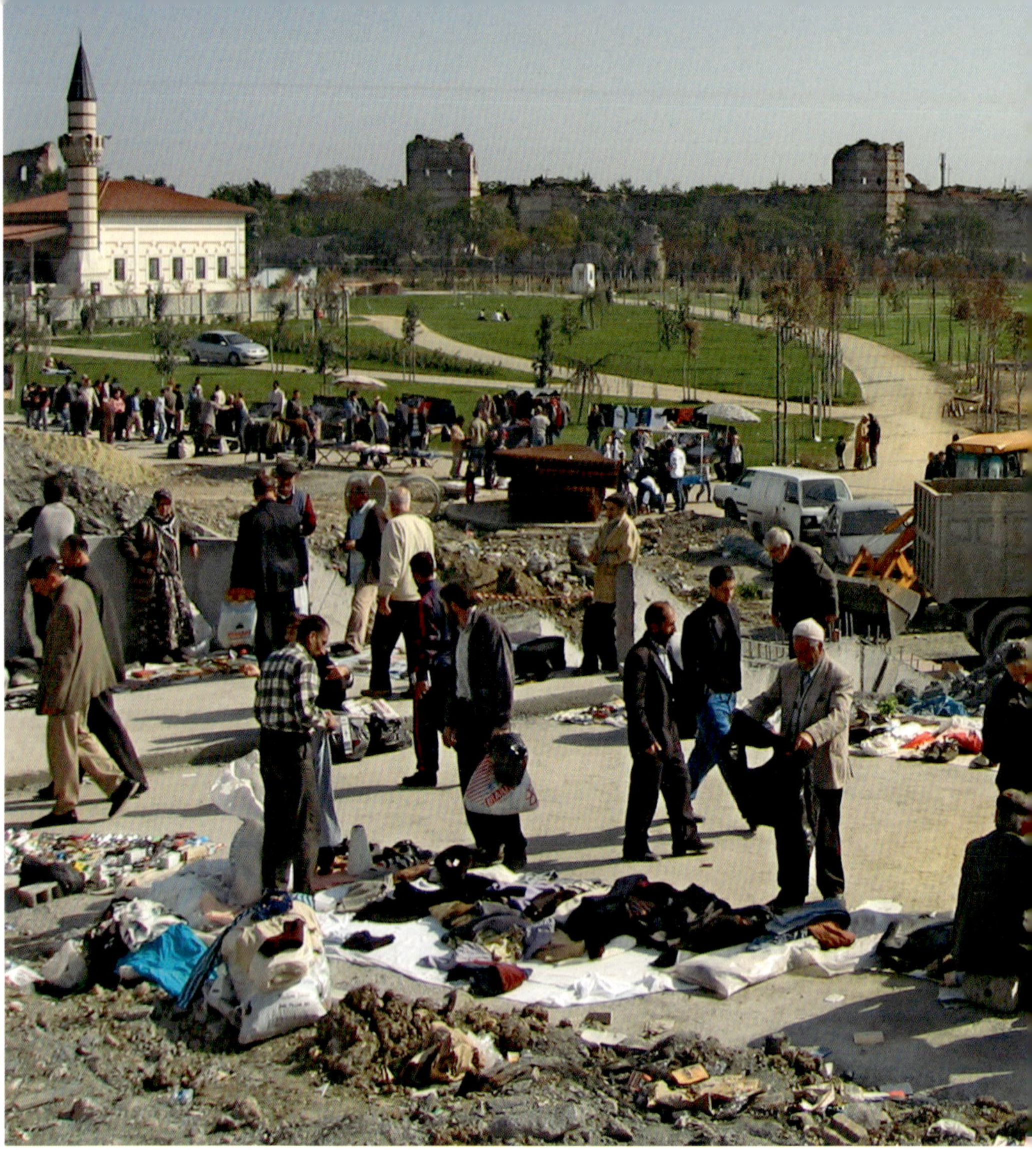

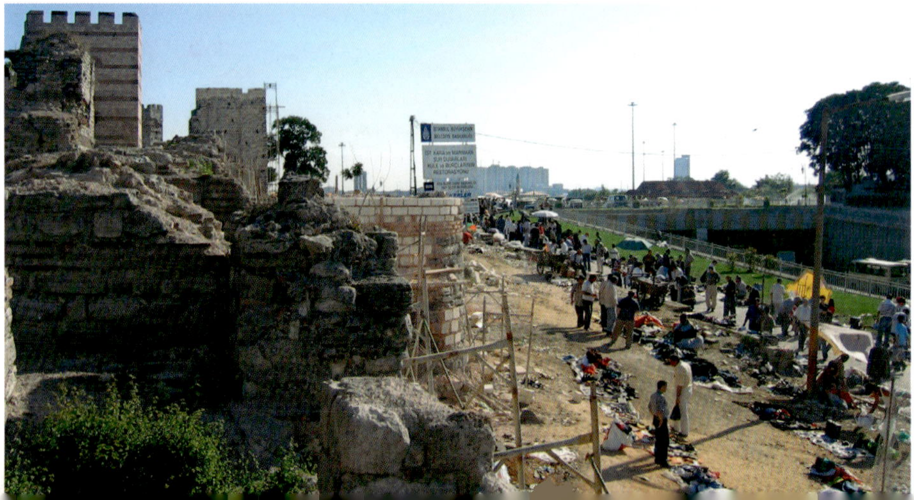

Informal market along the Byzantine city walls and Londra Asfaltı, an arterial road to the west, Istanbul Topkapı, 2005

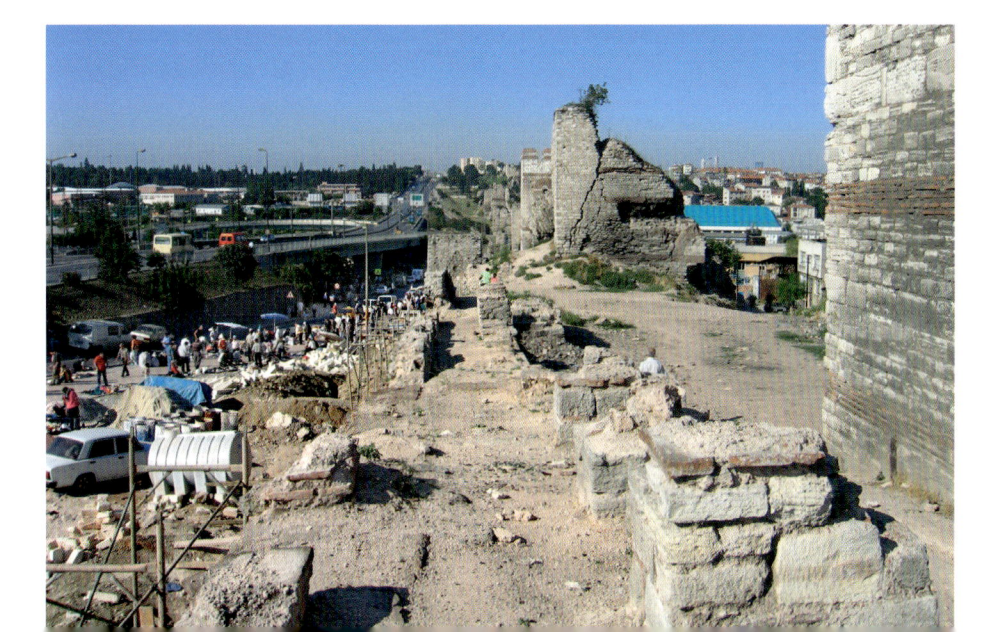

# Visiting Stalin
## Moscow Izmailovo

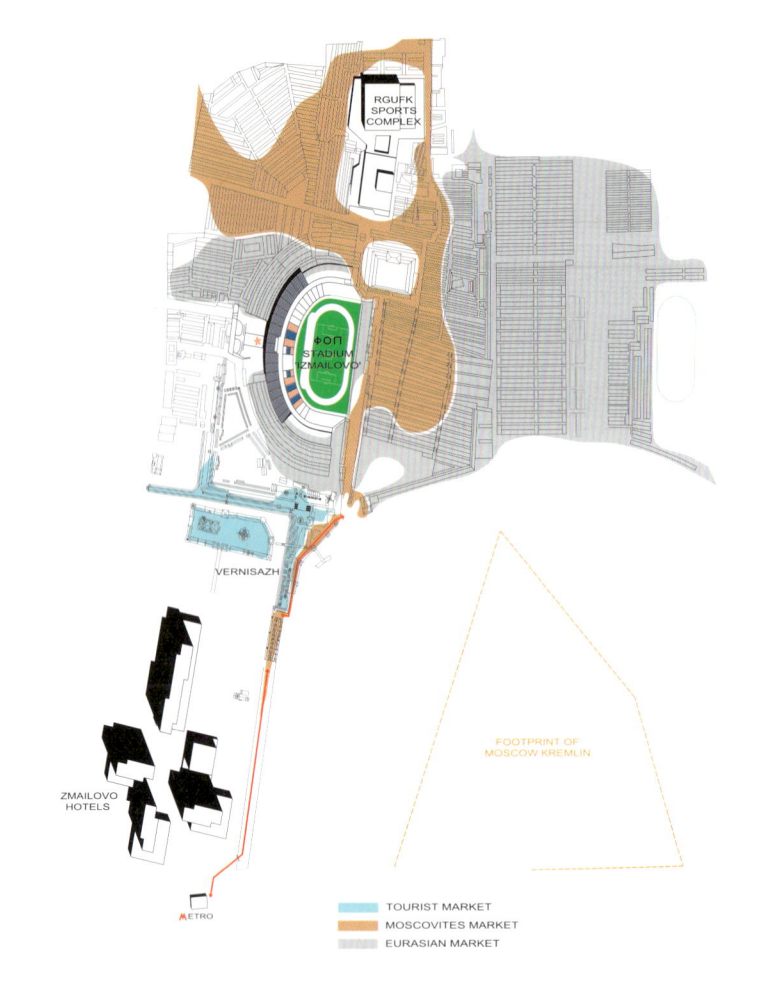

RGUFK SPORTS COMPLEX

ФОН STADIUM IZMAILOVO

VERNISAZH

IZMAILOVO HOTELS

FOOTPRINT OF MOSCOW KREMLIN

METRO

- TOURIST MARKET
- MOSCOVITES MARKET
- EURASIAN MARKET

Vernisazh
Mock Russian village with arts and crafts market catering for international tourists, Olympic Village of the 1980 Summer Games in the background, Moscow, 2006

Vernisazh, Moscow, 2006

Cherkizovsky Market, Moscow, 2006

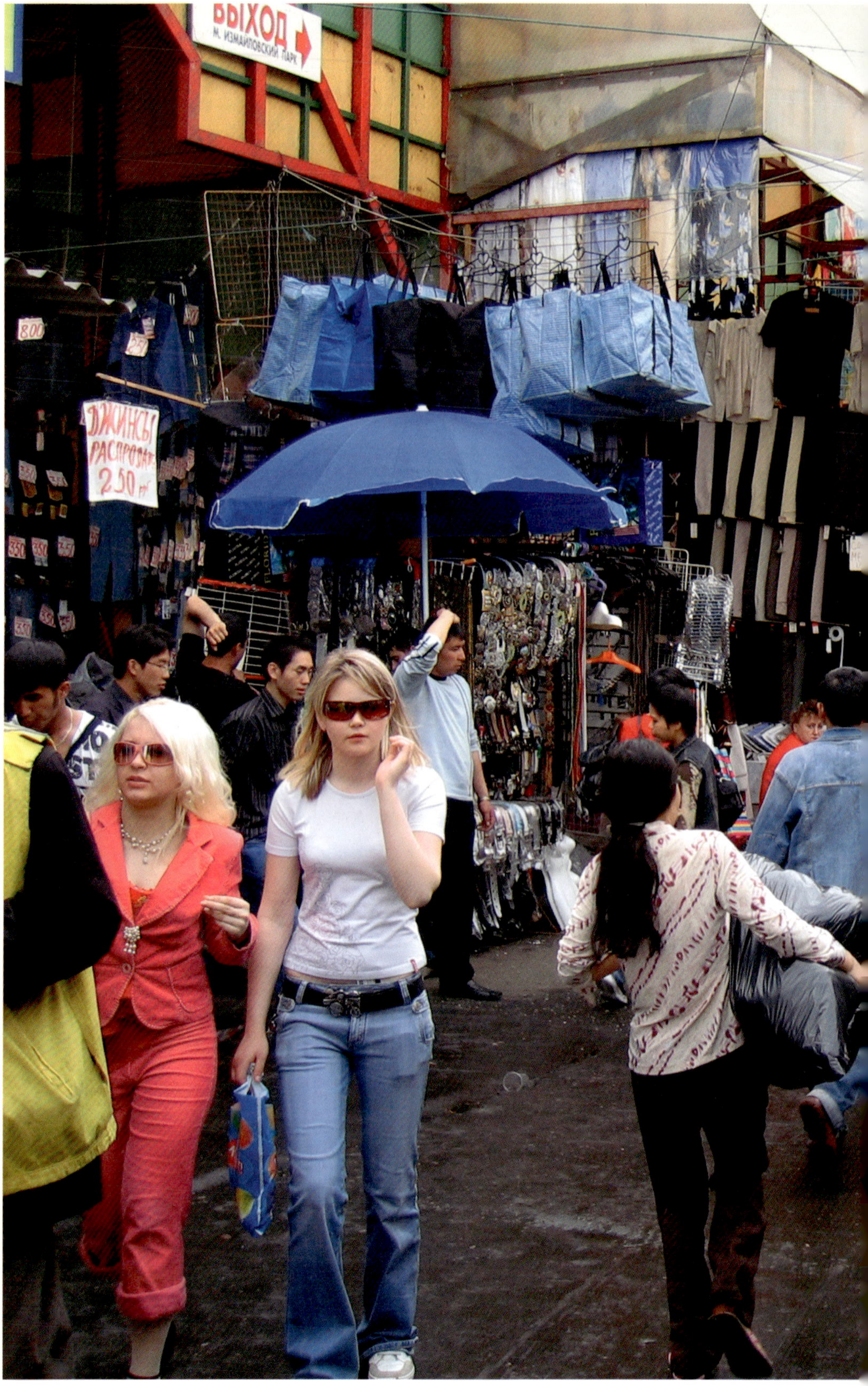
ВЫХОД
М. ИЗМАЙЛОВСКИЙ ПАРК
ДЖИНСЫ

Cherkizovsky Market
Large Eurasian market surrounding the former Stalinets Stadium in the northeast of Moscow, 2006

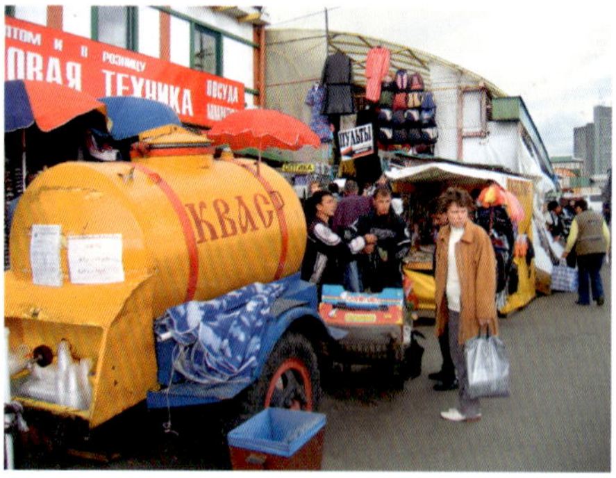
РОЗНИЦУ
ТЕХНИКА
ПОСУДА

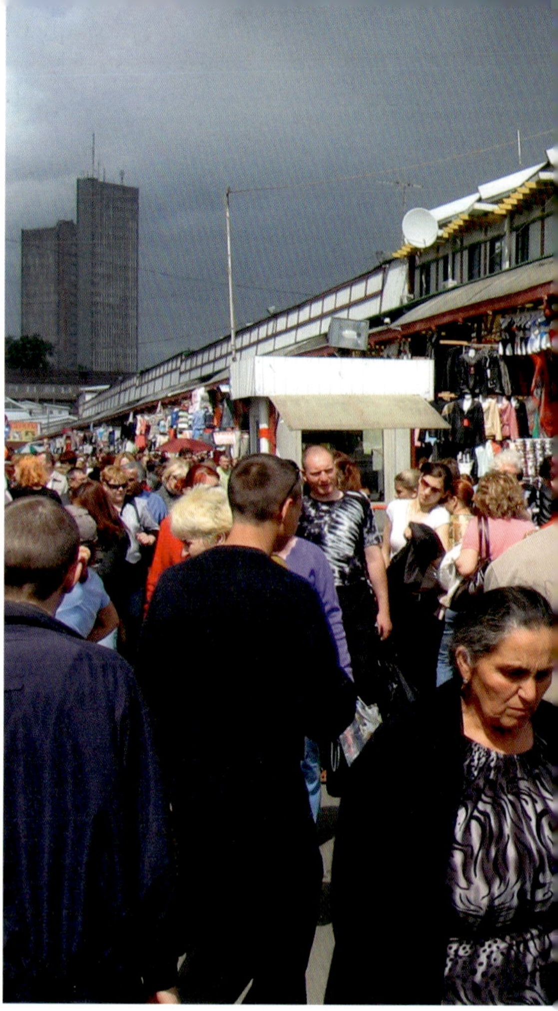

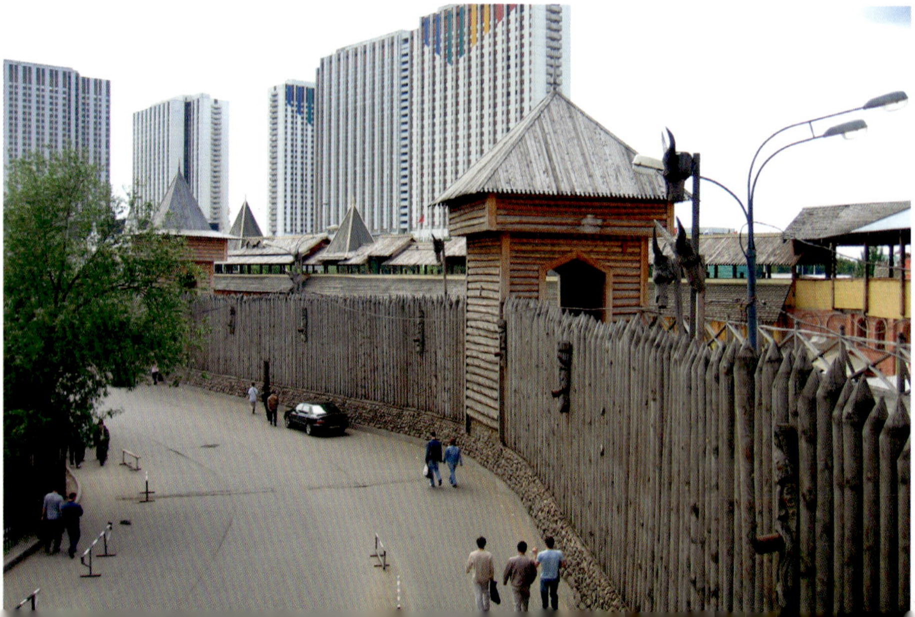

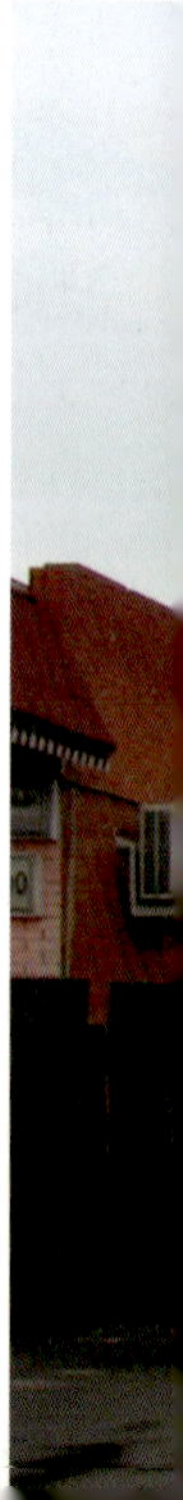

Cherkizovsky Market, Moscow, 2006

Vernisazh, Moscow, 2006

Vernisazh, Moscow, 2006

Cherkizovsky Market, Moscow, 2006

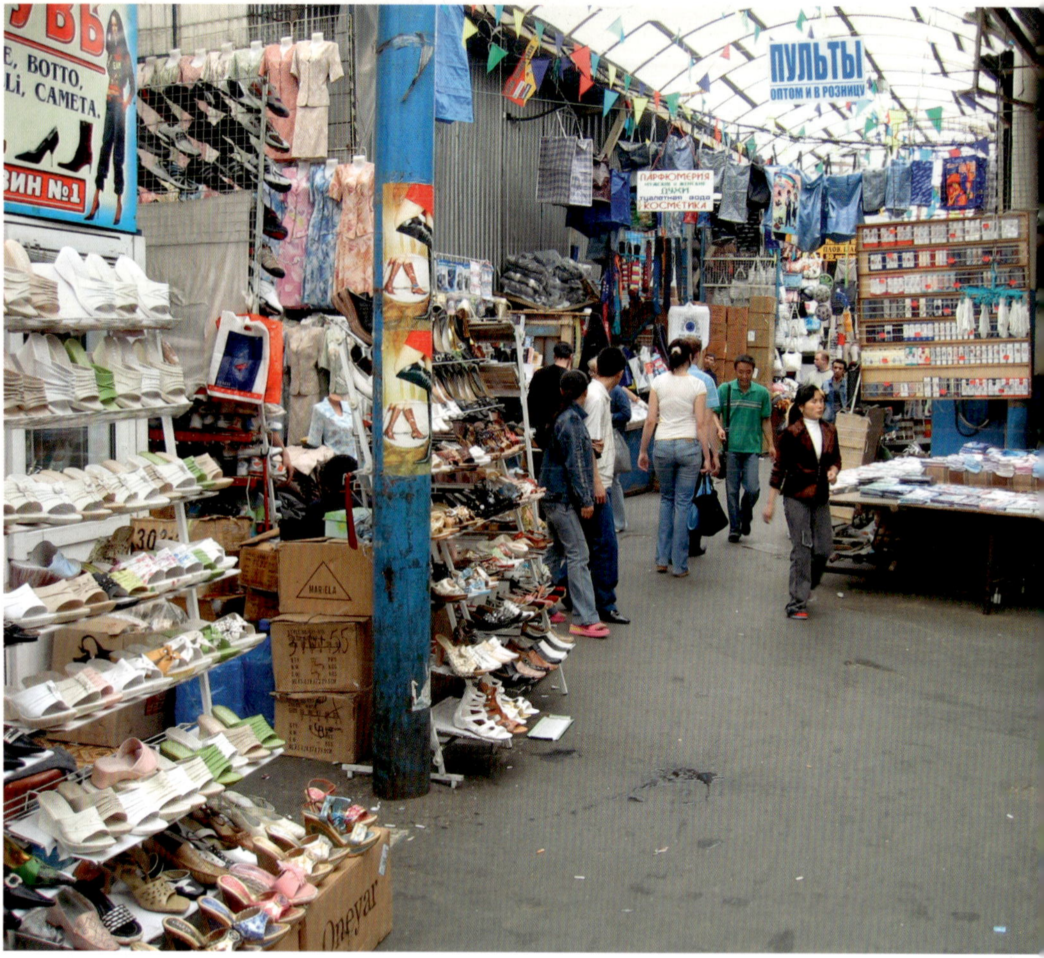
ПУЛЬТЫ
ОПТОМ И В РОЗНИЦУ
КОСМЕТИКА

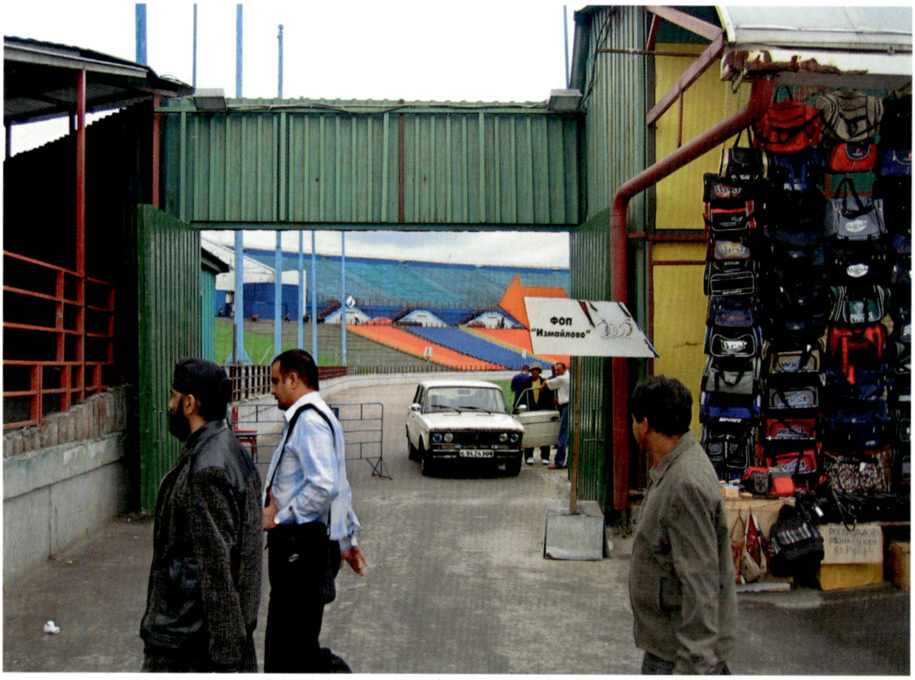
ФОП
"Измайлово"

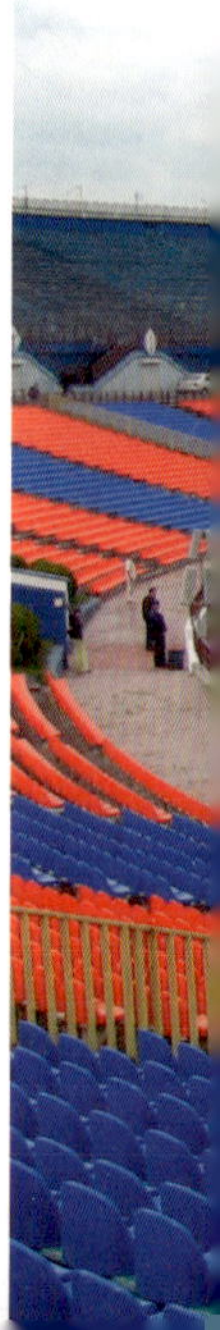

Cherkizovsky Market, Moscow, 2006

FOP Stadium
The former Staliners Stadium built above Stalin's secret bunker in the 1930s, Moscow, 2006

# The politics of 'cityness' and a world of deals

AbdouMaliq Simone

## INTRODUCTION: LIVING ON FRACTURES

How does the actual lived experience of increasingly heterogeneous and networked urban spaces redefine core assumptions about urbanization? What happens to the idea, the practice and the limits of the city when it appears, as is the case across much of the Global South, not as a planned convergence of productive forces, but a disjunction of disparate forces? As the city becomes a place where different kinds of actors are grabbing what opportunities they can, how is it possible to concretize collaboration among 'citizens' and constitute a shared set of references? The objective here is to begin to conceptualize an urban politics able to deal with the intensifying ambivalence generated by urban life – where possibilities and vulnerabilities are thoroughly entangled, and where there are no unequivocally clear trajectories of development or change. Thus, it focuses on the notion of 'the deal'.

Cities are largely fractured spaces. In the domains of regulation and governance, cities encompass areas where the prevailing practices of production, exchange and financial management are exempt from the law and regulations that would otherwise be applied, using either a specific geographical position (offshore), economic designation (export processing zone, special use area); or temporal period (state of emergency) to mark the exception.[1] There are also areas where state administrations and civil institutions lack the political and economic power to assign the diversity of activities taking place within cities – i.e. buying, selling, exchanging, collecting, dissembling, stealing, importing, fabricating, residing, etc. – to specific bounded spaces and rules of operation, or the responsibility of clearly designated actors.[2]

Much urban planning and regulation is simulated planning and regulation. In other words, these practices serve as a veneer for masking what are often highly speculative and unmonitored interventions into built and social environments. For example, at the outset, the massive redevelopment across Southeast Asia of centrally located industrial areas, ports, rail stations, warehouses, commercial districts and the residential districts articulated to them has no certain economic disposition. It is difficult to assess the terms through which the implantation of large residential and commercial complexes, research and development centres and entertainment zones could be considered economically viable, particularly as occupancy rates, sales volumes and outputs are interwoven with more ephemeral or symbolic considerations of value. Additionally, these developments are ensconced in a calculus of fungibles, where what they can be used for and spatially or financially connected to is potentially converted into something else than the original intent. As such these developments don't so much 'exist for themselves' as they aspire to become increasingly valuable facets of larger packages that bundle together real estate, varied financial instruments and shifting trajectories and forms of investments from which new conditions of management, urban politics and taxation schemes will become inevitable. At the same time, the massive size of some developments not only reflects the conjoining of new construction technologies and finance, but also practically and symbolically constrains what surrounding land and infrastructure could be used for in any foreseeable future.[3]

In other words, architecture, infrastructure and land development are being used as instruments to compel, some might say extort, new urban institutional and social relations, from how decisions get made, what is viewed as possible or useful to do in cities, how financial responsibilities are to be defined and risks assessed.[4] In most instances, low-income as well as many middle-income residents are pushed to the peripheries of the city, which once serviced and connected to major transportation grids themselves become objects of speculation as cheap land is acquired by those with the aspirations to build big in ways prohibited by more centralized locations. Where the presence of heterogeneous residents within the central areas of cities enabled a kind of mutual witnessing of how each implanted themselves in and operated in the city, if not elaborating various complementarities among them, the push to the periphery, while not necessarily stopping an inflow of low-income residents, at least in their pursuit of occupations, renders it an often opaque place.[5]

Surrounding the core of the city, the periphery, with its intersection of the scattered remains of old projects and those of the new in various states of completion – from factories, shopping centres, housing developments – persistent rural economies, informal and formal low-income settlements, poses an uncertain future for this core.[6] If the massive redevelopments of the centre compel new logics of urban regulation, they also imply an increasingly difficult process of attempting to understand and manage relationships between the core and a periphery whose social dynamics are increasingly difficult to understand and predict. If the resultant economic motivations operative within the central areas produce more substantial connections to exterior economies and cities, with heightened dependence on dynamics upon which any individual city exercises limited control, then the additionally resultant disjuncture between central and peripheral urban areas, as well as different categories of urban actors, introduces a large measure of vulnerability to these redevelopments in the long run.[7]

In the Global South, many so-called megacities are usually thought about in terms of an urban fabric that has been overwhelmed, of a sociality that no longer is subjected to coherent forms of articulation and aspiration, and of institutions that no longer are capable of exercising authority over the use of materials and space. But this conventional view might be productively tempered by instead thinking of urban capacity in terms of the ways in which all cities are things in the making by virtue of the speed and intensity of diverse positions and practices of inhabitation that are not, or at most weakly, channelled by clearly demarcated trajectories of operation, spatial use, resource appropriation and social interchange.[8] In other words, at the heart of city life is the capacity for its different people, spaces, activities and things to interact in ways that exceed any attempt to regulate them. While the absence of regulation is commonly seen as a bad thing, one must first start with the understanding that no form of regulation can keep the city 'in line'.

Complex municipal politics of everyday regulation prevail, where different actors who share communities, quarters or districts attempt to work out incessantly troublesome connections between land, housing, services and livelihood that are not held in any stable and consistent relationship with each other. In much of the urban world, this process still wards off power being fixed in the hands of narrow interest groups or sectors. This does not mean that 'big men' or 'big women' don't exist, nor does it mean that there are no boundaries between, for example, religious authorities, technical expert groups, political parties or civic associations. But through multiple and shifting memberships, overt and covert alliances across business and family activities, it is never crystal clear just what hat any actor or group may be wearing (operating through) at any given time. The process, then, of trying to figure out just what is going on requires people to expand the field of whom they talk and pay attention to – a game that in turn makes working relationships more complicated.[9]

But unless these working relationships are attempted in ways more capable of engaging the plurality of social mechanisms in operation, the bulk of formal economic, political and administrative interventions will spend too much of their money and time attempting to disentangle populations from the particular ways in which they organize relationships with materials, places and infrastructure that are often either weakly visible and comprehensible or dismissed as illicit and unproductive.

Additionally, residents then spend too much time preparing themselves for ways in which the application of new laws, policies, regulations and rules increases disorder because they impose specific mandates on who, where, and how urban residents are to legitimately gain access to space, opportunities and resources. Such disorder can be tripped up if individuals are already operating, knowing themselves, or taking livelihood through many different 'places' and 'roles' at once. But instead of the energies, intelligence and time of residents being spent trying to put together new forms of collaboration, these defensive manoeuvres sometimes reiterate the salience of the prevailing definitions of identities, territories, occupations and sectors – and residents simply try to 'distribute' themselves across as many of them as possible. Instead of overturning categories such as patron and client, leader and follower, artisan and worker, man or woman, people will attempt to split the conventional categories in multiple sub-categories and find opportunities to fit into them at different times.

Instead of operating as a way individuals come to act decisively and creatively within the public realm, these informalities can actively de-link more and more aspects of everyday life from the possibilities of generating a larger, common interest.

Still, it is clear that in many of Europe's most ethnically, economically and culturally mixed urban districts, the necessary articulations among different occupations, networks, and resources needed in order for such mixtures to be sustained emanated from often highly peculiar local initiatives that melded aspects of religiosity, carnival, recreation, guerrilla mobilization, showmanship, public relations and even illicit financial schemes.[10] Such platforms are not necessarily or even frequently organizations like political parties, voluntary associations or community based organizations. A written set of agreed upon rules and procedures seldom exists, nor do identifications of membership. In fact, such platforms are sometimes barely discernible as 'organizations' at all, but still exist as an almost invisible form of collective action – where people regardless of whether they consciously know it or not are acting in concert with others to make something happen. There is no one identifiable agenda, no consensus, not even clear results to which everyone could agree.

But the capacity many residential quarters demonstrate to do what they can to make some kind of viable urban life cannot be imagined, let alone do 'its job' without finding ways to draw lines – make connections – among the scores of gatherings, consultations, reciprocal favours, improvised work crews and business ventures, group prayers, publicly shared meals, clandestine exchanges of goods and hastily pieced together solutions to extended family or neighbourhood crises that take place in a wide range of settings across the urban terrain – from markets, abandoned hotel ballrooms, deserted factories and crowded intersections. Urban activists and planners must always look out for these more invisible, provisional or improvisational occasions for collective action that enable participants to try out new ways of acting and collaborating.[11]

## URBAN VIRTUALITIES

The progressive impoverishment and deindustrialization of many cities, coupled with the enormous demands made upon urban space, engenders a reliance on the sheer density of inhabitants, actions and their associational possibilities. The focus on the 'second-hand', on piracy, repair and the improvisational re-assemblage of cannibalized objects and information creates specific ways for people to feel and think in the city. Additionally, cities give rise to capacities to participate in specific networks specializing in their own forms of translocal flows and exchanges – for example, the vast trade in illicit goods or the extensive spread of religious economies.[12]

To speak of the virtuality of urban residents with limited means remains a necessary but dangerous task, undertaken without the confidence of clear political or ethical guidelines. It is clear that urban life is becoming more precarious for the poor, as their worlds are reduced to the basic confines of a 'bare life'. We conventionally understand this bareness as the narrowing of one's everyday conditions and spaces of operation to a minimal domain of safety or efficacy. In physical or social environments that are highly disordered, unhealthy or dangerous, it is usually assumed that individuals put together small islands of security or order from which they can better deal with the unhealthy or insecure conditions that surround them. For example, the way in which the inside of a one-room cardboard squatter's shack is meticulously maintained in the midst of overflowing refuse at the exterior, or the way in which so-called marginalized populations attempt to secure a predictable territory of operation and hold onto it tenaciously. But in circumstances where effective mediations capable of connecting urban residents to predictable sources of provisioning, meaning and collaboration disappear, the 'bareness' to which residents are left is the city in its 'cityness'. Here, people 'let go' of any prospects for consolidating a sense of stability, and instead disperse themselves across discrepant urban spaces. They become scavengers of any small opportunity.

After all, 'cityness' is a world of sentiments, gestures, gazes, talk and movement, all of which potentially could be intersected, interrupted and redirected in ways that draw the attentions of those who otherwise would not pay attention, or conversely, let people 'slip under the radar'. So the job of urban life is to maintain a heightened sense of engagement with all that could ensue from applying a barely indiscernible gaze, of overhearing a conversation, of securing an almost invisible yet strategic proximity to others, of interrupting the flow of events ever so slightly but powerfully so as to move something in another direction.

Of course such thickening engagements with the 'raw materials' of urban life – its sheer densities of affect, bodies, and action – is not necessarily virtuous. Increasingly, residents have to cope with an incessant preying upon their own vulnerabilities. For cities are environments of trickery and deception as well as the forging of solid relationships of mutual dependency. Because such dependency is often relied upon in order to make ends meet, residents are all the more vulnerable to deception. Fellow residents who otherwise might look out for each other can also give information to thieves about who may not be in their apartments at certain times. Sexual partners are especially held in suspicion as the rights each individual in the couple would normally grant also leave them vulnerable to being taken advantage of. Residents may be conscious about displaying any weakness, and continuously watch what they say about themselves, what they wear, the routes they travel, and the company they are seen with. Even in cursory relationships with neighbours or associates, a person cannot be construed as having significant relationships, in the event that others to whom these associates may owe money or are perceived to have harmed in some way decide to hold that person as somehow culpable. Chances must be taken without the availability of a reliable means of calculation or with calculations that are intensely singular.

Yet, as urban systems are placed under more complex and comprehensive regimes of calculation, the question becomes the following: to what extent are those residents who always have to come up with new tactics for living through these vulnerabilities acquiring important proficiencies for circumventing the efforts by various economic elite to make the city more secure just for them? As cities must manage the events relevant to their well-being across larger scales of consideration, there is a tendency to privilege new forms of calculation, modelling and surveillance. These reinforce the notion of cities as patchworks of impersonal and atomizing institutional controls applied to fragmented uses of particular places and services which, in turn, enforce a sense of normative consumption – where people are subject to institutionalized codes about what constitutes legitimate behaviour and over which they have little possibility of direct negotiation.[13]

How should actual or possible interrelationships between what are, on the surface, disparate forms of urban virtuality be conceptualized? Are there ways in which informatics, networks, practices and capacities produced from different materials and relations of power intersect to keep urban spaces open and available to different actors and aspirations? For example, in the historical commercial districts Sukhumvit-Petchaburi (Bangkok) and Deira (Dubai), a deteriorated yet still functioning infrastructure of urban services and built environment is appropriated by a wide range of African actors often working in different forms of syndicated arrangements with others of the same and divergent nationalities. Entrepreneurial groupings can be both well-defined, with stable participants and sectors, and also highly fluid and malleable, with different forms of collaboration and trade being constantly renegotiated. Each has to work out ways of operating in dense commercial spaces, forging competitive but often complementary relationships with local retailers, landlords, transportation agents, commercial brokers and local officials in order to support the transactions necessary to move goods, services and people along specific trajectories of exchange. While structured commercial associations and companies have been established, most of these transactions operate under the radar and move opportunistically across different kinds of goods and markets.

## THE ANATOMY OF THE DEAL

Access to land, under-priced yields of power and water, extensions of grids and service roads, vertical construction rights and exceptions to regulations of all kinds are the purview of deals that, if not directly countervailing the rules and normative planning procedures, often stretch them. Municipal regulations and planning systems do avail themselves of a wide range of participatory mechanisms, technical proficiencies and data bases. Yet, the ability to respond to political and economic exigencies and to get things done within the temporal frameworks of specific administrations and budgetary cycles frequently requires procedural short-cuts and the appropriation of potentially synergistic effects that stem from the capacities of particular 'operators' to mobilize labour, finance and other services that cut across sectors and territory.

Competencies and jurisdictions are often demarcated and institutionalized in ways that entail clear limits to what any given agency, organization or company is entitled and available to do. Therefore, projects and programs that require the application of many different kinds of entities at various times often require administratively complex negotiations and scheduling pertaining to the way these entities work together and apply their abilities to a particular site of intervention. Organizational structures tend to emphasize the efficient replication of responses through standardization. For what they do has to be applied to many different kinds of clients and situations. So those who can offer, for example, the ability to put together construction crews, cartage, waste removal, cut-rate overtime, supplementary finance, political connections and media spin in one – on the surface – seamless package are vital to municipal administrations and have to be rewarded in ways that are often difficult to accommodate within prevailing rules and norms.

This ability to mobilize certain potentialities inherent in the heterogeneity of the city is usually incumbent in those operations that are able to manipulate the networked effects that scale enables. Yet frequently, such operations emerge from highly localized yet intensive positions within specific sectors or neighbourhoods that capitalize on apparently incommensurable relations – i.e. the intersection of social identities, functions, and domains that usually wouldn't be expected to work together. So that those who can connect, for example, religious leaders, gangsters, financiers, professionals, journeyman and civic associations begin to cover a lot of ground and spread out across other territories. While big players such as multinational consultant firms, technicians, contractors and property developers may have the size and coverage to deliver unrivalled efficiencies, they may not have sufficient local knowledge to expedite getting things done.

So the terrain of the city, its enclosures and publicities, its variously configured channels of movement, its organization of different venues where people are assembled in different densities and forms of association and its applications of work and attention emerge as specific compositions of agitation, stillness and receptivity. Points that intersect different energetic possibilities – what Deleuze has labelled 'topological points' – then can produce many different kinds of physical arrangements, so that embedded in different urban sites is the capacity to produce different scenarios and knowledge that are present all along but may never yet have been actualized. The frenzy of market trading grounds next to the recesses of quiet conversations over tea next to the receptions of official delegations next to the openings for the inflows and outflows of people and goods all produce a productive volatility that continuously reopens the relationships that everything has with everything else. It reworks the forms of stability and interchange. The contiguities and relations of residences, offices, warehouses, roads, factories, entertainment halls, plazas, parks, stations, and ports constitute a 'combinatorial richness'[14] capable of generating various effects and scenarios that exceed being the imposition of an organizational frame.

The absence of such a frame is not chaos or unpredictable fluidity. Each emergent element – each concrete spatial arrangement that ensues as a particular crystallization of energetic encounter – can be held together by intercalary entities that enable these elements to be connected.[15] Although these dynamics can be elaborated across the different languages of physics, chemistry and the social sciences, the point I want to emphasize here is that in urban politics the intercalary element is that of the deal. The deal is the connecting tissue or the catalyst that brings together the different scenarios and dispositions continuously produced and transformed by the intersecting intensities of urban life – its different speeds, reactions, rhythms and affects.

Of course urban history is full of the evidence of deals of all kinds, and the purported maturity of urban political systems is signalled by the capacity to curtail, regulate and tame the nature of deal making. Yet attempts to domesticate the deal have often produced contractions in spaces of combinatorial richness that limit who and what can interact in any given circumstance or location.

While the struggles for concrete rights to shelter and livelihood for all urban residents remain critical to viable urban futures, whatever guarantees and supports that are accomplished by them remain insufficient to working with increasingly complicated entanglements of economies and transactions among spaces of the city that have become more segregated. For the social categories we use to understand specific ways of life and the identities of urban actors are not the political ones through which varying constellations of residents come to or will come to the stage – i.e. configure ways of acting, forms of recognition and styles of deliberation capable of engineering specific kinds of changes in the city.[16] Thus, notions of the poor, middle class, elite, and so forth, while designating real differences in interests and capacities, are insufficient to charting out the entanglements of agendas, identities and positions that residents, without secure footholds in the city, themselves incessantly try to bring about.

Thus, urban politics must go beyond its often facile appeals for inclusiveness or for making up a variety of lacks and speak to the ways in which residents continuously try to be different kinds of actors to different kinds of residents at different times and in different spaces. Slums are both exemplary of social detritus and cutting-edge assemblages suited for effective flows of information in relationship to larger service economies; the poor are not only driven by desperate opportunism but also by a proficiency at hedging possible livelihoods. Those that are apparently kept out of an increasing number of gated communities, shopping complexes and industrial developments can have a much broader knowledge of the city and its dynamics than those equipped with the most sophisticated monitoring systems.

Again, this is not to overestimate the capacities and resilience of the majority, but to open up large, previously underapprehended swathes of urban life to their 'proper' consideration. This is largely a matter of timing, since it assumes that no differences are prohibitive of interaction. Anything can be intersected or transacted; it is just a matter of finding an opportune time, following the rhythms of urban relations, as different actors move toward and away from each other. This is a matter of small and fine attunements, of finding ways to continuously engage schools, housing projects, corporations, public arenas – not with a definitive, once-and-for-all attitude, but in continuous and small improvisations, where all parties are challenged to see what work they can do with each other. It is a method of generating evidence about what could be possible and when. Urban politics has to be about the choreography of rhythms – how to speed up and slow down, accelerate and delay, seize and delay, of intervening and letting things 'take their course' – as much as it is about the composition of organizations and territories.

'Real urban governance', de-centred from stable institutional relationships, increasingly takes place in much more provisional arrangements between shifting constellations of local political power brokers and their relations to an also shifting set of external players, including, for example, both transnational corporations and more mafia-type syndicates. Critical relationships also exist among a host of management agencies dealing in corporate intelligence, strategic management, security, urban resource provisioning, public relations and 'capacity building'. Each of these domains has its own oscillating local, regional and transnational networks that intersect in various ways at different times. While the nature of their operations may be beyond the inputs of the majority of urban residents, they nevertheless are and can be subject to multiple interventions of various durations that alter the basis on which assessments – of profitability, viability or security – are made.

This is a political time when populations are increasingly 'held up' and 'delayed' in order to be scrutinized and viewed, and when populations are calculated to be guilty in advance of any action simply on the basis of such scrutiny. As Gustav Massiah has said, the poor must constantly prove their innocence in advance. Therefore, how differences between actors, localities and aspirations can coexist and act with capacity in any given context, as well as how to steer the intersection of diverse peoples and contexts toward and through each other, become urgent matters of concern. We are quite familiar with processes of representing specific urban populations and activities, accounting for what they are doing, targeting those with special needs or those who pose particular threats and forging multicultural policies and partnerships. In terms of spatial allocations and distributions, these practices tend to reinforce the dismissal or exclusion of certain possibilities and ways of being in the city. In other words, they tend to take out of consideration numerous ways in which different locales and peoples could make use of each other.

Theoretically, the expansive intelligences of diasporic movements, the experiences of cross-sectoral planning, the cultural circulations along increasingly globalized circuits of exchange, as well as interactive media transmission, could be mobilized to generate new forms of collaboration, institutional practices and popular sentiments about critical questions of justice and efficacy. Again, these considerations are too often perceived as matters of engineered spatial mosaics, rather than considerations of how the duration of impacts, the intensity of memory, the prolonging of contingency and the slowing down or speeding up of how things are viewed can be critical matters of intervention. What can be brought together and made to operate in a concerted and collaborative way is not just a matter of scale and composition but also a matter of timing, volatility and calm. Particularly in the rush to stabilize and regulate cities in Africa, many of the provisional projects undertaken by residents to feed, house and to remake themselves are not given the necessary time to unfold and connect with each other, to see what synergies might work.

Schools have to connect with localities, localities have to connect with consulting firms, consulting firms have to connect with media engineers, media engineers have to connect with the sentiments of the streets, the streets have to connect with regulatory agencies, and so forth. There are complicated pathways among all of these sites, and each harbours a wide range of intelligences and capacities that are not used and are, at the same time, not explicitly blocked or prohibited. There are many different ways any particular setting could 'do its work', could make things happen, and for creating different registers of consideration – from the almost invisible and incipient to the publicly debated. For the act of affecting events and situations, of making something happen, requires different ways of doing things, visible and invisible, at different times – as the common sense results of media manipulation and behavioural shaping have long demonstrated. In other words, persuasion, inducement, compulsion, seduction and resistance all work at different times – not all the time. As such, interventions have to combine reflections on efficacy, ethics, politics, justice and creativity at the same time, even though these processes may be at work in and through different times.

1. Rolan Palen, *The Offshore World: Sovereign Markets, Virtual Places, and Nomad Millionaires* (Ithaca, NY: Cornell University Press, 2003); Derek Gregory, *The Colonial Present* (Oxford: Blackwell, 2004).
2. Asef Bayat, 'Uncivil Society: the politics of the "informal people"', *Third World Quarterly* 18 (1997): 53-72; Daniel Goldstein, *The Spectacular City: Violence and Performance in Urban Bolivia* (Durham, NC and London: Duke University Press, 2004); Claire Robertson, *Trouble showed the way: women, men and trade in the Nairobi area 1890-1990* (Bloomington, IN: Indiana University Press, 1997).
3. M.K. Ng, 'Political Economy and Urban Planning: A comparative study of Hong Kong, Singapore, and Taiwan', *Progress in Planning* 51 (1999): 1-90; C. Hamnett, 'Gentrification, postindustrialism, and industrial and occupational restructuring in global cities', in *A Companion to the City*, eds. G. Bridge and S. Watson (Oxford: Blackwell, 2000), 331-41; K. Olds, *Globalization and urban change: capital, culture, and Pacific Rim mega-projects* (Oxford: Oxford University Press, 2001); R. Grant and J. Nijman, 'Globalization and the Corporate Geography of Cities in the Less-Developed World', *Annals of the Association of American Geographers* 92 (2002): 320-340; R. Marshall, *Emerging Urbanity: Global Urban Projects in the Asia Pacific Rim* (New York and London: Spon Press, 2002); T. Rohlen, 'Cosmopolitan Cities and nation States: Open Economies, Urban Regions, and Government in Asia', Working Paper of the Asian Pacific Research Center, Stanford Institute for International Studies, 2002; U. Kaothien and D. Webster, 'The Bangkok Region', in *Global City Regions: Their Emerging Forms*, eds. R. Simmonds and G. Hack (New York and London: Spon Press, 2000); H. Savitch and P. Kantor, 'Urban strategies for a global era: A cross-national comparison', *American Behavioral Scientist* 46 (2003): 1002-1033.
4. Neil Brenner and Nik Theodore, 'Cities and the geographies of actually existing neoliberalism,' *Antipode* 34 (2002): 349–379; E. Swyngedouw, F. Moulaert, and A. Rodriguez, 'Neoliberal Urbanization in Europe: Large-Scale Urban Development Projects and the New Urban Policy', *Antipode* 34 (2002): 543-77.
5. Mike Davis, 'The Urbanization of Empire: Megacities and the Laws of Chaos', *Social Text* 22 (2004): 9-15.
6. Philip F. Kelly, 'Everyday Urbanization: The Social Dynamics of Development in Manila's Extended Metropolitan Region', *International Journal of Urban and Regional Research* 23 (1999): 283-303; D. Webster and L. Muller, 'The Challenges of Peri-urban Growth in East Asia: The Case of China's Hangzhou-Ningbo Corridor', in *Enhancing Urban Management in East Asia*, eds. M. Freire and B. Yuen (Hunt, UK: Ashgate, 2002).
7. Saskia Sassen, *Global Networks/Linked Cities* (New York and London: Routledge, 2002).
8. Matthew Gandy, 'Cyborg Urbanization: Complexity and Monstrosity in the Contemporary City', *International Journal of Urban and Regional Research* 29 (2005): 26-49.
9. James Ferguson, *Expectations of Modernity: Myths and Meanings of Urban Life on the Zambian Copperbelt* (Berkeley, CA: University of California Press, 1999).
10. Joan Subirats and Joaquim Rius, *From the Xino to the Raval: Culture and Social Transformation in Central Barcelona* (Barcelona: Centre for Contemporary Culture of Barcelona, 2006).
11. Yves Pedrazzini, Jean-Claude Bolay and Vincent Kaufmann, 'Social practices and spatial changes', in *Social practices and empowerment in urban societies*, ed. NCCR North-South, IP5 (Lausanne: IUED, 2005).
12. Richard Banégas and Ruth Marshall-Fratani, 'Modes de régulation politique et reconfiguration des espaces publics', in *L'Afrique de l'Ouest dans la compétition mondial. Quels atouts possible*, eds. J. Damon and J. Igué (Paris: Karthala, 2003).
13. Paul Virilio, *Ground Zero* (New York and London: Verso, 2002).
14. To use Manuel DeLanda's term.
15. Manuel DeLanda, *Intensive Science and Virtual Philosophy* (London: Continuum, 2002).
16. Dmitri Philippides, 'Official city-planning and para-urbanism', in *Athens 2002 Absolute Realism*, ed. Hellenic Ministry of Culture, Association of Greek Architects. Catalogue for the Greek participation in the 8th International Exhibition of Architecture, Venice Biennale, 2002. Athens: SADAS-PEA (Association of Greek Architects) & the Commissioners; Jacque Rancière 'Who is the subject of the rights of man', *South Atlantic Quarterly* 103 (2004): 297-310.

# Thank You USA
**Prishtina**

Prishtina, Kosovo, 2006

Hillary boutique on Bill Clinton Boulevard, Prishtina, 2006

Centre of Prishtina during the 'Thanksgiving Days for USA', 20-25 November 2006

Post-war businesses, Prishtina, 2006

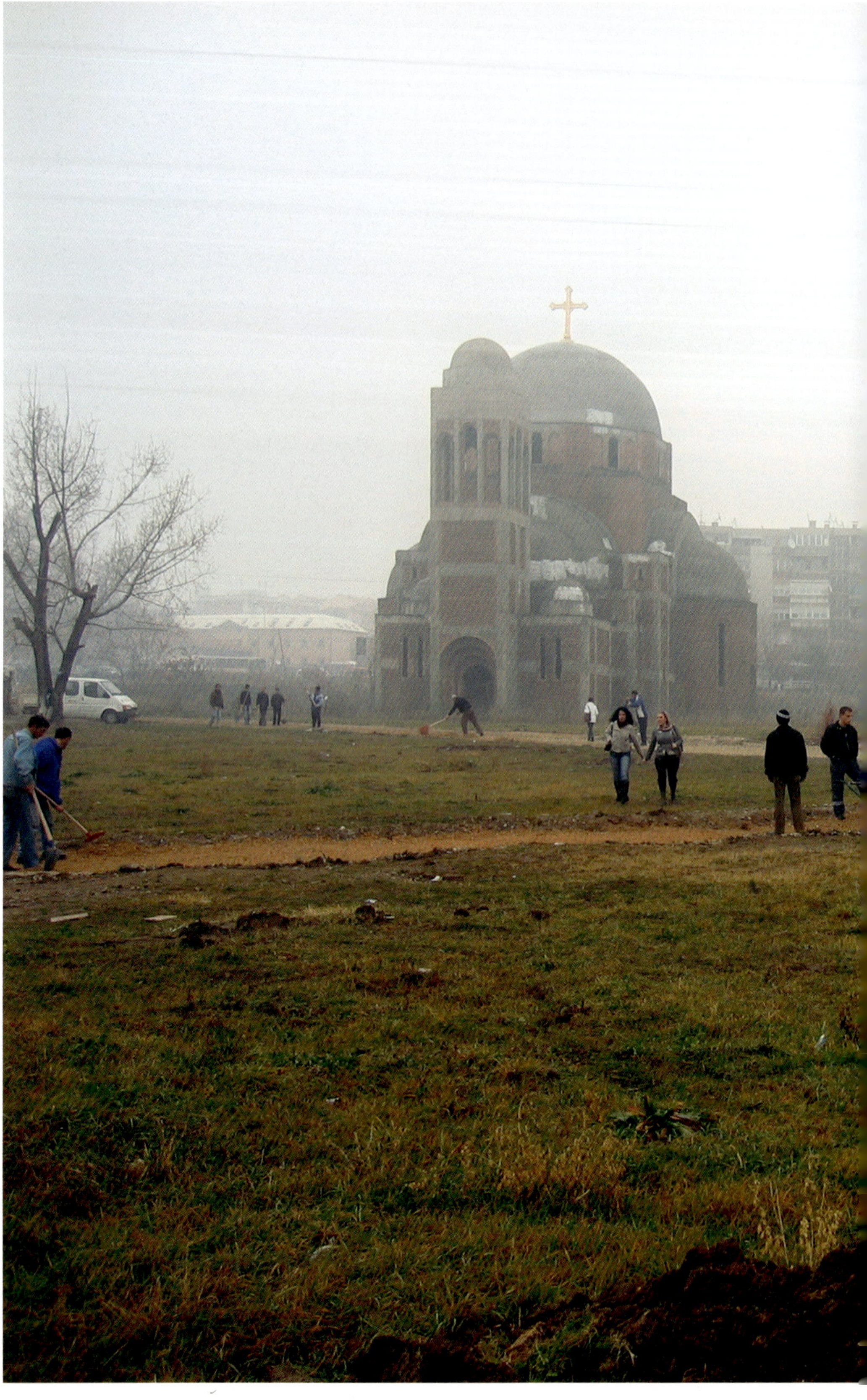

Serbian Orthodox Church next to the National and University Library, begun during the 1990s by the Milošević regime; the building project was abandoned but the shell still remains
Phristina, 2006

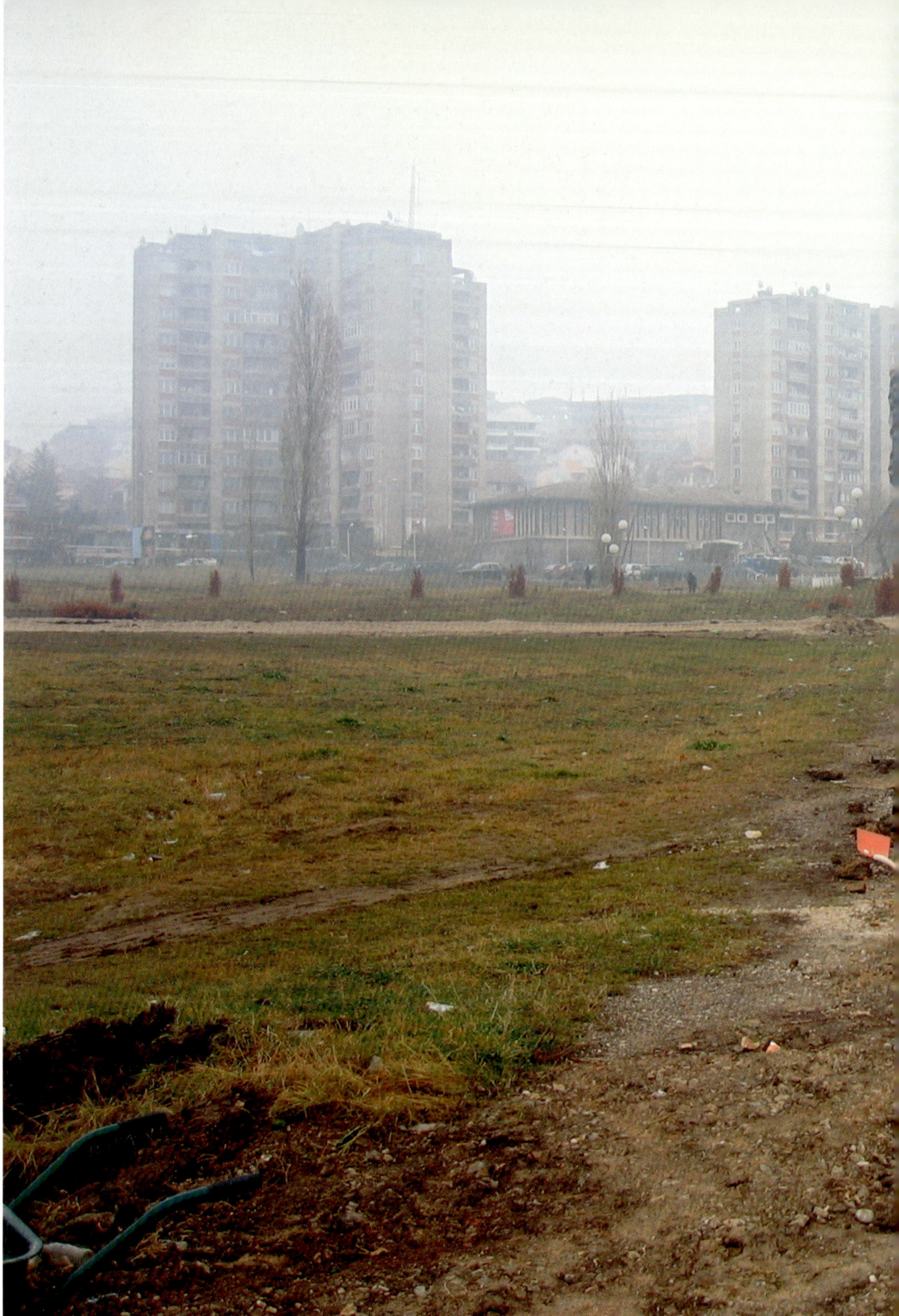

The National and University Library, designed by Andrija Mutnjakovic and completed in 1981; during the 1999 Kosovo war the building served as headquarters for the Serb military. Prishtina, 2006

Centre of Prishtina during the 'Tharksgiving Days for USA', 20-23 November 2006

*Forest Rising*
Marjetica Potrč
The Curve, Barbican Art Gallery, London, 2007

Rural school in the Brazilian state of Acre

Prishtina, 2006

## 219 Marjetica Potrc

**PM/HM**: In your exhibition work *Temporary Building Strategies* you trace moments of eruptions of new spatial realities in locations as distant from each other as Latin America and the Western Balkans. What is your interest in pursuing this kind of fieldwork?

**Marjetica Potrc**: I am interested in bottom-up initiatives and, yes, you can say that when I do this I am also tracing the dissolution of top-down initiatives, such as the modernist project. The modernist state is organized top-down and is large-scale. I believe that the future will be on a smaller scale, and that it will depend more and more on individuals who are socially conscious. For instance, the people in the Amazonian state of Acre, in Brazil, who manage extraction reserves, which are small-scale territories, are aware of their contributions to the world community. They propose a small-scale economy as a workable alternative in an age beyond the ideologies of communism or capitalism.

My practice is focused on on-site projects as well as on exhibition-based works. These latter are case studies. I started to exhibit case studies as a way of pointing to building practices across the world that are about self-sustainable architecture and are, typically, small in scale, which means they represent bottom-up initiatives. As an example, take *Xapuri: Rural School*, which I showed at the Sao Paulo Biennial in 2006. This is a case study of a primary school that has been built in a remote area of the Amazonian forest in the Brazilian state of Acre. Typically, such a school is equipped with extensive solar panelling and a satellite dish, in other words a source of energy and a means for communication with the world. The school stands for knowledge, the solar panels stand for power, and the satellite dish stands for communication. The Acreans call such schools 'power kits'.

I believe that architecture is a living language. You can read it. By reading architecture you can understand the value systems of the people who build it. The case study of the *Prishtina House* is a good example. I showed it twice, once at the Portikus in Frankfurt and a second time at the Kunstverein in Hamburg. Its decorative façade and the way it demarcates its territory point to the celebration of existence by the mostly rural population who have landed in Prishtina in recent years. Prishtina is the capital city of Kosovo, where currently you have three different governments; this means that no government really functions properly and the people themselves are constructing the city from the bottom up.

We say that in Prishtina a citizen is the smallest state. *Prishtina House* also points to successful survival in conditions where the state infrastructure has broken down. At times when there are electricity outages and the street lighting doesn't work, the *Prishtina House* provides the street light, which is powered from the house itself.

**PM/HM**: Talking about spatial developments in Prishtina and those new hybrid structures that are emerging in

220

many other cities in this region, there is a lack of terminology to describe the new aggregations of people and communities. Are they a side effect of globalized economies, a kind of globalized language aligned with more peripheral cultural connections?

**Marjetica Potrč:** When I travelled through the region of the Western Balkans with Kyong Park in 2005, we found there was one thing that was really obvious which struck me deeply: the shrinking of the ideal residential unit in the region. In the 1980s, you would have residential neighbourhoods with maybe 10,000 residents. Today in the Western Balkans, there are new architectural typologies of residential architecture that are dramatically smaller: the Urban Village and the Urban Villa. The Urban Village is a community of about 2,000 people, while the Urban Villa is a community of some 15 families. Today, the extent of people's desired co-existence is small in scale. Note that 15 years ago, modernist architecture, as well the modernist state, defined the mainstream way of life both in the Western Balkans and in the former Western Europe. The new typologies I'm talking about are entering the architectural language of the European Union only slowly and timidly. You can say that in this regard the Western Balkans is a faster region and the European Union is a slower region.

**PM/HM:** You articulate a strong belief in local governance rather than hierarchically organized forms of power, and the question then is how can we take care that these collaborations and forms of co-existence are played out in a sustainable and non-oppressive way?

**Marjetica Potrč:** I come from the former Yugoslavia, where the fragmentation of territories over the last 15 years was traumatic and terrible because of the wars in the 1990s. All the social structures collapsed. During this same period, in Brazil's western state of Acre, more than half the state territory was given to small-scale communities for self-management. These are extraction reserves populated by traditional communities such as rubber tappers and Indians. I call such fragmentation a happy fragmentation. It is also a great example of collaboration between the state of Acre and local communities. The self-dissolution of the state territory came about because both local communities and the state recognized the failure of large-scale modernist projects in Acre in the past (such as the large-scale extraction of timber, the large-scale extraction of rubber, the clearing of the forest for cattle pasture, and of course infra-

Prishtina, 2006

Prishtina, 2006

*Prishtina House*
Marjetica Potrč
*This Place is My Place – Begehrte Orte*, Kunstverein in Hamburg, 2006

*House in the Peyton area of Prishtina*

structural projects such as the railway and highway). But another reason was that they recognized a possible future: successful territories such as extraction reserves are self-sustainable and small in scale. It is also about survival. The communities in the Acrean forest say, 'If we survive in the forest, the forest will survive, and this is good for all.' In the Western Balkans, informality took off in the 1990s (with the informal city, the informal economy, the informal construction industry, etc.) because the state was non-existent. At some point, the informal economy in Belgrade and Tirana actually allowed these cities to survive. Informality also expressed the need to redefine the social contract. One must understand that eventually every kind of informality desires to become formalized in a new social contract.

Existence and co-existence are givens, but how you practice them is not a given. In my work, I point to the power individuals have when they try to build their lives, and in so doing re-formulate co-existence and existence.

I used to be uncomfortable when talking about the future, until I got involved with the *Europe Lost and Found* project and the *Lost Highway Expedition*. I always thought it was utopian to ask, 'What is the future?' I realize that I am using the word more and more. I am particularly interested in the future of territorialization. I am talking about acceleration into a fragmentation of territories, but I am also talking about individuals. When individuals are socially conscious, they are aware of, and can pursue, the common good. I am now talking about a concept called *singularité*. The term has been with us since the 1970s, if you think about theories of Yona Friedman and Constant's *New Babylon*, the *Mobile City*, and so on.

In Brazil, you see it if you look at Hélio Oiticica, who talks in 'Mundo Abrigo' ('world shelter') about the individual who is socially conscious, who understands himself or herself as a part of the world but also as contributing to it. In the 1960s, this was packaged as a kind of utopia. Note that the term Balkanization has been recently rethought. It used to be a negative term, describing the dissolution of a unity. These days, it is recognized as a force for democracy. It's about families, clans, communities, group identities, bottom-up initiatives, new citizenships and self-rule, all building up to a larger society.

221

*Visionaries of the '60s Meet Doers of 2006 II*
Marjetica Potrč

*Tirana, 2006*

**222** There are many successful and articulate bottom-up initiatives today. There must be a reason for this. One typical example that comes to mind is 'Barefoot College' in India, a project that started 30 years ago because of the failure of the state there. Today the group is successful not only because they can manage their own little settlement, but also because their strength actually comes from the fact that they collaborate with other rural communities across the world – in Kenya, Eritrea, Afghanistan, southern India, Nepal and so on. The network they produced is cross-national and a very good example of the strength of a network.

*VOID: A View from Acropolis*
An xurban collective installation project at Platform Garanti Contemporary Art, Istanbul, 2006

**PM/HM:** On the website of xurban_collective, there's a manifesto with 11 points, and in one of these you mention that as long as English continues to be the common language, the internet will remain the last and only transnational territory...

**Guven Incirlioglu:** This relates to global restrictions imposed upon the circulation of bodies. Some of our projects involve a kind of transfer, and this is a topic now high on our agenda. What is being globalized is capital and its circulation, as well as commodities. Yet at the same time, we increasingly see people locked up within their own territories and not free to travel at all. Interestingly enough, in Turkey, which is getting closer to becoming part of Europe – at least in negotiations – it is ever more difficult for Turkish citizens to get visas, especially Schengen visas. On the one hand, Istanbul receives more and more people from abroad, especially from Western Europe; on the other hand, people from Turkey aren't nearly as free to travel as they were before the Schengen Agreement. So this idea of the 'transnational' actually relates more to the web, though there's also a lot of news about how the internet might not, in fact, be totally accessible to everybody either. Recent news from China, for example, reports that – in collaboration with Google – the government can track search words and prosecute people who are surfing certain networks and websites, etc. Of course, for us the situation is different. We get invited to do exhibitions abroad and can travel more easily. But that's no indication of the situation. Let me, for example, talk about the proposal we handed in for the Istanbul Biennial in 2005 when it had a second venue in Eindhoven and it exhibited works from Istanbul there. For this space we formulated a proposal that proceeded from the idea of the European Union and the Turkish bid for EU membership. We came up with a kind of allegory of matrimony between our country and the EU. Actually, we don't know if this 'wedding' is ever going to happen, though either way one of the fears of European conservatives and national leftists is contamination. This has to do with the Turkish population living in Europe, with their not being integrated or refusing to be naturalized. So in the European subconscious there's always this stereotype about the Turkish Muslim. This has to do with the situation in Europe right now as well as history. For the exhibition, we suggested taking this idea of contamination and using it to provoke. We proposed picking up the garbage from brothels in Istanbul and taking it to Eindhoven to be put on display there, and then doing similar research in the neighbourhood, as the brothels in Istanbul were also very close to the venues of the Biennial. The idea had to do with transferring materials from Turkey and dealing with this transfer across transnational borders.

**PM/HM:** In light of your experiences with xurban's proposal for the 9th Istanbul Biennial, how do you perceive the current possibilities and perils of political art?

**Guven Incirlioglu:** I think we've more to do with the idea of 'art' than politics. Of course politics plays a very big role. In any case we try to come up with specific content and deal with specific issues. But in the end, what we're producing is art, a work of art. It always has something very particular, and a lot of times it can be very poetic. It's not just about writing or about manifesting something, nor is it just about commenting. A photograph or a video is something complete in itself, and although it might have a political

223   **xurban**

VOID: A View from Acropolis
Detail

**PM/HM:** Do you think that by working with these parameters there's a risk of producing colonial gestures in which one simply avails oneself of political or social realities in search of 'artistic' feedstock?

**Guven Incirlioglu:** Yes and, now that you mention the colonial, maybe I should go back to the context of Turkey, or Istanbul specifically. For example, Edward Said was for a long time very welcome in Turkey, in scholarly circles, and what he wrote in his book *Orientalism* was very relevant, or at least it seemed to be relevant for Turkey at the time. As you know, there are also many indications of this countrie's 'Orientalization', despite its being a former empire and much prouder (!) of its past than other colonial or post-colonial countries.

Now time has passed, and today I think the idea of colonization is not very relevant at all. I don't consider an artist who comes to Istanbul and works in Istanbul a neo-Orientalist. That's not how things work anymore: people are more mobile, and a lot of their experiences have become very ephemeral. Many of us Turks are tourists, too: we can do similar things when we go to Berlin, that is, stay for a couple of weeks, do stuff and exhibit. In this context, I see this as normal.

VOID: A View from Acropolis
Installation view

agenda, it's also an entity of its own – and this is important for us. I've always thought the turning point was probably in the 1990s. Until then, many artists were internalizing issues from their experiences. In the 1990s, it seems – at least with some exhibitions – that the idea of engaging oneself in political issues and trying to get the local community involved or working with it was part of the agenda. Even a look at the main theme of the Istanbul Biennial reveals that the issues shifted in the 1990s. The Biennial in 2001 was entitled *Egofugal,* 'Escape from the Ego', which sure made sense! In any case, that's what was needed. So, this trend started in the 1990s. Though in certain ways I see what's happening now to be something like a decline in art; at the same time there's a rise in politics and dissidence, and a siding with global resistance.

For example, this decline in art was very apparent in the Istanbul Biennial 2005. Not that works have to be perfectly crafted and exhibited, but I think the political content of many artworks doesn't get across due to the poor execution of the photographs, videos and/or materials used. The other problem has to do with confusing missionary or social work with art. These are completely different fields: people have been working in the Third World in Africa and Asia for many years; they have organized local communities to achieve certain ends and improve people's lives, and so on. This is a form of voluntary activism, but at no time have these individuals claimed they are doing art. In any case, what we see in a lot of artworks is a growing tendency to blend social activism with art, which is also problematic, I suppose.

224

xurban collective has researched, observed and investigated the framework of dialogues between the two neighbouring sites of Bergama and the area's gold minas. In their inquiry the idea of 'a dig' has been applied literally and conceptually to extract and collect evidence of spaces between the archaeological formation and the contextual framework that the site rests on. Earth taken from the area of Bergama and transported to Istanbul rests in a mound in the window of Platform Garanti as a symbol of digging, transferral and void. Large format photographs depict in minute detail the plants that blanket the archaeological ruins in a protective layer.

*VOID: A View from Acropolis*
An xurban collective installation project at Platform Garanti Contemporary Art, Istanbul, 2006

Admittedly, experiences are often more superficial, but this is true on all sides. What's more, the view is no longer unidirectional, from the West to the East, from colonizer to the colony. The phenomenon of superficial experience is global. Yet I wouldn't say I see some kind of conspiracy behind this, in terms of neo-colonization. If anything, the conspiracy is broader; for instance you have the US, the military industrial complex and multinationals involved in a country. The conspiracy is not on the level of ideas or views of a certain place. It's more about how, for example, the micro-economy of Istanbul is changing very fast, a lot of shops are closing, and a great deal of local production and exchange is giving way to global brands, multinationals and their subsidiaries.

*VOID: A View from Acropolis*
Detail

225

# Jesko Fezer

**PM/HM:** You work with a variety of very different formats in the field of architecture: you are part of the collective behind Pro qm bookshop, you are co-editor of *An Architektur* magazine as well as a practising architect. How do all these different formats interact with one another?

**Jesko Fezer:** I think it is quite impossible to practice architecture without talking about politics and it is impossible to work as in the cultural sphere without reflecting on the social dynamics of urban life. It is also impossible to think about these things without relating to other people working in the field and without trying to build a relationship with the public, no matter how such a public might be. So the formats – for example, doing a magazine, having a bookshop, working as an architect or as an artist – always have to do with the question of audience and users, with the question of discipline and self-reflection in terms of a political understanding of what cultural production means.

For me this has always been a step-by-step thing: you work on a certain project and then you realize that you need a certain format to fulfil what you want to do or say, and you need to cooperate with certain people, and find out about their ire interests and agendas. Or you realize that certain questions come up in the process of a project, and then you occupy yourself with the issue, you read a book about it, or you meet some people. On the other hand, of course, there are the financial dynamics behind all this, which means you have to have a job to make money for the next half year. Such a job, for example, a job in the academic context, where I have had different teaching positions, can enable you to develop a project. On the other hand, the idea of the bookshop developed in the context of doing project-based work over several years, like exhibitions or other cultural spaces for political discourses. It evolved out of the dilemma that you need, for instance, a bar or club that is working well in order to make your film. I thought it would be easier to create that kind of basic economic structure with a bookshop. So, in a way, it has been a very autobiographical development, and it would be difficult for me to find a more general line in this process.

**PM/HM:** How did *An Architektur* enter the equation?

**Jesko Fezer:** The magazine *An Architektur* was a continuation of an architecture student project we established in the mid-1990s at the University of Arts in Berlin. We founded an open group of 15 or 20 people called *Freies Fach* – it was a kind of self-training course on political and economic questions in the field of architecture and urban design. It was also an activist group against the revanchist redesign of Berlin in a neo-traditional manner that emphasized economic, budgetary matters. We had a lot of seminars, readings, discussions and regular demonstrations and public actions in Berlin. Just when we stopped working as *Freies Fach*, we were invited to the exhibition *Violence is at the Margin of All Things* organized by Andreas Siekmann and Alice Creischer. We took the occasion to rethink our work, though not solely in a Berlin-based context, because this was becoming in many ways too confined for us: all the issues of its dull conservative architecture, the ongoing privatization of the public realm and the racist discrimination that are still very important to discuss in this city. Especially our being critical of what was happening in Berlin architecturally became too narrow or too boring or was not connected to questions that we found important. And we thought it would be interesting to have a format like a magazine that claims to be a real architecture magazine and claims to have a real audience – a broad audience, or let's say a broad audience for architecture. In a way, we continued on with the same understanding of architecture as we had had in *Freies Fach*, but not on the level of activism but of discourse. With this exhibition, we had a budget to research the issue of security and its impact on architecture, so we thought: let's start up a magazine with that money and continue on.

**PM/HM:** Many of the things you are involved in have to do with education or self-education, such as the *Camp for Oppositional Architecture*. Why did you develop this particular approach and what were your experiences?

**Jesko Fezer:** The question of education is very interesting, though I had never thought about it in the way you just used it – as an underlying concept; but I can relate to it as something that is about the distribution of information and knowledge. If we define education

*An Architektur* 16
Material on David Harvey
Flexible Akkumulation durch Urbanisierung, cover, 2006

*Camp for Oppositional Architecture*
Sleeping accommodations, Berlin, 2004

as not being just about information, but also about legitimizing information, or empowering information, I think 'education' might be able to stand in a quite abstract sense for a very powerful social process of knowledge distribution. There is a kind of group or context, a big or small audience or public sphere where this information is shared, and where it has a certain

related to the idea of the platform and its social dimensions, the creation of knowledge, or the projective dimension of such a meeting. It was not easy at all to figure out what our common position in relation to mainstream architecture might be. So to give it as We were quitepeople the call and were even interested in .Twhere lot of .The mere idea of this camp generated meaning: one underscoring the existence of a kind of oppositional architecture. This might sound strange, because such architecture is regarded as impossible, but that was exactly the point. After the second *Oppositional Camp* in Utrecht last year, and preparing one in Vienna/Bratislava and in Istanbul, this seems to have been a good starting point for diverse theoretical and practical discussions.

**PM/HM**: How would you describe the relationship between your working methods and the political and economic realities of Berlin today, where there is not much official work for architects, yet an abundance of experimental projects on interstitial spaces?

**Jesko Fezer**: There are new restrictions and new political concepts of inclusion, but the question of how architecture works in the field of political economy is in a way still the same. The econ-

*'Hier entsteht'*
Jesko Fezer & Mathias Heyden, Volksbühne am Rosa-Luxemburg-Platz and *ErsatzStadt*, Berlin, 2003

omy and the political system modify themselves all the time, but how they relate to the built environment is still very problematic, and it is of course extremely important to think about how architecture might redefine its relation to the political and economic sphere. What is its role in the dominant conceptsin under people On the other hand, architecture has to discuss the role economies play in the formation of a city or even a local space. The only chance we have, as I understand it, is to invent certain spaces of freedom away from overwhelming economic pressures and political institutionalization.

plausibility, or is legitimized in the process of sharing it. Of course, our *Camp for Oppositional Architecture* was primarily about building up a social basis for sharing information. There is a certain offensive naivety

This can only be achieved by stepping actively and consciously into the flexible realms of the economic sphere, and the stable hierarchies and discourse of the political. As a rule this has been undertaken either as a neoliberal project that uses and reduces the state and thus politics in order to let the economy unfold its powers, or as a more or less socialist project that tries to restrain the economy by strengthening the state. Unfortunately this was what architects did throughout the last century – they brought in a bit more state and a bit more economy than they had originally intended. But how about a concept of politics that is not in need of a nation state and its regulations, one that gets rid of neoliberal considerations entirely? Yet to think about this and how it would allow architects to position social life in space, to reorganize the economy in space and to open political discourses in space, would be an interesting opportunity to start redefining such considerations. Of course, in moments of shifts in power, be it in the conception of the self, the economy or the political sphere, the ensuing confusion is – to put it optimistically – always a great chance.

227

# Tadej Pogačar

**PM/HM:** P.A.R.A.S.I.T.E. Museum is a virtual museum and was initiated in 1993, at a time when physical sites in the Balkans were highly contested. You proposed something that happens without proper physicality. What was the concept behind this move?

**Tadej Pogačar:** We can describe P.A.R.A.S.I.T.E. Museum as a notional, parallel art institution, a mobile spiritual entity that establishes specific interrelationships among a variety of subjects, societies, institutions, social groups and symbolic networks. The P.A.R.A.S.I.T.E. Museum of Contemporary Art doesn't have its own premises or staff but rather adopts territories, chooses different spaces and feeds on the juices of other institutions. As a 'parallel art institution' it serves as a critical model for analysing the systems and the institutions within it, and as a framework for the introduction of alternative forms of communication and the establishment of new connections. Its operations are not based primarily on the production of objects, but on the creation of situations and the cultivation of relationships.

Our early interventions in museums raised questions about order and knowledge: How are they produced and structured? How are they possessed, transmitted, and used? Another, closely related issue was that of social visibility: we question what we see and what we fail to see, what we consider 'natural' and what we find disturbing. We've intervened in art museums, permanent and private collections as well as history and natural history museums, etc.

ance, and power in everyday life, art and society. We remix, appropriate, redirect and confound recent states and orders. Some interventions have questioned the order and hierarchy of institutions; others, their ideologies and the hidden logic of their collections. An example: in a cultural institution in Ljubljana (which was temporary declared a P.A.R.A.S.I.T.E. Museum site) we prepared – in addition to an exhibition – an official meeting with the entire staff in order to introduce me as their new director. They were also informed that for the next month they would have to follow new rules and orders, for they were now employees of P.A.R.A.S.I.T.E. Museum. Of course they found this confusing…

**PM/HM:** You have produced a series of works on human trafficking and sex work in which you collaborate with far less institutionalized groups. How did this engagement with marginalized communities come about?

**Tadej Pogačar:** In the mid-1990s our interest shifted more to the city, especially to urban minorities and public space: uncoded spaces, non-spaces, appropriation of public space, etc. We introduced collaborative ways of working based on equal partnerships.

In 1999 we initiated the project *CODE:RED* as an ongoing collaborative, interdisciplinary platform for discussion and research into models of self-organization of urban minorities, global sex work, and human trafficking. This platform uses both real and virtual spaces, and takes the form of an open dialogue between artists, sex workers and the public in selected urban environments. *CODE:RED* employs various forms of public action, activism and subversions in media. It is clear that contemporary society still draws a sharp line between the groups it sees as inside society and those it views as outside. In order to survive, those excluded are forced to organize themselves and how they do so is radically different from those whose identity is part of a 'legitimate' social

monApoly – A Human Trade Game
Edition of 50 signed and numbered games, 2004

CODE:RED Bangkok
Lecture by Ana Lopes, Sparwasser HQ, Berlin, 2005

228

CODE:RED USA
Street media, New York, 2002

CODE:RED Venice
Red Umbrellas March, Venice, 2001

229 structure. Urban minority sex workers are among those excluded. They have no basic civil or human rights. In many countries their work is not recognized as work at all. They are stigmatized, victimized and brutalized. They must organize and raise their voices if they want to survive.

After the fall of the Berlin Wall, we experienced a massive flow of migrant prostitution into Western Europe. The Western countries were not prepared for this new situation. Countries that had developed an advanced policy towards sex work over the previous decades found themselves in a dilemma: due to the changed conditions of the new global economy, their legislation turned out to be outdated and useless – a situation that brought on a new state of chaos.

The World Congress of Sex Workers and New Parasitism in 2001 was the first public manifestation of the CODE:RED project. This project emerged as a consequence of our co-operation with Comitato per i Diritti Civili delle Prostitute from Pordenone, one of the leading organizations for the protection of sex workers in Italy. It took place within the framework of the 49th Venice Biennale in a public space, a tent, at Giardini and was called Prostitute Pavilion (Padiglione delle Prostitute). The congress was conceived as a creative platform for connections, exchange and information. The list of the participating groups and organizations included group activists and individuals from Taiwan, Thailand, Cambodia, Vietnam, Italy, Germany, the US and Australia. Another recent interesting joint project is CODE:RED Brazil, Daspu, initiated in collaboration with Davida. Davida is a non-profit organization founded in Rio de Janeiro in 1992 to promote the inclusion of prostitutes as citizens. The main tools of the Davida group are actions and interventions into the fields of education, health, documentation, communication and culture. In 2005 it established a fashion brand called Daspu. In less than a year this fashion brand became famous, nationally and internationally. Beside prostitutes, young designers and internationally renowned models joined to collaborate on the project. This is a true success story. Since then we have done projects with different groups from New York, Tirana, Madrid, Graz, Pordenone, Berlin, etc.

PM/HM: How do you feel about the strange blend of optimistic interest in transitional spaces that are characterized by self-organized networks on the one hand, and the resurgent obsession with specific geographies on the other?

Tadej Pogačar: In the heroic age of the Internet, optimism surged. ljudmila (ljubljana digital media lab) in Ljubljana was an important place for the international net art community. Yet reality once again caught up with us: we were being too idealistic when we ignored the basic rules of geography and politics underlying such locations. The art market is hungry and needs to rediscover Russia, China, Finland and even the Balkans. Without exception, recent shows from the Balkans have reflected Western stereotypes and prejudices; they do not give a proper picture of cultural production in the Balkan region. Yet there are still small, individual and self-organized initiatives in South America, the United States, Eastern Europe, Asia... They have not forgotten what notions like co-operation, the past or solidarity mean. What is more, they work locally and this makes it possible to change and improve local conditions. Once more I'd like to emphasize: for us strategies of mobility and adoptability are very important – like parasites in nature, we have to be small and clever to recognize hidden channels and paths through diverse territories.

# Parallel Worlds

# Gunners & Runners
## London

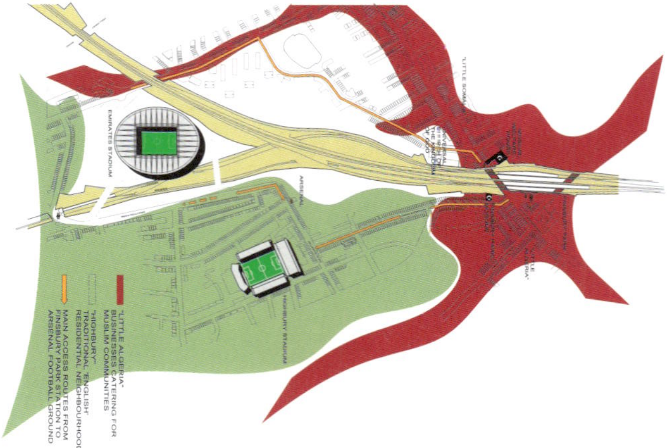

232

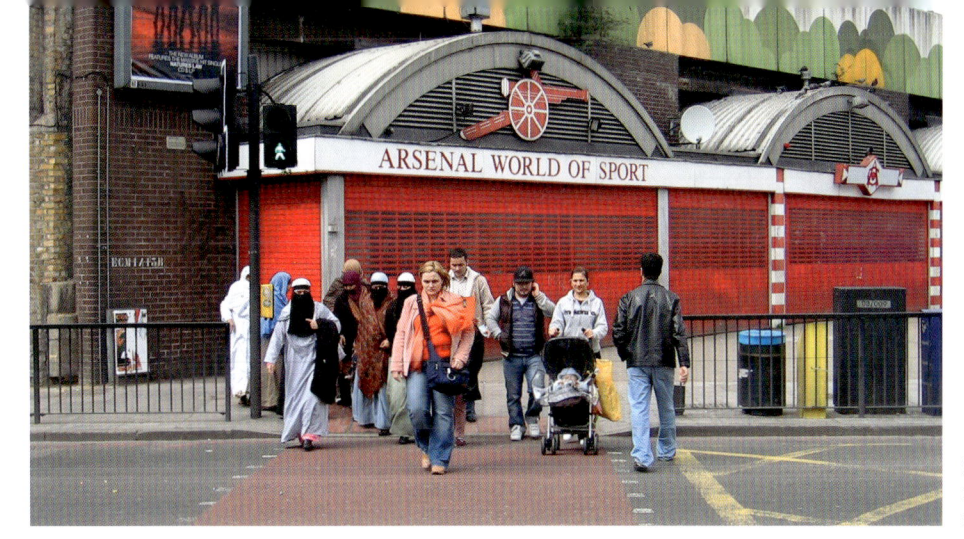

World of Sports
Arsenal club shop at Finsbury Park Station
London, 2006

The Home of Football
One of the last Arsenal games at the old Highbury Stadium
London, 15 April 2006

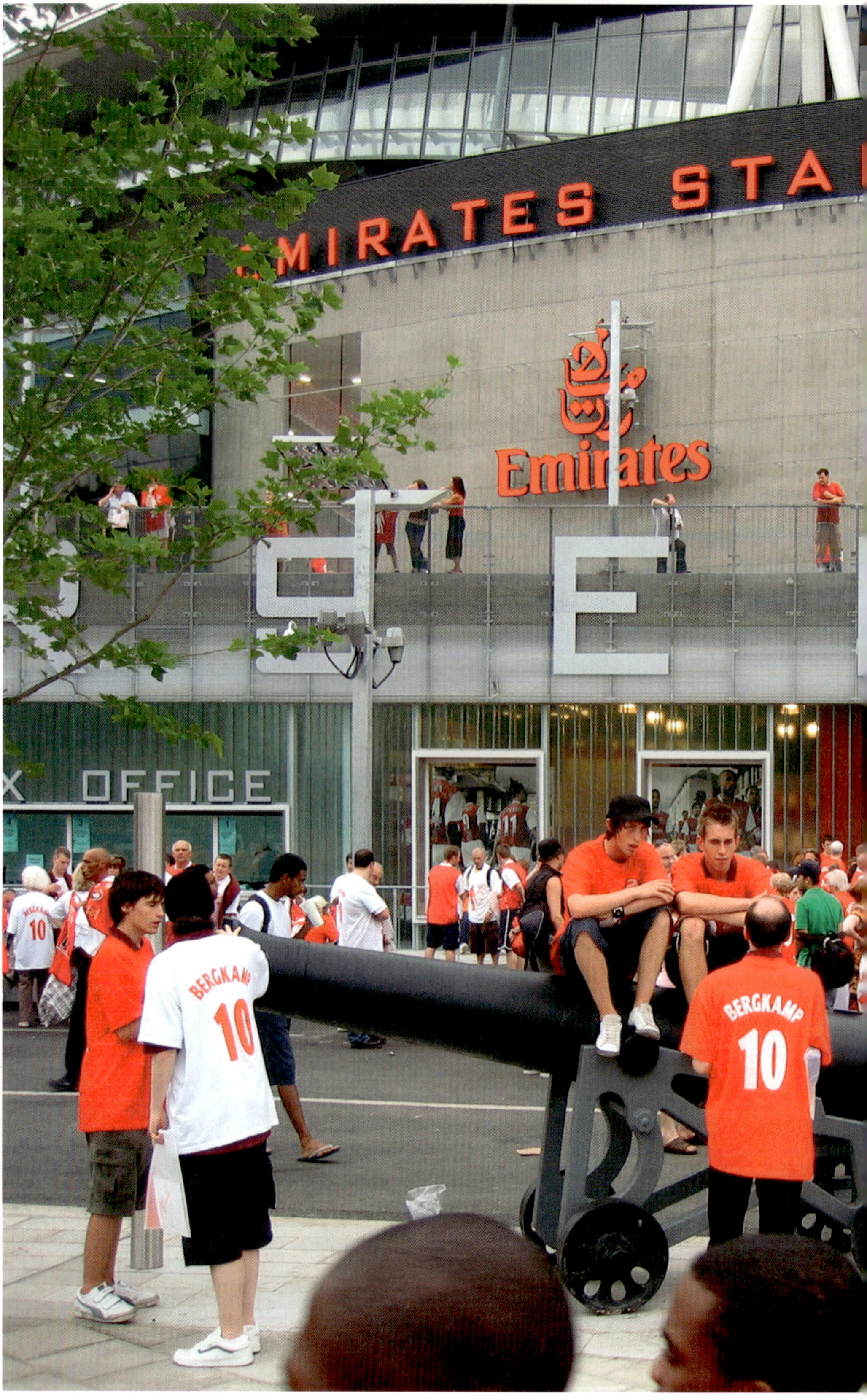
MIRATES STA
Emirates
OFFICE
BERGKAMP
10

Emirates Stadium
First Arsenal game at the new Emirates Stadium, London, 22 July 2006

Italian
Bedroom
Furniture
AMANDA
AFRICA
INDIA &
MOBILE
CALL VATAN

Finsbury Park
So-called 'Little Algeria' along Blackstock Road and
Seven Sisters Road in North London, 2006-2008

Emirates Stadium, 2006

Entrance to the North Bank Stand, shortly before the last Arsenal game at the old Highbury Stadium
London, April 2006

Emirates Stadium
First Arsenal game at the new Emirates Stadium, London, 22 July 2006

239

World of Sports
Arsenal club shop at Finsbury Park Station, London, 2006

## Parallel Worlds

### GUNNERS AND RUNNERS

*'When you first arrive to Highbury, you are saying, "Where is the stadium? Where is the stadium?" and then suddenly you are in front of it. You do not know why it is in the middle of the city. You are used to that here, but on the Continent we are not used to that – you see the stadium from three miles away. What I always like in England is that you feel the club belongs to the population around there – you can go out of the door and go to a football game. That does not exist anywhere else'.*
Arsène Wenger (Manager of FC Arsenal, *The Independent*, 3 May 2006)

*'When it comes to our essential values – belief in democracy, the rule of law, tolerance, equal treatment for all, respect for this country and its shared heritage – then that is where we come together, it is what we hold in common. It is what gives us the right to call ourselves British'.*
Tony Blair (*The Guardian*, 9 December 2006, extract from a speech by the British prime minister to an invited audience at 10 Downing Street)[1]

On 12 May 2006, Arsenal, a London football club steeped in tradition which is also known as the Gunners, played its last home game at Highbury Stadium, a venue equally rich in tradition. The name Gunners stems from the site on which the club was founded, the former Royal Arsenal munitions factory in the London suburb of Woolwich near the Thames, which in the nineteenth century was one of England's most important armaments production facilities. Its riverside location led to the Royal Arsenal becoming the most important military supply centre for the expansion of the British Empire. The factory workers' football team, which was founded in 1886 at the height of the expansion of the Arsenal into Europe's largest military industrial complex, represented an extension of military rivalry into civilian rituals of domination. Highbury Stadium, the home of the Gunners from 1913 to 2006, grew up around a playing field situated between gardens and backyards and was integrated seamlessly into the small-scale contours of a Victorian residential neighbourhood, where, on match days, kiosks, take-aways and souvenir stands were unceremoniously set up in front gardens and driveways. Every home game at the 'Home of Football' thus constituted an extravagant staging of the homeland: an opulent theatre of British culture that spilled out from the stadium into the neighbourhood and was perpetuated in numerous myths and legends.

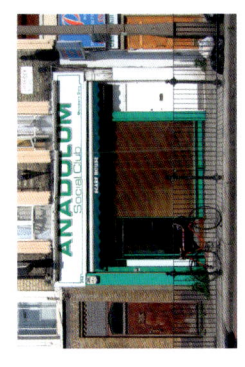

Scarf House
North London, 2006

In the weeks leading up to the closure of the stadium, British newspapers such as the *Evening Standard* and *The Guardian* devoted entire extra supplements to wistful obituaries for this historic London venue: 'Highbury wasn't just any stadium, Highbury was a cathedral of football'. The end of 'Highbury' also brought to an end the sacral practices with which the stadium was staged as a representation of British community. In Ashburton Grove, 500 metres away from the old venue, there is now a new stadium complex equipped with VIP lounges, luxury restaurants and a multi-media infrastructure that has been co-financed by Emirates, the Saudi Arabian state airline. The switch to the Emirates Stadium was 'necessary' in order to be able to continuing competing in the premiere league of global media presence. This transition from a cathedral of football to a cathedral of consumption marks not only a local but also a cultural change: from community-based pubs and fish-and-chip stalls to the comprehensive commercial use of multifunctional stadium structures, from a locally oriented, English working-class culture to a globalized world of flows. The upper end of this transformation is served by the flows of capital, the lower end by the flows of migration. Thus, two geographies of upheaval meet directly at the intersection point constituted by North London's Finsbury Park: the world of football and the post-colonial world of Islamic cultures in Europe. If the demolition of Highbury Stadium was mourned as the loss of a piece of British culture, it also constituted the loss of a monument that helped mask the realities around the stadium that had long exhibited a different image of 'Britain today'. Arsenal's move to the Emirates Stadium did not simply mean that a local population lost 'its' urban backyard stadium but that a stadium also lost 'its' population.

This atomization of an unambiguous relationship between sociality and space is taking place on two levels simultaneously. One level involves the confrontation of a locally shaped football culture with globally operating finance capital; this includes the purchase of naming rights for the stadium by the Dubai-based Emirates airline as it does the expectations linked with the stadium relating to London's claim to a place in the league of global cities. The other level concerns the intermixing of an introspective English residential neighbourhood with the networks of the global jihad. Nearby the stadium stands the Finsbury Park Mosque, which was opened in 1990 by Prince Charles and King Fahd of Saudi Arabia, and which, between 1997 and 2003, served as a gathering point for supporters of Islamic extremism inspired by the teachings of the resident radical cleric Abu Hamza al-Masri. It was during the run-up to the Football World Cup in Paris in 1998 that calls were first heard for Abu Hamza to be banned from the Finsbury Park Mosque due to fears of possible terrorist attacks.[2] 9/11 accelerated the investigation of possible subversive activities connected with the mosque. In January 2003 a raid by British anti-terrorist units uncovered not only fake passports and credit cards but also CS gas, hunting knives and hand guns. Conservative newspapers reacted by describing the mosque as a 'honey pot for terrorists' and as an 'arsenal for Islamic terror'.

After being stripped of his status as an imam, Abu Hamza continued to preach to his supporters in front of the mosque on St. Thomas's Road, on the very stretch of street used by Arsenal fans on their regular pilgrimage to their stadium. In the spring of 2006, recordings of these street sermons led to Abu Hamza's arrest and conviction for incitement to racial hatred and incitement to murder. Now under new leadership, the Finsbury Park Mosque – which was renamed the North London Central Mosque in 2005 – currently enjoys a high level of attendance, and the local network of businesses and facilities for immigrants from various parts of the Islamic world is growing rapidly. On match days the Arsenal fans now make their way to 'their' club through a multi-ethnic neighbourhood in which more than 120 languages are spoken, passing mosques and Muslim welfare houses, Halal butcher shops, internet cafés, Maghrebi snack bars and cafés with names like Salam, Aladdin and Paradise, specialized travel agents and bed-sit agencies, Islamic bookshops and scarf shops. These concentrated financial and migratory links with the Mahgreb and the Near and Middle East in Finsbury Park have led to a cultural and economic coexistence of religion and football, prayer rituals and pre-match anthems, international financial operations and local street culture. In the encounters and intermixing of English football fans with the migrant population, the urban space becomes a stage for the ambiguities of prosperity, legality and security with which the neo-liberal transformation of western society operates. The path that these encounters take is never prescribed, for outside an accidental confrontation on the street there are no roles or channels of coalescence for these separately existing spheres. Rather than generating a field of clear identitary positions, the different flows of cultural affiliations in Finsbury Park mark a departure from the belief in a stable concept of Britishness.

It is not only football but culture that is no longer, as the 1996 football hymn *Three Lions* put it, 'coming home'. The mourning of Arsenal's Highbury Stadium opened up a space for a more reaching farewell, a farewell to the idea that access to the understanding of culture is to be found in identitary configurations. The wistful final salute to the old Arsenal stadium marked a transformation that all European cultures are experiencing: a shift from an unambiguous socio-cultural belongingness and security experienced as familiar and homelike to a fragmented, kaleidoscopically refracted world in which our living spaces are no longer defined and shaped 'by ourselves' but in an interplay with the conditions and prescriptions of global capital. This process is proceeding hand in hand with a transformation of that which presents itself as community. This is a form of social upheaval that does not lend itself to mapping in terms of distinctive social events such as revolutions, demonstrations or political marches. Rather, it is taking place as a drama within the everyday and the insignificant, at the innumerable sites of the overlooked and the ignored. The uncon-

*Gunners & Runners*
Encounters between football fans, radical clerics and police in North London

FINSBURY PARK MOSQUE & MUSLIM WELFARE HOUSE

ABU HAMZA PREACHES IN THE STREET IN 2003

POLICE CORDONS ON MATCH DAYS

ARSENAL WORLD OF SPORT

MAIN ACCESS ROUTES FROM FINSBURY PARK STATION TO ARSENAL FOOTBALL GROUND

Finsbury Park

trolled acting out of this drama, with all its potential for deviation from prescribed patterns of behaviour, is not taking place in organized rallies on London's Trafalgar Square but in marginal actualities such as the encounters of massing football fans with radical Muslims praying on the street in St. Thomas's Road in Finsbury Park.

## ARTICULATIONS OF COMMUNITY

The case of Arsenal provides an example of an increasingly expanding geography of parallel worlds that are organized via networks and that become interwoven with other networks through situative opportunities. The dependence of such networks on the interests of the global market raises the question as to whether the dynamics of diffusion, segmentation and splintering in the contemporary 'space of flows', as Manuel Castells argues, are in fact increasingly rendering it impossible to share cultural codes or whether life in parallel universes is capable of generating new forms of sociality. According to Castells, an enforced global logic is preventing any kind of cultural, political and physical bridge being built between the different characteristics of this space. The distortion of different temporalities in different dimensions of a social hyperspace is driving apart social worlds that mutually imply one another without offering new contact points.[3] A search for forms of convergence can begin by looking at what emerges beyond the focus of this critique of the lack of a global sphere of connectedness, at the many self-organized situations of social praxis in which the dispersed spheres are bundled in different subjects and redistributed via them – a praxis of rich and varying textures of translocal sociality that present a range of possibilities for creating new sites of commonality. These sites can be located in close proximity to one another or far apart; they correspond to a fabric of complex temporal structures, of a *'time as lived*, not synchronically or diachronically, but in its multiplicities and simultaneities, its presences and absences'.[4] While the heterogeneity of these temporalities may as a whole have a centrifugal effect, this does not prevent them from flowing together at what are often the most unexpected places and generating something new.

Bijlmermeer
Around Kraaiennest station, before demolition of the elevated streets, Amsterdam, 1996

In what follows, we want to explore the potential of this spatially generative praxis and the possibilities for art and architecture to participate in shaping such a praxis. How can civil-societal solidarities be conceived of when the marketization of all existential contexts means that there is no apparent provision of spaces for the articulation of social coherence and cultural exchange outside the framework of the economic? What forms of reciprocity can be generated beyond the ideologies of global economic dependency? What alternatives can experimental forms of social and economic organization develop and what is the relationship between these alternatives and the production and distribution networks of the contemporary economy? Oliver Ressler's video project *Alternative Economics, Alternative Societies*, a continually augmented series of interviews with advocates of a diverse range of concepts, currently presents more than a dozen alternative social and economic models. These range from Takis Fotopoulos's 'Inclusive Democracy' and Michael Albert's 'Participatory Economics' to the Yugoslavian model of self-management and the workers' collectives during the Spanish Civil War and provide an outline of historical and contemporary blueprints that run counter to the logic of global capitalism. The logic of Ressler's work itself operates via a generation of communication rather than an idealistic plan. The incomplete speeches and narratives of the different speakers combine to produce a polyphonic permeation of a loosely connected sphere of economic and societal possibilities and a renewed 'market launch' of these ideas. The videos insist on the power inherent in the mobilization of language as a fundamental capacity to generate every type of statement without substantiation and thus unconstrained by economic pressures. Rather than foregrounding the examinatory function of language, they show how language can become a means of empowerment. Such a reclaiming of the possibilities of economy and society coalesces with the function of talk in the babble of voices at secret meeting points, improvised sites of exchange and makeshift sites of commerce. Rather than absolute knowledge, they cultivate an increased level of attention regarding an expanded linguistic capacity. Together they establish a model of language as a means of eluding the rational calculation of a thoroughly marketized life. An incessant speaking in order to incessantly renew the framework in which exchange can take place; a speaker who redefines him or herself through the act of speaking; talk as an instrument for a process of renewed signification.[5]

The potential of idle talk lies in its capacity to mobilize a force field the effective range of which extends beyond what is spatially manifested as a site of communication. As Paolo Virno emphasizes, it represents the raw material of post-Fordist virtuosity; as a fundamental principle of the performative it fulfils an important role in contemporary social production. Rather than referring to an existing, external condition, idle talk constantly creates this condition anew.[6] It invents and implements, while its communication breaks into the functional reference between words and things, into the relationship between the order of words and that of the body. On the one hand, this creativity of idle talk seems to serve the global instabilities fostered by capitalism, while, on the other, it also lays claim to the circuits of production as a source of dissent and disruption that takes effect not in an externally extant model but in the global flows of late capitalism itself: in its dubious business zones and in its politics of the commodity and the subject. Here lies one of the fundamental levels of communication that exhibits both artistic and economic organization – the inventive capacity of art together with the economic compulsion to subjective 'reterritorialization' (Guattari) in new frameworks of social power.[7] With his concept of the 'distribution of the sensible' (*Le Partage du sensible*), Jacques Rancière traces this back to a common mode of production that foregrounds the relationship between the production of modalities of experience and the possibilities of experiencing something. This distribution entails inclusions and exclusions in that it establishes what constitutes the horizon of the perceptible.[8] A space of action can be developed out of this argumentation by seeking alternatives to available forms of coexistence not via a recasting of stabile relationship patterns – via role reversal, altering features or reversing power relations – but via a reconfiguration of the topography of the possible. This expansion of the political sphere consists in the production of referential worlds within which decisions can be made.[9]

The words formulated by the different speakers in Oliver Ressler's video project *Alternative Economics, Alternative Societies* constitute the cells of such worlds – not only because they propose alternative models of production and co-existence but because they enter into a dialogic relationship with the words of others: the words of the Paris Commune, the words of the workers' movement or the words of radical political communities. This series of dialogues can be extended to many other groups and movements that, within the very wide field of radical alternatives to the dominant form of societal and economic production, help to form a theoretical context and trace a common engagement – from educational alternatives such as the Barefoot College in Rajasthan, India to more recent initiatives such as the anti-state No Border network and the digital open source movement. Hearing these presented talks, assimilating their terminology, tone and voices, creates a site of encounter with many parallel worlds. In Mikhail Bakhtin's concept of 'dialogism' words constitute subjectivity by generating a social space that is fundamentally interpersonal and thus facilitates a constant appropriation and transformation of the voice of the other. The radical directness of the voice and the polyphony of narrations shape a community of possibilities that enables speaker and listener to become co-producers of the community.[10] Temporally and spatially distant models of alternative sociality thus open themselves to a platform that facilitates a sharing and experiencing of parallel environments. What emerges at another level is not merely a reproduction of self-contained worlds but a complex map of intensities whose distribution, rather than according with a predetermined logic, develops out of reciprocal points of contact: out of a dispersed encounter between interest groups, out of models of other movements, networking processes and spontaneously co-ordinated actions. None of the links appearing between the models is required to be part of an overarching plan, part of the grammar of a common 'language project'. The networking process takes place in the acts of speaking and hearing not in the planning of a common language. This process avoids the limitations of a planned community and its instatement in the utopia of modern planned languages such as Esperanto, Ido, Interlingua and Volapük, which have all emerged from the desire to produce a new, global community by way of a consciously and systematically elaborated language project.[11] In this case the utopia of community refers to a far distant future that is tied to the pedagogical project of the acquisition of a shared planned language. The clearly recorded steps in the development of commonalities thus perpetuate a preconceived idea of community. They articulate community as a utopian product that is built on common goals the pursuit of which aims at the consummation of community. By contrast, a platform of speaking as seen in the case of *Alternative Economics, Alternative Societies* and many other projects in artistic and urban contexts localizes the utopia of community in a contemporary process. It is a manifestation of the community in the making.

Bijlmermeer, Amsterdam, 1996
Around Kraaiennest station in Bijlmermeer, showing the two levels of fast- and slow-moving traffic and a sprawling market along the lower level's pedestrian avenues and cycle paths

## COMMUNICATION IS NOT A BOND

If communication is not a product of work, then the communication between those who share a common horizon does not rest on a fixed alliance between contained entities. When Jean-Luc Nancy argues that 'communication is not a bond',[12] he is referring precisely to a form of communication that is not tied to the process of working towards a common goal but that rather emerges from the sharing of an ontological 'sociality'. This communication challenges the principles of shared economic identity because it does not proceed from an exchange between previously created subjects but rather sees the constitution of its community in the exchange itself, in a common exposition. The sharing of this exposition evokes a reciprocal and boundless interpellation, a communication without end. Such an evocation of communicative intertwinements and arrangements decouples the concept of networking from the economic sphere and the exclusive orientation to efficiency, progress and growth. It liberates the concept from the clasp of goal-orientation, professionalism and all that which Samuel R. Delany has characterized as 'the amount of need present in a networking situation'[13] and allows it to emerge from the question of community. Outside the attachment to work, on the everyday level of network migration and network support, relationships between networks and communities become discernible with which the separate discourses of contact as social interaction and networking as economic interaction begin to mesh.

In our search for such a structure in the interaction of artistic and spatial praxes, we want to move beyond a functionality that refers back to the operational character of 'community creation' and the ideological value of 'community achievements'. An architecture of coexistence that operates within the spatial without objectifying the spatial requires a different concept of commonality from which to proceed. Here, Jean-Luc Nancy's *The Inoperative Community* provides us with a useful critique of the ideological and economic project of the functional community. Nancy locates the weak point of this project in the concept of intersubjectivity and the principle anchored within it of reciprocal social recognition, in the fact that these ideas presume separately existing subjects in order to overlay them with the hypothetical reality of a social bond. Nancy counters this concept by maintaining that community is not founded on a work-based organization of separate existences but is constructed out of what Maurice Blanchot describes as 'unworking': an active renunciation of the activity of creating and completing in favour of disturbances, fragmentations and interruptions.[14] These pauses represent the creative moment of a community that does not realize itself by way of the belief in a collectively producible work – buildings, monuments, institutions, symbols – but via a repeatedly exercized resistance to immanent power.[15]

The shift from 'working' to 'unworking' also moves attention from the production of objects and contexts to the qualities of a situation and the possibilities that emerge from it. Instead of working on embedding qualities in objects or contexts, a current field of potentiality opens up whose autonomous existence is able to realize or hold back configuration. In the past, architecture, art and urban design have too often allowed themselves to be seduced by the apparent remedial power of a detailed plan of social utopias. However, the rigid structures of such a plan's operation cannot match the dynamically aggressive movements of fragmentation and deregulation in the globalized city, nor do they offer a field of engagement that could provide space for a fair competition between heterogeneous forces. But what if instead of simply putting aside the concept of utopia we were to redirect it and relate it to the potential of the present? If we anchor it in the midst of the everyday manifestations of social and cultural phenomena, utopia ceases to be positioned as an ideal blueprint and product of a distant future and becomes a communicative praxis that draws on the potentials of the present. Utopia thus becomes a process that negotiates its conditions and boundaries in the societal field of the present and effects transformations

Bijlmermeer, Amsterdam, 2006

within it. This shift of a distant ideal state into the here and now of the physical world presents not only a challenge to the ideational construct of the community but also a fundamental challenge to architecture as a planning discipline. It is confronted with two interrelated questions. What can architecture offer the community if community is not a project and therefore also not an architectural project? And how can it contribute to the constitution of community if the forces driving the latter are in principle non-spatial? The current crisis in the relationship between architecture and community indicated by these questions and the corresponding proliferation of spatial controls are both fundamental aspects of the search being conducted for architectures of coexistence. However, in the face of the excessive formation of obstacles to a utopian community of the present, how can a focus be brought into the debate around the formation of spatial coexistence that aims at more than exposing the negativity of domination?

This search for architectures of possibilities forms a guiding principle for many of the praxes and projects brought together in this book, including the two projects based in Paris that have intervened in the politics of urban planning via the articulation of communities. One project involves the creation of a place of retreat from the many ethnic and religiously determined groups in Sevran-Beaudottes, which was initiated by the Campement Urbain collective with its project *Je&Nous*. The other is the community garden *ECObox* by atelier d'architecture autogérée in La Chapelle. Both initiatives have been engaged over the long term in instigating a process of cultural appropriation of urban space and citizenry from the periphery. Numerous meetings, discussions and collectively organized events have been devoted to the modelling of structures within which spatial self-determination can take place. Who decides on the design of a collectively used space? Who controls access? Who takes responsibility for maintenance? Who is permitted to enter? Here, instead of healing the physical city, architecture expands and invents the means that it deploys: it uses a bricolage of art, propaganda, city policies and social relationships in order to intervene manipulatively in the context intended for urban renewal. Outside this context prescribed by authorities, hierarchies and by-laws, unplanned and self-empowered formations have emerged whose architecture is accorded a subsidiary role because it only takes on efficacy in connection with a network of participants – with the gatherings of residents; with collective actions; with the extension of the space of action in international exhibitions of the project; with the utilization and transformation of the created structures; with the myths that enable a community to emerge and the myths in which the community continues to exist.

Here, rather than producing an experimental model that is abstracted from one situation and can be transferred onto another, or an experiment that can be extrapolated if it proves successful, art practices engage in an experiment that is simultaneously its own outcome – one of many parallel worlds that represent the formation of new communities. It produces, as Giorgio Agamben formulates it, an indifference of the common and the respectively individual: 'Taking-Place, the communication of singularities in the attribute of extension, does not unite them in essence, but scatters them in existence.'[16] Its potential lies in enriching the location of a community of congregation amidst the decay of a single utopian society and the conflict of many essential communities. This 'common' occurs in the forsaking of the old communities shaped by ethnicity, religion, origin and social stigma with their respectively specific and uniform characteristics; in the opening up of ever new worlds that facilitate new forms of congregation in relation to shared horizons. The sharing of the horizon results from the production of a solidarity that consists neither in an appropriation and individualization of the common nor in the universalization of singular characteristics. Its reference point lies outside the characteristics that are anchored in the different expressions and communications of essential communities. The articulation of such solidarity requires neither an integration of the

Campo Boario, Rome, 2006

Campo Boario, Rome, 2006

specifics of all individual languages nor an equitable dissemination of a universally planned language. It requires a project of speaking that does not distinguish between a common nature of words and the spoken word. The displacements and frameworks that art can offer here facilitate a distancing from the old community and the cultivation of new connections, 'a space open to each individual and under the protection of all'.[17]

## NETWORKED AGENCY

A fundamental reference point in the formation of these worlds relates to the question of how collective agency can develop – how the plurality of dispersed forces can coalesce in forms of coordinated action and how these forms can gain relevance for the structuring of decisions, including in a political sense. Here, the model of the network can offer us a referential framework for the location of agency in so far as we discern the efficacy of action in the emergence of a new social form, in the transformation of organization in the sense of an expansion of reference points that links the different levels of economic, cultural and social activity to one another. Put another way, agency refers to a morphological process of comprehensive and continual network formation. The goal does not consist in finding the enterprise models that show how such a process acquires efficiency and how this efficiency can be applied to many spheres of everyday life. The difficulty consists in demonstrating how a certain autonomy of concrete action can establish itself within the structure of this process and how political possibilities thereby emerge. The task we face entails sketching a track that runs across the traditional separation of agency and structure, micro and macro levels, individual and collective in a way that reflects Manuel DeLanda's thesis that small autonomous organizational entities are reflected on a larger scale in other organizational entities, which in turn act autonomously. In this view, cities emerge from the interactions between the networks that form in the communication between individuals. Geopolitical structures in turn result from the interaction of cities, of networks and of individuals. DeLanda argues that even in a world shaped by alliances and connections the subject – as is the case on every other level of decisions regarding action – is not completely defined via its relationships to others.[18] At every scale level there are zones of self-organization that can generate resistance to other scales and form their own operational environment on the basis of this autonomy. Decisive here is the fact that the process in which this environment is configured cannot be explained in terms of its relationships to other spheres of influence but rather develops internal logics in the way it operates that allow for change. 'Autonomy within a community will not be realized by disciplinary regulation imposed by power, but by internal displacement, shiftings, settings and dissolutions that constitute a process of self composition: the self-regulation of a living society.'[19]

Spontaneously emerging architectures, intermediate uses, occupations, utilizations, self-organized meeting points and other temporary markings of communities, as well as the encounters between persons associated with them, are part of a route and a process, but they constitute neither the logical format nor a relationally defined goal of development. The concept of 'temporary architecture' frequently leads to the mistaken understanding of a certain aesthetic of improvised spaces as a desideratum of a community in the making and a corresponding staging of sites of the community. However, if we do not localize temporality in the aesthetics of constructional substance but rather in the different temporal rhythms of individuals, groups and communities, in the flowing movements of societal praxis itself, then we gain an insight into the extent to which the potential for the actualization of communities is spread across the individual zones of the city and roams across the different scales of social organization. Spaces that generate societal self-understanding thus take shape at every scale level of societal organization as an imprint of different temporalities that coalesce in the local and effect local shifts. That which is manifested spatially in these shifts can have many different qualities. It can be a sought-after form of expression, a camouflage, an object of defence, a contested placeholder, a point that provokes community or a mechanism in the discussion of the political question of spatial organization. All these spatial constructs refuse a clarification of the outlines of their field of action and introduce ambiguity to the classification of individuals and places. By operating against the unambivalent consolidation of constructional, social, historical or everyday-practical connections, they keep space open for what could be and at the same time reveal it to be a political question, a matter of community.

In *Homo Sacer*, Agamben proposes conceiving of the politics of community beyond its connections to actualization: as the autonomous existence of a potentiality that can counter imposed systems and restrain such a structured form of community while at the same time maintaining its capacity to become community elsewhere.[20] If we relate this capacity for the self-determined rearrangement of communities to the migrations of people, products, work and thought, then it would seem that mobility and parallelism are today the fundamental forms of expression for spatial distribution. The simultaneity of static and dynamic sites, the concurrence of zones of exception and regulated spheres, the overlapping of contradictory spatial systems – all this complicates the liminal spheres in which the transition from one organizational level to another takes place and obfuscates the reciprocal cognition of these spheres, not least the subject's self-knowledge. At the same time, as Judith Butler argues, a certain opacity of the subject constitutes a necessary part of its sociality. It is precisely due to this fabric of relationships that the subject can never give a full account of itself. Both levels can move in relation to one another, are open and can be used for change.[21] The relationships lying between these levels do not constitute an absolute dimension that infers the subject but rather an autonomous field that facilitates divergent action. Autonomy is thus not to be found on the level of a subject entirely known to itself but in the engagement with an unclear meshing of social relationships that shape and hold the subject. The state of not being completely representable to oneself, of being inconsistent or split, positions the space for a critique of norms that demand a certain behaviour of us in the field of the articulation of community with others – in a dispute over values, aesthetics and practices.

Campo Boario, Rome, 2006

There is thus also no perfect environment shapeable via art and architecture which could eliminate the pain associated with the experience of otherness. Exposure to the unknown and the uncertain is a basic experience that cannot be purged by aesthetic formation. Even if architecture is today endeavouring to meet the economic demands for the greatest possible degree of flexibility and situative adaptability, it cannot elude the confrontation with uninvited guests. Architecture can neither circumvent nor plan this experience just as it cannot produce an ideal site of coexistence. Coexistence is not a state that can be planned and therefore is available not as a blueprint but only as a political possibility.

As such a potential, coexistence, as Jean-Luc Nancy emphasizes, is particularly sharply defined at a point 'when there is no longer a 'city' or 'society' out of which a regulative figure could be modelled, at this moment being-many, shielded from all intuition, from all representation or imagination, presents itself with all the acuity of its question, with all the sovereignty of its demand. This question and demand belong to the constitution of being-many as such and, therefore, belong to the constitution of plurality *in* Being. It is here that the concept of coexistence is sharpened and made more complex'.[22] The community formulated as coexistence does not emerge via a staged merging of difference but rather reveals itself as a dispersed form

Campo Boario, Rome, 2006

based on changeable spatial configurations that interrupt this staging: spatial appropriations and take-overs, smuggling, counterfeiting and piracy. This moment of disruption becomes most explosive at the level where a common field of articulation is most lacking: in the thinking of coexistence on the scale of the global public sphere – its multiple fields of communication, its ailing forces and its indivisible common terrain. Addressing this form of community is a performative act.[23] It refers to the entire project of politics in a globalized public sphere in which the incongruity of different communal interests compels each group to creatively expand itself. Herein lies the difficulty for art and architecture: in the search for possibilities of revealing these expansions, of engaging with them and assessing them positively so that reciprocal concatenations and incorporations can form, levels of communication for a creative overlapping of different multiplicities.

In order to further develop such a concept of global coexistence and the global public sphere – one which refers to disruption and expansion – we would like to return to an idea we have already discussed in relation to the question of dealing with conflict, the idea of provisionality as compensation. What makes such an idea useful in this context is its shift in direction from the originality to the futurity. It replaces the mere toleration of contradictions and incongruities with an active moment of change. Sigmund Freud develops a psychoanalytic notion of *Ersatz* (substitute) in relation to magic and myth in his essay 'Totem and Taboo', where he suggests that art replaces an unattainable real object through an illusory one.[24] Aesthetic production and the pleasure obtained through it are in this way characterized by the figure of *Ersatz* in which the artist subscribes to a fantasy world rather than finding gratification in the real world. Freud sees no point in healthily sustaining the function of the surrogate throughout adult life. Rather, he thinks that the substitution operates as a retreat into compensatory gratification. But what if we were to recognize conflicts and disruptions in a sphere of connectedness and allow for a climate of sustained and permitted conflicts? This would constitute a step towards a possibly imperfect yet *perfectly appropriate* model of development. Such a model breaks with a clear separation of the world of fantasy and the world of reality.[25] It advocates a transformatory experience that localizes an experimentation with possible worlds in the world of existing relational structures. Competing systems and their construction of discontinuity are replaced by a shared praxis of maintained contradictions, a simultaneity of several worlds that creates space for change. 'To ask for recognition,' writes Judith Butler, 'or to offer it, is precisely not to ask for recognition of what one already is. It is to solicit a becoming, to instigate a transformation, to petition a future always in relation to the Other.'[26] Although the tension of perpetual contradictions may be accompanied by irritations, intrusions and exhaustion, what really matters is the capacity to repair and reconstitute relationships. The rejection of the concept of clear breaks and separations and a preference for perpetual contradictions point to an understanding of connectedness not as a model of enduring harmony but as an arc of tension that is maintained and altered by constant disruptions and repairs. In this model there is no normative ideal of balance that equates rifts with failure. Rather than acceding to the obsession with perfect realizations of a particular form of organization, it advocates a space in which the disordered and contradictory sides of creativity can act out their generative force and in the process precisely revise the conditions of growth.

This argumentation finds a dual echo in the often used relational construct of the multitude, as outlined by Paolo Virno in *A Grammar of the Multitude*. One aspect concerns the way in which the subject represents a zone of dispute between different forces that leave individuation incomplete and fragmentary. The mesh-like, amphibious subject of this confrontation is always tied to the force of the pre-

Campo Boario 2006
Between Monte Testaccio and the river Tiber in the XX district of Rome. The numerous courtyards of the former slaughterhouse are providing space for such diverse occupants as the *cavallari* and their three hundred horses, migrant Kurds, the caravans of the Calderasha community, the municipal police of the city of Rome, the School of Architecture of Roma Tre University and the Museum of Contemporary Art Rome (MACRO). *Villaggio Globale*, the social centre. At night the whole area around Monte Testaccio turns into one of the main nightlife districts for young Romans. There are plans by the municipality of Rome to turn the complex into a City of Arts.

Parallel Worlds

individual. The other aspect concerns the way network action acquires new models of social expression and interaction from a revision and redefinition of prevailing ideas and not from a transition from one point to another.[27] This assessment of the appropriation and reconfiguration of the network society thus rests on a concept of the substitute that has less to do with the principle of closure than with the practices of continued contradictions. This is a substitute that does not elude external reality. It neither represses this reality nor emulates it with the aid of a surrogate. It simply operates from the inside. This form of substitute is neither parasitic nor unfathomable. It is a structural mode that is conditioned by the same forces that have generated it, and it therefore shares their operational logic.

The most pressing challenge facing architecture today is that of creating possibilities for the emergence of dialogic forms of coexistence. This requires a reassertion of politics in the configuration of space and a new reoccupation of architecture as a field of collective action. Both aspects require a fundamental politicization of space as opposed to a classification of specific spaces for the conducting of politics, whether as a parliamentary forum, a public meeting or an activist group. Urban and geocultural configuration must be understood as a space of politics, and collective access to the utilization of this space must be facilitated. This in turn requires tools and means that are not borrowed from an existing repertoire but that can only be acquired within a framework of prevailing everyday realities, continually and anew. The development of such tools in dispersed experimental situations makes use of spatial and societal transition as an 'incomplete' yet 'completely appropriate' working model in order to constitute new forms of access. Here, community is not the goal of planning but rather the changeable and multifariously existent site of the acquisition of access.

Campo Boario, Rome, 2006

The approaches generated by the artistic and architectural practices brought together in this book can contribute to the further conceptual development of ways of dealing with a politics in which the maintenance of a state of exception becomes the predominant doctrine of a transformation that conforms to certain interests. They test a praxis that implants itself in this state of exception and provokes its own state of exception in order to develop and appropriate a potential for decision-making in an unregulated space of action and to reclaim the potential for transformation associated with it. Through their engagement with the predetermined material of the present, with momentary situations and with people who find themselves in a particular role, they are compelled to become inventive and to produce their own models of conflict negotiation without the security of being able to trust in expert models. It is precisely not in the application of existing expertise that their strength lies but in a constant renewal of the here and now.

In this way dispositions to action can develop that are not based on new hardening of identity traits but rather conform to a model of performative politics. Such an understanding of praxis does not invoke the role of opposition to a central power but rather breaks out of the imposed dualism of internal and external worlds and utilizes the fundamental dynamic of the network for itself – the dynamic of transformation in order to devise new relationships to the vis-à-vis. This performative praxis establishes contact and, in the process of exchange, pioneers compensatory paths that facilitate a transgression of the partitions and exclusions within the hegemonic order. Experimental spatial practices shape the substitute, the symbolic gesture that undercuts the exclusion of conflict. By giving space to lived subjectivities they facilitate the reintroduction of society in the negotiation of space. These project forms are thus not a secondary illustration of a political conflict but the terrain of the conflict itself.

1. 'Radical Muslims must integrate, says Blair', *The Guardian*, 9 December 2006, 4.
2. Sean O'Neill and Daniel McGrory, *The Suicide Factory: Abu Hamza and the Finsbury Park Mosque* (London: Harper Perennial, 2006).
3. Manuel Castells, *The Information Age: Economy, Society and Culture*, vol. 1, 2nd edition (Blackwell: Oxford, 2000), 458f.
4. Achille Mbembe, *On the Postcolony* (Berkeley, CA: University of California Press, 2001), 8.
5. Marina Gržinić, 'Performative Alternative Economics', in *Alternative Economics, Alternative Societies*, ed. Oliver Ressler (Frankfurt a.M./Novi Sad: Revolver/kuda.org, 2005), 24f.
6. Paolo Virno, *A Grammar of the Multitude: For an Analysis of Contemporary Forms of Life* (New York: Semiotext(e), 2004), 90f.
7. Félix Guattari, 'Du post-modernisme à l'ère post-media', in *Cartographies schizoanalytiques* (Paris: Galilée, 1989), 54. See also: http://brianholmes.wordpress.com/2007/07/21/swarmachine/
8. Jacques Rancière, *The Politics of Aesthetics: The Distribution of the Sensible* (London and New York: Continuum, 2004).
9. Jacques Rancière, 'The Abandonment of Democracy', in *Documenta Magazine*, no. 1-3 (2007), ed. documenta (Cologne: Taschen, 2007), 459.
10. Mikhail M. Bakhtin, *Problems of Dostoevsky's Poetics*, ed. and transl. by Caryl Emerson (Minneapolis, MN: University of Minnesota Press, 1984).
11. In this connection it is interesting to note that the steady expansion of the international Esperanto movement since the 1980s has not been based on a belated embrace of its original goals but on a complete transformation of its founding idea. The original goal of the Esperanto movement was to develop tools that would facilitate a better understanding between different cultures. However, contemporary supporters of the movement are now united by a 'conspiratorial' interest in the cultivation of their own 'Esperanto culture', i.e. in a form of communication employed in international congresses, online forums and personal meetings, hidden archives, politically oriented art circles and anti-globalization initiatives, the vehicle of which is Esperanto.
12. Jean-Luc Nancy, *The Inoperative Community* (Minneapolis, MN: University of Minnesota Press, 1991), 29.
13. Samuel R. Delany, *Times Square Red, Times Square Blue* (New York and London: New York University Press, 1999), 136.
14. Nancy, ibid. note 12, 31.
15. Ibid., 35.
16. Giorgio Agamben, *The Coming Community* (Minneapolis, MN: University of Minnesota Press, 1993), 19.
17. Campement Urbain, 'The I & Us Project', in *The [Un]common Place: Art, Public Space and Urban Aesthetics in Europe*, ed. Bartolomeo Pietromarchi (Barcelona: Actar, 2005), 206.
18. Manuel DeLanda, *A New Philosophy of Society: Assemblage Theory and Social Complexity* (London and New York: Continuum, 2006).
19. Doina Petrescu, 'Losing Control, Keeping Desire', in *Architecture and Participation*, eds. Peter Blundell Jones, Doina Petrescu and Jeremy Till (London and New York: Spon Press, 2005), 55.
20. Giorgio Agamben, *Homo Sacer: Sovereign Power and Bare Life* (Stanford, CA: Stanford University Press, 1998), 47.
21. Judith Butler, *Giving an Account of Oneself* (New York, NY: Fordham University Press, 2005).
22. Jean-Luc Nancy, *Being Singular Plural* (Stanford, CA: Stanford University Press, 2000), 43.
23. Susan Buck-Morss, *Thinking Past Terror: Islamism and Critical Theory on the Left* (London and New York: Verso, 2003), 22.
24. Sigmund Freud, 'Totem und Tabu (Einige Übereinstimmungen im Seelenleben der Wilden und der Neurotiker)', in idem, *Studienausgabe*, vol. IX, *Fragen der Gesellschaft/Ursprünge der Religion* (Frankfurt/M.: Fischer, 2000 [1912/1913]), 287-444.
25. A developmental model of conflictual praxis is sketched for example by Jessica Benjamin in 'Recognition and Destruction', *Like Subjects, Love Objects: Essays on Recognition and Sexual Difference* (New Haven, CT: Yale University Press, 1995).
26. Judith Butler, *Precarious Life. The Powers of Mourning and Violence* (London and New York: Verso, 2004), 44.
27. Virno, ibid. note 6, 80.

Campo Boario, Rome, 2006

# STEALTH

**PM/HM**: Marc and Ana, as members of STEALTH.unlimited you're currently based in Rotterdam, but it seems that the city of Belgrade has also played a formative role for the group. What is the story behind this translocal trajectory?

**Ana Dzokic**: Indeed, it all started with Belgrade and the mid-1990s, when together with a few friends I initiated an independent association called Projekt X. We were all students of architecture at the time, and in 1996 – a period of deep crisis in society – we organized an international event in an abandoned sugar factory, with 300 artists, architects and students. Through this project I began to realize that if you really want to make an impact and move things, a single person's efforts aren't enough. In 1998, Marc and I got interested in the transformation of the city of Belgrade and how, in less than a decade, a planned socialist society had turned into something completely new and difficult to describe. We started to collaborate with another colleague, Milica Topalovic, on a research project called *Wild City*. It focused on the massive, non-regulated development of an urban environment made by 'ordinary' people but ignored or even condemned by professional architects. It all began as research at the Berlage Institute in Amsterdam. Being in the Netherlands, we found it intriguing to draw a comparison to the Dutch planning context, as well as to the on-going debate on Vinex and *Het Wilde Wonen* ('Wild Living') and its institutionalized plea for far-reaching deregulation of housing. To have an actual connection with Belgrade, we approached a friend of ours, Ivan Kucina, who was teaching at the Faculty of Architecture there. *Wild City* became much more than a thesis project. It shaped our way of thinking, our approach and created a context in which to operate.

**PM/HM**: There's enormous interest in the 'Belgrade phenomenon'. How do you spread the knowledge you acquired while working on your thesis and digging deeper into Belgrade's situation? And how do you connect it all into an architectural discourse?

**Ana Dzokic**: One of the driving forces behind this project was to find out how to develop a collaborative approach and create a database on urban interventions by involving 80 students, while also having an influence on the discussion in Belgrade. The total discrepancy between the situation in Belgrade, where the whole system failed and control of spatial development was largely abandoned, and in the Netherlands, where each square centimetre of land is planned and given a function, became vital. What we find interesting is neither the one nor the other, but actually the situation in between. We're not only interested in bottom-up developments and what people do, but in the interaction of institutions with what people do. Is there something that evolves when they interact consciously or subconsciously, something from which we can gain knowledge and that can be integrated into our profession? We're not interested in cataloguing weird phenomena in order to exoticize issues existing in the Balkans, but to acquire knowledge from Belgrade's 'laboratory condition'. A challenging outcome of *Wild City* was that we became aware of the possibility of translating the urban (physical) complexity into the digital realm, of understanding and playing with the processes that shape the physical reality of the city, while at the same time getting to know the points where we might enter their trajectories in order to intervene. By connecting up with Mario Campanella, an aeronautics engineer with a master's degree in artificial intelligence, we developed

*Cut for Purpose*
Museum Boijmans van Beuningen, Rotterdam, 2006
STEALTH, project by Mario Campanella, Ana Dzokic, Marc Neelen

*Cut for Purpose*
Museum Boijmans van Beuningen, Rotterdam, 2006
Space cut out and used by participants
(Wendelien van Oldenborgh)

**Ana Dzokic:** The preoccupation of architects with the aesthetics of built objects is something we don't find very interesting. While researching on Belgrade, we weren't fascinated by its do-it-yourself aesthetics, but by the logic of this urban transformation, how it worked, and how it responded to economic success or failure. Not every situation worked well – some were quite problematic, but others went far beyond our professional imagination.

**Marc Neelen:** For a while during Modernism, there was the idea that architects could have a monopoly on space and its aesthetics. This period is definitely over. Let's speak about the situation in Europe. Control of who develops space is now distributed among many. Previously the state almost always set the conditions. In many countries today, the involvement of the state has decreased drastically and given way to private initiative, even on the lowest level of development. If this is, indeed, the context we're now dealing with, then things have gone far beyond aesthetics and are more about how you navigate developments in such conditions. To some extent you have to reinvent how you practise architecture. To be effective, you need to cooperate with others. One of the most impor-

*Wild City*, Belgrade, 1999-2001
STEALTH, project by Ana Dzokic, Ivan Kucina, Marc Neelen, Milica Topalovic

little room for this diversity to express itself spatially.

**PM/HM:** This brings up the question of the architect's role and possibilities in moulding future cityscapes. According to the traditional reading, the task of architecture is to come up with a certain spatial and visual configuration, one that is able to support a particular form of social organization. Do you see ways for architecture to engage in social dynamics other than by concerning itself with aesthetic production?

*Wild City*, Belgrade, 1999-2001
Village architecture densifies top floor of a city centre housing block

**Marc Neelen:** I would say that looking at Belgrade tells us a lot about some phenomena that are actually happening right here in Rotterdam but aren't so visible. In a crude situation like Belgrade's socio-political, cultural, economic crisis, you find a lot of transitions occurring right in front of your eyes. Similar things are happening in the Netherlands, even if not so directly, and if they don't affect your life as harshly, still they exist. In the project *Europe Lost and Found*, which we've been working on since 2005, the idea is to look at the former Yugoslav republics in order to have a better understanding of what is going on in the rest of Europe. Here in the Netherlands we're also dealing with a state that is cutting its responsibilities and becoming less powerful. We used to have a fairly regulated planning procedure in Holland; roughly each decade the state released a plan on how the country should be transformed. This is one of the things that has been given up recently. What the effects of this will be isn't at all clear, and we've no similar local experiences from which to take reference – so this is where Belgrade may be able to give us vital clues. If we look at the ways of living in these two cities, Rotterdam is definitely much more diverse in culture than Belgrade, but it leaves

the next incarnation of the project. It was called *ProcessMatter* and resulted in a digital simulation of the practice of street trade as observed in Belgrade.

**PM/HM:** How do you relate your initial research in Belgrade with investigating the situation in cities like Rotterdam? Is this about enriching the Dutch model with the Belgrade experience – or is a certain change already happening here as well, because different groups of people are also introducing different ways of living to Rotterdam all the time?

257

*Wild City*, Belgrade, 1999-2001
A private, one-man business and a public transport company run the same bus line (with buses of different type, size and colour)

**258** tant aspects of STEALTH's work is the co-authoring of urban space. As the city is a product of a multitude of interactions, it's important to tap into these energies – one single approach won't work. Hence, working in a network is vital to our profession.

van Beuningen in Rotterdam. Three young curators from its City Editorial Board wanted to push their activities beyond the institution and bring the dynamics of the city into the museum: with the Rotterdam art scene and its city audiences. So we decided to install a grid of 2,000 sheets of cardboard that would fill 400 square metres of museum space. Over a period of nine weeks and without any prearranged layout, a number of groups have been invited to excavate spaces for their activities within it. To set off the process, five simple spatial guidelines were provided. Here our tool has not been research, but the provision of a real physical structure as common ground – a 'larger-than-human' tool for co-authoring.

**Ana Dzokic:** One of the projects where this is being tested – and we're sitting in it now during this interview – is the project *Cut for Purpose*, made on the invitation of the Museum Boijmans

*Wild City*, Belgrade, 1999-2001
Semi-legal commercial activities occupy the pavement; the upper floor is used as a living space

**PM/HM:** How would you describe the motivations that formed the basis for atelier d'architecture autogérée (aaa) and what influence did these have on the structure of your work, for instance on the *ECObox* project you initiated in your own neighbourhood of La Chapelle?

**Constantin Petcou:** Two of the initiators, Doina Petrescu and myself, are from Romania, and when we came here we didn't know anything about liberal architectural practices. And maybe just because we were new to the West, we had the illusion we would find something more promising and visionary.

We were quite disappointed to discover that liberal practices in architecture didn't have real political and social concerns. We knew that in the UK and the US, where there was much less work at the time, a few architects were trying to develop other strategies. Step by step we attempted, in the 1990s, to develop another approach, one that was more political but independent from political lobbies and experimented with other ways of producing space. We started to develop strategies and tactics for provoking more from a user's perspective and acting as a 'catalyst'. We tried to re-position ourselves – neither at the top nor at the bottom, but somewhere in between. Like grass, in Deleuzian terms. And it was from this position that we tried to create transversal networks. The classic short-term, abstract and top-down assignment doesn't really work when one wants to invent practices embedded in urban realities and address the complex, mobile, transcultural dynamics of everyday life in a big city.

In a way it's difficult to say when all this started. It actually began before our experiences with aaa: in the 1990s we had tried to develop some projects in Romania. All the radical changes had left a legal void in the political system of Eastern Europe. So we took on a *bricolage* approach to our projects. We started aaa with the *ECObox* project in Paris, and for three years it was about the only aaa project, because it took all our energy. We were involved in this project in an everyday kind of way, because we were also inhabitants there. In other words, we lived in the area, which meant it was not an external project. It was a very interesting experience but also very intense and more or less a full-time activity. We created the preconditions for the project and at the same time for the group using it. Our strategy was to promote self-management. The first three years was a formative period for the group. When we had to move and the project disappeared as a 'place', it lived on as a group and this group was able to claim another space. Today *ECObox* has a new space and has become another self-managed, dynamic project. For a few months now, it has been run by a users' organization created by the people involved in the project. We keep in contact and try to maintain some kind of synergy.

**PM/HM:** Regarding the involvement of various communities and different professions or different kinds of activist groups, how did the *ECObox* project become a real communal project and not just a form of collaboration between different professionals on a temporary art project?

**Constantin Petcou:** Our tactic is to work over time with very long-term commitments and something like an

Nomad garden
The progressive construction of the *ECObox* garden between 2002-2004 in the yard of Halle Pajol, in La Chapelle area of Paris. Dismantling, displacing and temporary reinstallation on another vacant plot in the same area in 2005.

aaa

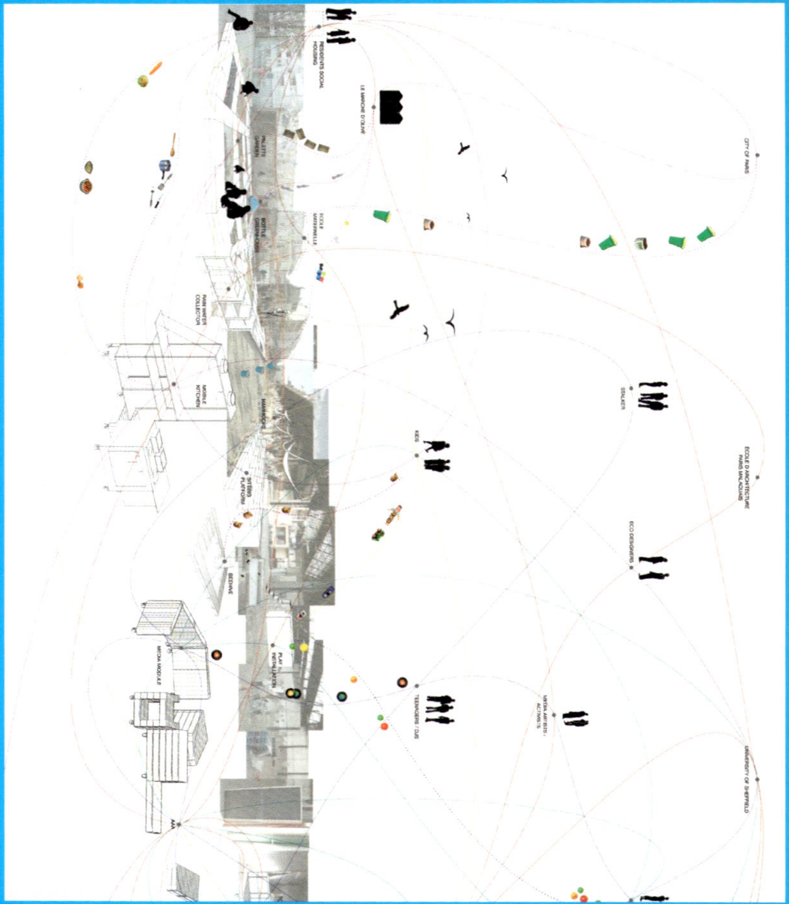

Participation and self-management
The collective programming of activities was based on a flexible use of space and the users' participation in its maintenance. This has progressively conducted to the self-management of the project.

say, different value systems. What was more, they all had different notions of an institution, local life, collective space, etc. So, we had to give people time to understand and agree on what kind of (non-) institution, group or organization we were, because it was not possible to classify us within existing ones. And bit by bit, as people started to talk to each other, a lot of other people arrived and began doing things, because somebody had told them that there was this place. That was how it worked, though not without conflicts, of course. We tried not to communicate too much through the media, because it was much better to let the information circulate through a physical network, one that had a certain proximity. Thus, over time, we succeeded in establishing a physical network that was both transcultural and -social. Though somehow the network created itself; we didn't actually do anything directly. We just enabled the situation, a possibility, and people generated the dynamics themselves. So this was one precondition. A second one had to do with claiming space and making it available for experimentation with what we might call a translocal platform. By chance, we managed to obtain a huge space, and this space – plus all the mobile infrastructure we established (e.g. a series

ECObox garden, Paris, 2002-2004

open translocal platform. A number of conditions are necessary for such a project to survive, and the first one is to give it time, to wait and not to propose anything specific at the beginning. In the case of ECObox, we tried – for political and pragmatic but also ecological reasons – to initiate a self-managed space. A precondition for this was to give ourselves a lot of time to build up people's confidence in us, whether they were from Europe, Central or North Africa, India or elsewhere – people who had different cultural backgrounds and, I would even

260

of mobile modules with micro-infrastructures for cooking, sound & media, reading & writing, joinery, composting, rainwater) – caused people gradually to propose certain activities: cultural events and economic activities, political meetings and debates.
In fact, we didn't do much but rather let things be, creating a possibility for things to appear or happen, enabling a certain momentum, something that doesn't happen in a 'normal' institution or urban structure. Nobody expects people to propose an activity and, for us as artists, this was very interesting.

Of course we also had our own network of friends and connections, which was important at the start and gave us some initial orientation, but everything afterwards depended on the people involved. They built up another network, whose dynamics were multi-layered: for example, last year this network focused more on media, i.e. tactical media. Before that, the network had been oriented more towards architectural eco-design and alternative energy, because these were compatible with the interests of the people involved. So it has all been diverse and flexible. Everything depends on who gets involved – ultimately I think we can speak here of temporary networks that create lasting projects.

**PM/HM**: How can one share the experience of such a networked project with a more translocal audience, be it through exhibitions, such as the berlin biennial for contemporary art, as in your case, or archival structures?

**Constantin Petcou**: Our strategy is not just 'architectural' – it's also political. And in a way, the project is both social and artistic. When I say artistic, I mean 'art' as a 'free space' for architecture. For an 'architect', ways of producing space are very standardized and restricted by norms and regulations, whereas for an 'artist', there's much more freedom to do things. So we wanted to go beyond the norms of architecture by opportunistically using another mode of spatial production, i.e. an 'artistic' one. But such transference can be critical. We know, of course, that an art space or commission can also be rather limiting at times, but what we wanted from it was the opportunity to criticize both architecture and art production by doing things in a different way. In this sense our approach is both interdisciplinary and extradisciplinary. We try to be extradisciplinary as architects and critically push the limits of our profession, which is, I guess, one of the reasons why we're invited to exhibit, to show in such spaces. In reality, however, we don't show anything in a usual way. Rather we use the art space to produce problems and to share them with others. This was the case with the berlin biennial and the GAK (Gesellschaft für Aktuelle Kunst) in Bremen, as well as other art events and venues where we used the exhibition to create a workspace for a self-organized team, and the institutional framework as an opportunity for people without means to do critical work and have visibility: the spaces we have created fluctuate between being

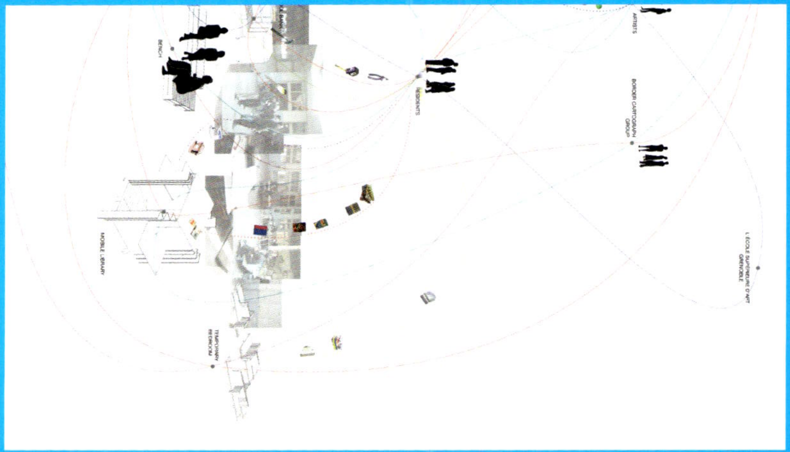

**Mobile modules**
A number of modules (kitchen, tool bank, radio station, library, water collector) have been realized by aaa and inhabitants, artists and students. They constitute the elements of a mobile architecture which allow multiple combinations of space and use, mixing different publics and users.

a public and/or meeting space, workshop or even personal space, if necessary. In Berlin we had a small space for 'cooking ideas' with two conference tables; step by step we used the wood from the tables to construct a mobile urban kitchen, which was then taken out into the city. What we showed or, let's say, 'made visible' was a meeting-working-cooking space accessible to a large number of people. All these experiences have been documented as processes, which means we now have a rather big video archive that includes most of the projects we've participated in. And we hope that one day, in addition to capturing memories of our past experiences, this archive will become a resource for others. Transmission might also be called a precondition for projects of this kind. We transmit projects in many ways: first know-how is passed directly on to others while the project is being implemented and experienced (as was the case with *ECObox*); and then specific transmission tools are created, for instance, an archive accessible under certain conditions to everybody interested, an infrastructural base that can be borrowed or shared as well as long-term assistance and friendship.

**262**

# Igor Dobricic

*Before and After the Show*
Seminar, Lisbon, 10–11 June 2006
ALMOSTREAL

**PM/HM**: You're coordinator of the ALMOSTREAL project at the European Cultural Foundation (ECF) in Amsterdam. What are the main goals of this networking project and how do they relate to the ECF's mission more generally?

**Igor Dobricic**: The ECF is a cultural foundation, which means we're not an art foundation and we're not funding 'art for art's sake'. So we've a certain social and cultural agenda for funding art, and this involves searching for a special kind of art that has social relevance. But we have noticed that funding policies often create a particular kind of art instead of discovering it. Foundations invest in what they consider 'engaged art' and by doing so make this art possible. Especially in eastern Europe a lot has happened that has made artists change how they work in order to get funding – this is an entirely unsatisfactory development. As a funding body, one shouldn't create an art scene through the way one invests money, but rather figure out how to identify aspects that are especially socially relevant in existing art practices. Funds should not be allocated to particular kinds of practices, but to practices individually selected for their specific characteristics. ALMOSTREAL marks an honest attempt – however clumsy it might seem – to move away from instrumentalizing the arts via funding policies and towards funding those projects in art whose relevance isn't dependent on their sources of financial support.

What's more, the results of funding often aren't sustainable in the long run. Let's say you're funding a certain activity and you're doing this somewhere in Europe where fewer resources are available. Well, the moment you pull out, this activity breaks down, because there's nobody to take over. So our major strategy with respect to this problem is to stimulate alliances, collaborations and partnerships, and the creation of a specific network – or a number of overlapping networks. These networks develop between artists and practitioners, who are supported by us so they can create platforms. The assumption is that this kind of networking with its exchange of information and flow of resources will sustain each individual organization better. This has been an important point in informing the structure of ALMOSTREAL.

Another important aspect of the project is that when we coordinate and fund we try to use the same tools as the artists themselves are using. In other words, we actually want to do what we preach. In this project we try to operate and interact with our partners by looking at how they – artists or art collectives or art initiatives – operate. This also means we create a structure that is unusual for various reasons. This structure is evolving and continuously changing – to a dangerous point of radical fuzziness – through the input of people who have become our partners. So we create a certain network with a number of interesting organizations, individuals and artists, and then we encourage them to re-create it with their input and critical thinking, and this makes it change and evolve accordingly.

**PM/HM**: In your writings you introduce intercultural competence – rather than the rhetoric of intercultural dialogue – as a more meaningful concept for facilitating an understanding of difference. How can intercultural competence be promoted through a funding body like the ECF?

**Igor Dobricic**: Competence implies making an effort to learn, which is why it's more appealing than the notion of dialogue, which is easily taken for granted as some kind of inborn, God-given ability. I think notions of learning/education/social emancipation are crucial for a different approach toward problems of difference. By calling it competence we also force ourselves to clearly identify exactly how we're failing today to 'teach and transmit this competence'. I was at a conference recently on intercultural communication – yet another such term – in Genoa, Italy: a highly academic event in a port city full of immigrants. You had these 20 people sitting in Genoa's City Hall, this beautiful Renaissance room, discussing the issue of intercultural communication – all very high-level, very intelligent, very insightful. Yet none of this informs any kind of practice. When you step out of City Hall onto the street, you're confronted by the reality of Genoa, full of African immigrants, which was why the conference was organized in the first place. For the most part, these two worlds remain separate. And the radicalism of this separation and the sheer shock of moving between these two worlds that exist in the same cityscape and don't communicate at all – are quite disturbing. So to trigger an understanding and exchange of differences, rather than regretting the lack of shared identities, we truly need to address the reality of parallelism and separation. The first thing involved is a competent engagement with difference, and the second, the hope that art will be able to provide a place where this encounter can be explored in a very complex and sophisticated – as well as accessible and experiential – form. Though this doesn't necessarily have to be done on a grand scale, but with honesty and without fear of misunderstandings and confrontations. For currently the exploration of difference in cultural and social practice is not really happening on a serious level due to fear.

To give an example of the precious experiences that small organizations can have in the context of an alternative/independent cultural scene, I would like to mention the Balkan region, where those who are dealing or operating in the proximity of the 'new' alternative media scene are communicating the most efficiently across national boundaries in the arts at the moment. They've developed and perfected certain skills and strategies that are quite fascinating in the context of Balkan fragmentation. I don't see any other artistic discipline or group doing the same. So for us and ALMOSTREAL, as a personal given, as a structure of consciousness. I think anybody who aims at programmatically exposing or accommodating the differences in other individuals without referring to his or her own internal processes of differentiation and alienation is doing something other than art. As an artist you somehow know that it's impossible to carry out a social or political mission without making and understanding it as a personal, internalized issue. If the mission to 'change the world' is completely externalized, the artist can no longer practice art; he or she is doing something else and immediately becomes implicated as merely another player in the social game of power. And from game theory we know: it's very hard to change the rules of a game if you're fully implicated in it. Since we live in a liberal capitalist context, we all experience this difficulty quite personally. This reference to the otherness in us is like a side exit from the maze, a place where the social game dissolves into the process of personal transformation. And this is where I see the role of artistic production: in exercising and exploring strategies of change that in many different ways go beyond self-expression (identity), but always proceed from self-examination (difference).

it has been really interesting to focus on a few key organizations – kuda.org and PRELOM in Serbia, WHW in Croatia, pro.ba in Bosnia – and try to develop a series of activities with them that we would want to support.

ALMOSTREAL works from the premise or belief that the power of art stems from the fact that by nature artistic activity deals with difference in, what I might call, a fundamental, existential way; i.e. individual difference is seen

*"It will be what we make it"*
Preparatory meeting, Lisbon, 1-3 July 2007
ALMOSTREAL

*"Karima meets Lisboa meets Miguel meets Cairo"*
ALMOSTREAL

264

Parallel Worlds Interview

# Parallel Worlds

## of Self-Education, Self-Organization and Self-Empowerment, and the Question of Biopolitics

### Marina Gržinić

The question of self-education, self-organization and self-empowerment is one of structural and institutional possibility, economy and agency in the deeply unbalanced (biopolitical) space of Europe. The process of self-empowerment is to be seen as a critique of contemporary official and institutionalized structures of presentation, mediation and articulation that concentrate in the last instance on only taking care of themselves.

First World capitalism has recently lost interest in former Eastern European space. Or rather, it never actually had any profound interest in it. This situation can be understood only on the level of the internal developments of contemporary global capitalism and in light of the fact that a once-divided Europe is gradually disappearing; it is now regarded as a union of 'Europeans'. Reasons for this sudden but complete indifference to Eastern Europe at the heart of Europe vary. Though all of them are connected with financial capital, the prevalent form of contemporary capital that accumulates differentially through circulation. Past divisions and the ideology of difference within Europe are seen as an obstacle to such circulation. Behaving as if Europe is already one common space makes it unnecessary to push inclusion through exclusion; instead it is enough to behave as if differences no longer exist. We all become identical through a process of evacuation, one that David Harvey defines as 'accumulation by dispossession' in his *Brief History of NeoLiberalism*. 'Accumulation by dispossession' was and is a process of expulsion, one that negates the possession of any possible difference. And where required for its completion, legal means have been used in combination with institutional, legislative, bureaucratic, infrastructural, theoretical and cultural devices. The process of 'accumulation by dispossession' may no longer be underway in Europe; many see it as already completed here. Yet it is still in progress elsewhere, for example in the Third World.

As a consequence of this change, Chris Wright and Samantha Alvarez argue against David Harvey's 'accumulation by dispossession' in their article 'Expropriate, Accumulate, Financialise'. Instead they propose another process characteristic for financial capital, one described by Michael Hudson in *Super Imperialism* in 1972 (and republished in 2003). Hudson says that we are witnessing a process that, instead of gaps in distribution, displays the contrary; he terms it 'the imperialism of circulation'. In my view, these processes cannot be seen as a simple shift between modes of accumulation of capital (one relegating 'accumulation by dispossession' to the sidelines): rather the one has constituted (through dispossession) the parameters for the other in order to dominate the present moment.

I have sketched out some of the most interesting aspects in the important debate about questions of accumulation and redistribution of financial capital. They have to be seen as constituting the backdrop for all serious debate on what has to be done at present with regard to questions of agency for possible emancipative politics within and/or against global capitalism. But what is particularly important for now is the process of what, in relation to Hudson, we may call the 'imperialism of endless circulation', a process that has its equivalent in another process, one

I can describe simply by referring to Jelica Šumić-Riha's article 'Jetniki Drugega, ki ne obstaja' ('Prisoners of the Inexistent Other'). According to her, what is impossible in today's world of capitalism is impossibility as such.

The imperialism of circulation without differences as the primary logic behind the conditions that produce global financial capitalism implies that what is being produced is money as financial power, though this bubble is also sure to burst sooner or later. Nevertheless, capital has only one agenda – surplus value – and this is more than just a programme or a Hollywood film conspiracy; it is a driving force. In its frantic attempt for ever more possibilities, the imperialism of circulation prevents subversion and the attack of a master entity. Everything circulates, is exchanged and clearly dispossessed of any difference; no obstacles are to be seen in the network that structures reality for us. Those once perceived as enemies – from individuals to institutions – are behaving as if we were all mired in the same situation and, now united, have to find the remedy to our problems and obstacles (which they created in the first place, though they forgot this immediately). Today it is impossible to say something is impossible.

Or to put it differently: in the past, subversive acts were possible as they were subversion against an unmistakable 'foreclosure' and division in society. The big Other, the virtual symbolic order or the network that structured and continues to structure reality for us, was what gave things 'a consistency' and nearly guaranteed interventions against it. The world today presents itself in an endless circulation (imperialism is an excellent concept to capture this force), and it is seen as 'friendly' and as an endless exchange. Therefore to solve expropriation, enslavement and neo-colonial interventions by capital, a single measure is proposed – 'coordination' (are we really so dumb as to pursue such a theory?). Of course those proposing this have a card up their sleeve: in order for things to circulate smoothly, it is necessary to coordinate things successfully, and this also means getting rid of those who still bother us with social and class antagonisms.

Setting boundaries for this inconsistency of the big Other means to act. Acting changes the very coordinates of such impossibility. For it is only by acting that I can effectively assume the non-existence of the big Other. This not only implies that I have to take the representation and articulation of a division into my own hands in order to set the boundary within this cynical situation, one in which the only thing that is impossible is impossibility as such, but it also, as argued by Šumić-Riha, implies that it is necessary to build the framework to effect a 'foreclosure' that will set the parameters and provide the coordinates of the political act. And yet, as Šumić-Riha reminds us and Jacques Lacan already argued in *Seminaire XVI*, if discourse has no foreclosure it does not necessarily mean an end is impossible. On the contrary: due to the disappearance of foreclosure, this topic is continually part of the agenda.

**ZAVZEMAMO PROSTOR**
**WIR GREIFEN RAUM**

*Zavzemamo prostor/WIR GREIFEN RAUM*, banner by the Research Group on Black Austrian History and Presence from Vienna, Araba Evelyn Johnston-Arthur and Belinda Kazeem, placed on the roof of Pavel Haus (Pavel house) in Laafeld, Austria (from July 2007 on), as part of the exhibition project *Toposcapes: Interventions into Socio-cultural and Political Spaces*, curators Marina Gržinić & Walter Seidl (Ljubljana/Vienna)

To recapitulate, what is impossible today is impossibility as such. This has clear repercussions on the level of resistance. But first to an example of a political act that does away with the inconsistency and non-existence of the big Other, and frees itself from being a hostage of the Other: the project *Zavzemamo prostor/ WIR GREIFEN RAUM* by the Research Group on Black Austrian History and Presence from Vienna, with its core members Araba Evelyn Johnston-Arthur and Belinda Kazeem, analyses the structural settings of contemporary racism, chauvinism and enslavement. With a statement in Slovenian and German,

*Zavzemamo prostor/WIR GREIFEN RAUM*, (WE ARE SEIZING AND CLAIMING SPACE) displayed as of July 2007 on a gigantic banner on the roof of the Pavel House – an intercultural meeting place and centre for the Slovenian minority in Laafeld, Austria – the Research Group connects two pressing issues of Austrian political and social reality.

Their first claim relates to Article 7, Paragraph 3 of the Austrian State Treaty concerning the rights of the Slovenian and Croatian minorities that stipulates: 'In administrative and judicial areas of Carinthia, Burgenland and Styria with Slovenian, Croatian and mixed populations, the Slovenian and Croatian languages, besides German, shall be permitted as official languages. Signposts and signs in these areas shall be in the Slovenian and Croatian as well as German languages.' Thus Article 7, Paragraph 3 of the Austrian State Treaty unambiguously defines the installation of bilingual signs. A problem arises because the Article does not define the areas or criteria for their installation, and so leaves room for interpretation (from 92 to 394 signposts). Ultimately there is the request to install a total of 394 bilingual signs, i.e. in all areas with more than 10 percent Slovenian-speaking inhabitants. The project of the Research Group on Black Austrian History and Presence must be seen as a precise intervention in this context. Their second claim relates to the group's aim of decolonizing Austrian history from established prejudices and recurring racist stereotypes that have been structurally, institutionally and historically incorporated into the present reality of the country.

A declaration of existence is the first step, argues Šumić-Riha, but what follows is the rigorous practice and logics of consequences in which the impossibility of the foreclosure of the capitalist discourse turns into the condition of a new possibility. It is the act that interrupts the consistency of the situation – indeed, it is the step outside. The Research Group on Black Austrian History and Presence explores the histories associated with our representational politics and how we reposition ourselves within a certain social, economic and political territory.

Global capitalism functions via the enactment of an iron law of worldwide sameness, and this is precisely what makes it possible for us to speak of a global world! (Capital is global!) Global capitalism means only capital is universal and free to move everywhere; capital is the only fully global citizen on our planet. Capital transforms processes of thinking into skills, depriving those who study and, therefore, 'the future citizens of the world without a world' of sustainable political and acting coordinates. The system of education becomes unified and 'easily understandable' and, even more important, easily transferable; education becomes a transparent machine for production and the circulation of skills. Therefore interventions by the EU, and beyond the EU, in education and knowledge have a precise agenda: to transform universities and academies into managerial institutions that will produce skilled students as future managers and submissive citizens. This agenda seems to be progressing well if we think of the current entrepreneurial applications at universities promoted by the Bologna Process. The Bologna Process, with its implementation of problematic reforms in education that dissociate education from social and political thought, is an EU initiative aiming to standardize education across the European continent and in the United States. It obviously favours industry or entrepreneurial applications and is against those practices of art that do not have the authority or institutional sanctioning of more traditional forms of art training.

On the one hand, we see the progressive privatization of education, a trend that is in stark opposition to what was propagated not too long ago as a milestone of neoliberal democracy, with its ideal of untouchable public space (which is also undergoing progressive privatization). On the other hand, in reference to Walter Mignolo, we see the devaluation of education. But privatization also means the privatization of histories, data, facts and views through a system that bears a paradoxical name: the universalization of knowledge. Though it should actually be obvious that only some histories and facts, views and systems – those of the ruling class – count as universal histories and universal views for all possible localities. Knowledge is not just a corpus formed from the 'outside' through administrative regulations and infrastructural deregulations. Inside it also hides class antagonisms and a colonial past.

Marina Garcés asks: 'What then does the production of critical and shared thinking consist of?' To answer this it is necessary to investigate official structures of knowledge and cultural production, along with how to build counter organizational frameworks. What I would like to say is that self-organization implies not only a process of criticizing universal knowledge, but also the detection of internal colonial situations. Garcés argues that if we only engage in asking what globalization has stolen from us, we find ourselves reduced to mere spectators, consumers or victims. By doing so we remove ourselves from any responsibility for local context and history. What is necessary is the political act of re-appropriating history and genealogies, an act that will result in re-capturing the materiality of a history yet to be constructed. History cannot be perceived as something purely virtual and fictionalized. If we take the path of being mere spectators, consumers or victims of the injustices capital has inflicted on us, we find ourselves prisoners and slaves of a system, as Garcés argues, that produces only a long list of wrongs.

Self-organization and self-referentiality are not reborn from empty space. The effects of critique cannot be measured only by what is said but also, according to Garcés, by the grounds on which we base our criticism. This takes us to our next claim, that universities are the outcome of the modern colonial expedition, such as emphasized by Walter Mignolo. What does this mean? That the universal is founded on a fake neutrality in order to hide, as Araba Evelyn Johnston-Arthur and Belinda Kazeem formulate it, its direct connection to the bloody histories of violence of a colonialism impregnated with enslavement, a looting of local histories, experiences and knowledge. Today the universality of knowledge has been cut off from the roots of modernity, and modernity can only be understood properly if seen in connection with the imperialistic colonial adventures of capitalism.

What is to be done? Instead of presenting ourselves as victims and outcome of a regulative policy that comes from the outside, it is necessary to think about the colonial from the inside. Walter Mignolo, in his endeavour to establish a new geopolitics of knowledge, talks about a radical proposition that means dismantling internal colonialism, and validating knowledge and power from the internal colonial difference. What matters is the construction of a new conceptual genealogy. Establishing such a genealogy means to wake up and rise precisely when we're knocked down by capitalism and post-socialist, transitional power relations and expropriations. Or even more to the point: 'The central issue of the geopolitics of knowledge is to understand ... what type of knowledge is produced "from the side of colonial difference" and what type of knowledge is produced 'from the other side of colonial difference"'. Such tasks differ in Latin America, the Caribbean, Asia, Africa, Europe, Germany, Serbia, Slovenia or Austria.

Going back to Araba Evelyn Johnston-Arthur's writings, I would like to emphasize that she proposes a new conceptual genealogy as a direct political gesture, as an act of intervention within local space. As said, Johnston-Arthur is one of the core members of the Research Group on Black Austrian History and Presence from Vienna, which organized itself to contest/provoke/decolonize deeply rooted colonial processes that have become a normal part of daily life in Austria.

Johnston-Arthur emphasizes that their work consists of exposing the systematically hidden histories of the African diaspora at local sites in Austria. She writes about how the current Viennese tradition is rooted in the bloody history of colonial violence and enslavement. Today this tradition has been normalized and trivialized. Then she goes on to argue that the re-staging of colonial scenes is an integral part of Viennese cultural practices and tradition. We encounter them in coffeehouses, pastry shops, as street names, as racist insults on the walls of houses and in public transport. She describes the situation of drinking coffee from a cup with a Meinl logo in a traditional Viennese coffeehouse. Meinl is an Austrian company whose wealth came from trading colonial goods. On a traditional coffee cup with the Meinl logo we see, as Johnston-Arthur points out, an orientalized black child as symbol of the fancy food industry, while in fact the logo restages Austria's colonial past. Johnston-Arthur writes: 'Enslaved Africans were mostly deported as children, made objects of the profitable "slave trade" in the eighteenth century. An essential element of this violent history of colonial oppression was and is the radical transformation of Africans into objects, into things.'

*Cafe Dekolonial – Sag der Mehlspeis leise Servus*, by the Research Group on Black Austrian History and Presence from Vienna, Araba Evelyn Johnston-Arthur, Belinda Kazeem and Njideka Stephanie Iroh, as part of the exhibition project *Toposcapes: Interventions into Socio-cultural and Political Spaces*, 2007, curators Marina Gržinić & Walter Seidl (Ljubljana/Vienna)

This also means, as Mignolo states, to act politically against the academic standard of scientific rigour in which the scientific obfuscates every possible criticism, and to insist on a decolonization that will interfere with 'proper' local history. It is necessary to analyse power structures in a local setting that allows us to behave completely detached from local history and the present.

In an essay written at the beginning of 2000 – just before the untimely death of Belgrade theorist and feminist Žarana Papić – entitled 'Europe after 1989: Ethnic Wars, Fascization of Social Life and Body Politics in Serbia', Žarana Papić argues that the '"chosen discourses of appropriation" of social memory, collective trauma and the re-creation of the Enemy-Otherness in image and event can become an integral, "self-participatory" agent in the Serbian pro-fascist construction of the social reality'. She goes on to say that the 'power over the representation of social reality' in Serbia can be seen as a strong discursive instrument of a political order. Its power lies in the position of the 'selective legitimization/delegitimization of social memory and social "pre-sence": through narration/negation of social trauma, transformable presence/absence of violence, the constitution/virtuality of the public sphere, and the formation of "collective consciousness". The legitimizing power of this dominant discourse lies in the construction of the "collective consensus"' with 'narcissistic rhetoric'; as emphasized by Papić, the outside world is the only factor and agency of misery inside Serbia and of de-privileging circumstances. With such a process, a field of self-victimization is opened and reconstituted, one that becomes active on every level of Serbian society, from the populist masses to intellectual and artistic practices. Papić describes this process of self-victimization as 'peregrination of the trauma', as a process of denial of any responsibility, for example, for war crimes in the former Yugoslavia.

Žarana Papić also speaks about a 're-invention of the chosen trauma' at the level of 'the public', one reinforced through the state media and as such a carefully planned revision of the historical balance sheet. To quote her: 'The media consistently forged... the Serb "indifference" towards the Other(s). The trauma became so internalized that Croatian and Bosnian victims could never reach the sacred status of the allegedly... 'greatest' Serbian, victims from 1941-42. One could perhaps even describe this as a "fictionalization of the chosen trauma".'

In relation to Žarana Papić's almost forgotten analysis – one that has even greater topicality today – it is important to understand that there is no outside to imperial or colonial difference. It is easier to adhere to the hegemonic genealogies of modern and post-modern Western thought (Mignolo) as well as much more fun and 'sexy' to adhere to the idea of being a victim, of being a product of the 'fictionalization of the chosen trauma'. It is easier to act for the big Other (Jelica Šumić-Riha) than to take the path of a radical political act that neither guarantees the same names nor immediate success. And precisely such a radical political act has been realized by the Research Group on Black Austrian History and Presence from Vienna.

References
- Austrian State Treaty, Article 7, Paragraph 3. See: http://www.mzz.gov.si/en/slovenian_minorities/
- Marina Garcés, 'The Experience of the US', *Zehar*, no. 60-61 (San Sebastian, 2007).
- http://magazines.documenta.de/attachment/000000343.pdf
- Marina Gržinić, 'Feminism is Politics', *Shedhalle*, no. 2 (Zurich, 2007).
- Marina Gržinić, 'The Impurity of Education, Knowledge and Self-Organization', *TKH: Journal for Performing Arts Theory*, no. 15 (Belgrade, 2008).
- David Harvey, *A Brief History of Neoliberalism* (Oxford: Oxford University Press, 2005).
- Michael Hudson, *Super Imperialism: The Origins and Fundamentals of U.S. World Dominance* (London: Oxford University Press, 2003).
- Araba Evelyn Johnston-Arthur (text) and Belinda Kazeem (visuals), *Reartikulacija/Re-articulation*, no.1 (Ljubljana, 2007). http://www.reartikulacija.org/pozicioniranje.html
- Jacques Lacan, *Le Séminaire livre XVI* (1968-1969), *D'un Autre à l'autre* (Paris: Seuil, 2006).
- Catherine Walsh, 'The geopolitics of knowledge and the coloniality of power: An interview with Mignolo', *Zehar*, no. 60-61 (San Sebastian, 2007). http://magazines.documenta.de/attachment/000000345.pdf
- Žarana Papić, 'Europe after 1989: Ethnic Wars, the Fascization of Social Life and Body Politics in Serbia', *Filozofski vestnik/Acta Philosophica*, no. 2, special issue *The Body*, ed. Marina Gržinić Mauhler, Institute of Philosophy ZRC SAZU (Ljubljana 2002): 191-205. http://www.komunikacija.org.yu/komunikacija/casopisi/sociologija/XLIII_3/d01/html_gb
- Jelica Šumić-Riha, 'Jetniki Drugega, ki ne obstaja' ('Prisoners of the Inexistent Other'), *Filozofski vestnik/Acta Philosophica*, no. 1, Institute of Philosophy ZRC SAZU (Ljubljana 2007): 81-103.
- Chris Wright and Samantha Alvarez, 'Expropriate, Accumulate, Financialize', *Eurozine, Mute* 5, 2007: http://www.eurozine.com/journals/mute.html (accessed on Sept. 1, 2007).

*Not a promised land but a delightful wandering*

new zeeland
not a promise land
but a delightfull
wandering

**PM/HM:** After years of negotiations you're now in the process of realizing a communal 'place of solitude' in Sevran on the outskirts of Paris. How does this protracted process relate to current urgencies of urban peripheries?

**François Daune:** It started with a competition, organized by the Evens Foundation, an originally private Belgian foundation. The subject was 'Art, Community and Collaboration'. We were asked to submit a proposal, but we replied with a *dispositif*, a kind of set-up or device that suggests new ways of collaborating between art and citizens. We wanted to initiate something, the beginning of a story, an urban fiction.
I'm an architect and at that time I was already working in an area of the city of Sevran. I thought it would be an interesting place to implement our project, *Je&Nous*. The town is located close to Charles de Gaulle International Airport, from where millions of passengers travel to the centre of Paris everyday on the RER train. And then you have thousands of inhabitants in Sevran's multicultural district, called Les Beaudottes, who've come from foreign countries all over the world. These two groups never meet unless some guys stop the train and rob things from passengers. Les Beaudottes station is renowned for such attacks. In contrast to the travellers who are constantly on the move, the people of Les Beaudottes are stranded there, trapped and – from the moment of their arrival – deprived of work and social status. Moreover, they've lost their mobility. The two groups live separately in two distinct worlds that form new territories of modernity.
The question for us was how to work with a community and use art as a means to promote collaboration between antagonistic communities. Living in Sevran-Beaudottes is economically difficult, but also and in particular because the French aren't welcoming towards immigrants, who are deprived of basic rights such as the right to vote and citizenship.
Many of them retreat into new forms of communitarism and/or patriarchal systems based on male authority. In this sense it was very interesting for us to try to initiate a project based on an exchange between 'alien' populations – a project that would address the question of community without archaic authority and 'make society' (*faire société*).
Our way of dealing with this enormous challenge involved a quite modest suggestion: we asked inhabitants not just to participate but also to 'share responsibilities'. We proposed creating

# 271  Campement Urbain

were Muslims. It was a very dense area and there were fights between the different communities. Before we submitted our proposal for the competition, we went to see the mayor to talk about the project. And this chap, the youngest (29!) mayor ever elected in France, said: 'Nothing's working here, so every new idea is OK with me. The city doesn't have any money to offer, but I'll support you.'

Well, we'd won the competition, but at first this was more of a nightmare because although it had been a nice, very utopian project to imagine, it wasn't going to be easy to put into practice. Our idea was to conceive a place that wouldn't be affiliated with any religion or ideology. Simply a place for – desired rather than imposed – solitude, where people would be able to escape for a little while from their own communities. And especially for Muslim women who have no other place to go but their homes.

**PM/HM:** Is there a connection between how the project works as a process and how you work within the Campement Urbain collective?

**Sylvie Blocher:** Well, for us the process of discussing the project with people was definitely more important than the actual production of an object. It was an object where an individual could be alone but that would be everyone's responsibility at the same time. All the communities would take care of the object while allowing people to get away from their respective communities.

In other words, people entering the object exit their communities. This means their communities have to accept that they're taking (an individual) time out when they go away and stay there. It's a place that might be able to trigger new practices. Though, since the project is the responsibility of the community, it exists only as long as people agree to keep the physical object intact. They have to discuss how to do this, how to use it, maintain it and so on. If discussion stops, the object will disappear. So discussing the meaning of such a space actually constitutes its beginning. Of course, there's also the question of how to convince people in the area to collaborate. So in simple terms, this was the project we submitted to the foundation – and we won the competition.

**Sylvie Blocher:** Sevran is a symbolic place. A new city, created in the 1970s for immigrants. Its first residents came from North Africa, from the Maghreb. Subsequently, Asian and then Indian communities arrived. Most of them

*Je&Nous*
Campement Urbain: Sylvie Blocher, François Daune, Josette Faidit
Project for a place of solitude in Sevran, France, 2003-ongoing

272

much more about the process and how we could work on it, because for us the process of how these people conceive themselves and become visible as subjects within the debate is essential. It's what we call 'a process of infiltration', which means infiltrating reality with art in order to upset its rules and conventions and so make room for the subject. For instance, we prefer talking things out and we don't vote. A suggestion has to be persuasive enough to convince the group. It's a long procedure – what we call in French *du temps dilapidé* – and the basis of democracy. It's also a process that has no intention to exclude. And it's the same one still used today by the Campement Urbain group. It took us eight months to get access to the area. Normally, people from outside don't go there. So we asked a sociologist to join the group. She started to go regularly into the area, to see what people were doing, what kind of associations existed and to understand all the unspoken laws. She sat for hours on a bench and in the beginning she was hassled, but after a while she became part of the landscape and started to converse with people. After eight months we organized our first meeting, but it was a disaster because the day we had chosen turned out to be the beginning of Ramadan – we'd thought it was the next day. So when we held the second meeting, we really thought nobody would come, but it was full.

Everyone was there and so we began to explain what we envisioned, i.e. to create a place of solitude together! We were actually quite worried as people from all the different communities were there. But then a woman looked at us and said, 'What you're proposing would be the "greatest luxury", because our apartments are so overcrowded, and the city so dense here.' Everyone was very firm and direct and said, 'OK, we understand, we like what you're suggesting, but who will make all the decisions?' Then a woman said, 'If we go there and it's not a mosque, a church or a temple, it'll have to be tremendously beautiful.' One man asked, 'Who will have the key to the place?' These two questions showed us that people understood the challenge of the project perfectly and the power issues it would involve. We explained that we wanted to create a new public space with them. Over a period of three years we've been there almost every week; together we've worked out what the object should look like and where it should be located in Les Beaudottes. We've also tried to work on our international image; for example, in 2003 curator Hou Hanru invited us to the Venice Biennial to participate in *Zone of Urgency*. With money donated by visitors to the Biennial, we were able to go there with some inhabitants of Les Beaudottes. We've presented the project at many international events. And as an artist, I've produced a video with 100 residents. We've also filmed the meetings in Sevran. To us, it seemed necessary to receive recognition internationally so as to force municipal, regional and state offices to consider 'sharing the responsibility'. Meanwhile, Campement Urbain has given the object a definite design based on the demands of the inhabitants. It will be a little public garden with a small structure floating with n it and perhaps a keeper to maintain solitude. Meanwhile the city has provided land. We've obtained permission to build. Though we still lack money and it isn't done yet. When we began, we'd no idea it would take so long… It has been a project full of happiness and pain.

**273**

*New Urban Spaces / Cultures and Peripheries / Infiltration*
Campement Urbain: Sylvie Blocher, François Deune, Josette Faidit
Detail of installation, Grand Palais, Paris, 2006

**PM/HM**: Istanbul has become a very popular site in the recent discourse on contested urban spaces, particularly in the art world. When you curated the 9th International Istanbul Biennial together with Charles Esche in 2005, you decided to use this opportunity to produce a biennial for and about Istanbul. What was the idea behind this decision?

**Vasıf Kortun**: The international community was welcome, but the exhibition was first and foremost for the residents of Istanbul. At the time we were operating in the districts of Galata, Beyoğlu and Tophane. These parts of the city are undergoing 'urban regeneration' and have become a main dumping site for event culture and entertainment. And then there is another district, right near us, behind the Platform Garanti Contemporary Art Centre, separated just by an avenue with a barrier in between. The barrier effectively eliminates the possibility of pedestrian flux for hundreds of metres in the epicentre of the city. This is the Tarlabaşı district, where people live in different conditions with a different economy and different ethnic composition. It's literally on 'the other side of the tracks', as Americans would say. There's a lot of research being done on Tarlabaşı, because it's convenient: you can always just drop by and then return to the smug comfort of Beyoğlu. Since the last master plan for Istanbul was drafted, the city has undergone radical restructuring, and part of this restructuring has given us a new and divided city. The Biennial took note of this on the urban level (Solmaz Shahbazi) and with regard to how it has affected people (Mario Rizzi). The Biennial was, in fact, more about situations between individuals and the artist than about larger conditions. This was also why we wanted to make the exhibition 'disappear' into the city and chose small buildings, as well as asked people to navigate and walk through places that they would not normally go to. Obviously, there were a few issues here. We wanted to address the fatigue felt with regard to biennials and their exhibitions in the 1990s: itinerant curators and itinerant artists – and new-economy knowledge workers who went from one place to another, and the knee-jerk reactions to the cities they knew little about. We wanted to get away from such responses, especially because Istanbul could be read through a kind of exotic frame. People tend to see it as lying somewhere between the Orient and the Occident. Here we don't understand these clichés about 'East and West' or about being 'between places'… So to prevent such non-reflective reactions to the city, we thought it would be much more important for people to come here and stay for a while, meet other people, read about the city and discuss with us, and *then* produce new works. Over 20 works were commissioned – works for which we thought it would be absolutely essential to slow down the pace. This fatigue with biennials also had to do with the number of artists in exhibitions. This kind of reinvention of the nineteenth-century world fair in the form of a biennial is problematic. It shouldn't require a 20-mile trek to see an exhibition, because then nobody will actually be able to see it all. Everyone just experiences the event. We decided to reduce the number of artists and give them a bit more presence as well as allow complex readings between the works themselves.

**PM/HM**: To pick up on that, what cultural and urban urgencies of present-day Istanbul did these works address?

*View from Deniz Palace Apartments across the new arterial road in Beyoğlu (Reyfik Saydam Caddesi – Tarlabaşı Bulvarı) towards the Golden Horn, Istanbul, 2005*

*Peggy Rug*
Paulina Olowska
Deniz Palace Apartments, 9th Istanbul Biennial, 2005

*Deniz Palace Apartments, Istanbul, 2005*

# 274 Vasıf Kortun

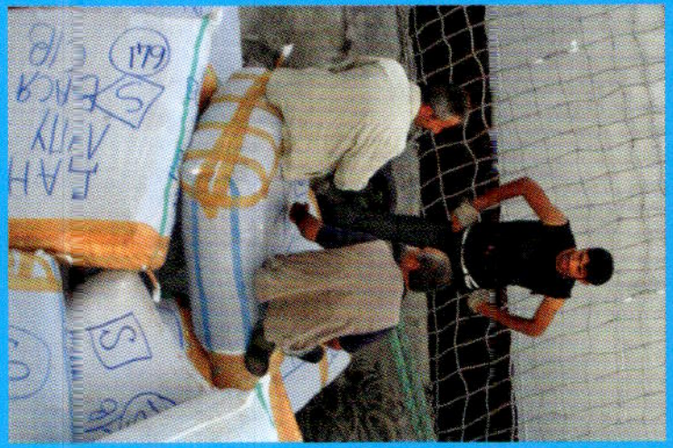

Scenes from around Istanbul Modern, a private museum devoted to modern and contemporary art, located in the former customs warehouse Antrepo no. 4 on the Bosphorus, 2005

Near Tünel Square at the southeastern end of İstiklal Caddesi in Beyoğlu, Istanbul, 2005

Taksim Square, Istanbul, 2005

**275**

**Vasif Kortun:** You know, Istanbul has just entered this unfortunate global city race and it's making large segments and various lifestyles of the city invisible. This is because it's all about cleansing and regulating, and since that's what it's about, the idea is to eliminate the (self-) representation of large parts of the city. The city is becoming a label and it's being marketed as such. It's a radical top-down transformation. This process neglects the most important and most interesting aspect of the city: its ad-hoc organic development and individuation in so many different zones. In terms of how we think of our cities, we haven't fully realized the potential of 'positioning' as opposed to mapping. Or to put it differently, it's not about deciphering the city, because Istanbul is actually a place where you can lose your bearings, as the actual, physical city itself is about disorientation. However, at the moment, a huge 'vacuum cleaner' is moving through the city.

**PM/HM:** What kind of counter-geography might be mobilized through active engagement with such disorientation in the urban field? And could this have an effect on the global distribution of network practices?

**Vasif Kortun:** I don't know how to answer that question. I operate from a particular zone in the city, one that is supposed to be the most public zone in the city, and yet this zone is actually in many ways not accessible to most of Istanbul's residents. Moreover, if you are old or have a phobia about crowds or confined spaces, you can't come here. The city spans too many miles for one centre to answer cultural needs. Many new communities and recent immigrants to the city have never even seen Beyoğlu or Galata, let alone the Bosporus. Coming back to your question, in recent years, immigration patterns have changed from how they previously were, for example, people once migrated to escape war in eastern Turkey. But today it's no longer possible for such people to be the architects of their own fortunes, because the government doesn't tolerate illegality anymore – and in the past this was a decisive factor in this self-made city. Certain districts are being destroyed because they're Roma neighbourhoods or they've a high density of 'undesirables'. NGOs are reacting to these processes, but in the end all that can be salvaged are memories and stories. Istanbul isn't – a city, but actually many cities loosely connected to one another. It's an agglomeration of villages and communities, strung together. I'm perhaps not the right person to address on networked practices. We might be able to house people and make them more visible or elevate them to another level of discussion, but we're by no means on firm ground here.

# Jochen Becker

**PM/HM:** You are one of the contributors of the project *ErsatzStadt*, which pursued various lines of critical engagement with contemporary urban realities. Some were more theoretical investigations, such as the book series *metroZones*; others had to do with direct interventions into the urban fabric. How does this particular approach of combining political engagement with enquiries into artistic and architectural practices resonate with the political and cultural climate in Berlin?

**Jochen Becker:** Actually, it was a critique of Berlin's recent discourses and a (temporary) farewell to Berlin, too. We were getting really bored with the ongoing description of the so-called *Europäische Stadt* (European City), which was one of the prime movers for Berlin's developers in (re-) constructing Berlin. In a lot of projects and initiatives, for instance *InnenStadtAktion* or *AnbauNeueMitte*, we fought against the reactionary perspective that often dominates the debate about Berlin. We asked which Europe they were talking about – that of Belfast, Belgrade or Istanbul? Berlin's developers tried to avoid US-American or Japanese cities. But from a broader perspective, there are many other models of urbanization, of daily activities, though at the time we still didn't know much about them. It was with the book *Metropolen*, which we were commissioned to write in a condensed format of only 95 pages, that we really started to discover the interesting new dynamics at work beyond the European City, and these – as we later learned and are still discovering – are influencing Berlin, too. We wanted to look at what is beyond the idea of *civitas*, such as written about by Richard Sennett in his book *The Conscience of the Eye: The Design and Social Life of Cities* with regard to civilized bourgeois society with its rules and regulations, well-functioning orders and the Fordist dream of a welfare state. We wanted to look beyond all this and adopt a more global perspective. We wanted to explore how informal structures emerge in the Global South, structures that are now obviously also evolving in the middle of Europe; how the welfare state is declining and people have to help themselves; or how the banlieues are trying to survive via self-organizational processes called 'shadow economies'. Migration and so-called liberalization – 'you'll have to help yourself, because nobody's going to help you' – the kinds of processes we read about in Istanbul, Lagos or Kabul, are growing significantly; I call this the International *Informal* Style. You notice that there are functioning structures and they're not at all exotic. But you have to be careful about saying, 'Hey, that's working in some ways, let's do it here, too', because that's really the neoliberal way of doing things. On the other hand, it's good to be prepared, to learn about what's coming, in order to keep what's good and emancipative, and get rid of what's either purely exploitative or terribly bureaucratic. This relates – in a very general way – to the idea of *metroZones*, and how to step beyond Berlin's perception of the European City.

**PM/HM:** Your current work is strongly concerned with reframing local issues by bringing them in touch with distant geographies that may initially seem unconnected. Can you give us some examples that highlight these oblique links between the urgency of Europe or the so-called European City and places elsewhere?

**Jochen Becker:** We started off by discovering that the idea of the European

Fashion Show for City of COOP (Buenos Aires & Rio de Janeiro), Prater der Volksbühne Berlin, 2003

Advertising for *City of COOP* (Buenos Aires & Rio de Janeiro), Berlin, 2003

277

City was also present in Leopoldville, the capital of the Belgian Congo, which had been shaped by King Leopold II and was renamed Kinshasa after liberation. This African city was a colonial product and is an example of how the European City exists not only in Europe but also all over the colonized world. And by exploiting the Belgian Congo, Leopold II was able to transform Brussels into what now looks like a European City, and it became the capital of Europe. He pursued a kind of Haussmannization, destroying old Brussels and building axes or, for instance, the imperial Palace of Justice. For what we now call the classical European City often evolved in the colonies. Though it was not something that happened separately, for relations were close between Europe and the colonies. And it was also not a one-way street: the situation was complex and is still so now. Due to current migration policies, the information society and so on, relations are even livelier today between the former colonies and postcolonial Europe. So our new, ongoing research project is called *From/To Europe* and explores such issues.

For years now, Mohammed has been the most common name chosen for boys in Brussels, and this really says something about how cities as worlds are emerging within Europe, within our European cities, in a very concrete sense: if you want to find a 'Nollywood' production, a DVD from Nigeria, you just have to go to the next 'Afro shop' – you don't have to order it from Lagos. Such communities exist here and – if you want to watch the DVD – you can find them just around the corner. Another example: the largest diaspora of Afghans in Europe lives in Hamburg.

We've discovered how close diasporic relationships are towards the respective country of origin, and that this is the case even within European cities; it is also a tendency that is bound to increase with the presence and practices of different peoples. How do peoples survive with the practices they bring with them – often out of sheer need or racial exclusion?

The state is destroying social and political welfare structures, and this is why people with precarious backgrounds are in general forced to exercise a kind of informality: in what ways do they have to betray the state to survive, as well as organize money illegally?

As a postcolonial structure, I think the banlieues reveal how extremely separate societies live in the middle of France. The country is divided in at least three groups: the very rich, who are living more or less directly in Paris; then the downgraded, protesting middle class, who say that Paris is too expensive and so they have to move outside the city – just like the proletarian or post-proletarian population had to do decades ago. The middle class now have to live in the suburbs, between housing estates in the banlieues, which is the third structure. The banlieues have other ways of earning money, and people try to survive and organize themselves socially, and this also includes gangster-like structures. There is hardly any communication between these three groups, a fact that has become very obvious in recent clashes – as has also the existence of an undiscussed colonial background that is related to the crisis in the banlieues. We worked on th s in the anti-colonial film group Remember Resistance, in our programme *Bourdieu in the Banlieue*.

With the project *City of COOP*, we discovered how post-crisis Buenos Aires – formerly the most European city in South America – became part of Latin America, though without g'ving up the idea of a better life. In Rio, on the other

the temporary structure of the project *Hier Entsteht* at Rosa-Luxemburg Platz in Berlin?

**Jochen Becker:** Well, compare it with *Dolmush Xpress* – a temporary art project in which you could take a privately owned taxi, solar boat, or horse carriage through Kreuzberg – the idea being to copy practices one-to-one from Istanbul to Berlin. I think this is a rather tenuous idea because it disregards what such things mean within the context of Berlin. True, a kind of temporary structure is also created, one that you might think is similar to *Hier Entsteht*. But there are differences, and I want to show this with an example: in the 1970s a lot of architects travelled to the Global South. There they discovered informal architectures that offered a kind of relief from what was going on in the post-illusional period after 1968. They also discovered a new freedom of planning, a sort of hybrid dream. When they returned, it turned out to be impossible to implant this into European structures and regulations, but they still tried in a number of ways to introduce participatory architecture as a form of self-made architecture within the laws of Europe. It was also within such an agenda that we connected to what the team of *Hier Entsteht* was doing. Reconstruction at this location was a form of participatory architecture, and we wanted to know: what does this mean today, and how might we demonstrate and study it within the structure of this project?

hand, a lot of people have been living in precarious situations for ages. They have no notion of the welfare state, but are used to dealing with crises, which distinguishes them from many people in Argentina who had had no previous experience with such situations. So I think we can all learn a lot.

**PM/HM:** How can we appropriate these new ways of learning you've described for local projects, such as for

*7 Islands and a Metro* (Mumbai/Bombay) *metroZones in ErsatzStadt*, Volksbühne Berlin, 2003

Gülsün Karamustafa at *Self Service City: Istanbul* Volksbühne Berlin, 2003

278

*Invisible Zagreb*
Initiated by platforma 9.81 in 2003

## Marko Sančanin

**PM/HM:** In the group Platforma 9.81 you've been investigating possibilities of translating various local situations and histories into each other. When pursuing a politics of connectivity, how do you deal with the problems of sharing and of allowing for a sense of commonality without resorting to notions of similarity and homogeneity?

**Marko Sančanin:** There are three things I can briefly say about this. The first has to do with comparing collaborative networks in western Europe and eastern or Non-EU Europe; the second, with architectural research and how it's displayed; and the third, with answering the general question of what we all have in common. I will start with the third: Do we actually have anything in common? To answer this, it would be necessary to make some local inquiries. Though there's one thing I'm certain about: we all lack something with respect to how the public domain is transformed, and hence how such transformations are governed. We all lack something that we aren't able to express – and yet we lack it together. This is probably the best possible diagnosis and forecast for cultural 'West-meets-East' experiments. I think it's difficult to work with us because we tend to produce excess meaning. Moreover, we often tend to rewrite our programme briefings and project proposals. We operate in loops – proceeding from the starting hypothesis while also probing practical parameters, and this is not a particularly efficient approach for a group of architects. A lot of time, energy and money goes into extra activities that are intended to increase institutional support for the non-institutional. This is a completely natural development. Since we've acquired a certain amount of knowledge and expertise via an ideological programme (though some-

visibility, and enables you to have an impact on policies... for example, urban policies. However many of these so-called research projects have more to do with displaying phenomena in a white cube than provoking real change. At the end it has more to do with social pornography than intellectually committed and engaged practices. It is sometimes almost impossible to collaborate with people who have no methodology, theoretical background or real interest in the new communitarian ideas embedded in architectural practice. Or at least this has been our experience.
When we talk about comparing collaborative networks in Western Europe and the Balkans, we're still speaking about a situation in which there is a complete lack of resources, and this situation actually forces people to collaborate, to share ideas, funds, infrastructure and equipment. In Western Europe the situation is different. It's one of plenty. Or at least this is what friends in Western Europe seem to be experiencing. Basically everyone involved in these activities is competing with each other, especially because of the growing demand on the market for these kinds of architectural practices. Every museum or gallery wants such projects to spice up its annual programme a bit.

times in opposition to the establishment), there is a clear need and love for truth and knowledge, as well as an epistemological imperative to develop institutions out of our own organizations. This is a developmental stage and through it we would like to reach a point where we can actually sustain our activities. The cultural market sometimes gives you more media

**PM/HM:** In what ways does Platforma 9,81 try to go beyond these limitations you've mentioned, for instance, limitations of institutional demand or individual authorship?

**Marko Sančanin:** In a collective, the question of the distribution of capital, whether it's material or cultural – or symbolic like authorship – is always a latent reason for antagonisms within the group. The way we negotiate these antagonisms and particular interests is connected with the degree to which the final product is also produced by others – non-architects in particular. If we manage to produce something that has been clearly made with knowledge outside our own expertise, then it's difficult to claim ownership and this influences the way the final product is interpreted, translated or displayed. Local circumstances have contributed to many organizations in Zagreb collaborating because they share common standpoints on the political, cultural and economic circumstances of transition. Organizations working in different fields – such as architecture, visual arts, performing arts or new media – are somehow able to understand each other and come together. Since a lack of resources also economically defines how we operate and share ideas and resources, it has been only natural for us to collaborate with people from the Multimedia Institute, the What, How and for Whom and the Centre for Drama Arts and other organizations. We also share a mutual interest in 'instituent' practices of knowledge production and have started parallel educational programmes. Establishing educational environments is a form of community work that examines the issue of authorship, what we produce and how, who invests how much and who benefits from it. This involves a totally different understanding from the one architectural practices usually have. Many other organizations from the Zagreb Cultural Capital 3000 platform have also participated in such activities.

**PM/HM:** Can these networked practices in the Balkans also provide a reference for engagement in the increasing fragmentation elsewhere?

**Marko Sančanin:** As an architect you have to borrow concepts to even think about a project. Architecture has always involved the application of already existing concepts. So I see nothing surprising in thinking that the uncertain state of the EU is a kind of big Balkan concept for a complex political system of unpredictable shape. Though I don't see any further implications here. Yes, we could say that Europe, in trying to solve the Balkan problem, has been Balkanized itself. Well, so what.
The collaborative practices of independent cultural scenes from Croatia or Serbia have nothing to do with this. At least I haven't seen any valid proof to the contrary. I can just say that the common platform that connects those of us from the Balkans who are involved in such architectural practices is probably the same one that causes us to collaborate with different organi-

*Operation City*
Peak of the *Invisible Zagreb* project
(10-day event with 15,000 participants), 2005

Installation of an environment made of bombed containers from Sarajevo and machinery of construction companies that went bankrupt

*Operation City*
Zagreb, 2005

281

zations locally. We share some of our ideological viewpoints, and they're in opposition to the way history is reproduced here; we also have in common some very similar phenomena happening in urban and rural environments; and we all come from the same type of economy and political system. And since we basically speak the same language, we understand each other better than we would be able to in English. So these are the reasons why we all work together. It's also why I am optimistic about future collaborations.

Sometimes I get a bit frustrated because I can't help thinking that European intellectuals, artists or cultural managers believe that some form of politico-cultural archaeology in the Balkans might provide them with fresh concepts for European cultural development in general. Apart from the fact that such a viewpoint is still extremely colonial, I don't think we can expect to understand the social experiments in the former Yugoslavia without understanding the multi-layering of cultural, political and economic relations that have been operating there from the start. You can't just turn 'socialist hedonism' or 'self-government' into a fetish. A rather hollow expectation exists, one that harbours the hope there is something tangible – a conceptual social system – that can be connected with the former Yugoslavia or the Balkans. There's a work by Andrei Tarkovsky that greatly resembles this situation. For the past couple of years we've all been something like guides through the 'Zone'. People are still coming from the West to interview us. We take them to see post-industrial wastelands or unexpected urban phenomena and to listen to the stories of artists who gave conceptual, body art performances before they were invented in the West, and all that kind of stuff.

But the problem is that this 'Zone' is now empty. There's no longer anything there for you to see or understand. The real truth is that when you visit the Balkans, you're most likely to find some neurotic fantasy, one you've brought with you yourself.

# Conversions
## Berlin

Berlin Alexanderplatz
The centre of former East Berlin, 2006

Former East Berlin, 17 years after the 'fall of the wall', 2006

RACCIATELLA
IMBISS
IMBISS
EIS SPEZIALITÄTEN zum Mitnehmen
KALTE GETRÄNKE
RME GET

Former Palast der Republik (Palace of the Republic) Berlin, 2006

# Orienthaus
## Wasserpfeife

Business & Communication Center

| Algerien | Kamerun | Russland |
| --- | --- | --- |
| Armenien | Kroatien | Serbien |
| Bangladesch | Kuba | Syrien |
| Bosnien | Libanon | Thailand |
| Bulgarien | Mazedonien | Ukraine |
| Eritrea | Marokko | USA / Kanada |
| Gambia | Nigeria | Türkei |
| Ghana | Polen | Tunesien |
| Jugoslawien | Rumänien | Vietnam |
| Kenia | | |

INFINITY.NET TELECOM

---

## TELE-INTERNET CAFE'
### LOCO Bluenet LOCO
Phone — Internet — Fax — Calling Cards

---

## Orient Friseur
### Damen & Herren

Kantstraße
Shops and service enterprises along
Kantstraße in former West Berlin, leading
from Bahnhof Zoo to Charlottenburg, 2006

## Oda Projesi

**PM/HM:** The name of your group – Oda Projesi (room project) – refers directly to your first project: *About a Useless Space*. Can you describe what importance this project had and why you incorporated it into the name of your collective?

**Seçil Yersel:** Our first project is the one we always somehow find ourselves going back to or referring to, either in between our other projects or during them. When we first moved to this neighbourhood in Galata we hadn't intended to start such a project, but after we started meeting our neighbours and working more with the dynamics of Istanbul, as well as thinking about the state of the art scene here, we asked how we might accommodate the way the neighbourhood functions within our own space. We didn't want to repeat the usual concepts offered by 'art' spaces to 'audiences', so instead we first tried to create a meeting point. We emptied one of our three rooms, and made it available for potential projects, while the other rooms remained more or less private. This one room never looked like a white cube or a gallery space. It was just empty and cleaner than the other rooms. And because it was empty and clean, it was like a gap in the neighbourhood, and the neighbours kept asking, 'Why is the room empty?' This is when we started talking about a space's possibilities. In a sense, it was really about a space that could become a place. Since it was open for shaping, we invited people to it, both our neighbours and people from the art scene, and had them read a text by George Perec called *About a Useless Space*. The text was about searching for a room that doesn't have a function, that is intentionally functionless. At first it's like an environmental space; it's every room in which you can possibly do something: a room for cutting your nails, a room for looking outside – in other words, Perec was writing about the possibility of a room that has no function in itself, a 'useless' room. Over the past eight years, the space has actually been 'useless': it has gained and lost its function during projects and daily life. It has not really been an 'art space', a living space, workspace or studio. In between, it has had many different uses.

**PM/HM:** To enable a space to continuously re-invent itself for such a long period, one needs to consider how to sustain a certain constituency. How did you go about this process of both continuation and change?

**Özge Açıkkol:** Maybe Istanbul itself helped us a lot… The process happened on its own, because the actions and even the 'curating' changed from project to project. For example, we carried out 'one-day' projects in which we invited people to the room: we told them that for this one day it would be *their* space, and about once a week they did their projects there. We also invited our neighbours to do the same. If a space doesn't present itself as an exhibition space, then the audience doesn't really become or act like an audience. Such a relaxed situation also opens up other possibilities. For instance, since people didn't actually know the closing and opening hours of the space; they would just drop by. Or it was possible that someone who was just passing by would see a light and say, 'What's happening here?' and then we would sit together and talk, and so on. The first people who came to see us or joined us were neighbours; then there were those we knew and emailed, but who didn't live in the neighbourhood – they would come by to see what we were doing; last there were those who just happened to pass by. So in a sense, it also has to do with the discussion we had with Vasif Kortun, whether what we were doing was public art or not. Though we did not really think about or discuss whether we were doing public art. The type of art we did emerged along the way as we did things: theory came afterwards – actions were what dominated. And as long as we've been here, and we've been in the same neighbourhood now for 8 years, we've had relationships that go beyond our being artists. We're simply part of the neighbourhood, even if we are somewhat strange neighbours. We've tried to shape this kind of role not just with the neighbours in Galata but also with the art scene in Istanbul!

*SO FAR SO GOOD – SO WEIT SO GUT*
Nadine Raschke Kindlimann, Oda Projesi courtyard, 29 June 2004

**PM/HM:** Apart from exposing yourself to everyday situations, this sort of creativity has to do with documenting and narrating such situations with respect to an outside audience. How do you feel about these different levels of your work – the local effect that is related to your work on a one-to-one basis and its effect on the discursive field through which it gets distributed globally?

**Seçil Yersel:** The local effect we've experienced in creating this multi-functional space has been mainly related to our not being read properly, misread or receiving no recognition at all. Though art critics have been able to write that an exhibition was opening at the Oda Projesi space. And since there were not so many artist-run spaces at the time in Istanbul, this aroused people's curiosity. Also the artists we worked with were happy to be invited to a place that was more than an exhibition space or a stage. The participant and the audience were more affected than the art scene in Istanbul. The effects became more visible on the scene after we left the neighbourhood and started becoming more mobile. As regards the discursive field, the effect was rather that we were viewed as an example of a 'Turkish artist group that works with the public!' We started receiving invitations, but we rejected them as they tended to read us wrong, extracting us from Istanbul and the context, seeing only our actions or just looking for results. There was also another effect with regard to the discursive field: we were thought of as an artist group that could be taken for granted between the many museums and classic exhibition spaces. Along the lines of: What can Oda Projesi do in such a space? How can we deal with them? You might call this a positive effect. Well, we've always been open to the fact that what we're doing in Istanbul might be interpreted from, let's say, Japan, in a variety of ways… For example, the project has one side that has a lot to do with the local context, but it also has a side that is more than that. We discussed such issues when we published an edition of *Annex* newspaper in Stockholm and how an art space functions in a city. The people we invited had a space in the peripheries of Stockholm, in an immigrant neighbourhood, and we wondered how it functioned, because we thought it might be a great tool and should have a power of its own. But afterwards we realized that the people in this area and the artists didn't have a relationship with each other, and the artists were just saying to themselves, 'It's so strange and interesting and nice to be in such a neighbourhood and work part time as an artist.' So, in this sense, no real discussion took place.

**PM/HM:** In view of such experiences, do you now see yourselves more concerned with the context of art production than in your first project, which focused on the actual space of a particular courtyard?

**Güneş Savaş:** Yes, because we think, as a rule, the power of art and artists has always been used on the same audience, in the same context, even in the same language – the same *understandable* language – and with the same people around. If we can work with musicians who have nothing to do with contemporary issues, or an actor, or with others from different disciplines, then we can also work with our neighbours. We feel that art has always been produced for and consumed by a very small circle of people. I mean, if you go to an exhibition space, modes of transmission are very limited. Experiences in the neighbourhood have shaped our project and enabled it to open itself up more. Like now we've become more mobile and no longer have a concrete space: we work, for instance, at a radio station or do projects in a minibus, we share our experiences in discussions out in the field, and carry out short-term projects… we've also become more deeply involved in art production. All this has been the effect of Istanbul as a city on us! Since we live in this city and produce with it, we're constantly trying to understand how this city stays alive.

Oda Meetings / *The Picture of My Life*
Belmin Söylemez & Orhan Cem Çetin, 8th Istanbul Biennial
*Poetic Justice*, 20 September – 16 November 2003

## Iacopo Gallico

**PM/HM:** Stalker is a network known for setting up encounters with other cultural networks and expanding the traditional scope of creative practice. For instance, Stalker started *Ararat* in Campo Boario as an art project, but it seems to have taken on a life of its own. Is this flow of agency something that is inherent to the idea of Stalker?

**Iacopo Gallico:** Stalker evolved mainly out of an attitude adopted by architecture students when they squatted at Valle Giulia, the Faculty of Architecture at the University of Rome La Sapienza. This was in 1990. A group of students, who were not associated with any particular ideology or political party, took a political action – 'squatting' – as their point of departure. They tried living in the university, and making it a space that would allow them to imagine a different world and a different way of viewing the relationship between culture and space. Hence, for us Stalker is a 'laboratory of urban art'. This means there is a group of people who want to identify with others and use space as a device to do so – and this is what determines Stalker. It's a flexible constellation of people operating in the moment, a moment shaped by on-going projects; there's a direct relationship between the project to be developed and the profile of the group who are in charge of developing it, and for us this is 'a network'. In projects like *Ararat, Xenobia: the City, the Strangers and the Becoming of Public Space (Ararat, Xenobia: la città, gli stranieri e il divenire dello spazio pubblico)* or *Imagining Corviale*, a network represents the project itself: if you take a map of everyone involved in a project, it doesn't just represent a configuration of people we relate to or follow, but also mirrors the complexity we've found. Such a map enables you to understand the kind of work that is emerging.

Campo Boario was a slaughterhouse situated in an industrial part of Rome at the end of the nineteenth century. When the city expanded, it became unusable and so was abandoned in 1975. At the time I was living not far from it. From my room it looked like it was empty and I often thought it was a shame that the city didn't make it available to the public. When I finally visited it, I realized that it was not vacant. In fact, there was an air of fear and suspicion about the place, and it was anything but empty: many communities of foreigners lived there – Kalderash, North Africans, people from eastern Europe and others who had just found shelter there. They all shared this space, which somehow was in a sort of dynamic balance. We first entered this 'microcosm' during the Biennial of Young Artists from Europe and the Mediterranean, which took place at the Campo Boario in 1999, though in a restored section of the complex. The topic of the exhibition was public space, and together with the community of Kurds who had arrived in Rome following the Öcalan affair, Stalker squatted in the veterinary building. The aim was to create a cultural centre in this 'promiscuous' public space – promiscuous in the sense that one and the same space fulfilled multiple purposes and so satisfied the needs of the community. Above all it was a place where different cultures could meet. This space constitutes a 'marginal area', what we call an 'actual territory'. This means a territory continuously in a state of becoming and transforming. It's strange to go to *Ararat*, as we named it, because you always encounter different people there – in fact, this aspect is even stranger than experiencing how the place itself is changing. Though this is so only because *Ararat* has remained an open space, a platform for meeting and exchange, a real hub; here we're actu-

*Via Egnatia*
Osservatorio Nomade, workshop, 2001

The squatted fourth floor of Nuovo Corviale, a 958 metre long estate on the southwestern outskirts of Rome housing more than 6,000 people (designed by Mario Fiorentino in 1972 and built between 1975-1982), Rome, 2006

Newroz, 2002
*Ararat*, intercultural centre and laboratory of urban art at the Campo Boario, Rome, initiated by Stalker in 1999

ally able to discover and experience what a network is and how it works. It's incredible to see how the Kurds are connected to each other, and it's extremely interesting and stimulating to be able to trace their networks as well as map the geographies of these new cultural identities in Europe.

**PM/HM**: How has this approach of tracing different cultural networks informed your work in Corviale, a huge housing block on the outskirts of Rome, which has become a symbolic site of urban conflict at the city's periphery?

**Iacopo Gallico**: The idea was to work on the many 'images' of Corviale. How do the inhabitants of Rome see and think of this location, and how do its inhabitants view the institution and municipality of Rome? We tried to proceed from people's perception of the place, to create new relationships with its inhabitants and go beyond common tales about it. What we discovered was that Corviale is the product of a mix of politics and architecture. It has 8,000 inhabitants and cost 11 million euros to build. Though perhaps even more important, the municipality has spent four times that amount in the past 20 years, and this was almost always in relation to elections. In fact, Corviale is

the time it was completely empty, so people decided to squat and live in it. We did our project on this fourth floor, and found a way to listen and understand. Everything starts with listening. In *Ararat*, we were also dealing with a strongly politicized community. At the beginning it was quite hard to define limits. Art allows you to cross the boundaries of politics. Yet if you begin by approaching problematic political issues, you'll find a wall, a wall of misunderstanding. But if you start with the space itself and how to organize it, share it, or the likes, it's totally different. In Corviale, things were no different. We earned the trust of its inhabitants; they understood that we weren't the usual municipal architects only interested in measuring their apartments. We wanted to comprehend more, for instance the geography of the relationships interwoven into the space.

We're now able to say that self-organization starts with the capability to adapt your needs to a context; this means having no outside interlocutors who impose rules about how you have to manage things. Our research is based on a concept reflected also in how we operate as a network. This network is not conceived hierarchically; members of Stalker are completely independent from one another. In our

a big box created for winning votes. Of course you can also say it's a wonderful *objet d'art*, a sculpture, a monument – everything you might desire except a place to house people. Nevertheless, people have been able to adjust to life inside Corviale. Left to their own devices, they have organized themselves and somehow come to terms with the place – especially on the fourth floor where there is this corridor running through the middle of the building. It was originally conceived as a linear service area. But at

society this is a precondition that has to be established in order to transform competition into collaboration. It involves the ability of autonomous individuals to work toward the same end, the same project. We can think very differently, but if we share the same project, we can collaborate together. This is the strength of networking.

**PM/HM**: How have these experiences of connecting identities, localities and

291

temporalities informed the network of Osservatorio Nomade, which you created to facilitate an understanding of the changing geographies of Europe?

**Iacopo Gallico:** Osservatorio Nomade is an interdisciplinary research project initiated by Stalker that proposes ways of intervention based on spatial practices of exploration, listening and relation, activated through creative tools of interaction with the environment and the inhabitants, and archives of memories. It's a meta-structure we developed for the project *On Egnatia, a Path of Displaced Memories* in 2004. The idea was to build a metaphorical and transnational monument with stones, Salentine stones. For us these stones were a symbol of pain as well as tradition, of the relationship between man and territory. We used the stones to collect stories from people who had migrated along the Via Egnatia. We returned the stones to locations where the speakers asked us to because something special had happened along the way to them there. The Via Egnatia is an ancient path that follows the Via Appia and goes to Istanbul; it was constructed during the Roman Empire to take the army to the border, but it has changed its course many times over the ages. Now the Greeks are building a very modern motorway there, called Egnatia Odos. It runs straight through the country, from Igoumenitsa to the Turkish border. Yet since historically the Via Egnatia passed through Albania, its re-establishment seems strangely connected with eastern Europe – and so for us, it has turned into a device to reveal the complexity of this part of Europe and its cities, where new communities of different peoples are emerging. In order to collect stories, we developed – in for example Rome, Athens, Paris and Berlin – agencies of the Osservatorio Nomade network, a transdisciplinary group of people capable of sharing their approach to a territory and a context, where context means not a static place but a complex and dynamic reality forged by connect ons and relationships between agents who interact with the territory. To reveal the complexity of this reality, we used the Osservatorio Ncmade network and involved different individuals who – due to their sensibilities and interests – would be able to monitor the very complexity it represents. And this is a complexity that is always also represented by another complexity, one manifesting itself in the representation of a system of relationships between agents and interlocutors.

Nuovo Corviale, Rome, 2006

Below Nuovo Corviale, Rome, 2006

*Would you like to participate in an artistic experience?*
20 painted steel objects circulating in Latin America, Europe and Africa, 1994-2007; documentation by the participants on www.nbp.pro.br; view of the installation at the Aue-Pavillon, documenta 12, Kassel, 2007

*diagram (passages)*
Ricardo Basbaum, 2001

For an artist this is really the playful part of artworks. If you think you know who you are and constantly take it for granted, you'll simply ruin your work. You need to go behind things, because it's all a game. I think one of the most interesting things for an artist is to let himself/herself be reinvented in some way and be carried away by the work he/she is doing. Though this has limits. It isn't that you're reborn each time, but that you're able to play and there are spaces with which you can play. If you're aware of this, you can incorporate it into how you work as an artist. So that's what I like and try to work with. I work with roles, though this doesn't just have to do with the roles of the artist, critic or curator, but also with my thinking and how I depart from different ways of creating these roles. Apropos the image of the artist, what kind of artist do you want to be? Do you want to be at the top of the market? Some artists want this extremely badly. It's true this is a possible position for an artist. You can play with fashion; you can play with marginality; you can play with suffering and the role of the romantic artist. In art history, there's also this game with the image of the artist – and it can be traced. So I have been playing more or less with these different roles (artist, agent, critic, curator) and with the image of the artist I would like to negotiate. In these roles I include a certain subjective component. Not that I'm completely conscious of this but it is, to an extent, an aspect that interests me.

**PM/HM:** Politically and socially engaged art is often conceptualized in relation to working with selected groups or communities. In what you describe, you seem to mistrust direct involvement in political situations and prefer a more playful negotiation of power. What kinds of politics and aesthetics emerge from this interaction?

**PM/HM:** Travel, role-play, transformation – there's a certain line of displacements to be found in your work. What role do such displacements play in the way you produce art?

**Ricardo Basbaum:** Artists should not control meanings, and how people play, project and imagine things in relation to their work. These things should remain open. It's interesting for artists to discover that they don't exist prior to their works, but are reinvented each time anew. Many thinkers have expressed such thoughts. Most obviously, Deleuze and Guattari, to whom I feel particularly close. They often talk about such matters. The subject comes after the rest; it's not what's in the foreground.

# Ricardo Basbaum

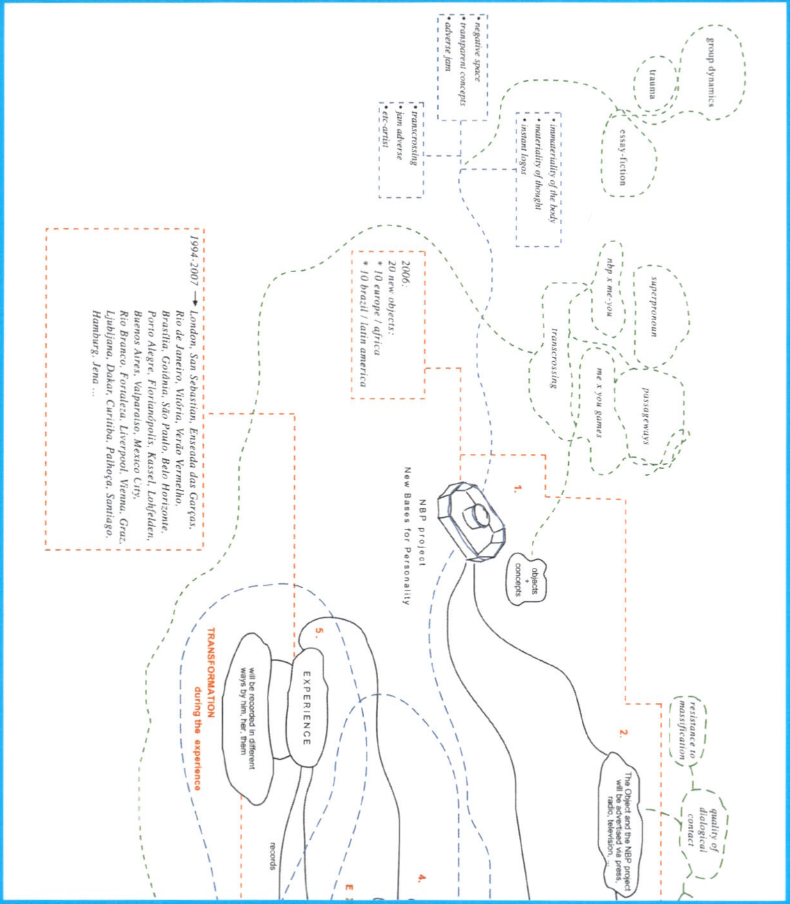

made person, the political person. It's really difficult to invent different subjectivities in a political role. That's why I think it's tricky and difficult to play with politics – though obviously, it's also very necessary. When you do so with art you really need to think a lot about how you play. So I think artists who play with politics really need to invent a way of positioning themselves in order to avoid the commonplaceness of the political person who has all sorts of sentences, all sorts of ready-made answers. I'm not speaking about content, but about how things are dealt with. Maybe because of my Brazilian heritage, art can't avoid being a fusion of sensory elements. If you try to avoid this, and just concentrate on content and statements, you lose a lot. Then it would be better to choose another route, not art.

**PM/HM:** Sometimes we feel that the major hope of the twenty-first century lies in the potential of different cultures to interact in an undauntedly creative manner. This is usually linked to the idea that, because of the differences between cultures, they constantly reinvent themselves to engage with one another meaningfully. Do you see any relevance in such optimistic or utopian thinking?

**Ricardo Basbaum:** You can play with the political in different ways and not necessarily only as an artist. I really don't know what's the most effective way of playing with politics. Is it by being an artist or an anthropologist or a civilian? Of course you can play with art in politics as well. I think my work deals with politics, but I'm sometimes uncomfortable with the fact. When you go into the political arena it's very difficult to re-invent yourself. The subjectivity of politics seems to be already prepared for you. It targets a ready-

*Would you like to participate in an artistic experience?*
Work in progress since 1994, participation Brigida Baltar,
Verão Vermelho, 1997

*Would you like to participate in an artistic experience?*
Ricardo Basbaum, diagram, 1994-2007

*Would you like to participate in an artistic experience?*
*Work in progress since 1994, participation Casa das Artes da Mangueira, Rio de Janeiro, 2006*

**Ricardo Basbaum:** It's complex. As someone who grew up in the 1980s I don't know to what extent a utopia is a productive thing. I don't believe in magical solutions. It's such a slow process. It's always about negotiating and moving through empty spaces. When I speak about Brazilian culture it's very clear to me that I have to specify what I'm referring to. When I say Brazilian culture, I don't mean official Brazilian culture, because I don't really care about or believe in it. I think the main parts of any culture aren't the official ones. So it's difficult today to believe in a big totality. It's always about small groups. Although small for a city is one thing; small for a country, another, and small for the world, a lot. It's really difficult, it takes time and has its own dynamics. Nevertheless, I think there are certain links that certain people just spread and create. And they can very slowly contaminate others. I believe this group of millions worldwide has a different speed, and they're aware of something others don't care about. And this is something I'd like to believe. Though it's not the totality of everybody who is interested. And I don't mean there'll be a kind of redemption – I don't think that will ever happen.

Anyway, it's always a game. A game played by certain groups that don't fit in completely or are more aware or caring. Not that these people are illuminated or special. It's just a kind of incitement that's interesting to cultivate and not everybody experiences the same incitement at the same time. I believe strongly in such dynamics. There's this art critic who was active during the 1950s, '60s and '70s: Mario Pedrosa. He died in 1981. He was a very important person for Brazilian art. He was extremely active against fascism and went to Europe in the 1930s and '40s. He made a very interesting and fitting comment about how Brazil is condemned to be modern. It's as if we have to make a revolution over and over again.

We don't have a background based on tradition, so horizons are open to invention. This means you can always try to create some sort of utopia. We don't have centres and models;

we can always still plan what might be next, because we are never already something.
This is all very interesting, but this utopian element also scares me. Though I actually believe a utopia can serve a good role when you're stuck and can't move. For then a utopia can generate movement. Nevertheless, I think today it's more important to be somewhat pragmatic, to cultivate certain kinds of conflicts or negotiate a great deal. You know you play a double role – sometimes inside and sometimes outside. But it's necessary to do both. I think it's much more important to learn how to play with such movement and not be stuck just in one place or, if you have to negotiate with larger powers, to be able to escape somehow, too. It's very difficult to play with such displacements.

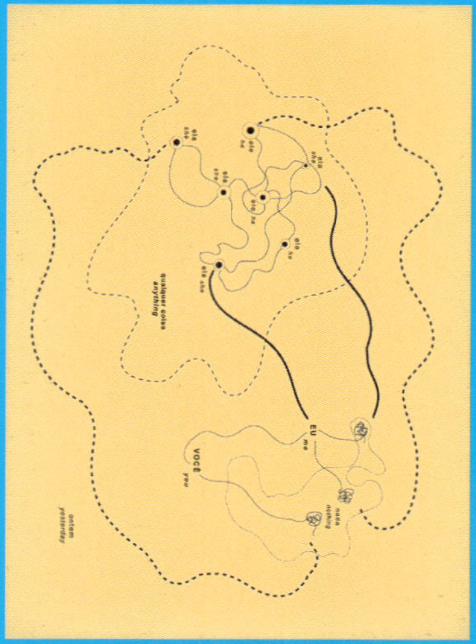

**PM/HM:** Notions of playfulness and reinvention are also important in your long-term project: *Would you like to participate in an artistic experience?* After showing at the documenta12 in Kassel, how is this project to evolve in the future?

**Ricardo Basbaum:** This project consists of an object that I let people use as they wish for a month. They can do whatever they want with it, all they have to do is send me some kind of documentation. The project has been going on for thirteen years (since 1994) and now it's entering its third stage. It can virtually go on forever – for instance, for the next two hundred years – because it's based on a mechanically produced object.
I'm still learning from the project, because even though it has been going on for 13 years, I haven't worked on it properly yet. I've archived the documentations, I have set up a website and now I'm preparing myself for this next stage.
At the same time, my experiences with it are very complex in terms of notions of conceptual art or theories of contemporary art; though it can also be regarded as just a very direct, painted steel object. And a very useful item: you can use it in your kitchen, your toilette or to bathe the baby. So it has both the role of being useful and of being a conceptual piece at the same time. Though so far it hasn't been used to its full potential. What's more, I would like to take the project to different cultures and play with different groups. Sometimes an artist is only able to play with the art world. However, I would also like to gain access to other worlds I haven't reached yet.

*diagram (me-you series)*
Ricardo Basbaum, 2000

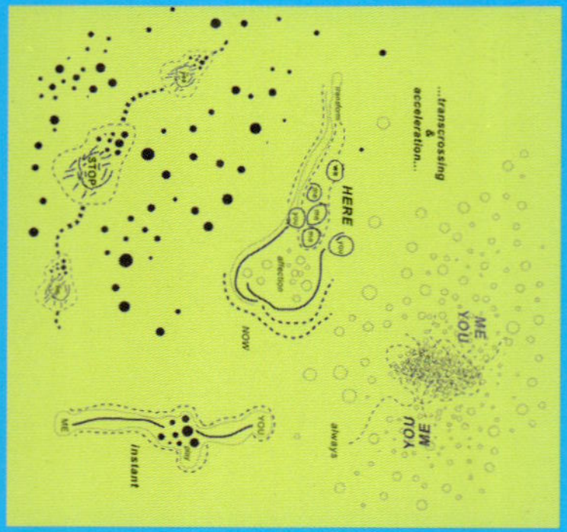

*diagram (me-you series)*
Ricardo Basbaum, commissioned by the museum in progress, Vienna, for the urban tension project, 2002

*obs. + system cinema + superpronoun*
Installation view at CAAM, Las Palmas, 2005

296  Parallel Worlds  Interview

# Horizons
## Rio de Janeiro

Universidade do Estado do Rio de Janeiro (UERJ), 2005

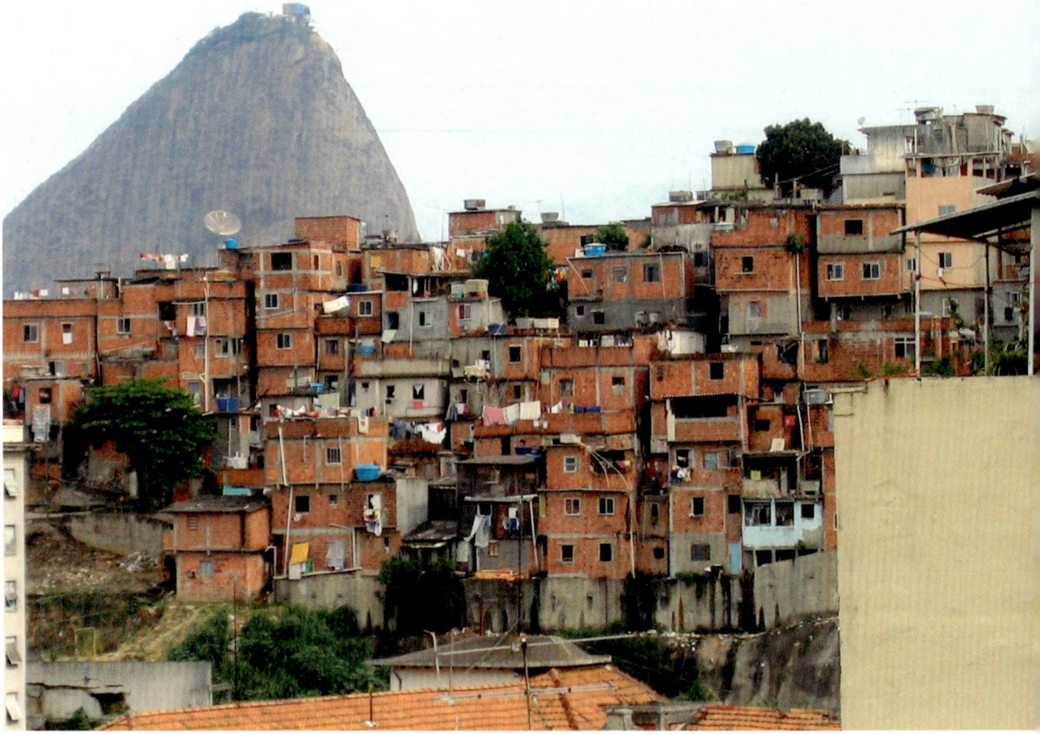

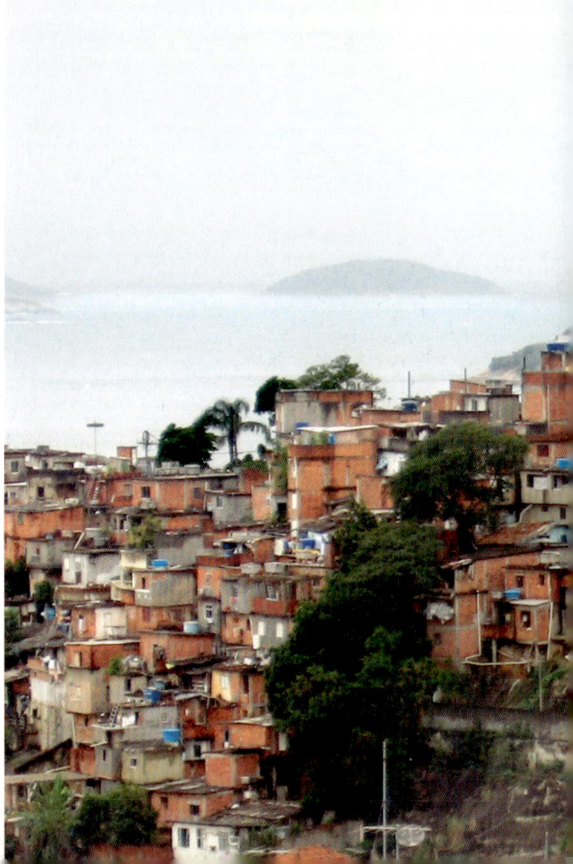

Francisco de Castro-Santa Teresa
One of the 500 favelas in the Brazilian metropolis
of Rio de Janeiro, 2005

Catedral Metropolitana de Rio de Janeiro, 2005
Designed by Edgar de Oliveira da Fonseca, inaugurated in 1979

Cidade Universitária
Unfinished building of the university hospital, Rio de Janeiro, 2005

Rua Dez, elevated street built on top of the Favela Parque da Candelária near the campus of Universitário Francisco Negrão de Lima, 2005

Universidade do Estado do Rio de Janeiro (UERJ), 2005

Universidade do Estado do Rio de Janeiro (UERJ), 2005
Pavilhão Reitor João Lyra Filho, located on the campus of Universitário Francisco Negrão de Lima, designed by Flávio Marinho Rego and Luiz Paulo Conde, inaugurated in 1976

303

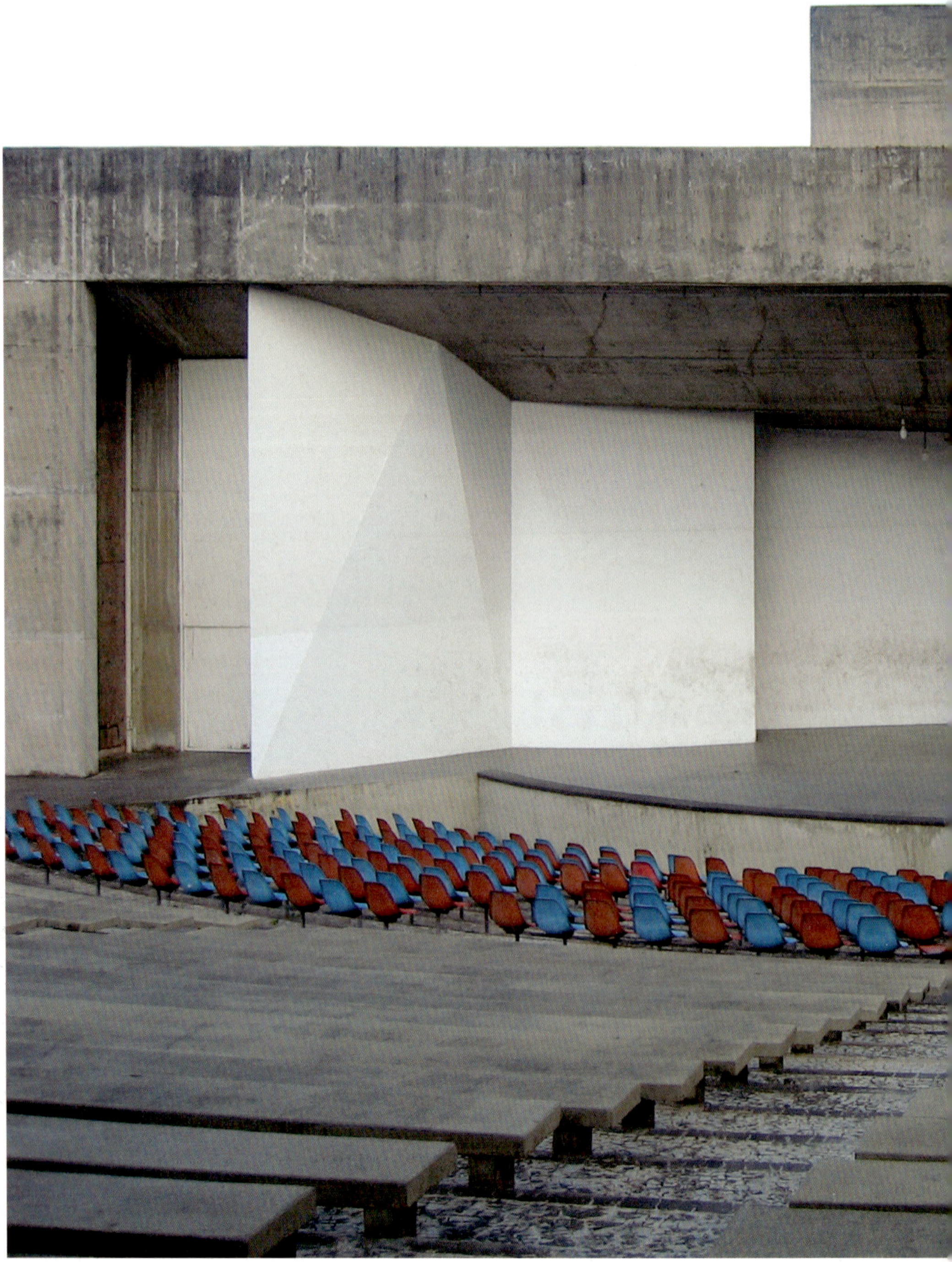

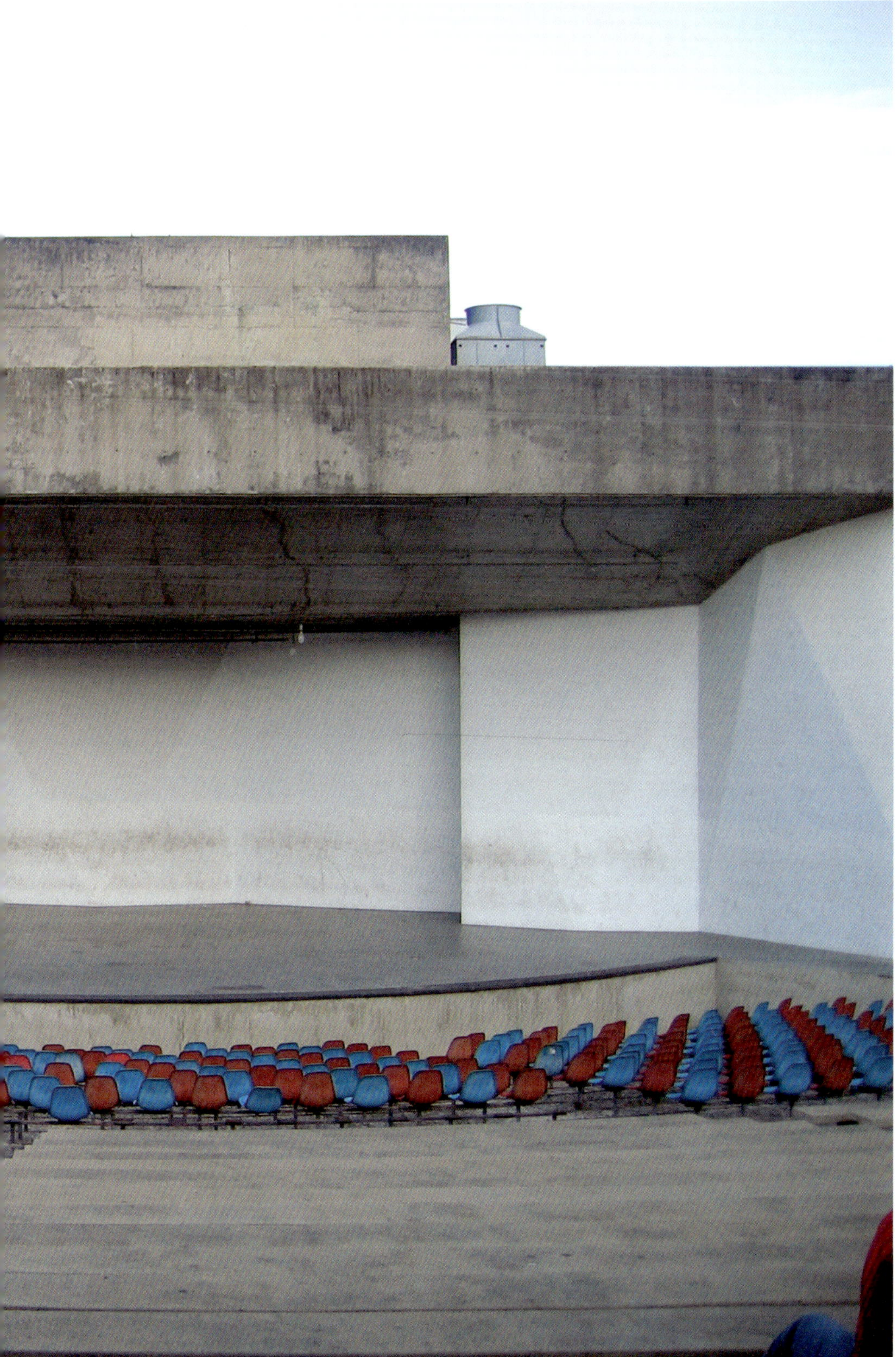

Universidade do Estado do Rio de Janeiro (UERJ), 2005

# Biographies

## ESSAYS

**Adrian Blackwell**
is an urban and architectural designer, artist and researcher, whose work focuses on the spaces and forces of uneven development produced through processes of post-Fordist urbanization. His art and urban research have been exhibited across Canada, at the 2005 *Shenzhen Biennale of Urbanism / Architecture* and *LACE Gallery* in Los Angeles. Blackwell co-edited *Unboxed: Engagements in Social Space,* with Jen Budney and co-curated *Detours: Tactical Approaches to Urbanization in China* with Pei Zhao. In 1997 he won Toronto's Nathan Phillips Square Design competition in collaboration with PLANT Architects, STI & Partners, and Peter Lindsay Schaudt. He teaches architecture and urban design at the University of Toronto, where he initiated al&d's China program in 2004, and has been a visiting professor at Chongqing University and the University of Michigan.

**Marina Gržinić**
is a philosopher, artist and theorist. She is professor at the Academy of Fine Arts in Vienna, Institute of Fine Arts, Post Conceptual Art Practices, and researcher at the Institute of Philosophy at the ZRC SAZU (Scientific and Research Center of the Slovenian Academy of Science and Art) in Ljubljana. Gržinić also works as a freelance media theorist, art critic and curator. She has been involved with video art since 1982. In collaboration with Aina Smid, Gržinić has produced more than 40 video art projects, a short film, numerous video and media installations, several websites and an interactive CD-ROM (ZKM, Karlsruhe, Germany). Her most recent book is *Re-Politicizing Art, Theory, Representation and New Media Technology* (Akademie der bildenden Künste Wien, SCHLEBRÜGGE.EDITOR 2007). She lives and works in Ljubljana and Vienna.

www.grzinic-smid.si

**Irit Rogoff**
is a writer, theorist and curator who works at the intersections of the critical, the political and contemporary artistic practices. She is Professor of Visual Culture at Goldsmiths College, London University and was Director of 'Translating the Image – Cross Cultural Contemporary Arts' (AHRC Research Project 2001-2006), from which two volumes will be published by Koenig Verlag in 2008. Irit Rogoff is currently heading the Ph.D. programme in Curatorial/Knowledge at Goldsmiths. She is the author of *Terra Infirma – Geography's Visual Culture* (Routledge 2001). Her upcoming books *Unbounded* and *Looking Away – Participating Singularities – Ontological Communities* will both be published in 2008. Recent curatorial projects include 'De-Regulation with the work of Kutlug Ataman' (Antwerp 2006, Herzylia 2006, Berlin 2008), 'Academy – Learning from the Museum' (Van Abbemuseum, Eindhoven 2006) and 'SUMMIT: Non-aligned Initiatives In Education Culture' (Berlin 2007).

**AbdouMaliq Simone**
is an urbanist with particular interest in emerging forms of social and economic intersection across diverse trajectories of change for cities in the Global South. Simone is presently Professor of Sociology at Goldsmiths College, University of London, and Visiting Professor of Urban Studies at the Wits Institute for Social and Economic Research, University of Witwatersrand. His work attempts to generate new theoretical understandings based on a wide range of urban practices generated by cities in Africa, the Middle East and Southeast Asia, as well as efforts to integrate these understandings in concrete policy and governance frameworks. Key publications include *In Whose Image: Political Islam and Urban Practices in Sudan* (University of Chicago Press 1994) and *For the City Yet to Come: Urban Change in Four African Cities* (Duke University Press 2004).

## INTERVIEWS

**aaa**
Constantin Petcou and Doina Petrescu co-founded aaa (atelier d'architecture autogérée) in 2001. aaa is a research and action platform revolving around urban mutations and the cultural, social and

political practices emerging in the contemporary city. Its team has a variable geometry and includes architects, artists, researchers, residents and users of the spaces it creates. In the La Chapelle area of northern Paris aaa has initiated a series of self-managed projects that encourage residents to access and critically transform temporarily misused or underused spaces. This strategy valorizes a flexible and reversible use of space and aims to preserve urban biodiversity by encouraging the co-existence of a wide range of lifestyles and living practices. aaa is currently involved in the European Platform for Alternative Research and Action on the City (PEPRAV).

www.urbantactics.org

### Ayreen Anastas
writes in fragments and makes films and videos. *Pasolini Pa\* Palestine* (2005), *m\* of Bethlehem* (2003), the *Library of Useful Knowledge* (2002) have been shown internationally in festivals, museums and cinemas but not yet broadcast on television. *The New Shorter Oxford English Dictionary* was published in *Rethinking Marxism*, Volume 16, Number 3, July 2004. She has no affection for the proclamation of victory. Troubled by any image of herself, suffers when she is named.

www.campcampaign.info

### Ricardo Basbaum
is an artist and writer who was born in 1961 and currently lives and works in Rio de Janeiro, Brazil. Recent solo shows include *la société du spectacle (& NBP)* (kunstraum lakeside, Klagenfurt, 2007) and *psiu-ei-oi-olá-não* (A Gentil Carioca, Rio de Janeiro, 2004). In 2007 Basbaum exhibited at Documenta 12 (Kassel) and presented work at *Imagine Action* (Lisson Gallery, London), among other group shows and projects. In 2006 he co-curated *On Difference #2* (Kunstverein Stuttgart) and *pogovarjanja/conversations/conversas* (with Bojana Piskur, Škuc Gallery, Ljubljana). He is the author of *Além da pureza visual* (Zouk, 2007) and a contributor to *Art after Conceptual Art* (ed. Alexander Alberro and Sabeth Buchmann, Generali Foundation, MIT Press, 2006). He works at the Instituto de Artes, Universidade do Estado do Rio de Janeiro.

www.nbp.pro.br

### Helmut Batista
was born in 1964 in Rio de Janeiro, Brazil. He is the director of the non-profit contemporary art space CAPACETE at the Escola de Cinema e Audiovisual Darcy Ribeiro in downtown Rio de Janeiro. Between 1985 and 1997 he worked as an artist, set designer and camera assistant in Paris, Vienna and Milan. Batista has exhibited worldwide and given talks at all kinds of cultural institutions. His books include *Public Intervention* (1991), *The Interventionist* (1994) and *You Do Not Need to Pay, But You Have to Consume It* (1997).

www.capacete.net

### Jochen Becker
lives and works in Berlin as a critic (*taz/die tageszeitung, springerin*), project teacher (Hochschule für Gestaltung und Kunst, Zurich) and cultural producer (Baustop.randstadt,-/NGBK, Berlin, 1998; MoneyNations2/Kunsthalle Exnergasse, Vienna, 2000; Urban Control/Forum Stadtpark, Graz, 2001; Werkleitz Biennale, 2002). He is a founding member of BüroBert, co-editor of *Copyshop – Kunstpraxis & politische Öffentlichkeit* (1993), editor of *BIGNES?* on recent urban development, and co-editor, with Stephan Lanz, of *Metropolen* (2001), *Space//Troubles* (2003), *Hier Entsteht* (2004), *Self-Service City: Istanbul* (2004), *City of COOP: Buenos Aires/Rio de Janeiro* (2004), *Kabul/Teheran 1979ff* (2006) and *Architektur auf Zeit* (2006). In 2007 he launched the mediaZones book line, whose forthcoming titles include *Nollywood*, *EuroMaps* and *Roaming Around*.

www.metrozones.info

### Matei Bejenaru
is an artist and initiator of the *Periferic* Biennial in Iasi, Romania. Established in 1997 as a performance festival, *Periferic* has evolved into an international contemporary art biennial that offers a platform for discussions on the historical, socio-political and cultural context of Iasi. Together with a group of artists and philosophers from Iasi, Bejenaru founded the contemporary art institution Vector Association in 2001 and is also a member of the editorial board of *Vector*, a publication dedicated to the artistic and cultural situation in the transition countries of southeastern Europe and in the Middle East. In 2005, he published and exhibited a

*Travel Guide* for illegal Romanian workers. Most recently, he developed the project *Impreuna/Together* (2007), which involves the Romanian community in the UK and was shown at Tate Modern London.

www.periferic.org

**Ursula Biemann**
is an artist, theorist and curator working on the gendered dimension of geopolitical displacement and migrant labor. Border and mobility are recurring themes in her video essays from *Performing the Border* (1999) to *Contained Mobility* (2004). She initiated the collaborative projects *Kültür* (1997) on Istanbul's urban politics and *B-Zone*, Kunstwerke Berlin (2005) which includes her video research *Black Sea Files* (2005) on the Caspian oil geography. Her multi-channel video, *Sahara Chronicle* (2006-2007), was first exhibited at Arnolfini, Bristol in September 2007. Biemann curated the exhibitions *Geography and the Politics of Mobility*, Generali Foundation, Vienna (2003), and *The Maghreb Connection*, Townhouse Gallery, Cairo (2006). She has published numerous books and essays including *Geobodies*, a monograph of her video essays (2008), and is a researcher at the universities of art and design in Zurich and Geneva.

www.geobodies.org

**Stefano Boeri**
was born in 1956 and currently works as an architect in Milan. His office (Boeri Studio) focuses on architecture and urban design. He is the founder of the international research network Multiplicity and professor of urban design at Milan Polytechnic. His studies on the contemporary urban condition pay particular attention to, and taxonomically describe, the 'real-time' dynamics of the mutation surrounding urban facts. Stefano Boeri has also served as curator for the Architectural Department of the Milan Triennale, creating in 2002 *USE –Uncertain States of Europe*, a study focused on the social and territorial future of Europe. Between 2004 and 2007 he worked as editor-in-chief of the international magazine *DOMUS*, and since September 2007 he has run, as editor-in-chief, the international magazine *Abitare*.

www.stefanoboeri.net
www.multiplicity.it

**Campement Urbain**
is a group of architects, artists and theorists that was set up – with variable geometry – in 1999 and advocates the decompartmentalization of each one of its members from his or her own discipline. In compliance with its commitments, Urban Encampment production stems from 'non-specialized' work, where the admixture of praxis and knowledge (non-hierarchized) combines with the contributions of local inhabitants and figures to collectively prompt a temporary experimentation with 'treasures of nothings', such as new kinds of urban fictions. Their project *Je & Nous* (2003-2008) is located in Sevran-Beaudottes, Paris.

www.campementurbain.org

**Sarah Carrington** and **Sophie Hope**
worked in partnership from 2000-2006 as B+B. Together they organized exhibitions, workshops and events as well as developing an ongoing archive, researching and writing on socially engaged art practice in the UK and internationally. Past B+B curatorial projects have included *Notion Nanny*, a touring project around the UK with artist Allison Smith (various venues, 2005-2006), *Real Estate: Art in a Changing City*, as part of *London in Six Easy Steps* (Institute of Contemporary Arts, London 2005), *Trading Places – Migration, representation, collaboration and activism in contemporary art* (Pump House Gallery, London 2004) and *B+B at Home*, a six-month programme of residencies, exhibitions and events (Austrian Cultural Forum, London 2003). Since 2006 Sarah and Sophie have worked on independent projects and research.

www.welcomebb.org.uk
www.reunionprojects.org

**Branka Ćurčić**
works as an editor in the infocentre department of kuda.org, a new media centre in Novi Sad in Serbia. She also serves as co-editor in kuda.read, the centre's publishing arm. Her work focuses on critical approaches to new media culture, technologies, new cultural relations, contemporary artistic practice and the social realm.

www.kuda.org

### Igor Dobricic

is a dramaturge, theatre-maker and arts programme officer at the European Cultural Foundation (ECF). He studied dramaturgy at the Academy of Dramatic Arts in Belgrade, Yugoslavia, and worked for the Belgrade International Theatre Festival (BITEF). Dobricic also carried out experimental theatre work with a group of teenagers, with whom he established the Theatre of Growing UP. In 1999 ECF offered him a position as coordinator of the arts programme and he decided to move to Holland, where he was admitted to the postgraduate course at the De Amsterdamse School of Advanced Research in Theatre and Dance Studies (DasArts). Parallel to his position with the ECF, he started working in 2004 as a dramaturge and advisor for a number of theatre projects. Since 2005 he has been a visiting professor of concept development at the School for New Dance in Amsterdam.

www.almostreal.org

### Ana Dzokic and Marc Neelen

have been working together since 1996. In 2000 they established STEALTH, a collective based in Rotterdam and Belgrade in which they have collaborated with Milica Topalovic, Ivan Kucina and Mario Campanella. STEALTH has established and participated in a number of projects on the complexity and inconsistency of the contemporary city, such as *Wild City* (Belgrade), *Urban Catalyst* (Amsterdam), *Adaptations* (Apexart, New York, and Fridericianum, Kassel), *Challenging the Conservative Brain* (Kunstverein Munich), *Cut for Purpose* (Museum Boijmans van Beuningen, Rotterdam) and *Europe Lost and Found* (Western Balkans). Ana and Marc are members of both the Centrala Foundation for Future Cities and the School of Missing Studies, an interdisciplinary network that engages in the experimental study of cities marked by abrupt transition.

www.stealth.ultd.net

### Joan Escofet

was born in 1965 and is a member of *Straddle3*. He takes a special interest in the complex configuration of the inhabited environment. Trained in architecture and art, he has developed projects that deal with the construction of architectures, content structures and visual images in different formats and that establish a visual dialogue and call for a personal alchemy of meaning.

www.straddle3.net

### Jesko Fezer

was born in 1970 and currently lives in Berlin, Germany. He is co-owner of the thematic bookshop 'Pro qm' and editor of the political architecture magazine *An Architektur*, which initiated the *Camp for Oppositional Architecture*. Fezer has held several teaching positions for architecture, and in 2005/2006 he served as guest professor for architectural theory and urban research at the Academy of the Arts in Nuremberg. He has participated with Axel John Wieder in solo and group exhibitions such as the 3rd Berlin Biennale, the 9th Istanbul Biennal and the first European Kunsthalle show in 2007. At present he is working together with the office 'ifau und Jesko Fezer' on a range of architectural projects in Graz, Utrecht, Berlin and Stuttgart. His latest publications are: Fezer/a42.org: *Planungsmethodik gestern*, Fezer/Schmitz: *Lucius Burckhardt: Wer plant die Planung?*, Fezer/Heyden: Hier entsteht: *Strategien partizipativer Architektur und räumlicher Aneignung* and Fezer/Reichard/Wieder: *Martin Pawley's Garbage Housing*.

www.anarchitektur.com
www.oppositionalarchitecture.com

### Asya Filippova

was born in 1969 in the Far East of the USSR and currently lives in Moscow. She graduated from the economics department of Moscow State University in 1992 and received an MBA in production management in 2003. In November 2003 she was appointed director of the 'October' paper factory in the historic centre of Moscow. In January 2005 she launched the cultural project PROEKT_FABRIKA, located in the factory's former industrial workshops. The project includes an exhibition hall (513 square metres), a theatre venue (250 square metres, 80 seats), an open-air site, studios, offices and a printing shop. It is devoted to supporting emerging artists, creating a new cultural landscape and developing social projects.

www.proektfabrika.ru

**Rene Gabri**
is interested in the complex mechanisms that constitute the world. He works alone as well as collaboratively within the folds of cultural practice and politics. Through his involvement with 16 Beaver (16beavergroup.org), Rene has helped organize public readings, discussions and social activities. Along with Erin McGonigle and Heimo Lattner, he also works under the name e-Xplo (e-Xplo.org), which has resulted in a variety of public art projects exploring social, economic and political forces.

www.campcampaign.info

**Iacopo Gallico**
was born in 1971 and took a graduate degree in architecture at La Sapienza University of Rome. Since 1999 he has been a core member of the Rome-based architectural collective Stalker, researching the marginal areas of the contemporary city. He has lectured on environmental and social topics at various universities, including Università Roma III, Universitat Internacional de Catalunya, École Supérieure des Beaux Arts de Toulouse and Universität Hannover. Dividing his time between Rome and Berlin, he is currently collaborating on two projects with the Osservatorio Nomade (ON) network: the first, *Kurds on the Map*, deals with the Kurdish diaspora in Europe, the second, *Wall(k)*, focuses on the metabolization of conflicts in the city of Berlin.

www.osservatorionomade.net
www.stalkerlab.it

**Nataša Ilić**
is a freelance curator and critic. She is a member of the independent curatorial collective What, How & for Whom (WHW). A non-profit organization for visual culture, WHW was formed in 1999 and is based in Zagreb, Croatia. Its other members are the curators Ivet Curlin, Ana Dević and Sabina Sabolović, and the designer/publicist Dejan Krsić. Since May 2003 WHW has been directing the programme of Gallery Nova – a non-profit, city-owned gallery in Zagreb. WHW's international shows include *What, How & for Whom*, which commemorated the 152nd anniversary of the Communist Manifesto (Croatian Association of Artists, Zagreb, 2000; Kunsthalle Exnergasse, Vienna, 2001), *Looking Awry*, Apexart, New York (2003), and *Collective Creativity*, Kunsthalle Fridericianum, Kassel (2005). Nataša Ilić co-curated the Cetinje Biennial V entitled *Love it or Leave it* (2004). She currently lives in Zagreb.

www.whw.hr

**Katrin Klingan**
was born in Lienz, Austria, and majored in comparative and Hispanic studies at the Universities of Vienna and Madrid. She received a research scholarship from the Fundación Ortega y Gasset in Madrid and conceptualized and organized various cultural events in Vienna. From 1995 to 1997 she served as assistant to the Viennese councillor for cultural affairs, and from 1998 to 2001 she worked as a dramaturge for the Vienna Festival, co-curating various projects dealing with performance, visual arts and film. From 2001 to 2002 Klingan was an adviser for cultural affairs at Erste Bank Group in Austria, Slovakia, the Czech Republic, Hungary and Croatia. In 2003 she was appointed artistic director of *relations*, a project initiated by the Federal Cultural Foundation in Germany. At the moment Klingan works out of Berlin, Germany.

www.projekt-relations.de

**Vasıf Kortun**
is a curator and the director of Platform Garanti Contemporary Art Centre, Istanbul. His texts have appeared in many different books, magazines and exhibition catalogues. *Szene Türkei: Abseits aber Tor!*, a book on Turkey co-authored with Erden Kosova was published in 2004. The co-curator of the 9th Istanbul Biennial in 2005, Kortun received the 9th annual Award for Curatorial Excellence given by the Center for Curatorial Studies at Bard College in 2006.

www.platform.garanti.com.tr

**Erden Kosova**
is an art critic living in Istanbul. As a writer and editor, he has contributed to *artist* and *Resmi Gorus*, two contemporary art magazines based in Istanbul. Kosova co-authored the book *Szene Türkei: Abseits aber Tor!* (Jahresring & Walther König, 2004), and he is also a member of the post-anarchist collective that runs the

magazine project *Siyahi*. He recently co-curated *Leaps of Faith*, an exhibition that was held in both sections of the divided city of Nicosia in 2005. He currently works for the Istanbul-based socialist newspaper *Birgun*, and is a PhD candidate at the Visual Cultures Department of Goldsmiths at the University of London.

**Olga Lopoukhova**
art director of the cultural centre ART-Strelka (since 2004). Curator, art manager. PhD in ancient history (1986). Executive producer of Innovation, the National Russian visual arts award (since 2006). Consultant at the All-Russian museum competition *The Changing Museum in the Changing World*, presented by the Vladimir Potatin Foundation (since 2007). Curator of the group exhibition *This is Not Food* (Era Foundation, 2007). Director of the cultural programmes of the Open Society Institute – Soros Foundation (1995 - 1998). Executive producer and editor of the catalogues for ARTKliazma, an annual open-air festival of contemporary art (Moscow region, 2003 - 2005). Co-curator of the Russian pavilion at the 51st Venice Biennale (with Ljubov Saprykina, 2005).

www.artkliazma.ru
www.artstrelka.ru

**Margarethe Makovec** and **Anton Lederer**
are the founding directors of < rotor >, a Graz-based art initiative that has been focusing on art production in central and southeastern Europe since the late 1990s. They have been involved in numerous projects on societal processes, including *Land of Human Rights* (2007-2009), *Balkan Konsulat* (2002-2003), *Wir sind wer wir sind: Aspekte vom Leben der Roma in der zeitgenössischen Kunst* (2004-2006) and *No Space is Innocent!* (2006). Often their projects address aspects of the production of public space, e.g. *Never Stop the Action* (2001) and *real\*utopia: Kunst im Grazer Stadtteil Gries* (2003).

www.landofhumanrights.eu
www.rotor.mur.at

**Oda Projesi**
is an artists' collective based in Istanbul. Its three members, Seçil Yersel, Özge Açıkkol and Güneş Savaş, turned their collaboration into an art project in 2000. They first met in 1997 and decided to rent and share an apartment in Galata as a studio. This apartment evolved into a multi-purpose private and public place. Between 2000 and 2005 the group worked in the neighbourhood and was invited to many events and projects abroad. Due to the gentrification of the area, the group had to leave their studio. They are now mobile and considering options for new places. In each of its projects, Oda Projesi works with different tools and strategies, and Istanbul as a city has had a great effect on their projects and tactics.

www.odaprojesi.org

**Philipp Oswalt**
is an architect who was born in 1964 in Frankfurt am Main (Germany) and currently lives in Berlin. Between 1988 and 1994 he served as editor for the architectural journal *Arch+*. In 1996/1997 he worked for the Office for Metropolitan Architecture/Rem Koolhaas in Rotterdam, and between 2000 and 2002 he served as a visiting professor for design at the Technical University of Cottbus. Since 2006 Oswalt has held a professorship for architecture theory and design at Kassel University. In 1998 he won the international competition for the design of the memorial site at the former women's concentration camp in Ravensbrück. In 2006 he took the second prize at the international competition for the temporary design of the former premises of the Berlin City Palace. He initiated and acted as coordinator for the European Research project *Urban Catalyst*, which dealt with temporality in urban space (2001 to 2003). He has worked as chief curator of *Shrinking Cities*, an international research and exhibition project of the German Cultural Foundation (2002 to 2008).

www.shrinkingcities.com
www.urbancatalyst.net

**Kyong Park**
is acting associate professor of public culture at the Department of Visual Arts at the University of California, San Diego, US. He was the founding director of the Centrala Foundation for Future Cities in Rotterdam (2005), a co-curator of *Europe Lost and Found* and a founding member of *Lost Highway Expedition* (2006). He served as editor of *Urban Ecology: Detroit*

*and Beyond* (2005), a co-curator for *Shrinking Cities* in Berlin (2002-2004), the founding director of the International Centre for Urban Ecology in Detroit (1999-2001), a curator of the Kwangju Biennale in South Korea (1997), and the founder/director of Storefront for Art and Architecture in New York (1982-1998). Working as an artist, architect, curator and theorist, using texts, photographs, videos, installations and multi-media, he has produced research reports, documents and representations of urban landscapes that delineate economic, political and cultural borders and that chart out the territories of contemporary social geography.

www.europelostandfound.net

### Tadej Pogačar

is an artist, educator and curator. He studied art history, ethnology and fine art at the School of Humanities, University of Ljubljana, Slovenia. From 1994 to 1999, he was the editor in chief of *M'ARS* magazine, published by the Museum of Modern Art, Ljubljana. He is the founder and director of the P.A.R.A.S.I.T.E. Museum of Contemporary Art, a virtual critical institution, established in 1993. Tadej Pogačar has exhibited at the 10th Istanbul Biennial; 47th Sao Paulo Biennial; 49th Venice Biennial; PR 04, Puerto Rico; Art in General, New York; Museo de Arte Carillo Gil, Mexico City; Stedelijk Museum, Amsterdam; Moderna Museet, Stockholm; Galerie für Zeitgenössische Kunst, Leipzig; ZKM Karlsruhe. His video works have been shown at the University of Maryland, Baltimore; The 3rd San Francisco Sex Worker Film and Video Festival, San Francisco; APEX, New York; 16 Beaver, New York.

www.parasite-pogacar.si

### Poka-Yio

is an artist and curator who lives and works in Greece. He received a BA in fine arts and a Master's in digital arts in Athens. He creates installations, drawings, video art and performances and has participated in numerous exhibitions in Greece and abroad. Poka-Yio was a member of the experimental music group Ilios from 1993 to 1996 and a founder of the artist group Political Body (1994 to 1996). He is also the co-founder and director of A-Station (the Athens Centre for Contemporary Art), and co-founder of the Athens Biennial. He co-curated the first Athens Biennial *Destroy Athens* together with Augustine Zenakos and Xenia Kalpaktsoglou.

www.athensbiennial.org

### Marjetica Potrc

is an artist and architect based in Ljubljana, Slovenia. Her work has been exhibited extensively throughout Europe and the Americas, with solo shows at the Guggenheim Museum (New York, 2001), the PBICA (Lake Worth, Florida, 2003) and elsewhere. Her many on-site installations include *Dry Toilet* (Caracas, 2003), *Balcony with Wind Turbine* (the Liverpool Biennial, 2004) and *Solar-Powered Desalination Device* at the Sharjah Biennial 8 (Sharjah, UAE, 2007). She has taught at several well-known institutions in Europe and North America, including the Massachusetts Institute of Technology (2005), and has published a number of essays on contemporary urban architecture. She is the recipient of numerous grants and awards, most notably the Hugo Boss Prize (2000) and the Vera List Center Fellowship for Arts and Politics at The New School, New York (2007).

www.potrc.org

### Gerald Raunig

Philosopher and art theorist, lives in Vienna; works at the eipcp (European Institute for Progressive Cultural Policies), Vienna; co-ordinator of the transnational research projects *republicart* (2002-2005) and *transform* (2005-2008); university lecturer at the Institute for Philosophy, University of Klagenfurt, Austria; (co-) editor of two series of books: *republicart. Kunst und Öffentlichkeit* and *es kommt darauf an. Texte zur Theorie der politischen Praxis*; member of the editorial board of the multilingual webjournal *transversal* and the Austrian journal for radical democratic cultural politics, *Kulturrisse*. Recent books: *Kunst und Revolution. Künstlerischer Aktivismus im langen 20. Jahrhundert* (2005), *Art and Revolution. Transversal Activism in the Long Twentieth Century* (2007), *PUBLICUM. Theorien der Öffentlichkeit* (2005, ed. by Gerald Raunig and Ulf Wuggenig), *Kritik der Kreativität* (2007, ed. by Gerald Raunig and Ulf Wuggenig), *Tausend Maschinen* (2008).

www.republicart.net
www.eipcp.net

### Oliver Ressler
was born in 1970 and currently lives and works in Vienna, Austria. He produces theme-specific exhibitions, projects in public space and videos on issues such as global capitalism, forms of resistance, social alternatives, racism and genetic engineering. Past works include *Doom!* (with David Thorne), *European Corrections Corporation* (with Martin Krenn) and *What Would It Mean To Win?* on the protests against the G8 summit in Heiligendamm (with Zanny Begg). In co-operation with Dario Azzellini, Ressler has produced the films *Venezuela from Below* (2004) and *5 Factories – Worker Control in Venezuela* (2006). He has participated in more than 100 group shows, including the art biennials in Prague, Seville and Moscow and the Baltic Biennial. In 2002 his video *This Is What Democracy Looks Like!* won the first prize at the International Media Art Awards of the ZKM Karlsruhe.

www.ressler.at

### Josep Saldaña
was born in 1956 and works as an independent analyst/programmer. He is a main contributor to the projects *Context* and *Openfridays*. Devoted to net-driven research and development, *Openfridays* seeks to appropriate and disseminate emerging culture as a new *art de vivre*. From 2004 to 2007 he actively participated in urban movement around Can Ricart/Parc Central in Barcelona.

www.straddle3.net

### Marko Sančanin
was born in Zagreb. In 2000, with a group of architecture students, he founded the architecture and media collective Platforma 9,81 to explore spatial and urban phenomena in the context of shifting political, economic and cultural identities. Using cross-disciplinary educational and research networks, Platforma 9,81 promotes activism and new urban techniques through public events and mass media. Its projects reflect on the spatial implications of contemporary public and cultural spaces (*Invisible Zagreb*), the urban phenomena of tourism development on the Adriatic coast (*3D Žurnal – Tourist Transformations*), cultural cross-disciplinary and tactical networking (*Zagreb Cultural Kapital 3000*), territorial installations of geopolitics, military and economic control on Cyprus (*Cyprus Territory*) and models of participatory urban planning and bottom-up development at seven locations on the Adriatic coast (*Croatian Archipelago NL*).

www.platforma981.hr

### Despoina Sevasti
is an artist and freelance curator who lives and works in Athens. She took a BA in archaeology and a BA in fine arts in Athens and studied contemporary art theory at the Department of Visual Cultures at Goldsmiths, London. She mainly works with installations, video and photography and has participated in exhibitions in Greece and abroad. Between 2002 and 2006 she collaborated with A-Station (the Athens Centre for Contemporary Art), and she currently works as a project manager for the Athens Biennial.

www.athensbiennial.org

### Pablo de Soto
is a researcher and practitioner in the fields of media architecture and social cybernetics. Together with chaser and osfa, he forms the core of hackitectura.net, a collaborative network that conducts practical and theoretical research into the emerging territories of information and communication technologies, new social networks and traditional physical space. hackitectura.net has produced such events as *La multitud conectada* and *Fada'iat*. Pablo de Soto also promotes the Technology Observatory the Straits and co-edited the book *Fada'iat: Freedom of Movement, Freedom of Knowledge*. He co-curated *Emergent Geographies*, the second edition of *Technology, Creativity and Society* in Extremadura, and he is currently working on the project *Situation Room* at La LABoral. He holds a master's degree in architecture from KTH Stockholm.

www.hackitectura.net
www.fadaiat.net

**Srdjan Jovanovic Weiss**
is an architect and founder of NAO (Normal Architecture Office) as well as a founding member of the School of Missing Studies. He is currently a lecturer at the University of Pennsylvania in Philadelphia and is pursuing his PhD at Goldsmiths, University of London. In 2006-2007 Jovanovic Weiss collaborated with Herzog & de Meuron architects on research and design projects. His book *Almost Architecture*, published by Merz&Solitude and kuda.nao in 2006, explores the roles of architecture vis-à-vis democratic processes. His *Lost Highway Expedition Photobook*, co-edited with Katherine Carl, was released in October 2007.

www.thenao.net

**Eyal Weizman**
is an architect and Director of the Centre for Research Architecture at Goldsmiths College, University of London, and has worked with a variety of NGOs and human right groups in Israel/Palestine. He co-edited the book *A Civilian Occupation* (2003), to accompany a major exhibition of the same name, and is the author of *Hollow Land: Israel's Architecture of Occupation* (2007). Weizman is a regular contributor to many journals, magazines and books, and is an editor at large for *Cabinet* magazine (New York). He received the James Stirling Memorial Lecture Prize for 2006-2007.

www.goldsmiths.ac.uk/architecture

**xurban_collective**
Functioning as an international collective since 2000, xurban has members in Istanbul, İzmir, Linz and New York City. Initiated by Guven Incirlioglu and Hakan Topal, whose transatlantic collaborations have taken the form of installations and on- and offline projects in the new media, the collective has since expanded to include Ahmet Atif Akin, Mahir M. Yavuz and other contributors of mostly Turkish origin. xurban's mission is to provoke a questioning, examination and discussion of contemporary politics, theory and ideology. It takes an intercontinental perspective in considering these issues. Documentary photography, video and text are often combined to render visible the multiplicity of information layers inherent in the subjects or situations explored.

www.xurban.net

**Claudia Zanfi**
is an independent curator and art critic with an interest in emerging cultures and micro-geographies. She is a contributor to art magazines and has authored texts for many group and monographic publications. In 2000 she founded the cultural agency aMAZElab, and she also directs MAST (Museo di Arte Sociale e Territoriale). She promotes a range of cultural and editorial projects, with a particular emphasis on social and geopolitical topics. Past work includes *A Ticket to Baghdad*, *Sofia Photographic Biennial*, *Cyprus Day*, *Transcrossing Memories (Nicosia)*, *Re-Thinking Beirut*, *New City Territory (Venice Biennale)*, *Communities and Territories*, *Atlante Mediterraneo* (with projects in Istanbul, Beirut, Nicosia, Tel Aviv, Alexandria and Barcelona) and *Going Public,* an ongoing project on public art and contemporary life.

www.amaze.it

# Index

3Cs: counter cartographies collective, 47
5 Factories – Worker Control in Venezuela, 185
16 Beaver group, 114-117

A/S/L (Age/Sex/Location), 17
A-Station, 130-131
aaa (atelier d'architecture autogérée), 248, 259-262
About a Useless Space, 288
Academy Remix, 35
Açıkkol, Özge, 288
Agamben, Giorgio, 24, 47-48, 76, 80-81, 89, 114, 248, 250
Akšamija, Azra, 14, 56, 143
ALMOSTREAL, 263-264
Alternative Economics, Alternative Societies, 184, 244-246
Altvater, Elmar, 154
Alvarez, Samantha, 265
aMAZElab, 88
AMO, 55
An Architektur, 226
Anastas, Ayreen, 76, 112-117
Annex, 289
Ararat, Xenobia: the City, the Strangers and the Becoming of Public Space, 290-291
ARTKlyazma, 64-65
ARTStrelka, 64-65, 182
Association Apsolutno, 58
Attalides, Katerina, 123
Azzellini, Dario, 185

B+B, 29, 174-175
Babić, Žarana, 269
Baci, Adrian, 88
Backyard Residency, 177
Bajevic, Maja, 88
Bakhtin, Mikhail, 245
Balkan Konsulat, 28-29
Barbrook, Richard, 30
Barefoot College, 222, 245
Barnett, Thomas, 53
de la Barra, Pablo Leon, 89
Basbaum, Ricardo, 293-296
Basualdo, Carlos, 89
Batista, Helmut, 178-180
Becker, Jochen, 276-278
Bejenaru, Matei, 176-177

Berardi, Franco, 23
Bhabha, Homi, 85
Biemann, Ursula, 76, 90-93
Blackwell, Adrian, 100-109
Blanchot, Maurice, 247
Blocher, Sylvie, 272-273
Boeri, Stefano, 132-134
Border Crossing Services, 185
Bourdieu in the Banlieue, 277
Bruegger, Urs, 159
Buck, Daniel, 104, 107
Buden, Boris, 32
Burgin, Victor, 76
Burkett, Paul, 100
Butler, Judith, 85, 114, 250-251

Callon, Michel, 157-158
Camp Campaign, 76, 112-117
Camp for Oppositional Architecture, 226-227
Campanella, Mario, 256
Campement Urbain, 248, 271-273
Can Ricart, 66, 71, 77
Canetti, Elias, 82
Carl, Katherine, 14
Carrington, Sarah, 174-175
Castells, Manuel, 244
Centrala Foundation for Future Cities, 13, 56
Centre for Research Architecture, 118-119
City of COOP, 277-278
CODE:RED, 228-229
Comitato per i Diritti Civili delle Prostitute, 229
Constant, 221
context weblog, 66-67
Conti, Gianmaria, 88
Costales, Victor, 179
Creischer, Alice, 226
Croatian Association of Artists, 30
Cuomo, Raphael, 93
Čurčić, Branka, 58-59
Cut for Purpose, 258
CZKD (Centre for Cultural Decontamination), 17

Daune, François, 271-272
Davida, 229
Davis, Mike, 154-155
Debord, Guy, 102
DeLanda, Manuel, 249
Delany, Samuel R., 246
Deleuze, Gilles, 47, 51, 100, 206, 259, 293
Deng, Frederic, 105
Derieg, Aileen, 33
Derrida, Jacques, 48, 50
Dobricic, Igor, 263-264
Docklands Community Poster Project, The, 174-175
Dorkbot Barcelona, 66

Dubossarsky, Vladimir, 64-65
Dunn, Peter, 174
Dzokic, Ana, 14, 256-258

East Art Map, 34
ECObox, 248, 259-262
ErsatzStadt, 276
Esche, Charles, 274
Escofet, Joan, 66-68
Esen, Orhan, 146
Europe Lost and Found (ELF), 52, 221, 257
European Cultural Foundation (ECF), 263
European Institute for Progressive Cultural Policies (eipcp), 32-33
EXIT, 34
Expósito, Marcelo, 33

Fada'iat, 67-68, 77, 136-137
Fezer, Jesko, 226-227
Filippova, Asya, 181-183
Foreign Office Architects, 71, 77
Foucault, Michel, 49, 106-107, 132, 156-157
Free School of Art Theory and Practice, 176
Freud, Sigmund, 251
Friedman, Yona, 55, 221
From/To Europe, 277

Gabri, Rene, 76, 112-116
Gallico, Iacopo, 290-292
Garcés, Marina, 268
Geers, Kendell, 123
German Federal Cultural Foundation, 34, 54
Global 500, The, 184
Going Public, 88-89
Granovetter, Mark, 158
Gregos, Katarina, 121
Gregotti, Vittorio, 132
Griesemer, James, 158
Grupo de Arte Callejero, 30
Gržinić, Marina, 17, 265-270
Guattari, Félix, 22, 245, 293
Güngör, Aylin, 130-131

hackitectura, 68, 77, 135-137
Hannula, Mika, 22
Hardt, Michael, 15, 81-82
Hari, Hariklia, 89
Hart-Landsberg, Martin, 100
h.arta, 176
Harvey, David, 265
Hegyi, Dora, 176
Heidelberg Institute for International Conflict Research (HIIK), 78-79
Heller, Charles, 91
Herzog & de Meuron, 55, 57, 70-71, 77

315

*Hier Entsteht*, 278
Ho, Samuel, 106
Holmes, Brian, 114, 159
Hope, Sophie, 174-175
Horelli, Laura, 177
Howard, Ebenezer, 105
Huang, Youqin, 105
Hudson, Michael, 265
Hummer, Andrea, 32

Ibrahimi, Astrit, 29
Içsöz, Oguz, 130
IG Kultur Österreich, 32
Ilić, Nataša, 30-31
*Imagining Corviale*, 291
Incirlioglu, Guven, 223-225
Indymedia Barcelona, 67
Indymedia of the Straits (Indymedia Estrecho), 77, 135-137
International Centre for Urban Ecology (iCUE), 54
Iorio, Maria, 93

Jameson, Frederic, 30
*Je&Nous*, 248, 271-273
Johnston-Arthur, Araba Evelyn, 266, 268

Kaufmann, Therese, 32
Kazeem, Belinda, 266, 268
Klingan, Katrin, 34-35
Knorr Cetina, Karin, 159
Koleček, Michael, 28
Kortun, Vasıf, 274-274, 288
Kosova, Erden, 121-123
Krenn, Martin, 185
Kucina, Ivan, 14, 256
kuda.org, 17, 58-59, 264
Kuprina, Elena, 181
Kwon, Miwon, 18

Lacan, Jacques, 266
Laclau, Ernesto, 84, 148
Landau, Sigalit, 121
Lang, Susanne, 59
Latour, Bruno, 21, 83, 157
Law, John, 157
*Leaps of Faith*, 86, 121
Lederer, Anton, 28
Leeson, Lorraine, 174-175
Lefebvre, Henri, 78
Lembke, Thomas, 106
*Leonardo*, 68
Lester, Gabriel, 179
Lin, George, 106
Linke, Armin, 93
ljudmila (ljubljana digital media lab), 229
Lopoukhova, Olga, 64-65
*Lost Highway Expedition (LHE)*, 8, 12-14, 16, 18, 52-53, 56-57, 221

*Maghreb Connection, The*, 90-91
Mahnkopf, Brigitte, 154
Makovec, Margarethe, 28-29
[mama], 12, 17, 30
Marx, Karl, 104, 107
Massiah, Gustav, 208
Massumi, Brian, 46, 48-49, 120
MAST (Museo di Arte Sociale e Territoriale), 88
Melitopoulos, Angela, 14
Mennel, Birgit, 33
Metelkova, 17
*metroZones*, 276
Mignolo, Walter, 267-269
*Migrations*, 54
Minichbauer, Raimund, 32
*Missing Identity*, 34-35
*Mobile City*, 221
Modé, João, 179
Mouffe, Chantal, 84
*MSE Meeting*, 28-29
Multiplicity, 75-76, 133-134

Nairobi People's Settlement Network (NPSN), 25
Nancy, Jean-Luc, 246, 250
Neelen, Marc, 14, 256-258
Negri, Antonio, 15, 23, 81-82
*New Babylon*, 221
No Border Network, 245
*No Comment*, 181
Normal Architecture Office (NAO), 55-56
Nouvel, Jean, 69-70, 77
Nowotny, Stefan, 32-33

Observatory of the Straits (Observatorio Technologico del Estrecho), 68, 90
Oda Projesi, 288-289
Oiticica, Hélio, 221
*On Egnatia, a Path of Displaced Memories*, 292
Onar, Anber, 122
*Openfridays*, 66
Osservatorio Nomade, 291-292
Oswalt, Philipp, 94-96

Paci, Adrian, 88
Papadimitriou, Maria, 88
Papastegiadis, Nikos, 48-49
*P.A.R.A.S.I.T.E. Museum*, 228
*ParcCentralPark*, 66-67
Park, Kyong, 14, 52-54, 56, 220
Pedrosa, Mario, 295
Perec, George, 288
*Periferic*, 176-177
Perjovschi, Dan, 29, 86
Perjovschi, Lia, 29
Petcou, Constantin, 259-262
Petrescu, Doina, 259
Plant, Amy, 175

Platforma 9,81, 279-281
Podnar, Gregor, 28
Pogačar, Tadej, 228-229
Poka-Yio, 130-131
Pollock, Griselda, 50
Ponger, Lisl, 175
Potrc, Marjetica, 14, 52, 56, 89, 219-222
Prelom kolektiv, 17, 264
Press to Exit, 17
*Prishtina House*, 219
Prlja, Nada, 174
pro.ba, 264
*ProcessMatter*, 257
Proekt Fabrika, 65, 181-183
*Project For an Inhibition in New York or How To Arrest A Hurricane*, 112
Pun, Ngai, 104, 107
*Pure Data Beta Rave*, 135

Radek Community, 31
Rancière, Jacques, 78, 114, 245
Raqs Media Collective, 17, 21
Raunig, Gerald, 32-33
*Real Estate*, 174
*real*utopia*, 29
*relations*, 34-35, 54
*Remote Sensing*, 92
republicart, 32-33
Research Group on Black Austrian History and Presence, 266-270
Ressler, Oliver, 184-185, 244-245
*Reunion*, 175
Rizzi, Mario, 274
*ROAD project*, 178
Rogoff, Irit, 46-51
Rometti, Julia, 179
Rossi, Aldo, 132
< rotor >, 28-29, 122

Said, Edward, 54, 224
Saldaña, Josep, 66-68
Sančanin, Marko, 279-281
Sassen, Saskia, 154
Savaş, Güneş, 289
*Scan Istanbul – Suburbs of a 21st Century Metropolis*, 130
Schmitt, Carl, 48
Schneider, Florian, 59
School of Missing Studies (SMS), 13, 55-56
Sevasti, Despoina, 130-131
Shahbazi, Solmaz, 274
*Shrinking Cities*, 94-95
Siekmann, Andreas, 226
Sieverts, Thomas, 102
Simmel, Georg, 85
Simone, AbdouMaliq, 161, 202-209
Sitorego, Andreas, 131
Škuc, 28
Smith, Christopher, 104

*Solid Sea*, 75, 134
Soros Centres, 29
de Soto, Hernando, 156
de Soto, Pablo, 135-137
Stalker, 290-292
Star, Susan Leigh, 158
STEALTH, 256-258
Stein, Gertrude, 23
Steyerl, Hito, 32
Straddle3, 66-68, 77
*Suburbia – the Vast Cityscape of the Athenian Suburbs*, 130
Šumić-Riha, Jelica, 266-267, 270

Tafuri, Manfredo, 133
Tarkovsky, Andrei, 281
*Temporary Building Strategies*, 219
Terkessidis, Mark, 30
*Timescapes*, 14
Tiravanija, Rirkrit, 88
Topalovic, Milica, 256
*Trading Places*, 174
Trans Europe Halles, 182
*Trans_European_Picnic*, 7, 58-59
*transform*, 33
*translate*, 33
*transversal*, 32
Tupyseva, Elena, 181

*Urban Catalyst*, 94

V2_Institute for the Unstable Media, 59
Vector Association, 176-177
Veltz, Pierre, 153
*Venezuela from Below*, 185
Vidler, Anthony, 82
Virno, Paolo, 19, 107, 245, 251

Wang, Hui, 101
Weiss, Srdjan Jovanovic, 14, 55-57, 142
Weizman, Eyal, 75-76, 85, 118-120
WHW (What, How and for Whom), 30-31, 264, 280
*Wild City*, 256
Winzavod, 65, 182
*World-Information.Org*, 58
*Would you like to participate in an artistic experience?*, 296
Wright, Chris, 265

*Xapuri: Rural School*, 219
xurban, 223-225

Yersel, Seçil 288-289

*Zagreb Cultural Capital 3000*, 280
Zanfi, Claudia, 88-89
*Zavzemamo prostor/WIR GREIFEN RAUM*, 266-269
Žižek, Slavoj, 30

# Credits

## IMAGES OVERALL

Peter Mörtenböck and Helge Mooshammer (front cover, 5, 6, 8, 12-15, 17-25, 27, 36-45, 60-63, 69-71, 74, 77, 79-81, 83-84, 97-99, 110-111, 124-129, 140, 143-147, 149-150, 152-153, 155-156, 158-160, 164-171, 186-201, 210-218, 232-241, 243-253, 255, 282-287, 297-305), kuda.org (7), Marjetica Potrc (9), Srdjan Jovanovic Weiss / NAO (16), Multiplicity (76), Dan Perjovschi (86), Adrian Blackwell (101), David Christensen / Adrian Blackwell (106, 109), Azra Akšamija (143, 162, 172-173), Research Group on Black Austrian History (266, 269)

## IMAGES INTERVIEWS

**aaa (atelier d'architecture autogérée)**
aaa (259-262), aaa, Nishat Awan, Claudia Amico (260-261)

**Ayreen Anastas and Rene Gabri**
Ayreen Anastas and Rene Gabri (112-117)

**B+B (Sophie Hope and Sarah Carrington)**
Loraine Leeson (174), B+B (174), Charim Gallery, Vienna (175)

**Ricardo Basbaum**
Daniela Mattos (293), Ricardo Basbaum (293-295), Nacho González (296)

**Helmut Batista**
Helmut Batista (178), Judith Augustinovic (178-180)

**Jochen Becker**
metroZones (276-278)

**Matej Bejenaru**
Vector Association (176-177), h.arta (176), Laura Horelli (177)

**Ursula Biemann**
Ursula Biemann (90-92), Charles Heller (91), Ursula Biemann and Hosoya Schäfer architects (92), Raphael Cuomo and Maria Iorio (93), Armin Linke (93)

**Stefano Boeri**
Boeri Studio (132), Multiplicity (133-134)

**Campement Urbain**
Campement Urbain (271-273)

**Branka Ćurčić**
kuda.org (58-59)

**Igor Dobricic**
ALMOSTREAL (263-264)

**Jesko Fezer**
Katja Eydel (227)

**Asya Filippova**
Peter Mörtenböck and Helge Mooshammer (181-183), Proekt_Fabrika (183)

**Iacopo Gallico**
Andrea La Rocca (290), Stalker Archive (290-291), Peter Mörtenböck and Helge Mooshammer (291-292)

**Nataša Ilić**
WHW (30-31)

**Katrin Klingan**
Maria Ziegelböck (34-35)

**Vasıf Kortun**
Peter Mörtenböck and Helge Mooshammer (274-275)

**Erden Kosova**
Sigalit Landau (121), Anber Onar (122), Katerina Attalides (123), Kendell Geers (123)

**Olga Lopoukhova**
ARTStrelka (64), Peter Mörtenböck and Helge Mooshammer (65)

**Margarethe Makovec**
< rotor > (28-29)

**Oda Projesi**
Oda Projesi (288-289)

**Philipp Oswalt**
flag (94-95), Nikolaus Brade and Falk Wenzel (94, 96), Peter Mörtenböck and Helge Mooshammer (95), Christoph Petras / StadtimBild (95)

**Kyong Park**
Kyong Park (52-54)

**Tadej Pogačar**
Tadej Pogačar and Dejan Habicht, P.A.R.A.S.I.T.E. Museum (228-229)

**Marjetica Potrc**
Marjetica Potrc (219-222), Lyndon Douglas (219), SEPLANDS and PRODEEM, the State of Acre, Brazil (219), Fred Dott (221)

**Oliver Ressler**
Oliver Ressler (184-185)

**Marko Sančanin**
platforma 9,81 (279-281)

**Despoina Sevasti and Poka-Yio**
Aylin Güngör (130-131), Andreas Sitorego (131)

**Pablo de Soto**
observatorio tecnológico del estrecho (135-137)

**STEALTH**
Ana Dzokic (256-258)

**Straddle3**
Straddle3 (66, 68), Peter Mörtenböck and Helge Mooshammer (67)

**Srdjan J. Weiss**
Ana Dzokic and Marc Neelen (55), Arnoud Schuurman (55), Srdjan Jovanovic Weiss (56-57)

**Eyal Weizman**
Eyal Weizman (118-120)

**xurban**
xurban_collective (223-225)

**Claudia Zanfi**
aMAZElab archive (88-89)


**DVD**

**Network Creativity**
Network map of kuda.org and School of Missing Studies: Srdjan J. Weiss/NAO; kuda.org map: kuda.org; USE installation in Bordeaux: Multiplicity; *Aussage*, Ezra Ersen, images: mrs-lee.com; 4th MSE Meeting, Prishtina, illustrations: Šejla Kamerić

**Contested Spaces**
Cartography of the geopolitical territories of the Straits of Gibraltar: observatorio tecnológico del estrecho, Marta Paz, Pablo de Soto; context network graph: Straddle3; Centre régional de la méditerranée: Boeri Studio; swarm strategy diagrams and *Moving Through Walls*: Eyal Weizman; Camp Campaign map: Ayreen Anastas and Rene Gabri; various untitled drawings, 2005: Dan Perjovschi; *Crossing the Line*: Šejla Kamerić; *Legislated Nostalgia/Now Denial*: Katerina Attalides; *THIS I SNOT AM ERICA*: Kendell Geers; *100's of Aircrafts*: Demetris Neokleous; *Rule Britannia*: Sigalit Landau; *Crossroads at the Edge of Worlds*, video still: Charles Heller; *The Maghreb Connection* and *Sahara Chronicle*: Ursula Biemann

**Trading Places**
Contemporary Building Strategies, Prishtina: Marjetica Potrc; *Prishtina House* at Kunstverein in Hamburg, 2006, Marjetica Potrc, photo by Fred Dott; *Xapuri: Rural School*, How to Live Together, 27th Sao Paulo Biennial, 2006, Sao Paulo, Brazil, photo by Wolfgang Draeger, courtesy of Marjetica Potrc and Max Protetch Gallery; Jacarezinho and Célula Urbana do Jacarezinho, Rio de Janeiro, photos by Judith Augustinovic; *5 Factories – Worker Control in Venezuela*, installation shot, Berkeley Art Museum, 2006: Oliver Ressler and Dario Azzellini; *Shrinking Cities* world maps: *Shrinking Cities*/project office Philipp Oswalt with Tim Rienits; *CODE:RED* and *monApoly – A Human Trade Game*: Tadej Pogačar, Dejan Habicht, courtesy of the P.A.R.A.S.I.T.E. Museum and Tadej Pogačar; *Academy: Learning from the Museum*, Van Abbemuseum Eindhoven, 2006, curator: Irit Rogoff, images: Church Of London Design

**Parallel Worlds**
*A Useless Space*, floor plan: Oda Projesi; Sevran town hall and *Je&Nous* at Grand Palais, Paris: Campement Urbain; *Ararat*, *Via Egnatia* and *Flying Carpet*, Campo Boario, Rome: Stalker Archive; market stalls in Lagos, photo by Ines Weber; *Would you like to participate in an artistic experience?*, diagram, 1994-2007: Ricardo Basbaum

This publication appears on the occasion of the project **Networked Cultures**, initiated by the editors in association with Goldsmiths, University of London in 2005.
www.networkedcultures.org
info@networkedcultures.org

### ACKNOWLEDGEMENTS

We would like to thank all authors and interlocutors for their contributions. This research is supported by a Marie Curie Intra-European Fellowship and a Marie Curie European Reintegration Grant within the 6th European Community Framework Programme. Additional support is provided by Goldsmiths, University of London.

### PUBLICATION

**Editors**
Peter Mörtenböck, Helge Mooshammer
**Translations**
Catherine Kerkhoff-Saxon, Robin Benson, Adam Blauhut, Joseph O'Donnell
**Copy editing**
Pierre Bouvier
**Design**
Thonik, Amsterdam
**Printing and lithography**
Drukkerij Die Keure, Bruges
**Binder**
IBW, Oostkamp
**Paper**
Arctic Volume, 130 grs
**Project coordination**
Solange de Boer
**Publisher**
Eelco van Welie, NAi Publishers

### DVD

**A film by**
Peter Mörtenböck, Helge Mooshammer
**Post-production**
RAUM.FILM, Vienna
**Editing and video graphics**
Ines Weber
**Label design DVD**
Thonik, Amsterdam
**Duplication DVD**
Prima, Katwijk

© 2008 the authors, NAi Publishers, Rotterdam
All rights reserved. No part of this publication may be reproduced, stored in a retrieval system, or transmitted in any form or by any means, electronic, mechanical, photocopying, recording or otherwise, without the prior written permission of the publisher.

NAi Publishers is an internationally orientated publisher specialized in developing, producing and distributing books on architecture, visual arts and related disciplines.
www.naipublishers.nl
info@naipublishers.nl

Available in North, South and Central America through D.A.P./Distributed Art Publishers Inc, 155 Sixth Avenue 2nd Floor, New York, NY 10013-1507, tel +1 212 627 1999, fax +1 212 627 9484, dap@dapinc.com

Available in the United Kingdom and Ireland through Art Data, 12 Bell Industrial Estate, 50 Cunnington Street, London W4 5HB, tel +44 208 747 1061, fax +44 208 742 2319, orders@artdata.co.uk

Printed and bound in Belgium

ISBN 978-90-5662-059-2

Cover image: Istanbul, Topkapı, informal market along the Byzantine city walls
Back cover image: *Camp for Oppositional Architecture*, Berlin, 2004